ReFocus: The Films of Amy Heckerling

ReFocus: The American Directors Series

Series Editors: Robert Singer and Gary D. Rhodes

Editorial Board: Kelly Basilio, Donna Campbell, Claire Perkins, Christopher Sharrett, and Yannis Tzioumakis

ReFocus is a series of contemporary methodological and theoretical approaches to the interdisciplinary analyses and interpretations of neglected American directors, from the once-famous to the ignored, in direct relationship to American culture—its myths, values, and historical precepts. The series ignores no director who created a historical space—either in or out of the studio system—beginning from the origins of American cinema and up to the present. These directors produced film titles that appear in university film history and genre courses across international boundaries, and their work is often seen on television or available to download or purchase, but each suffers from a form of "canon envy"; directors such as these, among other important figures in the general history of American cinema, are underrepresented in the critical dialogue, yet each has created American narratives, works of film art, that warrant attention. ReFocus brings these American film directors to a new audience of scholars and general readers of both American and Film Studies.

Titles in the series include:

ReFocus: The Films of Preston Sturges
Edited by Jeff Jaeckle and Sarah Kozloff

ReFocus: The Films of Delmer Daves
Edited by Matthew Carter and Andrew Patrick Nelson

ReFocus: The Films of Amy Heckerling
Edited by Frances Smith and Timothy Shary

ReFocus: The Films of Kelly Reichardt
Dawn Hall

www.edinburghuniversitypress.com

ReFocus:
The Films of Amy Heckerling

Edited by Frances Smith and Timothy Shary

EDINBURGH
University Press

Edinburgh University Press is one of the leading university presses in the UK. We publish academic books and journals in our selected subject areas across the humanities and social sciences, combining cutting-edge scholarship with high editorial and production values to produce academic works of lasting importance. For more information visit our website: www.edinburghuniversitypress.com

Edinburgh University Press Ltd
The Tun—Holyrood Road
12 (2f) Jackson's Entry
Edinburgh EH8 8PJ

Typeset in 11/13 Monotype Ehrhardt by
Servis Filmsetting Ltd, Stockport, Cheshire,
and printed and bound in Great Britain by
CPI Group (UK) Ltd, Croydon CR0 4YY

A CIP record for this book is available from the British Library

ISBN 978 1 4744 0461 7 (hardback)
ISBN 978 1 4744 0462 4 (webready PDF)
ISBN 978 1 4744 0463 1 (epub)

Contents

Figures

Acknowledgments

We must first thank our series editors, Robert Singer and Gary Rhodes, who approached us with the idea of editing this book for their *ReFocus* series, even though we had never met. At Edinburgh University Press, our thanks go out to our commissioning editors, Gillian Leslie and Richard Strachan; our desk editor Eddie Clark; our cover coordinator Kate Robertson; and our copyeditor Michael Ayton, who put all the final touches on the book you now see. There are two anonymous reviewers whom we naturally cannot name, but you know who you are, and we thank you for your helpful suggestions in shaping this volume. We of course would not have this collection without our great contributors, and we thank them for their insights, labor, and patience as this project came to fruition.

Frances would specifically like to thank her family for their ongoing support, and, naturally, the wonderful Mr Metcalf, a cheerleader for *Clueless* without whom no sentence would ever be written.

Tim specifically thanks Richard Brown, Ilana Nash, and Elizabeth Patterson, for lively discussions about Amy Heckerling. He dedicates this study of a creative, intelligent, and determined woman to his wonderful daughter Olivia Xendolyn, who is so totally awesome.

Notes on Contributors

Lindsey Alexander has an MFA in poetry from Purdue University. She is a Kentuckian, a Cher Horowitz-wannabe, a writer, and an editor. For more information, visit her website at ldalexander.com

Susan Berridge is Lecturer in Film and Media at the University of Leeds. Her research interests include narrative forms, the teen genre and screen representations of gender, sexuality and sexual violence. She has published on these themes in *Feminist Media Studies*, *New Review of Film and Television Studies*, and *Journal of British Cinema and Television*.

Zachary Finch is a PhD student in English with a concentration in Film, Media, and Digital Studies at the University of Wisconsin-Milwaukee. He is a graduate of the University of Wisconsin-Eau Claire and North Carolina State University. He is the co-editor of the *Directory of World Cinema: Scotland* (2014).

Mary Harrod is Assistant Professor in French Studies at the University of Warwick. She has published journal articles and book chapters on both Hollywood and European cinema, and released two books in 2014: *French Romantic Comedy: Gender and Transnational Identity in Contemporary Cinema* and *The Europeanness of European Cinema: Identity, Meaning, Globalization* (co-edited with Mariana Liz and Alissa Timoshkina).

Claire Jenkins is Lecturer in Film and Television Studies at the University of Leicester. She has published work on superhero families, metrosexuality and costume in British television, older "bird" chick flicks, and Hollywood's wedding romcoms. She is the author of *Home Movies: The American Family in Contemporary Hollywood* (2015).

Betty Kaklamanidou is Lecturer in Film History and Theory at the Aristotle University of Thessaloniki, Greece and Visiting Research Fellow at the University of East London, UK. She has written *Genre, Gender and the Effects of Neoliberalism: The New Millennium Hollywood Rom Com* (2013), and co-edited *The Millennials on Film and Television* (2014), *HBO's Girls: Questions of Gender, Politics, and Millennial Angst* (2014), and *The 21st Century Superhero: Essays on Gender, Genre and Globalization in Film* (2010), among several book chapters and essays in peer-reviewed journals. In 2011 she was awarded a Fulbright scholarship to conduct research in New York. Her fields of study include film and politics, adaptation theory, genre and gender, and contemporary Greek cinema.

Murray Leeder holds a PhD from Carleton University (2011) and is currently teaching at the University of Manitoba. He is the author of *Halloween* (2014), as well as numerous other articles, many on vampire films, and is editor of the forthcoming collection *Cinematic Ghosts* (2015). He is also contributing an article partially about *Vamps* to the forthcoming collection *Laugh Until You Bleed: Vampires and Humor* (2015).

Stefania Marghitu is a PhD student at the University of Southern California's School of Cinematic Arts within the Division of Critical Studies. Her research focuses on feminist media studies, television, modes of authorship and media industries. Her paper on *Girls* can be found in *Gender Forum*, and her chapter on *Mad Men* can be read in the edited collection *Smart Chicks on Screen: Women's Intellect in Film and Television* (2014).

Kimberly M. Miller is an Associate Professor of Communication Studies at Grove City College in Pennsylvania. She holds a BSc in Writing, an MA in English, and a PhD in Composition. Her interests include screenwriting, poetry, and novel writing.

Andrea Press is Professor of Media Studies and Sociology, University of Virginia. She has published numerous essays, articles, and chapters on feminist media theory, social class and media, and media audiences.

Lisa Richards is a Teaching Fellow in film, television, and media studies at Aberystwyth University. Research interests include hybridity in the teen genre on film and television, and the performance of masculinity in the British police procedural drama.

Ellen Rosenman is Provost's Distinguished Service Professor of English, Professor of Gender and Women's Studies, University of Kentucky. She has published work on Virginia Woolf, and is currently co-editing a reader entitled *Transnational History of Feminist Thought*, with Susan Bordo and Cristina Alcade, as well as a book-length manuscript on the social imaginary of the Victorian penny dreadful.

Timothy Shary is the author of *Generation Multiplex: The Image of Youth in Contemporary American Cinema* (2002; revised 2014) and *Teen Movies: American Youth on Screen* (2005), as well as co-editor with Alexandra Seibel of *Youth Culture in Global Cinema* (2007). His work on youth cinema has been published in numerous books and journals since the 1990s, including *The Journal of Film and Video, Film Quarterly, The Journal of Popular Culture,* and *The Journal of Popular Film and Television*. He has also edited *Millennial Masculinity: Men in Contemporary American Cinema* (2012) and will be the co-author of a book with Nancy McVittie, *Fade to Gray: Aging in American Cinema*, to be published in 2016.

Frances Smith holds a PhD from the University of Warwick and teaches Film, Media, and Screen studies at the University of Winchester, the University of West London, and Syracuse University's London Programme. She has published articles and book chapters on gender and class in the Hollywood teen movie, contemporary female stardom, and the construction of British masculinity.

Lesley Speed is a lecturer in Humanities at Federation University Australia. Her research interests include youth films, popular genres, Australian comedy and early cinema, questions of taste, discourses of generation in relation to popular culture, and the historical and cultural contexts of entertainment.

Film and Television Work
by Amy Heckerling

It's Showtime (no credited director, United Artists), 1976
   researcher
Getting It Over With (independent), 1978
   director, writer
Fast Times at Ridgemont High (Universal Pictures), 1982
   director
Johnny Dangerously (Twentieth Century Fox), 1984
   director
European Vacation (Warner Bros.), 1985
   director
Fast Times (Universal TV), 1986
   television show: producer; writer and director of three episodes:
   "Pilot" (1986)
   "What is Life?" (1986)
   "The Last Laugh" (1986)
Life on the Flip Side (NBC), 1988
   television show: producer
Look Who's Talking (TriStar Pictures), 1989
   director, writer
Look Who's Talking Too (TriStar Pictures), 1990
   director, writer
Baby Talk (Columbia Pictures Television), 1991–2
   television show: character creator
Look Who's Talking Now (Tom Ropelewski, TriStar Pictures), 1993
   co-producer, based on characters created by

Clueless (Paramount Pictures), 1995
director, writer
Clueless (United Paramount Network), 1996–9
television show: creator, executive producer; writer and director of four episodes:
"Pilot" (1996)
"I Got You Babe" (1996)
"Do We With Bad Haircuts Not Feel?" (1996)
"As If a Girl's Reach Should Exceed Her Grasp" (1996)
A Night at the Roxbury (John Fortenberry, Paramount Pictures), 1998
producer
Molly (John Duigan, MGM), 1999
executive producer
Loser (Sony Pictures), 2000
director, writer, producer
The Office (NBC), 2005–13
television show: director of one episode:
"Hot Girl" (2005)
I Could Never Be Your Woman (Bauer Martinez Studios), 2007
director, writer
Vamps (Anchor Bay Entertainment), 2012
director, screenplay
Gossip Girl (CW Television), 2007–12
television show: director of two episodes:
"Monstrous Ball" (2012)
"Father and the Bride" (2012)
The Carrie Diaries (CW Television), 2013–14
television show: director of three episodes:
"Express Yourself" (2013)
"Hush Hush" (2013)
"Date Expectations" (2014)
Suburgatory (ABC), 2011–14
television show: director of one episode:
"Victor Ha" (2014)
Rake (Fox Network), 2014–
television show: director of one episode:
"Three Strikes" (2014)

CHAPTER I

Introduction

Frances Smith and Timothy Shary

Figure 1.1 Amy Heckerling in 2012.

"As if!" The Prince Charles cinema in London's West End throngs with women relishing the California vernacular of Cher Horowitz, Alicia Silverstone's character in *Clueless* (1995). Although it is a cold evening in mid-November of 2014, the prospective audience members stoically grit their teeth as the breeze circles around their replica yellow tweed blazers and short, tartan skirts that instantly conjure up the character's signature style. Nearly twenty years since its release, the cinema has organized several successful quote-along screenings of *Clueless*, and dressing up as a favorite character is strongly encouraged. A loose adaptation of Jane Austen's novel *Emma*, the teen-oriented literary adaptation was an unusual cinematic prospect in 1995. Would teenagers really be tempted to spend their free time watching updated film versions of the books they pored over during their schooldays? Contrary to expectations, *Clueless* was a hit, grossing $57 million at the US box office and still more in video and DVD rentals and sales.[1] Unsurprisingly, the film spawned a series of imitators in the form of a lucrative cycle of similarly updated adaptations of canonical European literature, with *Pygmalion* morphed into *She's All That* (Robert Iscove, 1999), *The Taming of The Shrew* reworked as *10 Things I Hate About You* (Gil Junger, 1999), and *As You Like It* becoming *Never Been Kissed* (Raja Gosnell, 1999).[2] By 2003, Robin Wood deemed a literary antecedent one of the central tenets of the teen genre.[3]

Clueless has certainly enjoyed a lasting and widespread cultural resonance. Charlie Lyne's recent documentary, tellingly titled *Beyond Clueless* (2015), takes the film as the centerpiece of the modern teen genre. Yet, despite the crowds compelled to central London to watch and quote along with *Clueless*, undoubtedly few could identify its director, Amy Heckerling. Indeed, despite a thirty-year career spanning and influencing a number of popular genres, Heckerling is far from a household name. Our aims for this collection are twofold: to unpick the often complex presentations of gender, language, and desire in Heckerling's film and television work, and in so doing, to go some way toward examining her contribution to the landscape of contemporary popular Hollywood cinema. In common with other volumes in the *ReFocus* series, we seek to re-examine, and ultimately to restore, Heckerling's place in Hollywood.

The specter of auteurist criticism inevitably haunts attempts at uncovering the significance of a particular director's work. The arguments against this type of work are well-rehearsed: that filmmaking, particularly in Hollywood's industrial context, is an inevitably collaborative process of compromise that doesn't correspond to the romantic ideal of the all-controlling auteur; and in any case, to know something of the director is not necessarily an effective means of gaining a greater understanding of that individual's body of work. What is more, the rise of postmodern and post-structuralist thinking has radically displaced the supposed sovereignty of the auteur in favor of a diffuse meaning-making system in which signification is at least as much determined by the polysemous landscape of the receivers' individual cultural background, and the auteurs themselves are seen to take their creativity from across the cultural spectrum.

Yet the auteur is not dead, or not quite. Heckerling, a screenwriter as well as a director, undoubtedly retains a signature style that can be seen across a large number of her film and television works, even in early productions such as *Fast Times at Ridgemont High* (1982) and *National Lampoon's European Vacation* (1985), which were allocated to Heckerling not for her nascent status as an auteur, but given to her as a hired hand, or *metteur-en-scène*, to borrow Truffaut's terminology.[4] Heckerling retains certain key actors across her work, including Alicia Silverstone, Stacey Dash, Paul Rudd, and Wallace Shawn. Further, her work appears centrally concerned with transitional periods in life. Heckerling's teen movies explore characters' coming-of-age processes. Elsewhere, Heckerling would explore how women negotiate impending parenthood, and an identity as a single mother, in *Look Who's Talking* (1989) and *Look Who's Talking Too* (1990). In turn, the later *Loser* (2000) portrays the transition from high school to college, and indeed, the movement from rural to urban identities. Similarly, her most recent films, *I Could Never Be Your Woman* (2007) and *Vamps* (2012), explore the transition between youthfulness and old age, and the cultural requirements mandating women in particular to resist nature and maintain an appearance of youthfulness. Throughout, Heckerling retains a sense of play: these identities are not fixed, inevitable realities, but may be reworked.

In seeking to recuperate Heckerling's place as a contemporary director, this collection may be regarded as feminist in its ambition. Indeed, as Sean Redmond and Deborah Jermyn note in their collection on Kathryn Bigelow, Andrew Sarris's pantheon of directors who may be regarded as auteurs is universally male, a fact that goes unacknowledged in his work.[5] To grant a book-length consideration to the work of a female director may thus in itself be regarded as a feminist act.[6] At the time of writing, Bigelow remains the only woman to have won the Academy Award for Best Director, in 2009 (and in the 87 years during which the awards have been bestowing Best Director, women have been nominated only four times from over 400 nominations). In turn, the proportion of female directors working in Hollywood on the most successful films remains a lowly 7 percent, a figure that has actually *declined* since 1998.[7]

In contrast to Bigelow, who has consciously sought to deny the importance of her gender when considering her work, Heckerling places gender— particularly the construction of femininity—center stage.[8] In addition to *Clueless*, the work for which Heckerling remains best known is *Fast Times*, a film whose reputation has changed markedly over time. In 1982, an incensed Roger Ebert deemed it a tonally wayward "scuz-pit of a movie," not least for its salacious portrayal of Jennifer Jason Leigh as the protagonist Stacy.[9] However, the film has subsequently been the subject of a critical reprieve. Writing in

2003, Wood described the film as "disarming and exhilarating," successfully balancing what he describes as the "necessary" concessions to heterosexism and the commodification of sex with a striking portrayal of emergent female sexuality.[10] What's more, *Fast Times* is unusual for its matter-of-fact presentation of Stacy's abortion, and, less obviously, the shift from the school to the mall as the locus of American teenage lives.

With the aid of hindsight, the film's use of stock characters can be seen to pave the way for John Hughes's influential mid-1980s teen movies. Nonetheless, Heckerling's portrayal of teen femininity differs starkly from Hughes's portrayal of virtuous, vulnerable girlhood so memorably incarnated by Molly Ringwald. While Andie (Ringwald) in *Pretty in Pink* (Howard Deutch, 1986)[11] studies hard, urges her father to find employment, and angrily fends off advances from Steff (James Spader), *Fast Times* sees Stacy deceive her parents, shinning down a drainpipe in order to see her boyfriend, to whom she has also lied about her age.

Heckerling's career in film and television has been an influential force within contemporary Hollywood. In order to understand how her career has developed, we supply a biography that traces key moments in her life. With the caveats delineated above, this potted history is not intended as the key to understanding Heckerling's work, but rather, as enabling us to observe that there is a person here, one who is informed by the particularities and specificities of a life.

Amy Heckerling was born in the Bronx, New York, on May 7, 1954, and grew up in New York City in a working-class Jewish family. In addition to her enjoying movies on television as a child with her grandmother, it was the late '60s cinema scene of the metropolis, especially movies at the Museum of Modern Art, that afforded her the opportunity to pursue her love of older and foreign films, which she did even more as a student at Manhattan's High School of Art and Design. She tells a prophetic story about her first day at the new school, an experience that speaks to the feminist inspiration behind many of her films:

> we had to write compositions detailing what we wanted to do in life . . . I wrote that I loved musical comedies and I wanted to be a writer/artist for *MAD* [magazine]. The guy sitting next to me wrote that he wanted to be a director. I was really annoyed because I thought that if an idiot like that guy could say he wanted to be a director, then so could I, and I certainly should be a director more than he should. It had never occurred to me that that was a job possibility. He put the thought in my head because until then I would never have thought of saying that I wanted to do that; it didn't seem to be one of the jobs in the world that could be open to me.[12]

After high school, she eagerly enrolled at New York University's Tisch School of the Arts, where she earned her BA in film in 1975. New York City did not have much of a film industry then, so Heckerling followed the example of her NYU friend Martin Brest (who would go on to become a successful director himself, and whom she briefly dated), and moved to Los Angeles after earning a fellowship to attend the American Film Institute. She later took a job as an assistant editor with the Warner Bros. studio, raising money to finish her Master's degree in directing at the AFI. Heckerling then wanted to make Hollywood movies, which was a daunting prospect, because of the 7332 movies made by the studios between 1949 and 1979, a mere fourteen had been directed by women.[13]

Her second-year film at the AFI, *Getting It Over With* (1977), comically tackled the taboo subject of a girl wanting to lose her virginity on the eve of her twentieth birthday, and its appeal led to a contact at Universal, which helped her through the ordeal of landing an agent. In the meanwhile, Heckerling also had to overcome a serious car accident, and then her agent sent her back to Warner Bros., where she developed a script that she considered "a female version of *Carnal Knowledge*," the sexually candid 1971 film about two college buddies whose attractions to women lead them in divergent and problematic directions.[14] After sexist brass at Warners' passed on the project, she befriended producer Art Linson at Universal, who was seeking films for younger audiences, such as an adaptation of a book by a young writer named Cameron Crowe, based on his research while posing as a student in a San Diego high school. Heckerling thought that *Fast Times at Ridgemont High: A True Story* (1981) deserved a better script than the one Universal was currently developing, and Linson appreciated how she incorporated a shopping mall as a locus of activity and showed the importance of jobs in the teen characters' daily lives. She went to work with Crowe on refining his book into a new screenplay, and was later assigned to direct it as her debut, sans the book's subtitle.[15]

Even with a minimal marketing campaign and expressed doubt from Universal executives, *Fast Times* became a solid box office hit in the fall of 1982, earning $27 million at the domestic box office.[16] Unlike the raunchy Canadian import *Porky's* (Bob Clark), which brought in surprisingly huge revenue that summer, and distinct from the numerous teen comedies that followed (*The Last American Virgin* [Boaz Davidson] and *Homework* [James Beshears] later that year; *Getting It On* [William Olsen], *Joysticks* [Greydon Clark], *My Tutor* [George Bowers], and *Risky Business* [Paul Brickman] the next year), Heckerling's film featured the experiences of girls as well as their male counterparts, providing a rare gender balance in the new cycle of salacious teenage sex romps.[17] Heckerling not only had an uncanny way of discovering young screen talent such as actors Jennifer Jason Leigh, Sean Penn, Phoebe Cates, and Forest Whitaker: she also tapped into numerous themes—sex, drugs, music, school, and that crucially dismissed topic of employment—that were ripe for Reagan-era youth.

Heckerling had married David Brandt in 1981 at the age of 27, a union that soon dissolved in 1983 just as she was achieving widespread success. She was then inundated with scripts to consider, which were "mostly . . . about girls losing their virginity," but she wanted to head in a different direction.[18] Her subsequent feature did just that, by parodying the classic gangster films she grew up with: *Johnny Dangerously* (1984), while clever and reverential, was met with considerably less success than *Fast Times*. One unexpected outcome from that project was her work with writer-director Neal Israel during pre-production, whom she had asked "to polish the script," a collaboration that led to their marriage.[19] Heckerling directed her next film, *National Lampoon's European Vacation*, the following year, and it managed to gross nearly twice as much as *Fast Times* despite tepid critical reviews and ostensible lack of social relevance. (Israel had a similar sensibility for fluffy comedies, launching the unlikely *Police Academy* [Hugh Wilson] franchise with his 1984 screenplay and directing the Tom Hanks hit *Bachelor Party* that same year.)

Perhaps sensing momentum, Heckerling adapted *Fast Times* into a TV series for CBS, although it ran as a mid-season replacement in the spring of 1986 and was cancelled after just seven episodes. She briefly put her career on hold after having her only child, Mollie, in 1985, then slowly returned to work by producing a short TV series pilot, *Life on the Flip Side*, in 1988. The next year, she found her greatest success yet when she wrote and directed *Look Who's Talking*, featuring an interior monologue voiced by very bankable star Bruce Willis and marking one of many comebacks for John Travolta. Heckerling originated the idea while she was pregnant with Mollie and wrote the script during her daughter's infancy.[20] The low-budget comedy brought in $140 million at the American box office and another $157 million worldwide, thus earning an astonishing 40 times its production cost, which is remarkable for a film outside the action and sci-fi genres. Production of a sequel was swift in an effort to capitalize, yet *Look Who's Talking Too*, which Heckerling co-wrote with Israel and released just thirteen months later, earned barely a third of the original. Nonetheless, Heckerling's effective comic concept motivated ABC to launch a TV series retitled *Baby Talk*, which ran across the 1991–2 seasons for 35 episodes, with little input from the creator herself. Similarly, she had a minor producing credit on a third feature film, *Look Who's Talking Now* (1993), which was a flop by all accounts.

After a somewhat fallow period in the early '90s, Heckerling returned to the teen genre with *Clueless* in 1995, a well-reviewed and soon revered summer hit set in contemporary Los Angeles with wealthy high schoolers, assuring temporary stardom for lead Alicia Silverstone. The success of this farcical comedy inspired another adaptation of a TV series with the same name, which enjoyed a much longer run than her previous episodic endeavors, going to 62 episodes between 1996 and 1999 on the youth-friendly UPN network, even though Heckerling herself only wrote or directed four episodes and produced fourteen others.

By now, her career achievements had become evident, and in 1998 Heckerling was awarded the Franklin J. Shaffner Award by the AFI, which is given annually to an alumnus "who best embodies the qualities of the late director [for which the award is named]: talent, taste, dedication and commitment to quality filmmaking."[21] In 1999 the advocacy group Women in Film presented Heckerling with its Crystal Award, which honors "outstanding women who, through their endurance and the excellence of their work, have helped to expand the role of women within the entertainment industry."[22] Around this time she worked as a producer on the mildly lucrative *A Night at the Roxbury* (John Fortenberry, 1998) and directed some uncredited scenes, until she resumed writing and directing two years later with the oddly earnest college comedy *Loser*. Alas, the title of the film would prove predictive, as it lost money and displeased critics, and Heckerling again took a hiatus from the industry.

In 2005, she began work on another romantic comedy, *I Could Never Be Your Woman*, this time disparaging the television industry and the mythologies of female aging. While delivering on the star presence of Michelle Pfeiffer and Paul Rudd, whose lively affair is complicated by their age difference, the

Figure 1.2 Amy Heckerling directing the 2000 movie *Loser*.

film unfortunately had dubious funding sources that effectively prohibited its theatrical distribution. It languished for two years awaiting release while Heckerling coped with her ill elderly parents, until it was relegated to a DVD release in 2007, when it earned warm critical praise yet went largely unseen.[23] She waited five more years before writing and directing another feature, *Vamps*. This contemporary vampire comedy was also doomed to the video market, despite reteaming Heckerling with Alicia Silverstone, and despite the ongoing cultural fascination with all things vampiric.

Heckerling has since returned to consistent work in directing for television, helming occasional episodes of *Gossip Girl* (2012), *The Carrie Diaries* (2013–14), *Suburgatory* (2014), and *Rake* (2014). Along the way, she developed *Clueless* as a Broadway musical in 2014, having written the book and lyrics, and expressing interest in pop stars Katy Perry or Iggy Azalea playing Cher.[24]

While Heckerling is generally known as a comedy director, her films about youth have distinguished her oeuvre the most, and she was passionate about the genre into her mid-forties, when she made *Loser*. She said at that time:

> There are so many things about life that you're just figuring out [in your teens], and it's all new and exciting and heart-breaking. A teenager has to decide what they're going to do with their life, and that's one of the most important decisions that you'll make. To try to figure out who you are, how good you are at various things and how happy you are doing them, nobody [in the film industry] deals with that unless it's about somebody who wants to sing or dance.[25]

This concern for conveying something of real teenage experience goes back as far as *Fast Times*. Reflecting on her experience of making the film several years later, she states:

> [Consider] the fact that they were under 18 and they're having sex and you are seeing it. Not to say that that isn't exploited in a lot of the cop shows, but to have that be just a regular part of a girl's life. The disconnect between what's going on in schools and what's allowed to be shown in movies has gotten really bad because girls in junior high are having oral sex and getting bracelets for it, and in movies everybody's got to be 30 years old to have sex. It's very bizarre. At that little sliver of time I was allowed to do something—even with a lot of fighting—but was actually allowed to show something about a real teenager's life.[26]

Notably here, Heckerling draws attention to the distinction between the characters of *Fast Times* and those of, say, *Grease* (Randal Kleiser, 1978), whose youngest actor, John Travolta, was already 26.

This concern for the experience of real teenagers in the 1980s can be seen to recall the work of her contemporary, John Hughes, who likewise mined a rich seam of ordinary, Midwestern, middle-class, suburban teenagers in the spate of six films he wrote, produced, and/or directed between 1984 and 1987. Arguably, Hughes's "brain, princess, athlete, basket case, and criminal," so well-known from *The Breakfast Club* (1985), draw from the social types Heckerling delineated in *Fast Times*, although the coziness of Hughes's narratives contrasts with the raw, hard-won life lessons of Heckerling's earlier hit. Like Hughes too, Heckerling soon abandoned the teen genre to work in the burgeoning family genre with her successful *Look Who's Talking* films. She returned to the teen genre in the 1990s with *Clueless*, whose sharply informed satire, thirteen years after the humor and poignancy of *Fast Times*, adds weight to Heckerling's claim that she was somebody who wanted to deal with the lives of the majority of ordinary teens. *Loser* was certainly a weaker effort—perhaps owing to its over-reaching into social commentary on date rape drugs and the immorality of college hierarchies between and among students and faculty. Nonetheless, she maintained her agenda to lend humor to serious issues for youth.

Heckerling's latest two films, *I Could Never Be Your Woman* and *Vamps*, evade easy categorization as youth films per se. However, the former maintains a youth subplot, as the film's protagonist produces a teen television show. In turn, although the protagonists of *Vamps* are far older biologically than their teen movie counterparts—one is well over 100—the film can nevertheless be seen to allegorize the difficulties that teenagers face in keeping up with contemporary lingo and trends. What's more, the focus on characters supposedly attending college allows Heckerling to stay a part of the world of youth, while also permitting a nostalgic reflection on the process of aging.

The book opens with a consideration of the work for which Heckerling remains best known: her work in teen film, and increasingly, television. In addition to *Fast Times* and *Clueless*, which have been considered elsewhere, this section also investigates her lesser-known *Loser*. Susan Berridge's essay on female friendship investigates the crucial—and underexplored—area of medium specificity in this area of scholarship. In turn, Zachary Finch considers the complex portrayal of female sexuality in Heckerling's teen work. Lastly, Mary Harrod observes the polygamous referentiality of Heckerling's films, and considers how Heckerling's work can be regarded as part of a recent wave of postmodern female-oriented work.

The book's second section concentrates on one of the most noticeable aspects of Heckerling's work, namely her innovative use of language. Andrea Press and Ellen Rosenman adopt an unusual focus group methodology to examine how different groups of students articulate the construction of class in *Clueless*. In turn, Lisa Richards provides a linguistic analysis of the unique teen lexicon used in the film. In both cases, the authors deconstruct Heckerling's construction of particular youth communities with this central aspect of her film work.

The third section of this collection studies Heckerling's treatment of femininity, aging, and postfeminism. Throughout her career, Heckerling has portrayed female identities in transition. While her teen work explores the characters' sexual coming of age, her contribution to the 1990s family film, in the form of *Look Who's Talking* and *Look Who's Talking Too*, portrays a woman negotiating single parenthood. As the author of the first essay in this section, Claire Jenkins, observes, Heckerling's treatment of family dynamics is notably more liberal in tone than that found in the films of many of her contemporaries. Still today, the gender politics of *Look Who's Talking* remains striking. This section continues the investigation of femininity in transition with Betty Kaklamanidou's postfeminist examination of femininity and aging in *I Could Never Be Your Woman* and *Vamps*. Similarly, Murray Leeder analyzes the characters' careful maintenance of youthful appearance in *Vamps* in the light of the literary tradition of vampires for whom aging is impossible.

The book's concluding section looks at Heckerling's work in retrospect, examining the themes and overall shape of her work as a whole. Stefania Marghitu and Lindsay Alexander explore the reception practices and lasting cultural resonance of Heckerling's most popular film, *Clueless*. Turning her attention to Heckerling's contribution to the teen genre overall, Kimberley Miller compares her directorial style to that of the more celebrated John Hughes. The collection is completed by an update of Lesley Speed's essay investigating Heckerling's contribution to what she describes as "low comedy." Substantially revised in the light of developments in Heckerling's own career, and the growing academic and popular interest in women's comedy, Speed's work presents an opportunity for reflection on the lasting legacy of Heckerling's film and television work. This collection will thus recuperate the image of Heckerling as a key director within contemporary Hollywood cinema, and contribute to a growing body of work on female practitioners in the film industry.

NOTES

1 Unless otherwise cited, all box office figures in this book are determined by Box Office Mojo: <http://www.boxofficemojo.com/movies/?id=clueless.htm> (last accessed 26 February 2015).

2 Robin Wood also cites *Whatever It Takes* (David Raynr, 2000), adapting *Cyrano de Bergerac; Cruel Intentions* (Roger Kumble, 1999), adapting *Les Liaisons Dangereuses;* and *Get Over It* (Tommy O'Haver, 2001), adapting *A Midsummer Night's Dream*. In Robin Wood, *Hollywood: From Vietnam to Reagan . . . And Beyond* (New York: Columbia University Press, 2003), p. 319.

3 Wood, p. 290. Although Wood refers to the Teen Movie as a cycle, the term "genre" best describes this category of filmmaking. The cycle can be described as a "temporally brief but numerically and aesthetically significant outpouring of films" (Jane Feuer, "The international art musical: defining and periodising the post-1980s musical," in Steven Cohan (ed.), *The Sound of Musicals* (London: BFI, 2010), p. 55. However, the teen movie has had a lengthy lifespan, and, as we have argued elsewhere, can be seen to possess certain distinct narrative structures: Frances Smith, "Rethinking the norm: Judith Butler and the Hollywood teen movie," unpublished PhD thesis (University of Warwick, 2013), p. 36; Timothy Shary, *Generation Multiplex: The Image of Youth in American Cinema Since 1980* (Austin, TX: University of Texas Press, 2014), pp. 1–20.

4 François Truffaut, "Une certaine tendence du cinéma Français," *Cahiers du Cinéma*, #31, January 1954, p. 21.

5 Sean Redmond and Deborah Jermyn (eds.), *Hollywood Transgressor: The Cinema of Kathryn Bigelow* (London: Wallflower, 2003), pp. 3–4.

6 Ibid. p. 3.

7 According to a 2015 report, of the top 250 highest-grossing domestic films in the USA (excluding foreign titles) in 2014, women were directors of only 7 percent, which is actually a decline from 9 percent in 1998 when the study began. During those 17 years, the percentage of women in *all* key production positions—directors, producers, writers, editors, and cinematographers—was never greater than 19 percent nor less than 16 percent, and was at 17 percent as of 2014. See Martha M. Lauzen, "The celluloid ceiling: behind-the-scenes employment of women on the top 250 films of 2014," Center for the Study of Women in Television & Film. Available at <http://womenintvfilm.sdsu.edu/files/2014_Celluloid_Ceiling_Report.pdf> (last accessed 14 February 2015).

8 Ibid. p. 4.

9 Roger Ebert, "Fast times at Ridgemont High," *Chicago Sun-Times*, 1 January 1982. Available at <http://www.rogerebert.com/reviews/fast-times-at-ridgemont-high-1982> (last accessed 16 January 2015).

10 Wood, p. 192.

11 Although *Pretty in Pink* was directed by Deutch, it was also written and produced by John Hughes, and may be consequently considered an example of his work.

12 Nicholas Jarecki, *Breaking In: How 20 Film Directors Got Their Start* (New York: Broadway Books, 2001), p. 143.

13 Patrick Robertson, *Film Facts* (New York: Billboard Books, 2001), p. 136.

14 Jarecki, p. 148.

15 Melissa Silverstein, "Interview with *Vamps* director Amy Heckerling," *Women and Hollywood*, 9 April 2012. Available at <http://blogs.indiewire.com/womenandhollywood/interview-with-amy-heckerling> (last accessed 13 February 2015).

16 *Fast Times* earned nearly $27.1 million in theatrical release between August and October of 1982. See <http://boxofficemojo.com/movies/?page=main&id=fasttimesatridgemonthigh.htm> (last accessed 13 February 2015).

17 While these and other sex romps continued to focus on boys—including *Hollywood Hot Tubs, Hot Moves, Snowballing, The Wild Life* (all 1984); *Hot Chili, Hot Resort, Paradise Motel, Private Resort* (all 1985)—the only other films in this cycle that featured girl protagonists were directed by another pioneering woman director, Martha Coolidge, who made *Valley Girl* (1983) and *Joy of Sex* (1984). See Shary, pp. 250–8.

18 Jarecki, p. 153.

19 Kristin McMurran, "Mixing marriage and movies is a mirthly delight for directors Amy Heckerling and Neal Israel," *People Weekly*, 23: 19 (13 May 1985), p. 104.

20 Mary G. Hurd, *Women Directors and Their Films* (Westport, CT: Praeger, 2007), pp. 24–5.

21 American Film Institute, "Franklin J. Shaffner Award". Available at <http://www.afi. com/conservatory/alumni/schaffneraward.aspx> (last accessed 13 February 2015).

22 Women in Film Los Angeles, "Crystal Award". Available at <http://www.wif.org/past-recipients> (last accessed 13 February 2015).

23 Silverstein.

24 Ryan McPhee, "As if! Amy Heckerling's *Clueless* musical could be coming to Broadway, starring Katy Perry," *Broadway.com*, 11 July 2014. Available at <http://www.broadway. com/buzz/176693/as-if-amy-heckerlings-clueless-musical-could-be-coming-to-broadway-starring-katy-perry/> (last accessed 5 March 2015).

25 Serena Donadoni, "Hormonal pyrotechnics 101," *Detroit Metro Times*, 26 July 2000. Available at <http://www.metrotimes.com/detroit/hormonal-pyrotechnics-101/ Content?oid=2168746> (last accessed 5 March 2015).

26 Silverstein.

Heckerling in Teen Film and Television

Introduction to Part I

This volume aims to demonstrate the breadth and significance of Amy Heckerling's film and television work, an oeuvre most closely associated with the teen genre. Released in 1982, *Fast Times at Ridgemont High* draws from the male-oriented sex quest film of the time, such as *Porky's* (1982). However, with a focus on female characters, and a proto-feminist perspective in the film's nonchalant treatment of abortion, *Fast Times* saw Heckerling carve out a particular space for herself within the genre. Heckerling did not return to the teen film until 1995, with the enormously successful *Clueless*, which made a star of the film's lead, Alicia Silverstone. Markedly less successful was *Loser*, which, five years later, followed Jason Biggs as a rural outcast finding his feet at university in New York City.

Heckerling fully capitalized on the growth of teen television as a result of a widespread expansion of cable and satellite television networks that occurred in the 1990s. As a result, she produced television series following up on the characters of *Fast Times* and, later, *Clueless*. Examining the latter in particular, Susan Berridge explores differences in medium specificity as they relate to the romance narrative of *Clueless*. While the film version draws from the romantic comedy genre, centering on the burgeoning attraction between Cher (Alicia Silverstone) and Josh (Paul Rudd), Berridge observes the differences in television as a medium that allow the *Clueless* series to grant greater importance to the friendship between Cher and Dionne. As a result, Berridge's essay contributes to ongoing debates on the relationship between medium, genre, and narrative.

Secondly, Zachary Finch investigates the sexual politics of Heckerling's work in teen film. Observing Stacy's emotional growth throughout *Fast Times*, which sees her reject casual dalliances in favor of meaningful romance, and

Cher's proud status as a virgin in *Clueless*, Finch questions the sexual politics of Heckerling's teen work. Examining the nuanced presentation of Paul in *Loser* as sensitive yet virile, Finch concludes that Heckerling's construction of masculinity and femininity alike does much to dispel the myths of the sexual aggressor and gatekeeper respectively.

The final essay in the section, by Mary Harrod, takes its cue from the multi-layered and endlessly referential qualities of Heckerling's teen work. As part of a wider study of women's genre cinema, Harrod notes how mainstream female directors are frequently sidelined in favor of more obviously artistic fare. What's more, observing the recent trend for allusive women's cinema, Harrod argues that Heckerling presents an important precursor to this work, which provides new possibilities for spectatorial engagement.

CHAPTER 2

Cher and Dionne BFFs: Female Friendship, Genre, and Medium Specificity in the Film and Television Versions of Amy Heckerling's *Clueless*

Susan Berridge

At the center of both the film and the television versions of Amy Heckerling's *Clueless* is the friendship of Cher (Alicia Silverstone and Rachel Blanchard, respectively) and Dionne (Stacey Dash, in both versions). Of all the central teenage relationships featured in the film, this is the only one to occupy an equally prominent space in the spin-off television series, which originally premiered on ABC in 1996, before moving to UPN in 1997 for its final two seasons and ending in 1999. While Cher and Dionne's friendship remains central in the television version, other key relationships from the film, such as their friendship with Tai (Brittany Murphy/Heather Gottlieb) and Cher's romance with her stepbrother Josh (Paul Rudd/David Lascher), are much more peripheral.

Writing about contemporary romantic comedies, Celestino Deleyto directly identifies *Clueless* (the film) as indicative of the increasing emphasis of the genre on friendship over romance. He argues that, while female friendships are typically codified in romcoms as "conventionally previous to the arrival of 'true love,'" the true narrative interest of *Clueless* lies with the female friends.[1] This is perhaps partially due to the film's generic hybridity, blending elements of the romantic comedy with the teen genre. Same-sex friendships are key to the teen genre, as exemplified by Heckerling's earlier teen film *Fast Times at Ridgemont High* (1982) as well as by more recent films such as *The Sisterhood of the Travelling Pants* (Ken Kwapis, 2005) and *Superbad* (Greg Mottola, 2007), offering a relatively safe space in which teenage characters can work through issues—often related to sex and romance—as they negotiate the transition from childhood to adulthood. In turn, teen films and television series, including *Clueless* along with teen dramas such as *The Carrie Diaries* (The CW, 2013–14) and *Gossip Girl* (The CW, 2007–12), both of which Heckerling directed episodes for, and teen sitcoms such as *Girl Meets World* (Disney Channel, 2014–), are often centrally concerned with shifts in these relationships as characters gradually mature.[2]

Owing to the shared centrality in them of teenage characters and concerns, teen films and television series are frequently conflated in scholarship.[3] And yet, notably, friendship narratives in *Clueless* play out very differently in Heckerling's film and television versions, pointing to the powerful ways in which not just genre but also medium specificity intersects with how narratives are framed. Through a comparative analysis of female friendship in both the film and television versions of *Clueless*, this essay will explore these differences in more depth. (I will focus exclusively on the first season of the television spin-off, owing to Heckerling's lack of involvement with subsequent seasons.) I argue that the prominence of Cher and Dionne's friendship to both texts potentially challenges the conventional notion of women being largely passive and dependent on men and, in turn, is indicative of Heckerling's contribution to the teen genre, placing female perspectives, concerns, and relationships at the center of her work.[4] However, the separate film and television media offer very different narrative—and ideological—possibilities for how this friendship is portrayed. The closure enforced on the film, as well as its indebtedness to romantic comedy conventions, mean that ultimately Cher and Dionne's friendship is marginalized in favor of Cher's relationship with Josh. This marginalization is reflective of broader gendered inequalities in Hollywood, where women, particularly those who do not need men for personal fulfillment, are frequently sidelined to make room for heteronormative romance. In contrast, the cyclical and repetitive form of the teen television sitcom creates a more conducive space for the portrayal of Cher and Dionne's relationship, which assumes a much more central role in the series than any of Cher's romantic encounters.

SCHOLARSHIP ON THE TEEN GENRE

As Steve Neale notes, critics, theorists, and historians of film genre have rarely paid attention to teen films, despite this genre's importance to Hollywood as an industry.[5] Yet, while the distinct cinematic teen genre is under-researched, scholarship on it remains more prevalent than work on teen television, with books, articles, and subsections in books on film genre devoted exclusively to identifying shared textual markers across teen films.[6] Nevertheless, a coherent teen genre remains difficult to define. Timothy Shary explains, "the teen film poses an interesting challenge to formulaic genre studies, if only because this genre is defined not so much by its narrative characteristics (although there are considerable generic similarities among teen films) as it is by the population that the films are about and to whom they are directed."[7] Neale similarly notes that teen films are marked by generic diversity, as reflected in teen film scholarship that typically emphasizes the generic hybridity of teen films.[8] Shary, for example, separates the chapters in his 2002 book, *Generation Multiplex*, according to subgeneric categories such as "Youth in School" and "The Youth Horror Film". *Clueless* itself is a blend of a teen high school movie and a romantic comedy, and it is notable that, while it features most prominently in Shary's school chapter, it is also referenced in a later chapter on "Youth in Love and Having Sex".[9]

Similarly, scholarship on teen television rarely conceptualizes this programming as a coherent generic category with distinct textual markers. Instead, programs tend to be studied in isolation, divorced from broader generic frameworks. As well as the wealth of scholarship on *Buffy the Vampire Slayer*[10] (The WB/UPN, 1997–2003), there are book-length studies on individual series such as *Beverly Hills, 90210* (Fox, 1990–2000) and *My So-Called Life* (ABC, 1994–5) and essays on programs including *Sabrina, the Teenage Witch* (ABC/The WB, 1996–2003) and, more recently, *Veronica Mars* (UPN/The CW, 2004–7).[11] As with the work on teen film, when genre is discussed, it is frequently in relation to the generic hybridity of particular texts, such as *Buffy*'s use of horror elements or the blend of teen and supernatural elements in *Sabrina*. Therefore, in this work the teen series is paradoxically and implicitly defined by its very *lack* of distinct generic markers.

The lack of scholarly attention paid to the specifically *teen* aspects of the genre can partially be explained by its low cultural status. Lesley Speed identifies this low status as a key reason for the common affiliation between female directors, such as Heckerling, and teen films, as this is a genre that often relies on small budgets with little need for big stars.[12] The teen genre has a paradoxical claim to "quality," as traditionally the teenager as a figure (both in film and media and in real life) has not enjoyed critical approval. There is, therefore, a tension for the adult academic in studying texts that are arguably aimed at a much younger audience, which is typically manifest in two main ways. The first is for the adult academic to rather pessimistically dismiss what the teen genre may offer to (adult) viewers.[13] The second and more common way in which this tension is exemplified is by adult scholars attempting to justify their critical interest in the teen film or television programmer by celebrating the "quality" aspects of these texts. As teenagers lack social power, the "quality" status of individual teen texts is almost always configured on adult terms. It is no coincidence that teen films and television programs with cross-generational appeal are repeatedly discussed at the expense of those with more exclusively teenage appeal. Indeed, teen film and television scholarship, in keeping with wider scholarship on children's media, has tended to focus on the potential impact of particular texts on young viewers' behavior and expectations, at the expense of analyzing these texts for their meanings.[14] This concern is often justified by an underlying assumption that young viewers are more susceptible to media imagery than adults and, thus, in need of guidance on what to watch.

This tendency to argue for a film or program's "quality" status by highlighting its uniqueness illustrates a key bias against the concept of genre. As Jane Feuer explains, the French term "genre" literally means type, and "genre theory deals with the way in which a work may be considered to belong to a class of related works."[15] Thus, traditionally, genre analysis has sought to identify and highlight similarities across bodies of texts. With its emphasis on textual repetition, then, genre analysis works against common standards of evaluation that are based on "a romantic theory of art that places the highest value on the concepts of originality, personal creativity, and the idea of the individual artist as genius."[16] As Feuer further notes, the concept of genre was initially used in film studies to condemn mass-produced films for their lack of originality.[17] Conversely, many genre analysts focus on generic hybridity and variation, but again this is often in the service of arguing for an individual film or program's exceptionality from other generic texts.

This is heightened in the case of teen television owing to the fact that the medium itself is denigrated, frequently associated with domesticity, commercialism, repetition, and diversion.[18] As television is not culturally revered, it follows that criticism of teen series that seeks to elevate the quality status of these programs tends to marginalize their televisual aspects. For example, when making claims for the quality status of individual teen series, Matt Hills emphasizes the program's cinematic elements, such as high production values, and the crossover of cinematic stars and directors.[19] Further reflecting this bias, it is notable that the film version of *Clueless* has had access to critical approval in a way the television spin-off has not.[20] While there is little focused scholarly writing on *Clueless* (film), it is still often cited, albeit briefly, in books and articles on teen cinema, and a recent edition of *Cinema Journal* devoted an entire section to the film.[21] To my knowledge, there is no equivalent scholarship on the television series. Moreover, teen television scholarship focuses almost exclusively on teen *drama* series—programs that are often melodramatic in their mode of address and deal with serious issues—rather than comedic teen sitcoms, pointing to the way in which television genres also exist on a highbrow/lowbrow cultural axis.[22] And yet, a comparative analysis of portrayals of female friendship in the film and television versions of *Clueless* reveals that, despite being a denigrated genre, the teen sitcom potentially offers a more accommodating space for the complex portrayal of female relationships than film and should not be so readily dismissed.

This tendency to focus on teen dramas at the expense of other formats including teen sitcoms is reflected in two recent collections of essays on teen television by Glyn Davis and Kay Dickinson, and Sharon Marie Ross and

Louisa Ellen Stein.[23] Both books state a desire to address teen television seriously and each takes a fluid approach to genre, aiming to challenge existing preconceptions about what "teen television" encompasses by combining textual analysis with considerations of industry and reception. However, at the same time, they equate teen television largely with teen drama series. Almost all the essays in these anthologies focus on this particular format with no acknowledgment of this bias. Nevertheless, these books are helpful in positioning individual programs in relation to a broader structure that considers teen television as a coherent genre, and both are framed by introductions that usefully challenge the notion of teen television as unworthy of academic attention.

In many ways, this expansive and inclusive approach to genre is refreshing, aiming to challenge the narrow focus of much existing teen television scholarship on "quality" dramas with crossover adult appeal. And yet, it can risk losing sight of the televisual specificity of these texts, because there is a tendency in scholarship on the teen genre to conflate films and television series. This is reflected in Roz Kaveney's book *Teen Dreams*, in which she alternates between discussions of teen films and television series with little attention paid to medium specificity, displaying a strong bias toward the films, including *Clueless* as well as *Heathers* (Michael Lehmann, 1988), *Mean Girls* (Mark Waters, 2004) and *Sixteen Candles* (John Hughes, 1984).[24] When she does discuss teen programming, looking at series such as *Buffy* and *Veronica Mars*, it is typically to consider the influence of teen film on these texts, examining cinematic references and crossover stardom. Notably, these television programs are subsumed into an all-encompassing "filmography" at the end of the book.[25] Teenage characters and themes certainly transcend formats, genres, and media. However, to conflate teen film and television risks obscuring the powerful ways in which medium specificity intersects with genre, altering the ways in which particular narratives are framed, as a study of Heckerling's film and television versions of *Clueless* reveals.

FEMALE FRIENDSHIP AND ROMANCE IN THE FILM VERSION OF *CLUELESS*

As Yvonne Tasker observes, although "the elaborate description of sentimental, homoerotic relationships between men is commonplace in popular cinema," films that focus on female friendships have traditionally been relatively unusual.[26] It is useful here to draw on Karen Hollinger's work, as she identifies a rare spate of female friendship films in mainstream cinema from the 1980s to the early 1990s, including *Desperately Seeking Susan* (Susan Seidelman, 1985), *Beaches* (Garry Marshall, 1988), and *Fried Green Tomatoes*

(Jon Avnet, 1991).[27] She considers the role that female friendship plays across a range of films during this period, identifying progressive qualities, such as the emphasis on a female sensibility, pleasures of identification, and sympathetic heroines. Hollinger creates a typology of female friendships in these films, drawing on the five categories of literary female friendship representations developed by literary critic Janet Todd.[28] These categories include sentimental friendship (exemplified by the psychologically enriching female friendships in *Steel Magnolias* [Herbert Ross, 1989]), erotic female friendship (illustrated by lesbian relationships in *Go Fish* [Rose Troche, 1994]), manipulative or anti-female friendship (such as the controlling friendship in *Single White Female* [Barbet Schroeder, 1992]), political friendships (exemplified by *Thelma and Louise* [Ridley Scott, 1991], in which the friends fight against wider gender inequalities), and social female friendships (illustrated by the nurturing friendships in *Mystic Pizza* [Donald Petrie, 1988]).[29]

While Hollinger does not discuss *Clueless*, her definition of the female friendship film—films that feature a central female address, protagonists, and concerns—could arguably be applied to the film. *Clueless* most easily falls under the title of a social female friendship film, because it features supportive female friendships that encourage the psychological development of the female characters. Notably, like *Clueless*, two of the main films that Hollinger uses to illustrate this category—*Desperately Seeking Susan* and *Mystic Pizza*—are films that were targeted at, and particularly successful with, youth audiences. Female friendships in this type of film are not overtly political in that they do not necessarily challenge the patriarchal status quo, but rather facilitate women's smooth transition into normative gender roles. Hollinger explains, "through the teaching of female wisdom or the granting of a sympathetic ear, women in these works aid and sustain each other, perhaps by promoting a friend's heterosexual romance."[30] Thus, these films often carry a conservative message and, in turn, could be dismissed as instruments of patriarchal society with women encouraged to find fulfillment in "the private sphere of feeling."[31] However, as Hollinger notes, "Although social female friendship does not in any way attack patriarchal society, and even works to facilitate women's integration into the existing social structure, it still challenges articulations of conventional femininity in two ways: by portraying female friendship as an alternative to women's complete dependence on men and by qualifying traditional concepts of feminine passivity."[32]

Writing specifically about 1990s female-fronted teen films, Mary Celeste Kearney also identifies a growing trend toward films that privilege same-sex female friendship over heterosexual romance, emphasizing confidence, self-respect, and assertiveness, and in doing so, challenging traditional female coming-of-age narratives.[33] She attributes this shift to the increase in the number of female producers, directors, writers, and studio executives who have, at times, lent more legitimacy to feminist ideas and female perspectives.[34] While Kearney is primarily interested in independent teen films with more overtly feminist themes than *Clueless*, such as *Girls Town* (Jim McKay, 1996) and *Foxfire* (Annette Haywood-Carter, 1996), both of which deal explicitly with themes of sexual violence, Heckerling is certainly a writer and director who often privileges a central female point of view as well as feminist concerns. As Lesley Speed argues, "While her films exemplify Hollywood's tendency to absorb and de-politicize feminist values, Heckerling's career also reflects the role of contemporary female film directors in expanding teen film and low comedy beyond their traditional masculine preoccupations."[35]

In keeping with its literary origins in Jane Austen's *Emma*, *Clueless* institutes a strong, central female perspective. Indeed, using *Clueless* as one example along with films such as *Little Women* (Gillian Armstrong, 1994) and *Mrs. Dalloway* (Marlene Gorris, 1997), Hollinger argues that "many [1990s] classic adaptations represent attempts by female screenwriters, directors, and production executives to recapture for a contemporary female audience the distinctive voices of prominent women of the past, either real or fictional."[36] This distinctive female point of view is highlighted by the use of Cher's voiceover throughout, providing the viewer with intimate access to her thoughts and concerns as she navigates her personal relationships. In turn, the film privileges traditionally feminine spaces, such as Cher's bedroom and the shopping mall, with female friendships heavily emphasized within these contexts. The centrality of Cher and Dionne's friendship is established from the film's opening montage, which features several shots of the pair laughing together while socializing with their peers.

Figure 2.1 Cher and Dionne's close female friendship.

Dionne is more formally introduced by Cher within the first three minutes of the film, when she goes to pick her up on the way to school. Notably, Dionne appears several minutes before Josh, the eventual love interest, highlighting the importance of female friendship to the narrative. Through her voiceover, Cher explains that Dionne "is my friend because we both know what it's like for people to be jealous of us," further stressing their compatibility in relation to their mutual love of fashion and their names—both are named after "great singers of the past who now do infomercials." The framing, and their clothes, reinforce their closeness: they are framed side by side as Dionne gets into the car, wearing complementary outfits of tartan mini-kilts and blazers. In a shot/ reverse shot exchange, the dialogue captures their intimacy as they jokingly mock each other for their fashion choices and Dionne gently teases Cher about her driving. The following scenes in the high school further emphasize the closeness of their dyadic friendship, with the pair framed walking side by side toward the camera as they chat about Dionne's relationship problems. Further, despite being only fleetingly apart, Cher immediately phones Dionne after her class ends to rant about her report card, and the two briefly reunite in the corridor, suggesting their inseparability.

With this central narrative emphasis on intimate female friendship, *Clueless* fits not only with the female friendship film identified by Hollinger, but also with a spate of romantic comedies from the mid-1990s onwards that privilege same-sex friendship over heterosexual romance, including *The Women* (Diane English, 2008), *Baby Mama* (Michael McCullers, 2008), and a more recent film written and directed by Heckerling, *Vamps* (2012), which also starred Alicia Silverstone.[37] In particular, *Clueless* can be seen as a precursor to the more contemporary phenomenon of the "girlfriend flick," identified by Alison Winch.[38] Directly developing upon Hollinger's assertions, Winch defines the girlfriend flick as women-centered (romantic) comedies, in which men play little part and the narrative is driven by female friendship.[39] Although Winch views the girlfriend flick as a post-2008 phenomenon, many of the features of these types of films also apply to *Clueless*. As Winch explains, "Whereas the rom com typically portrays boy meets girl, boy loses girl, boy gets girl, these films relate the ups and downs of intimacy between women, while dispensing a knowing cynicism towards romance."[40] The girlfriend flick, thus, privileges intimate female friendship, with friends supplying "significant emotional and moral support, playing a fundamental role in validating each other's identities," and in doing so, offers an important and potentially cathartic space for female viewers to reflect upon the complexities of women's relationships.[41]

Like *Clueless*, the girlfriend flick also commonly features a savvy voiceover, through which the female protagonist addresses female spectators with (supposedly) female concerns, such as how to juggle romantic and familial relationships and overcome body issues.[42] This emphasis on a style of address common to self-help books echoes Alice Leppert's assertion that the form of *Clueless* as well as "its narration, and visual style . . . evoke teen magazines," in terms of its aspirational, hopeful mode of address and emphasis on advice for making over wardrobes, social lives, and romantic relationships.[43] Indeed, makeovers—both physical and psychological—feature prominently in *Clueless*, in keeping with both the girlfriend flick and teen genre more widely. Early on in the film, Cher and Dionne make over their teacher, Miss Geist (Twink Caplan), in an attempt to make her more attractive to her colleague, Mr Hall (Wallace Shawn), and in turn, encourage him to raise Cher's grade as a result of his newfound romantic bliss.

The most central makeover involves Cher and Dionne befriending and making over new student Tai (Brittany Murphy in the film), as a kind of "project" to make her acceptable to the popular crowd. The friendship between Cher, Dionne, and Tai speaks to Winch's assertion that "girlfriendship is an investment in the individual as girlfriends are essential in enabling feminine normativity."[44] Their makeover of Tai involves making her look more conventionally "feminine" by washing out her red hair dye to reveal a more natural color, motivating her to diet and work out, changing her clothes from loose fitting T-shirts and trousers to short skirts and skimpy tops, and encouraging her to wear more make-up. Cher also gives her vocabulary lessons and schools her on social etiquette. This speaks to Hollinger's assertion that the social female friendship film, while prominently featuring close female friendships, often works to reinforce patriarchal social structures by reaffirming traditional gender roles.[45] As Winch adds, these "strategic friendships ossify certain power structures and these prohibit women from investing in relationships that might devalue one's femininity."[46] Illustrating this, Cher and Dionne directly intervene to stop Tai from associating with slacker skater Travis (Breckin Meyer), fearing that this friendship/potential romance would jeopardize Tai's popularity.

On the one hand, then, *Clueless* privileges female friendship as a space of support, and helpful advice. Cher and Dionne's care of Tai is viewed by them as a selfless act of solidarity, a way to facilitate Tai's integration into the top social group at their school. Upon meeting Tai for the first time, Cher asks a reluctant Dionne, "Don't you want to use your popularity for a good cause?" Later, she describes Tai as a "lost soul," telling Josh that she is "rescuing [Tai] from teenage hell" and that "her life will be better because of me." This chimes with Hollinger's arguments about the female friendship film offering an alternative to women's dependence on men as well as challenging notions of feminine passivity.[47]

On the other hand, these friendships are paradoxically put in the service of reinforcing traditional gender norms for the purpose of *attracting* men, as illustrated by Tai's makeover. As Winch argues in relation to girlfriend flicks more widely, the regulation of female bodies through female friendships means that "hegemonic power structures are both perpetuated and obfuscated through girlfriend culture."[48] Notably, in *Clueless*, it is women who look at women, while the male gaze is friendly and largely benign. Winch expands on the girlfriend flick in stating that, "whereas the girlfriends sustain the post-feminist dream of representability and help each other realize it, heterosexual men provide relief from the scrutinizing gaze."[49] Although Winch makes no reference to *Clueless* in her analysis, it is notable that Travis's attraction to Tai is signaled from the very start of the film, prior to her makeover. The benign-ness of the male gaze does not, however, alleviate the compromises the female characters make in wanting to be more attractive to men.

It is striking that Tai's makeover and the three friends' shopping trips take place at a point in the narrative when Cher's cluelessness is at its most pro-nounced. As Gayle Wald notes in her insightful analysis of the film's represen-tation of national citizenship, *Clueless* conflates Cher's "consumption with her cluelessness," which "in turn portends the film's representation of romance as the rationale for the revision of Cher's gendered identity."[50] This is exempli-fied by the fact that it is Cher's realization of her love for Josh that acts as the catalyst for the waning of her interest in shopping and physical makeovers, replacing these activities with more "worthy" pursuits such as organizing the school's Pismo Beach Disaster Relief. If consumption is "a primary means of sociability among girls, who alternately 'bond' over shared (or similar) purchases," then it follows that upon replacing Cher's love of shopping with her love for Josh, the film also inadvertently suggests that she has given up on socializing with her girlfriends.[51]

Indeed, Dionne is narratively marginalized in the final third of the film, a turning point that arrives when Cher realizes she wants a boyfriend. This epiphany occurs directly following a disastrous driving lesson between Dionne and her boyfriend, Murray (Donald Faison), with Cher in the back seat, which ends up with all three teens narrowly escaping a car crash on the Los Angeles Freeway. Initially, the three teens are framed side by side in the car with Cher in the middle. However, Cher quickly becomes obscured as Dionne and Murray kiss passionately in relief at avoiding an accident. The camera cuts to a close-up of Cher's sad facial expression as she looks on, her voiceover noting that, "After that, Dionne's virginity went from technical to non-existent, and I realized how much I wanted a boyfriend of my own." While Dionne is mostly absent for the rest of the film, Cher's friendship with Tai still features, although it is now marked by jealously, and competition, as the two clash over Tai's crush on Josh. In the film's final twenty minutes, Cher's developing romantic feelings for Josh take precedence.

In keeping with the generic conventions of the romantic comedy, the narra-tive of the film is resolved when Cher and Josh finally admit their feelings for

Figure 2.2 The final shot of *Clueless* privileges heteronormative romance over female friendship.

one another and kiss, leading to a happy ending. This moment immediately cuts to a wedding scene, temporarily tricking viewers into believing that they are watching Cher's wedding, only for the film to swiftly turn this on its head through Cher's dismissive voiceover and the revelation that it is actually Miss Geist and Mr Hall being wed. Referring to this scene, Deleyto argues that, in some ways, the ending of *Clueless* subverts generic norms, acting as a reminder that the true narrative interest of the film is firmly on the relationships between the female characters rather than on heterosexual romance. He argues that "the happy ending here strengthens the friendship bond between the teenagers to the detriment of the heterosexual couple," attributing this emphasis on teenage peers to the film's generic teen/romantic comedy hybridity.[52] However, while Cher, Dionne, and Tai are framed sitting together at the wedding and it is implied that they will remain close friends, it is significant that their topic of conversation is their own future weddings. The three friends are all romantically paired up by the film's end, with Josh, Murray, and Travis respectively, who look on in mock horror at their marriage discussion. Further, in one of the final scenes, the girls are depicted competing, fairly aggressively, over who will catch Miss Geist's wedding bouquet as their bemused boyfriends watch. Cher wins, her main motivation being that Josh has placed a bet with the other boyfriends. The film's final shot is a close-up of a lengthy kiss between Cher and Josh, accompanied by the non-diegetic song "Tenderness" by General Public. The lyrics of the song—"Seems like without tenderness there's something missing"—reinforce the prioritization of heteronormative romance over female friendship at the film's closure.

As Tasker notes, "across a range of genres, the cost of heterosexuality and of the narrative that enacts this as a journey, is the death of female friendship."[53] One reason for this common narrative trajectory suggested by Tasker is the fear of lesbianism posed by the female friendship film. While she notes that not all female friendship films necessarily imply lesbianism—and certainly, I would argue that *Clueless* does not—"nonetheless, both women's friendships and cinematic portrayals of lesbianism operate in a shared terrain which involves female characters acting in a space not defined by male characters or by a narrative progress towards heterosexuality."[54] Indeed, female friendship is often positioned implicitly in film as something "to be grown out of," a temporary stage.[55]

This could be a reason why close female friendships in teen films, such as *Clueless*, are more common than in films featuring adult women. As teenage characters are in a liminal stage between childhood and adulthood, same-sex friendship is arguably less threatening to the heteronormative patriarchal order than adult female relationships, as it is commonly suggested that these teenage friendships are fleeting. Nevertheless, the film's ending speaks to Tasker's assertion, positioning Cher and Dionne's friendship as the precursor to her romantic relationship with Josh. Writing specifically about female-centered teen films, Kearney identifies a similar trend to Tasker, arguing that "most mainstream representations of female adolescents suggest that girls must leave their same-sex friendships behind as they enter womanhood (a position naturalized in such films as heterosexual)."[56] While *Clueless* does not suggest that this romance equals the death of same-sex friendship, ultimately, the film recuperates all three teen females into heteronormative relationships, suggesting that their personal fulfillment relies on their finding men. In turn, this narrative resolution recalls Winch's argument that, "like the films from the 1990s that Hollinger analyses, the girlfriend flick reinstates conservative principles as each girlfriend slips into the seeming security of the middle class heterosexual matrix."[57] The television version of *Clueless* offers alternative narrative and ideological possibilities for the portrayal of female relationships by privileging Cher and Dionne's friendship over any romantic relationships.

CLUELESS AS TEEN SITCOM

Significantly, in a parenthetical aside, Gayle Wald notes that the television version of *Clueless* locates Cher in a "'pre-Josh' period, allowing for the formulation of plots centering on Cher, her friends, and their various 'clueless' adventures, rather than the determining 'master-plot' of heterosexual romance".[58] The "pre-Josh" setting of the show is narratively ambiguous—certainly Josh is a less central character in the television version, but Tai is still present, albeit peripherally, and Miss Geist and Mr Hall (Twink Caplan and Wallace Shawn, also from the film) are already married. This section explores representations of female friendship in the television series in more depth, arguing that with the removal of a "master-plot" or overarching narrative of heteronormative romance, this version of *Clueless* offers a potentially more subversive portrayal of Cher and Dionne's relationship, one that is not ultimately compromised by their relationships with men as it is in the film.

The television version of *Clueless* can arguably be categorized as a teen sitcom, fitting with Lawrence Mintz's definition of the sitcom as a half-hour series, featuring self-contained episodes in which the same characters, settings and premise are encountered each week.[59] As Mintz continues, "the most important feature of sitcom structure is the cyclical nature of the normalcy of the premise undergoing stress or threat of change and becoming restored," thus leading to a happy ending.[60] More recently, some television scholars have taken issue with the narrowness of Mintz's definition of the sitcom, arguing that it operates to exclude other programs that might break from these typical narrative conventions.[61] Nevertheless, Mintz is helpful in identifying important narrative features of the traditional sitcom: the circular, repetitive premise that continually returns to a state of equilibrium by the end of each episode. I am particularly interested here in how this narrative form impacts upon the way female friendship and, in turn, heterosexual romance are framed.

At the beginning of each episode of *Clueless*, Cher has a new experience: she joins a drama class, she takes over as "Miss Buzzline," the school magazine's advice columnist, she volunteers to help save a neighborhood park. And, in turn, she quickly encounters a new dilemma: how can she get the attention of the boy she likes, what kind of advice should she give, how should she help save the park? The weekly dilemma is solved by the episode's conclusion, and order is restored, bringing a happy ending. As Davis and Dickinson argue in relation to teen television more widely, makers of teen programming often feel a responsibility to educate young viewers about relevant issues.[62] Reflecting this generic norm, several episodes of *Clueless* veer toward didacticism, with Cher learning an important lesson at the end, such as not to betray her father's trust (season 1, episode 2: "To Party or Not to Party") or the value of community work (season 1, episode 3: "City Beautification"). However, unlike the film version, which prominently features the psychological transformation of key teen characters over the course of the narrative, characters in the television spin-off largely remain unchanged from week to week. Cher may learn a lesson at the end of each episode, but she returns the following week as clueless as ever. This, in turn, reflects the narrative conventions of the traditional US sitcom, in which episodic storylines are typically circular rather than linear.[63] As Lisa Williamson asserts, "the result [of this form] is that sitcom characters are often described as learning nothing from their experiences within individual episodes and of having no memory from week to week."[64]

If the film suggests that Cher must overcome her cluelessness in order to achieve a heteronormative romantic happy ending, then it is notable that in the television version her cluelessness remains largely constant. Additionally, her friendship with Dionne remains a stable entity each week, not to be replaced by boys and romance. Theirs is the only relationship to fully carry over with the same intensity from the film, with Tai appearing only sporadically and Josh occupying a more fraternal role rather than that of a love interest. Other actors and characters carry over from the film, such as Dionne's boyfriend Murray (Donald Faison, also from the film) and their peer/frenemy, Amber (Elisa Donovan), as well as teachers Miss Geist and Mr Hall, but these figures remain less central than Dionne and Cher.

The television spin-off stresses Cher and Dionne's closeness in almost every episode. For example, "To Party or Not to Party" opens with Cher joining Dionne's drama class. Pairing up together to do a class exercise, Cher and Dionne both mistake the notion of "mirror work" to mean gazing at their reflections in their compacts. Further, when Cher has to mime out a scene, it is only Dionne who can understand what she is trying to convey. The main plot of the episode centers on Cher falling in love with fellow drama student Donal (Christopher Daniel Barnes), only to later discover he is unworthy. However, in the following episode, Donal is absent, never to be seen again, and instead it opens and ends with Dionne and Cher shopping and praising each other's new clothes.

The television version of *Clueless* continually privileges female friendship over heteronormative romance. While several episodes in the first season feature Cher falling in love, none of these romances lasts beyond one episode.[65] This emphasis on Cher and Dionne's friendship is particularly stressed in the final episode of the first season (#18), entitled "Secrets and Lies". The episode finds Cher happily in a relationship with her classmate, Noah (Jason Marsden), and is set around (and was also broadcast on) Valentine's Day. The problem-of-the-week occurs when Cher accidentally tells Murray that Dionne once dated his best friend, Sean (Sean Holland), leading to Murray and Dionne temporarily breaking up and Dionne refusing to speak to Cher. Cher's loneliness is stressed by the camerawork and mise-en-scène, as she is framed in a long shot standing alone in an empty classroom, the cool blue decor of the room reinforcing connotations of sadness. Her accompanying voiceover stresses her misery at spending Valentine's Day with only Noah, rather than her female friend, further affirming the series' emphasis on friendship over romance. Indeed, throughout the episode, Cher and Dionne wear nearly identical outfits of pink dresses and red tops, highlighting their separation all the more as they sit apart from each other in class.

It is striking that an episode about Valentine's Day, usually marked by romantic storylines across the teen genre, is centrally concerned with Cher and Dionne's relationship rather than Cher's relationship with Noah, who features only briefly. Toward the end of the episode, Cher sits glumly alone at a Valentine's Day fundraising stall, selling lollipops to be distributed as Secret Valentines' presents. Her mournful voiceover notes that "Secret Valentines are okay, but make sure you remember the people who matter the most—your best friends." In keeping with the episodic narrative form, by the episode's end the dilemma is resolved when Dionne and Murray make up and Dionne subsequently apologizes to Cher. The episode ends with Dionne joining Cher at the stall and wishing a "Happy Valentine's Day to my major best. Boyfriends will come and go, but you and me are forever." The coincidence of this episode with the end of the season reinforces the fact that the central narrative interest of the television version of *Clueless* lies with Cher and Dionne's friendship, in striking contrast to the end of the film. In the film, the compromise of Cher's romantic "gain" of Josh is the marginalization of her female relationships. Yet, the lesson learnt by Cher and Dionne at the end of season one of the television version is not to prioritize boys and romance over their friendship.

CONCLUSIONS

Catherine Driscoll explicitly identifies *Clueless* (the film), along with *Heathers* and *Mean Girls*, as representative of the diversification of girl characters in teen film from the late 1980s onwards, noting that these films differ from earlier mainstream teen films in terms of the centrality in them of female relationships.[66] The female friendships in *Clueless*, though, stand out from those in these other two films. While female relationships in *Heathers* and *Mean Girls* are mostly characterized by aggressive competition and rivalry, the friendships in *Clueless* stress support and loyalty. Although Cher and Tai fall out temporarily, this disagreement is short-lived and Cher and Dionne's friendship remains constant throughout the film. This emphasis on female solidarity can arguably be attributed to Heckerling's central role as writer and director, placing a female perspective and female relationships at the heart of the film. While it would be naïve to suggest that a female director/writer automatically results in a feminist film, it is notable that Heckerling's wider film work regularly foregrounds feminist issues. *Fast Times* challenges typical gendered portrayals of teenage female sexuality, both *Clueless* and her later college film *Loser* (2000) include moments of sexual violence (Cher is sexually harassed in a car by a classmate, while *Loser* features three college boys who try to drug and rape their female peers), and her more recent films *I Could Never Be Your Woman* (2007) and *Vamps* both touch upon gendered inequalities in relation to aging.

And yet, a comparative analysis of portrayals of female friendship in the film and television versions of *Clueless* reveals that genre and medium specificity have a powerful impact upon the transgressive potential of Heckerling's work. The representational differences in each version speak to Tasker's assertion that the common filmic narrative trajectory positions female friendship as a temporary stage on the way to heterosexual romantic fulfillment.[67] The teen film, in particular, has been described as a "sexual coming-of-age narrative," typically ending with teens recuperated into romantic relationships.[68] Ultimately, in the film version of *Clueless*, same-sex friendship is pushed to the side in favor of a focus on Cher and Josh's romance. In stark contrast, in the television version, narratives of same-sex friendship and heteronormative romance remain structurally distinct. In the *Clueless* television series, Dionne doesn't need to be marginalized to make way for the "true" (heteronormative) happy ending as in the film—rather, her friendship with Cher is framed as more constant, more enduring, more satisfying than any romantic relationship.

It would be interesting to carry out further research into the production context of both versions of *Clueless*, particularly around institutional constraints in relation to the film and television industries, as this will arguably affect the representational politics of Heckerling's work. In a recent interview with *Entertainment Weekly*, Heckerling and Twink Caplan (Miss Geist in both versions of *Clueless*, but also an associate producer on the film) reflected upon difficulties in getting the original pitch approved by studio executives.[69] Inspired by the female-fronted 1960s teen sitcom *Gidget* (ABC, 1965–6), Heckerling had originally intended *Clueless* to be a television series entitled *No Worries*.[70] However, her pitch was rejected by Fox because, as Caplan recalls, "They thought the script needed more boys in it. They were afraid that if they focused on girls, we wouldn't get any guys to see it."[71] While it is ironic that ultimately the television spin-off from *Clueless* rather than the film prioritizes female relationships, Caplan's comment speaks to a longer-standing tradition of the marginalization of women in/by Hollywood—particularly of those who are not centrally concerned with men.

NOTES

1   Celestino Deleyto, "Between friends: Love and friendship in contemporary Hollywood romantic comedy," *Screen*, 44: 2 (2003), p. 175.
2   See *The Carrie Diaries*: "Hush hush" (season 1, episode 8); "Express yourself" (season 2, episode 2); "Date expectations" (season 2, episode 10); and *Gossip Girl*: "Father and the bride" (season 5, episode 12); "Monstrous ball" (season 6, episode 5).
3   For an example, see Roz Kaveney, *Teen Dreams: Reading Teen Film and Television from Heathers to Veronica Mars* (London: I. B. Tauris, 2006).

4   Karen Hollinger, *In the Company of Women: Contemporary Female Friendship Films* (Minneapolis, MN: University of Minnesota Press, 1998), p. 8.

5   Steve Neale, *Genre and Hollywood* (London: Routledge, 2000), p. 125.

6   For book-length studies of teen cinema, see Thomas Doherty, *Teenagers and Teenpics: The Juvenilization of American Movies in the 1950s* (Boston, MA: Unwin Hyman, 1988); Jon Lewis, *The Road to Romance and Ruin: Teen Films and Youth Culture* (New York: Routledge, 1992); Jonathan Bernstein, *Pretty in Pink: The Golden Age of Teenage Movies* (London: St. Martin's Press, 1997); Timothy Shary, *Teen Movies: American Youth on Screen* (London: Wallflower Press, 2005); Stephen Tropiano, *Rebels and Chicks: A History of the Hollywood Teen Movie* (New York: Back Stage Books, 2006); Catherine Driscoll, *Teen Film: A Critical Introduction* (London: Berg, 2011); and Timothy Shary, *Generation Multiplex: The Image of Youth in American Cinema Since 1980*, rev. edn (Austin, TX: University of Texas Press, 2014). For essays on teen cinema, see Timothy Shary, "The teen film and its methods of study," *Journal of Popular Film and Television* 25: 1 (1997), pp. 38–45; Steve Neale, "Teenpics," in his *Genre and Hollywood* (London: Routledge, 2000), pp. 118–25.

7   Shary (1997), p. 39.

8   Neale (2000), p. 124.

9   Shary (2014).

10 Notably, like *Clueless*, *Buffy the Vampire Slayer* originated as a film before being made into a television series. However, the film was strikingly different from the television version, and, somewhat inverse to *Clueless*, the film was a flop while the television series was highly successful.

11 For but a few examples of scholarship on *Buffy*, see Rhonda Wilcox and David Lavery, *Fighting the Forces: What's at Stake in* Buffy the Vampire Slayer (Oxford: Rowman & Littlefield, 2002); Elana Levine and Lisa Parks, *Undead TV: Essays on* Buffy the Vampire Slayer (Durham, NC and London: Duke University Press, 2007); Anne Billson, *Buffy the Vampire Slayer* (London: BFI, 2005). Book length studies of other teen series include E. Graham McKinley, Beverly Hills 90210: *Television, Gender and Identity* (Philadelelpia, PA: University of Pennsylvania Press, 1997), and Michelle Byers and David Lavery, *Dear Angela: Remembering* My So-Called Life (Lanham, MD: Lexington Books, 2007). Essays on individual programs include Sarah Projansky and Leah R. Vande Berg, "Sabrina, the teenage . . .?: Girls, witches, mortals and the limitations of prime-time feminism," in Elyce Rae Helford (ed.), *Fantasy Girls: Gender in the New Universe of Science-Fiction and Fantasy Television* (Oxford: Rowman & Littlefield, 2000); Rachel Moseley, "Glamorous witchcraft: gender and magic in teen film and television," *Screen* 43: 4 (2002), pp. 403–22; Caralyn Bolte, "'Normal is the watchword': Exiling cultural anxieties and redefining desire from the margins," in Sharon Marie Ross and Louisa Ellen Stein (eds.), *Teen Television: Essays on Programming and Fandom* (Jefferson, NC: McFarland, 2008); Andrea Braithwaite, "'That girl of yours—she's pretty hardboiled, huh?' Detecting feminism in *Veronica Mars*," in Ross and Stein (2008).

12 Lesley Speed, "A world ruled by hilarity: gender and low comedy in the films of Amy Heckerling," *Senses of Cinema*, 22 (2002). Available at <sensesofcinema.com/2002/22/heckerling/> (last accessed 25 November 2014).

13 For an example, see Doherty (1988).

14 Shary (2014) offers a similar argument, pp. 20–4. For examples of research on the behaviour and expectations of young viewers, see Karin Beeler and Stan Beeler (eds.), *Children's Film in the Digital Age: Essays on Audience, Adaptation and Consumer Culture* (Jefferson, NC: McFarland, 2014); Becky Parry, *Children, Film and Literacy* (Basingstoke:

Palgrave Macmillan, 2013); Sarah Smith, *Children, Cinema and Censorship: From* Dracula *to the* Dead End Kids (London: I. B.Tauris, 2005); Barrie Gunter and Jill McAleer, *Children and Television* (London: Routledge, 1997).

15 Jane Feuer, "Genre study and television," in Robert C. Allen (ed.), *Channels of Discourse, Reassembled: Television and Contemporary Criticism*, 2nd edn (London: Routledge, 1992), p. 138.

16 Ibid. p. 142.

17 Ibid.

18 Ian Goode, "Value and television aesthetics," *Screen* 44: 1 (2003), p. 106.

19 Matt Hills, "*Dawson's Creek*: 'Quality teen TV' and 'Mainstream cult'?" in Glyn Davis and Kay Dickinson (eds.), *Teen TV: Genre, Consumption, Identity* (London: BFI, 2004), p. 65.

20 Gayle Wald, "Clueless in a neocolonial world order," in Frances Gateward and Murray Pomerance (eds.), *Sugar, Spice, and Everything Nice: Cinemas of Girlhood* (Detroit, MI: Wayne University Press, 2002), p. 103.

21 For examples, see Shary (1997), (2005), (2014); Neale (2000), p. 124; Kaveney (2006); Driscoll (2011), pp. 56–61. See also "In focus: *Clueless*," *Cinema Journal* 53: 3 (2014).

22 Jason Mittell, *Genre and Television: From Cop Shows to Cartoons in American Culture* (New York and London: Routledge, 2004), p. 15.

23 Davis and Dickinson (2004); Ross and Stein (2008).

24 Kaveney (2006).

25 Kaveney (2006), pp. 187–8.

26 Yvonne Tasker, *Working Girls: Gender and Sexuality in Popular Cinema* (London & New York: Routledge, 1998), p. 140.

27 Hollinger (1998).

28 Ibid. pp. 6–9.

29 Ibid.

30 Ibid. p. 8.

31 Ibid. p. 9.

32 Ibid. p. 8.

33 Mary Celeste Kearney, "Girlfriends and girl power: female adolescence in contemporary U.S. cinema," in Gateward and Pomerance (2002), p. 125.

34 Ibid. 130.

35 Speed (2002).

36 Karen Hollinger, "From female friends to literary ladies: The contemporary woman's film," in Steve Neale (ed.), *Genre and Contemporary Hollywood* (London: BFI, 2002), p. 78.

37 Deleyto (2003); Suzanne Ferriss and Mallory Young (eds.), *Chick Flicks: Contemporary Women at the Movies* (New York: Routledge, 2008); Alison Winch, "'We can have it all': the girlfriend flick," *Feminist Media Studies* 12: 1 (2012), pp. 69–82; Alison Winch, *Girlfriends and Postfeminist Sisterhood* (London: Palgrave Macmillan, 2013).

38 Winch (2012), p. 69.

39 Ibid.

40 Ibid.

41 Ibid. pp. 69–71.

42 Ibid. p. 70.

43 Alice Leppert, "Can I please give you some advice?': *Clueless* and the teen makeover," *Cinema Journal* 53: 3 (2014), pp. 131–2.

44 Winch (2013), p. 2.

45 Hollinger (1998), p. 8.
46 Winch (2013), p. 3.
47 Hollinger (1998), p. 8.
48 Winch (2013), p. 5.
49 Winch (2012), p. 77.
50 Wald, p. 113.
51 Ibid. 112.
52 Deleyto, p. 175.
53 Tasker, p. 140.
54 Ibid. p. 153.
55 Ibid. p. 151.
56 Kearney, p. 133.
57 Winch (2012), p. 79.
58 Wald, pp. 119–20.
59 Lawrence Mintz, cited in Brett Mills, *The Sitcom* (Edinburgh: Edinburgh University Press, 2009), p. 28.
60 Ibid.
61 See for example Mills (2009); Lisa Williamson, "Contentious comedy: negotiating issues of form, content and representation in American sitcoms of the post-network era," (unpublished PhD thesis, University of Glasgow, 2008); Jason Mittell, *Genre and Television: From Cop Shows to Cartoons in American Culture* (New York and London: Routledge, 2004).
62 Davis and Dickinson (2004), p. 3.
63 See typical episodes of other US sitcoms such as *Friends* (NBC, 1994–2004) and *Frasier* (NBC, 1993–2004) for examples.
64 Williamson, p. 9.
65 See (all from season 1): "Kiss me Kip" (episode 8); "I got you babe" (episode 9); "Romeo and Cher" (episode 11).
66 Catherine Driscoll, *Teen Film: A Critical Introduction* (London: Berg, 2011), pp. 56–7.
67 Tasker, p. 140.
68 Jane Feuer, *The Hollywood Musical* (Bloomington, IN: Indiana University Press, 1993), pp. 125.
69 Chris Nashawaty, "*Clueless* (1995)," *Entertainment Weekly* (5 October 2012). Available at <http://www.ew.com/ew/article/0,,20639761,00.html> (last accessed 25 November 2014).
70 Ibid.
71 Ibid.

CHAPTER 3

Fast Times with Clueless Losers: Lessons on Sex and Gender in Amy Heckerling's Teen Films

Zachary Finch

John Hughes is nearly synonymous with the teen film, having written, produced, and/or directed several of the 1980s' most successful and acclaimed films of the genre. However, the less recognized Amy Heckerling deserves reappraisal as an important teen film director, with three key efforts in the genre in three separate decades. Lesley Speed writes, "Heckerling's career also reflects on the role of contemporary female film directors in expanding teen film and low comedy beyond their traditional masculine preoccupations."[1] Indeed, with *Fast Times at Ridgemont High* (1982), *Clueless* (1995), and *Loser* (2000), Heckerling mixes comedy and drama as her young protagonists find themselves out of their depth, and taking on adult situations, often without knowing what they are doing. Stacy (Jennifer Jason Leigh) in *Fast Times*, Cher (Alicia Silverstone) in *Clueless*, and Dora (Mena Suvari) in *Loser* are trying to be adults; they think of themselves as adults, and all learn various lessons through their misadventures. These characters ultimately discover that adulthood is about asserting one's agency, and making informed choices regardless of society's proscriptions or peer pressures. Heckerling's teen films prominently express this lesson on adulthood through the spheres of sexuality and gender roles. In each of her teen films, Heckerling argues that teenage women should respect and educate themselves in sexual matters, and follow a path that makes them most happy. Her films also point out the absurdity of patriarchal demands upon young men to fulfill traditional gender roles, specifically the role of sexual conqueror. In doing so, Heckerling's works achieve nuanced representations of teens that are more than fodder for comedy or cautionary tales as they skillfully contemplate the transition from childhood to adulthood.

Sex and the negotiation of gender roles are key aspects of adolescent and young adult maturation. Unlike many teen films of the 1980s and 1990s, which handled sex in terms of polarities between, as Timothy Shary puts it, the "frivolously unenlightened"[2] and the "tortuously somber,"[3] *Fast Times*, *Clueless*, and *Loser* treat sex as a key element of youth education. Central to Heckerling's teen film work are plotlines that feature Stacy, Cher, and Dora as they negotiate their sexual activity (or inactivity). Sex is not all fun and games in these films as it is in comedies like *Porky's* (1982) and *American Pie* (1999), nor is it a death sentence as in *Kids* (1995). Instead, sex is part of the process of enlightening the heroines as they endure the trials of growing up. Additionally, teens in the real world work through gender norms and expectations, and Heckerling's works display this, too. For example, these films interrogate the cultural assumption that young men possess uncontrollable sex drives unless they are gay, weak, or emasculated. This assumption is, to an extent, challenged in *Fast Times*, *Clueless*, and *Loser*. For instance, the lead male protagonist of *Loser*, Paul (Jason Biggs), is nurturing (during scenes when he cares for newborn kittens) and protective (when he beats up his ex-roommate for slandering Dora), as well as sexually virile (at the end of the film when he takes Dora in his arms and passionately kisses her).

All three films appeared in historical and cultural contexts in which proper sexual behavior for young women and the traditional roles for young men were reassessed, and, to an extent, arguments for older notions of both made a comeback. As Lisa M. Dresner points out, *Fast Times* is situated within a brief moment between the sexual revolution of the late 1960s and 1970s, with its gains in women's sexual choices, and a backlash (to use Susan Faludi's term[4]) that included, for example, abstinence-only education and the renewed cultural conservatism in the 1980s of the Reagan administration.[5] Faludi describes the period generally, stating: "By the early '80s, the fundamentalist ideology had shouldered its way into the White House. By the mid-'80s, as resistance to women's rights acquired political and social acceptability, it passed into the popular culture."[6] Later, feminist critic Jessica Valenti interrogated the history of the abstinence-only movement, writing that "abstinence education was really born in 1981, thanks to the passage of the Adolescent Family Life (AFL) Act under the Reagan administration,"[7] which funded pregnancy prevention programs, but only those that advocated abstinence, excluding other birth control methods. Valenti concludes that this was really about retracting the rights of women and reinforcing traditional gender roles.[8] One of the key points of Valenti's critique is the idea that young women are ultimately and wrongly judged by their so-called "purity," which in US culture means whether or not they are sexually active and nothing else.[9] In her debut feature effort, *Fast Times*, Heckerling argues against the pure/impure binary (which is still very much at play in patriarchy) by portraying Stacy's sexual experiences and learned lessons as part of a process of education and maturation, not a simple matter of purity or impurity.

Stacy encounters negative sexual experiences in *Fast Times*, but the loss of her virginity and an unplanned pregnancy leave her wiser, not ruined, as her new romantic relationship with Mark (Brian Backer) at the end of the film indicates. In fact, because of these experiences, she is able to reach the conclusion to make decisions on her own terms, without following the bad advice of her friend Linda (Phoebe Cates) or other social pressures. Dresner argues that *Fast Times* is a "truly feminist"[10] teen film because it is not exploitative in its treatment of sex, and because of Stacy's agency and ultimate decision to "pursue avenues of fulfillment that are arguably ultimately more useful to her,"[11] such as female friendships and, possibly, future romance. She is correct to point out that Stacy ultimately exhibits far more agency than many girls in the teen films of the era and before, like Samantha (Molly Ringwald) in *Sixteen Candles* (1984), Carrie (Sissy Spacek) in *Carrie* (1971), Deanie (Natalie Wood) in *Splendor in the Grass* (1961), and Melanie (Yvette Mimieux) in *Where the Boys Are* (1960). However, Stacy's assertion of her own agency is the endpoint, rather than her starting place. Stacy's pursuit of sex at the beginning of the film is driven by peer pressure from Linda, which complicates the claim that Stacy acts entirely of her own volition. Stacy loses her virginity during unsatisfying sex with Ron (D. W. Brown) early in the film; some time later Stacy attempts to initiate sex with Mark, who is too shy to do much more than kiss. After Mark rejects her overtures, Stacy mutually commences sex with his friend, Mike (Robert Romanus), which results in an unplanned pregnancy. The sum of her experiences leads her to choose to "take it slow" and strike up a relationship with nice-guy Mark at the end of the film. Stacy arrives at this decision because her instances of intercourse in the film are at best unfulfilling (she gets nowhere with Mark, and no pleasure from Mike) and at worst dangerous (including sex with a near-stranger, Ron). By the end of the film, Stacy is educated about sex and eventually comes to her own conclusions rather than continuing to follow Linda's advice.

Stacy ends up as a more mature character because of her newfound respect for herself and her ability to make her own decisions regarding sexual activity. Her decision to refrain from sex is a result of some negative experiences, but none of those negative experiences results in truly devastating consequences, such as sexually transmitted diseases or social shaming, which might be expected during an era of renewed cultural conservatism (or from a more conservative filmmaker). Stacy's experiences are painful and awkward, and her sex with Mike leads to an unplanned pregnancy, but Stacy is able to arrange an abortion in a private and informed way. This un-glamorized (and un-humorous) treatment of teenage sex was a point of consternation for contemporary test audiences and reviewers. Some felt that the sex in *Fast Times* was too graphic and that it promoted unsafe teen sex. In a video interview with the Women In Cinema organization, Heckerling states that test screenings of

Fast Times in Orange County, California (a socially and politically conservative region) were very poorly received simply because teen sex was portrayed frankly and not romanticized.[12] Heckerling states that the initial test audiences felt that the film exploited teens (though Phoebe Cates, then 19, was the only teenager among the principal cast) and that the film advocated for abortions.[13] This reaction seems absurd today, but it does speak to the way abortions were represented in teen films of the early 1980s before they were vilified and nearly eliminated from teen film plotlines later in the decade and after. As Shary notes, abortion, in this film and others of the era like *The Last American Virgin* (1982) and *Teachers* (1984), addressed "emotional and moral issues,"[14] but not issues of "legality and availability."[15] Stacy's abortion is legally procured and safely performed, but it is not without some dismay, as Mike fails to both pay his share of the cost of the procedure and give her a ride to the clinic, leaving her alone to deal with the consequences of unprotected sex. The abortion itself is less traumatic than another rejection by a potential romantic partner. Writing about this moment in the film, Shary observes that Stacy is "more upset that Mike fails to help her than that she's aborting a child after only two sexual contacts."[16] Stacy's embarrassment is salved by her non-judgmental brother, Brad (Judge Reinhold), as he promises to keep this event a secret between the two of them. These scenes reveal the awkwardness, shame, and other difficulties facing young women with unplanned pregnancies, but abortion is portrayed as a viable option.

These conditions notwithstanding, the unfavorable Orange County test screenings led Universal to shelve the film for a time and later release it to a minimal 200 west coast theatres.[17] Roger Ebert called the film "a scuz-pit of a movie," disliking the representations of the teenagers, in particular the way Jennifer Jason Leigh's character engaged in sexual activity.[18] However, many of the contemporary reviews were more positive, such as Janet Maslin's, which states that the film offers a "fresh perspective" on teen life.[19]

If much of *Fast Times*'s original audience noticed that the film represents teen sex matter-of-factly (and even uncomfortably), few recognized that the film does not out-and-out advocate for it. In the commentary to the DVD of *Fast Times*, screenwriter Cameron Crowe argues that one of the goals of the film was to show that the kids engage in sex "without knowing the emotional weight of it."[20] In the same commentary, Heckerling acknowledges the attempt to capture the spirit of the time during which, for teens, "sex was not a big deal"[21] and everyone was doing it, but really they were "children experiencing all this stuff too fast."[22] The problem, for Crowe and Heckerling, is not simply that teens were having sex (which *is* the problem for the cultural right wing), but that they were doing so without the proper education and recognition of the consequences. As Heckerling points out, one of the goals of the film is to portray the activities of clueless adolescents as they played at, or made attempts at, adult activities including jobs, relationships, and, of course, sex.[23] The forthright view of teen sex in *Fast Times* may have influenced subsequent teen films as the 1980s wore on because, as Shary attests, "This is not to say that teenagers did not have sex in films after 1986, but they no longer lost their virginity in the carefree ways of the early 1980s."[24] The process leading up to Stacy's loss of virginity in *Fast Times* may begin as carefree, but her actual sexual activity proves to be anything but.

The assertion of agency is the key to Stacy's journey in *Fast Times*, rather than any particular stance toward sexual activity. The film argues that teens must learn to make decisions for themselves in order to actually become the adults they pretend to be during these years, as they jump into activities like driving cars, acquiring jobs, and relationships. *Fast Times* shows that many teens do not make adult decisions about sex, but rather they succumb to peer pressure. One of the early scenes begins with Linda encouraging Stacy to flirt with 26-year-old Ron. She lies about her age, and he asks for her phone number. A moment later, Linda implores Stacy to take the initiative and call him in order for her to lose her virginity, because, after all, Linda "did it when she was thirteen. It's no huge thing; it's just sex." Later, Linda matter-of-factly coaches Stacy on how to perform fellatio by using a carrot as a prop. These are clear examples of what Jean Schwind refers to as "cool coaching,"[25] in which slightly older and/or more "experienced" teens give advice to their peers. While Schwind argues that *Fast Times* does reflect the positive aspects of cool coaching, such as friends providing sounding boards for each other and sympathetic ears, the early scenes in *Fast Times* reveal a dark side to this kind of peer advice that pushes Stacy toward what will ultimately be unfulfilling sex.[26] Linda's glibness and Stacy's vulnerability to peer pressure convey the idea many teenage girls do not make informed decisions about sex—instead, they are playing at being adults.

Stacy's not-quite-childlikeness and vulnerability are visually reinforced in the scenes depicting her "date" with Ron, again reminding the viewer that this is not yet an informed agent making responsible sexual decisions, but a teen out of her depth. Just over sixteen minutes into the film, we see Stacy in her room, lying in bed. She is tucked in by her mother, who says "Goodnight" and turns out the light. The details in the frame emphasize Stacy's youthful status. A teddy bear rests in the background. A toy dog sits in the foreground. Her blanket is printed with flowers. As she climbs out of bed, we see that she is fully dressed and ready for a date. As she hoists herself out of her bedroom window, she steps over a doll and other stuffed animals. The decor and details within the frame remind the viewer that this is, or was, a young girl, not a responsible woman, sneaking out of her safe, home environment for sex with an older man. In addition to these indicators of childhood and childlikeness, we see that Stacy reveals an older savvy that deceives her mother and arranges a date,

Figure 3.1 Stacy in front of a wall that bears ominous graffiti in *Fast Times*.

even if she does not anticipate any negative consequences. In this scene, Stacy physically propels herself from a childhood space into a more adult world of sex and dating by climbing through a window. This movement through the window from bedroom to outside world shows Stacy's liminality, as she moves from childhood to adulthood, but does not fully inhabit either zone.

Stacy's first sexual experience is presented as somewhat painful and confusing, and the visual compositions reinforce this liminal phase of Stacy's development. Stacy may be ready for sex physically, but not mentally or emotionally, and therein lies the potential for danger. After Stacy sneaks out of her bedroom, she stands alone on a street corner until Ron picks her up.

In a wide shot, Stacy waits under a streetlight, and a sign on the building behind her reads "Wasted Youth," advertising the LA punk band of the era, but also perhaps commenting that Stacy's youth is about to be "wasted" by her giving her virginity to Ron, or that "the youth" are wasted by engaging in adult activities too soon. In the same shot, Ron's car pulls up and, wordlessly, she gets in. The compositions and the actions in this scene evoke images of prostitutes standing on street corners and climbing into the clients' cars. The film does not overtly condemn Stacy as promiscuous, but the details of the frame suggest that this activity is possibly dangerous, or illicit.

The scenes depicting Stacy and Ron's "date" argue that rushing into sex may be painful and unfulfilling. The two make their way to an isolated, dark baseball dugout—hardly a romantic or comfortable setting. They awkwardly sit for a moment while he begins to take off his clothes; he asks her if she is really nineteen, and again she lies about her age. Satisfied with that answer (and supposedly absolving him of any further responsibility for sex with a minor), Ron proceeds to lie on top of her, undress her, and have sex with her. The camera is placed over Ron's shoulder for much of the scene, and the viewer is able to watch Stacy's facial reactions to intercourse. Her expressions indicate that she is in pain, and shots of her face are intercut with shots from her point of view as she looks at the graffiti on the ceiling of the dugout. The effect of this cutting enhances the disorientation and perplexity of the moment from Stacy's point of view. The graffiti on the ceiling and walls of the dugout emphasize the grunginess (white walls marred by spray paint) of the setting. The baseball dugout—a masculine space—highlights her submission, and alludes to baseball metaphors that refer to the various stages of male sexual conquest (first base, second base, etc.).

The music and lyrics of these scenes indicate Stacy's lack of agency—she may have initiated the date, but she certainly loses control. Throughout the sequence, Jackson Browne's upbeat 'Somebody's Baby' plays on the soundtrack. The upbeat tune and lyrics, "She's got to be somebody's baby, she's so fine" and "Gonna shine tonight, make her mine tonight," provide contrapuntal sound and words when the images are read as uncomfortable and unromantic. She has submitted to Ron—"She's got to be somebody's baby . . . make her mine tonight"—and she is not an equal partner. Even though Stacy has made a choice to have sex, the lesson is that having sex in such a manner is wrong because it was the result of peer pressure and general ignorance.

Soon after the dugout scene, Ron has stopped calling, leaving Stacy disappointed and a little depressed. After an unsuccessful attempt to initiate sex with the shy Mark, Stacy and Mike have unsatisfying sex in Stacy's family's poolhouse. They are both awkward, but the sex lasts only a few seconds because Mike finishes prematurely. Medium close-up shots of Stacy's face indicate no pleasure, and Mike's embarrassment causes him to leave abruptly. The sex is brief, awkward, and unfulfilling. Stacy deals with the subsequent unplanned pregnancy without help from Mike, who becomes fairly nasty about the situation. He questions her on whether "it's his," implying that Stacy is promiscuous. Mike also says to Stacy, "It was your idea. You wanted to do it. You wanted it more than I did." He suggests that she get an abortion, and that it is "no big deal." This dialogue tells the viewer that Mike blames Stacy for their sexual intercourse—as if it were not mutual, and as if it were solely her responsibility to prevent the pregnancy. She agrees to the abortion, and requests that he pay for half of the procedure and give her a ride to the clinic. He does neither. Both of these teens, including "cool coach" Mike, are woefully ignorant about the possible consequences of sex.

However, as the film progresses, Stacy learns to assert herself by learning from these experiences. Dresner states that because Stacy responsibly researches and plans for the abortion, this is evidence of a growing agency and even feminism as she negotiates her unplanned pregnancy.[27] Stacy has sex

Figure 3.2 Mark enjoys a quick kiss from Stacy at the mall in *Fast Times*.

twice in the film—the first time results in pain and a bit of heartbreak, and the second in an unplanned pregnancy. At the same time, the abortion is not portrayed as devastating either to Stacy's family (only brother Brad knows about it) or to her future prospects for relationships (she is able to form a relationship with Mark late in the film), so the film's stance on abortion itself is not condemning. The problems for Stacy are her own ignorance and Mike's irresponsibility, for even though he suffers some humiliation for not helping Stacy (his car and locker are marked with the word "prick"), it is ultimately up to her to deal with the situation. In doing so, she grows as a character and arrives at a place in which she is able to make her own, informed decisions. As Stacy says near the end of *Fast Times*, "I've finally figured it out. I don't want sex. Anyone can have sex. I want a relationship. I want romance." Though the 1980s saw a conservative backlash against women's empowerment and female teen sexual activity as described by critics like Faludi and Valenti, *Fast Times* argues that it is not sexual activity itself that is the problem, but rather teens' lack of agency and their inability to make informed decisions regarding their sexualities. Rather than taking an abstinence-only stance (as many legislatures and Reagan-era conservatives did), *Fast Times* shows that teens will act as if they are adults in sexual and other ways, but they lack the knowledge, education, and experience that is indicative of adulthood. Therefore, they need more education rather than simple condemnation.

Heckerling's return to the teen film in 1995 with *Clueless* deals with sex in somewhat different ways, but Heckerling's emphasis on the importance of teen girls' assertion of their agency and making their own choices remains. In contrast to Stacy, Cher appears to have all the answers and knowledge she needs regarding sex and every other important matter. This impression is undercut later in the film as she, too, is shown to be a faux adult. Throughout the film, Cher Horowitz is portrayed as a strong-willed, savvy, and virginal teen girl. She insists on remaining chaste and is unwilling to have sex unless the circumstances are perfect. Unlike Stacy, whose cool-coached objective is to lose her virginity and have enjoyable sexual intercourse, for much of the film Cher has the goal of romance and a committed relationship with an older boy. She thinks she does not need to engage in sexual activity in order to be an expert on it. What is more, Cher is not just the main protagonist, but also the lead cool coach, instructing the other female characters on the proper conduct for young women. Cher seems like a credible authority on the basis of her encyclopedic knowledge of outfit combinations, her proper party conduct, and her skill at manipulating those around her (including the orchestration of her teachers' romance in order to improve her grades). These qualities give the impression that she is an informed agent, unlike Stacy in *Fast Times*, whose clueless status is the starting point. Cher's journey, in contrast, leads to the realization of her own cluelessness regarding sex and other matters like driving and Christian's (Justin Walker) sexuality. After Cher fails her driver's test (which undercuts her expertise and shows she is not yet part of the adult world), Tai (Brittany Murphy) exclaims to her during a moment of tension over stepbrother Josh (Paul Rudd): "Why am I even listening to you to begin with? You're a virgin who can't drive!" This statement questions Cher's previous authority and her self-assurance. In the following scene, Cher concludes that she does not know everything, after all. Like Stacy near the end of *Fast Times*, Cher has an epiphany in which she realizes her own lack of knowledge, as well as what she thinks she *really* wants—her stepbrother, Josh. Her stubborn avoidance of (or indifference to) sex does not mean that she is necessarily acting in the way that is best for her or her friends. Rather, she is unaware of her ignorance, and her path is the discovery of that fact. As Cher acknowledges her own feelings and inexperience, she positions herself to, perhaps, make more informed and conscientious choices.

Alice Leppert makes a convincing case that *Clueless* is something of a film version of 1990s teen magazines, dispensing advice on a wide variety of issues, not the least of which is sex.[28] Citing the film's (and many teen magazines') "tone of urgency,"[29] Leppert points out that advice about fashion and dating are given by Cher to other characters, especially Tai, and the intended audience for *Clueless*—primarily teen girls.[30] Though much of the tone of the film is tongue in cheek, as Leppert also attests, and at times Cher is shown to be "clueless" herself (like when she fails to recognize Christian's homosexuality), there is no doubt that Cher is considered to be the primary authority in the film. Not only is Cher the expert on a variety of subjects in the world of *Clueless*, but also, as Kyra Hunting notes, "*Clueless* became a nearly instant teen classic, influencing the language, fashion, and style of a generation and challenging the popular opinion that a film whose core audience was teen girls wasn't financially lucrative."[31] (Indeed, I remember returning to middle school in the fall of 1995, confronted with many eighth-grade girls ready to make a "W" with their thumbs and forefingers, and tell me "As if!") Leppert is correct that the film imitates the rhetoric, topicality, and even the imagery of teen magazines. However, the many moments in which Cher's advice and authority are shown to be questionable (like when Cher justifies her unsolicited advice to Tai by stating that she is a month older) seem to reveal Heckerling's critique of such magazines and the advice they dispense. The film shows that Cher herself is clueless, again pointing out that advice from cool coaches like Cher (and teen magazines) on topics like sex should be met with some skepticism.

If *Clueless* is something of a satire of teen magazines and their advice, Cher's attitudes toward sex seem particularly important. Approximately four minutes into the film, Cher's voiceover narration states: "I don't know why Dionne's going out with a high school boy, they're like dogs." In a tracking shot of Cher walking to class, a high school boy comes up to her and puts his arm around her. She gasps in disgust and throws him off. She exclaims, "Ugh! As if!" This comic scene establishes Cher's revulsion regarding high school boys, and she is certainly not interested in sex with any of them.

Cher's attitude toward dating and sex with high school boys is legitimized by her position as the hero of the film; she is the expert that the characters (and audience) should emulate—at least until she admits her own cluelessness. Cher's clothing shows that she is wealthy and confident about her looks. Her placement in the center of the frame in most shots indicates that she is not only the center of the film, but also the center of attention wherever she goes. The film's early tracking shots emphasize this, as most of the other students look at her as she passes by. She is the teen queen—the one who sets the trends (much like teen magazines), and this includes virginity.

If Cher's commitment to virginity seems naïve in the 1990s, an era in which sex became far more prevalent (but also far more vilified) in the media, it is significant that Cher defends that virginity at various points in the film. During a scene in a restaurant in which Cher, Dionne (Stacey Dash), and Tai discuss the attractiveness of a waiter, Tai is surprised when she learns that Cher is a virgin. Cher defends herself by saying, "You say that like it's a bad thing." Cher goes on to say, "I'm just not interested in doing it until I find the right person. You see how picky I am about my shoes, and they only go on my feet." These statements by Cher are a powerful argument for her virginity, and sexual inactivity for teenage girls more generally, if Cher speaks as the teen mag voice of the film. Cher's friend, Dionne, is also a virgin throughout much of the film, and even when she is no longer "technically a virgin," she is in a monogamous relationship. Only Tai is sexually experienced, and she is "made over" by the other girls, implying that if Tai were less clueless, she might also have been more selective in the past about sexual partners. Much of Tai's makeover centers on changing her attitudes toward liking the right kinds of boys and not rushing into sex. As Valenti argues, making oneself a valuable "commodity"[32] by remaining pure, yet appealing in the right sort of way, is a means by which patriarchy ultimately defines women by their sexual organs and experiences, not their intrinsic qualities. At the same time, Cher's inexperience with sex prompts Tai's "virgin who can't drive" comment, undermining Cher's position as an authority on something she has never experienced. The fact that Tai's makeover is conducted by someone who may not completely know what she is doing calls into question the reliability of Cher's knowledge regarding sex and boys. It also points to larger cultural dilemmas that demand teen girls be sexy but not slutty, and savvy but not too worldly-wise.

The implications of waiting to have sex until it is with exactly the right person are shown with some irony during the final scenes of *Clueless*. Late in the film, Cher comes to the realization that she loves her stepbrother, Josh. After a montage of shopping and soul-searching, Cher works out her feelings through voiceover narration and flashbacks.

She comes to the realization that she is "butt crazy in love" with Josh, and later he affirms his attraction to her as well. The two strike up a relationship, and in the film's final scene, Cher catches the bouquet at her teachers' wedding. The last shot of the film is a medium close-up of Cher and Josh kissing while she holds the flowers. This suggests that their marriage may be in the future, or at the very least they are firmly entrenched in a committed

Figure 3.3 Cher has a momentous insight about love as a fountain erupts with spray in *Clueless*.

relationship. Cher mentions in the final voiceover that she is too young to get married, but her partner remains her stepbrother.

Cher's revulsion to most high school boys contributes to a new romantic relationship with a quasi-family member. The potentially uncomfortable or incestuous implications of this relationship go unexplored by the film, especially when it comes to Cher's and Josh's future sex lives. Rather, the picturesque setting, romantic kisses, and loving looks in the final scenes of *Clueless* seem to reinforce the virtue of waiting for the right guy. However, the fact that the "right guy" is a stepbrother cannot be ignored, which makes the ending of the film a bit tongue-in-cheek. Shary argues that this moment in *Clueless* depicts a point in teen film history (the mid-1990s) where "we are left to infer that the world of sexuality has become so difficult for teens to navigate that Cher's choice of her stepbrother for a boyfriend is completely rational despite its dilemmas. Literally 'staying close to home' may ironically be the smartest sexual choice of all."[33] If one is picky enough and resistant enough to the exploration of sexuality, potential partners become so limited that one is unable to go outside of the immediate family, if even that far. Even though Cher has learned a lot, this coupling with her stepbrother proves she may still have a lot more to learn. *Clueless* provides a comic send-up of over-simplified teen magazine advice on sex (and other matters) that contributes to Heckerling's position in her films that teens, especially female teens, should learn to think for themselves in order to do what is best for them. Uninformed abstinence, succumbing to peer pressure and having sex simply to just do it, and following glib teen magazine advice on what shoes to wear or when and when not to have sex, are all ignorant choices.

Heckerling's most recent contribution to the teen film genre, *Loser*, pushes beyond the question of having intercourse. The lessons college students Paul and Dora learn are about power relationships and becoming an informed agent. Paul's roommates attempt to drug and rape their female classmates in an effort to deprive them of sexual choice and assert their dominance. For much of the film, Dora is not able to act on her own terms owing to financial hardships and an unequal dynamic in her romantic relationship with Professor Alcott (Greg Kinnear). In part because this film takes place in college (during the 2000s), it is assumed that most of the characters are having sex; the key issues for Heckerling in this film are power, respect, and agency.

Paul's dorm roommates, Adam (Zak Orth), Chris (Tom Sadoski), and Noah (Jimmi Simpson), present a frightening vision of young college men as sexual predators. Like many males in teen films, they are preoccupied with having sex, but their preferred method of obtaining partners is through date rape drugs ("roofies"). For Adam, Chris, and Noah, women are objects to be coerced and conquered. Their behavior and attitudes clash with Paul's so much that they cast him out of their dorm suite. Eventually, Paul finds new housing in the back room of an animal hospital. Later, the three former roommates impose upon Paul by planning a party during off-hours at his new residence. As the three decorate, they plan to covertly slip women date rape drugs during the party. Dora is persuaded by Chris to attend and she becomes a victim of their scheme (and thus misses her date with Paul that she originally planned), though, fortunately, she is not raped. A jilted Paul comes home late that night to find Dora drugged and unconscious. He takes her to the emergency room—using his limited funds to catch a cab—and allows her to stay in his room at the animal hospital to convalesce. When Paul questions Chris about drugging Dora, Chris victim-blames Dora, saying that she is one of the "bridge and tunnel girls. They sleep around to avoid the commute." Late in the film, the roommates purchase an additional $200-worth of roofies, but Paul replaces the drugs with ginkgo biloba. Unequal power in sexual relationships and relations between the sexes in *Loser*, whether they are between young men and unconscious women, or professors and students, are dangerous.

Dora's dilemmas in *Loser* exemplify the problems many young women face in a patriarchal society. As a student at an expensive university in New York (assumed to be NYU, but never named), Dora must work to pay tuition, but the only job she can find that pays enough is as a waitress in a strip club. She trades her looks/sexuality for money (though she is not a stripper), which is not a shameful thing in itself, but the labor conditions prove this to be an unwise occupation for her. Her supervisor, Sal (Bobby Slayton), steals from her tips. Later, the club owner, Victor (Robert Miano), fires her because she brings in less money than the other servers. Victor suggests that the reason for this is that she does not act flirtatious enough. When sympathetic co-worker Gena (Twink Caplan) says "Victor, she's working her way through college," he responds with an authoritative "Did I ask you?" Dora's attempts to better herself through education are met with financial hardship, forcing her to do whatever she can to pay for school. Dora attempts to get a job working the night shift at a convenience store, but the store only hires men because nights are "too dangerous" for women. Another frustrated attempt to get a job at a lithography shop ends because she is not in the union. Financial aid workers prove less than helpful, too. Dora nearly decides to sell her ova in order to pay for tuition, which amounts to literally selling part of her physical body. Discrimination, lack of opportunity, and sexist power relations in the workplace are interrelated with sex and gender expectations (such as the kind of work Dora is or is not fit for) in *Loser*.

Sexual relationships in *Loser* are significant for their unequal power relations. Dora comes to realize by the film's end that her relationship with Professor Alcott is unhealthy for several reasons. As her teacher, he holds a position of authority over her education. He explicitly states that he does not want to go to that "domestic place," but Dora eventually moves in with him and serves the roles of maid and concubine in return for a place to stay. This occurs because Paul's roommates blackmail Alcott when they learn about his relationship with Dora, and he decides that he might as well get the most out of her if he is going to "suffer the consequences," as he puts it. Alcott treats Dora in a condescending manner, saying to her while she mends his clothes, "I was just thinking how beautiful you looked while you were being quiet." He decides that Dora will attend Thanksgiving dinner with his family under the guise of his teaching assistant, revealing his desire to keep her as "the girl I can have fun with," but not an equal partner. Late in the film, Dora recalls her time spent with Paul (they sneak into Broadway shows, go out to eat, and enjoy the sights of Manhattan), and how he treated her much more respectfully. She ultimately realizes that the relationship with Alcott was unhealthy and that Paul is a romantic partner who will treat her as an equal.

Heckerling's meditations on sexual activity in her teen films are intertwined with issues the films raise about traditional gender roles, particularly masculine ones. Under patriarchal gender norms, men are incapable of controlling their sexual behavior. A traditionally masculine male is a sexual conqueror. There are a number of examples of this type of male in Heckerling's teen films. Valenti criticizes this element of culture by arguing that "positioning women as naturally nonsexual and men as innately ravenously sexual sets up not only a dangerous model that allows for sexual violence and disallows authentic female sexual expression, but also further enforces traditional gender roles."[34] When Stacy in *Fast Times* enters the world of sexual activity, she encounters "innately ravenously sexual" young men and there are negative consequences. Ron does not hesitate at all, and even if he doubts Stacy's age, he is more than ready. Even though at first Mike shows some hesitation or nervousness to engage in sex, bailing out is not an option and he actually proves so eager he ejaculates prematurely. In contrast, Cher knows what the score is when she says high school boys are "like dogs." Chris, Adam, and Noah are very much like "dogs" in *Loser*, as they pursue sex by illegal means, hedonistically consume alcohol, and avoid their studies.

For some young men in teen films, second thoughts about sexual activity may indicate a status of diminished masculinity, reinforcing the patriarchal requirement that males must be overtly virile. This is a trope that Heckerling uses, but also complicates and critiques through other male characters. When Stacy attempts to seduce Mark, he becomes shy and flees her room. Screenwriter Cameron Crowe confesses that, when Mark fails to have sex with Stacy, audiences in theatres at the time of the film's release yelled "Pussy! Pussy!" at the screen.[35] Indeed, Mark is coded as less masculine than Mike or Ron. For instance, Mark drives his parents' station wagon, but Ron drives his own, sportier car. Mark goes to Mike for romantic advice (though it is laughably bad) because Mike at least projects a macho swagger at many points in the film. Mark is also physically smaller than Mike and Ron, diminishing his masculinity further as he literally "looks up" to Mike. His smallness is emphasized at certain points in the production design: for instance, when he and Stacy are on a date in the German-themed *brauhaus*, the chairs they sit in are gigantic, emphasizing their childlikeness and further diminishing Mark's physical size. When Mike makes an appearance in the very same scene, he never sits. Rather, he stands over Mark, and a reaction shot of Stacy indicates a budding attraction to the larger (and more masculine) Mike. When Stacy later decides on abstinence and romance, Mark is the best partner with whom to do so, in part because he is a less traditionally masculine male (but a better overall partner, the film argues).

Not every male in Heckerling's teen films falls into the innately ravenous/less masculine binary. Spicoli (Sean Penn) in *Fast Times* is far more preoccupied with surfing and getting high than pursuing sex, yet his masculinity goes unquestioned. Travis (Breckin Meyer) is a similar Spicoli-type—the lovable stoner/skateboarder who ends up a good match and a respectful partner for Tai in *Clueless*. Paul in *Loser* provides the best example of a teen male character who displays a wide variety of behaviors that defy traditional gender roles, yet he retains his status as a masculine figure. He is one of the most hopeful male figures in Heckerling's teen films, precisely because he shows that young men can be masculine without being sexual predators. When Paul takes up residence at the animal hospital, his responsibilities for living there include basic care of the dogs and cats, and he takes these duties seriously, administering medications and gently handling the animals. Midway through the film, Paul and Dora discover a newborn kitten struggling to survive. They save it and reunite the kitten with its mother and siblings. Paul shows strong caregiving skills (including nursing Dora after her near-overdose), a trait not often associated with traditional masculinity. Though Paul is obviously attracted to Dora and women in general, he takes a firm moral stand against his roommates' roofie-schemes. He is polite and thoughtful, yet he displays strength often associated with traditional masculinity. Late in the film, Chris confronts Paul about the theft of the drugs and proceeds to insult Dora saying, "There's no velvet rope at Club Dora. Any asshole can get in." Paul beats up Chris in a display of chivalry (and traditional masculine power à la John Wayne, etc.), then apologizes to, and assists, an injured bystander. Paul is an overwhelmingly positive character, and he shows that young men may be sensitive, intelligent, and strong. Through him, Heckerling makes her strongest arguments against a narrow definition of masculinity, as he contrasts with his roommates, and other Heckerling characters like Ron and Mike.

The ways Heckerling's teen films deal with growing up through representations of sex and gender roles elevate her contributions to the genre. Unlike some teen films that treat these matters as jokes (like the aforementioned *American Pie*, as well as *American Pie 2* [2001], *Can't Hardly Wait* [1998], *Porky's* [1982], and others), *Fast Times*, *Clueless*, and *Loser* use comedy but ultimately convey serious lessons (without totally delving into the tragic and cautionary tale territory of films like *Kids*, *Thirteen* [2003] and *Havoc* [2005]). Through the experiences of Stacy, Cher, and Dora, we see that sexual activity for young women should be considered in light of making informed choices and claiming one's agency, rather than blindly following peer or magazine advice on whether to simply "do it" or not. Regarding young males, we see that the role of sexual conqueror is not appealing, but potentially dangerous, and that being a man means more than scoring.

NOTES

1 Lesley Speed, "A world ruled by hilarity: gender and low comedy in the films of Amy Heckerling," *Senses of Cinema*, 22 (2002). Available at <http://sensesofcinema.com/2002/filmmaker-profiles/heckerling/> (last accessed 22 July 2014).

2 Timothy Shary, "Virgin springs: a survey of teen films' quest for sexcess," in Tamar Jeffers McDonald (ed.), *Virgin Territory: Representing Sexual Inexperience in Film* (Detroit, MI: Wayne State University Press, 2010), p. 67.

3 Ibid.

4 Susan Faludi, *Backlash: The Undeclared War Against American Women* (New York: Crown, 1991).

5 Lisa M. Dresner, "Love's labor's lost? Early 1980s representations of girls' sexual decision making in *Fast Times at Ridgemont High* and *Little Darlings*," in McDonald, p. 174.

6 Faludi, p. xix.

7 Jessica Valenti, *The Purity Myth: How America's Obsession with Virginity is Hurting Young Women* (Berkeley, CA: Seal Press, 2009), pp. 111–12.

8 Ibid. p. 48.

9 Ibid. p. 9.

10 Dresner, p. 196.

11 Ibid. p. 185.

12 "2012 WIC Master Class with Amy Heckerling, Part 2". Available at <http://www.youtube.com/watch?v=3KC5LmwNYjE&list=UUvJLeboMEf-DbpH6InT7B2g> (last accessed 30 August 2014).

13 Ibid.

14 Timothy Shary, *Generation Multiplex: The Image of Youth in Contemporary American Cinema* (Austin, TX: University of Texas Press, 2002), p. 247.

15 Ibid.

16 Ibid.

17 "2012 WIC Master Class with Amy Heckerling, Part 2". Available at <http://www.youtube.com/watch?v=3KC5LmwNYjE&list=UUvJLeboMEf-DbpH6InT7B2g> (last accessed 30 August 2014).

18 Roger Ebert, "Fast times at Ridgemont High," *Chicago Sun-Times*, 1 January 1982). Available at <http://www.rogerebert.com/reviews/fast-times-at-ridgemont-high-1982> (last accessed 12 July 2014).

19 Janet Maslin, "Ridgemont High," *New York Times*, 3 September 1982. Available at
    <http://movies2.nytimes.com/mem/movies/review.html?_r=1&res=9507E7DA143BF9
    30A3575AC0A964948260&oref=slogin> (last accessed 15 November 2014).
20 Screenwriter and Director Commentary, *Fast Times at Ridgemont High* DVD, Universal,
    2004, 01:08:25–01:08:30.
21 Ibid. 01:09:14–01:09:25.
22 Ibid. 00:13:45–00:14:00.
23 Ibid. 01:07:00–01:07:45.
24 Shary (2010), p. 61.
25 Jean Schwind, "Cool coaching at Ridgemont High," *Journal of Popular Culture*, 41: 6
    (2008), p. 1019.
26 Ibid.
27 Ibid. p. 187.
28 Alice Leppert, "'Can I please give you some advice?' *Clueless* and the teen makeover,"
    Cinema Journal 53: 3 (2014), p. 131.
29 Ibid. p. 132.
30 Ibid.
31 Kyra Hunting, "Furiously franchised: *Clueless*, convergence culture, and the female-
    focused franchise," *Cinema Journal* 53: 3 (2014), p. 145.
32 Valenti, p. 30.
33 Timothy Shary, "'The only place to go is inside': confusions about sexuality and class
    from *Kids* to *Superbad*," in Murray Pomerance and John Sakeris (eds.), *Popping Culture*,
    7th edn (Upper Saddle River, NJ: Pearson Education, 2013), pp. 5–13.
34 Valenti, pp. 175–6.
35 Screenwriter and Director Commentary, *Fast Times* DVD, 00:42:35–00:42:55.

CHAPTER 4

"As If a Girl's Reach Should Exceed Her Grasp": Gendering Genericity and Spectatorial Address in the Work of Amy Heckerling

Mary Harrod

The work of Amy Heckerling is synonymous with a postmodern, allusive, anti-hierarchical and, above all, boundary-blurring aesthetic. The generic allegiances of her films thus throw up problems of categorization. *Fast Times at Ridgemont High* (1982) and *Clueless* (1995) are widely recognized as having been influential in shaping the post-1980s cycle of the cinematic teenpic, while the television show, video game, and book series spin-offs to which the latter has given rise stretch generic parameters in sometimes unexpected directions.[1] In between these two films, Heckerling had considerable success with family-oriented comedies like *National Lampoon's European Vacation* (1985), *Look Who's Talking*, and *Look Who's Talking Too* (1989 and 1990). However, Heckerling's later films *I Could Never Be Your Woman* (2007) and *Vamps* (2012) prove harder to classify in generic terms despite drawing explicitly on the director's teen narratives.

My interest here is specifically in the feminist potentials of Heckerling's uses of intertextual references and pastiche in *Clueless*, *I Could Never Be Your Woman*, and *Vamps*. I argue that these films create an effect comparable to that referred to by Roberta Garrett in a different context as "metagenericity," or the "playful, self-reflexive mixing of well-known cinematic formulas."[2] That is, they frequently reference previous texts, with varying degrees of self-consciousness, and they do so in such a promiscuous way that the viewer's engagement in this domain is likely to come not just from spotting specific references but also, in large measure, from appreciating a generalized sense of familiarity linked to "well-known cinematic [or more broadly textual] formulas."[3] As genre is "a functional interface between the cinematic institution, audiences, and the wider realm of culture," discussions of genre are always also discussions of spectatorial address.[4] This essay seeks to examine more fully the gendered implications of the mode of address such generic referentiality implies, including the question of how Heckerling's narratives may make us feel—an issue central to yet often sidelined in analyses of genre storytelling. In other words, the analysis accords priority not just to form but specifically to the interrelation of style, tone, and affect in mainstream narrative cinema, in a manner that, as we shall see, is ideologically loaded in the context of female authorship.

Garrett's study of *Postmodern Chick Flicks* in global (Hollywood) cinema has in fact provided the inspiration for this research, which forms the first stage of a larger project concerned with genre and pastiche practices in films made by women since around 1990. Her 2007 study claims that postmodernity has allowed highly "feminine" narratives that were frowned upon under second-wave feminism, notably romances and secondarily the melodrama, to flourish since the early-to-mid-1990s.[5] Garrett's central argument is that "new female-oriented cycles have increasingly incorporated self-consciousness and framing devices associated with postmodernist aesthetics and often used precisely to ameliorate the sentimentalism and feminine naïvety associated with older female-identified forms," and so make them more palatable for female viewers.[6] Her examples include *You've Got Mail* (Nora Ephron, 1998) and other melodramatic romcoms by Ephron, *Down with Love* (Peyton Reed, 2003), and the *Bridget Jones* films (2001, 2004) from popular cinema, but also art-house fare such as *Orlando* (Sally Potter, 1992) and *The Piano* (Jane Campion, 1993).

Garrett makes a persuasive case for the self-reflexivity of the recent female-oriented films she examines. However, the issue of female authorship does not enter into her conceptualization of "chick-flicks," although several of her examples are directed by women. Meanwhile, at the same time as female-directed avant-garde and art films have been overrepresented in feminist scholarship—with those of both Potter and Campion enjoying prominence—few analyses have considered the significance of women's recent contributions to mainstream genre filmmaking.[7] This situation is doubtless partly due to the relatively low figures for women in film industries, including Hollywood, where numbers of female directors are reported to have fallen from 9 percent in 1998 to only 5 percent in 2012.[8] Nonetheless, US-based filmmakers including, in addition to Heckerling, Kathryn Bigelow, Sofia Coppola, and Kimberly Peirce—who have received a limited amount of critical attention—as well as Catherine Hardwicke, Nancy Meyers, Karyn Kusama, and others—who have received almost none—are directing commercially impactful films across a range of genres.

What is striking about such directors' work is precisely the heightened genericity of their forms, the very over-determinacy of their dieges, which contain myriad allusions to pre-existing texts. Sometimes, as we shall see, these allusions are specific; at least as often, however, the issue is one of diffuse generic referentiality, the palimpsest effect on which genres rely for their effective engagement of viewers: films recall a generalized story arc and evoke the pleasures (or otherwise) of what Rebecca M. Gordon has referred to as a "feeling shape" associated with it.[9] It is for this reason that the term "heightened genericity" is more apt in this case than simply metagenericity, which seems to imply self-awareness—initially on the part, as it were, of the film and ultimately in the mind of the viewer it addresses—given the literal meaning of *meta* as *post*, here suggesting less an affective "feeling shape" than a later stage in cognitive processing. Silvan Tomkins's well-known theory of affects, which has been influential in film studies, outlines the way in which repetition of a similar experience "either results in habituation [and thus relative imperviousness] or sensitization and generalization"; the most powerfully affective genre films arguably engage the latter processes.[10] Yet it seems intuitively obvious that elements of this experience occur in spite of our intentions as viewers (as when we are irritated to cry while viewing excessively "sentimental" narratives). In other words, affects can operate beyond the consciously controlled realm of our behaviors. Additionally, Evan Thompson has summarized Husserl's model of time-consciousness to argue: "The retentional continuum is characterized by decreasing clarity and affective force as it sinks back into the past but it is also renewed at each moment, simultaneously being filled with new content while old content perpetually slips away into a sedimented and ultimately unconscious substratum."[11] In other words, part of the reason we cannot control affective responses created by generic sensitization is surely because they trigger associations with previous mediated experiences whose memory is unconscious. Applying these ideas to the present discussion, I contend that part of the effectiveness and affectiveness of genre films by Heckerling and other filmmakers whose work is characterized by heightened genericity—a particularly pervasive, promiscuous and generically determined sphere of intertextual relay—is located at or beyond the borders of consciousness. This is not to discount the importance of active, conscious moments of recognition triggered by her work for most spectators; the point is that these two types of response are frequently indistinguishable, which problematizes existing categories for understanding how films engage us.

Heckerling's work might not in fact initially appear a particularly obvious candidate for this model. In the first place, it is important to note that such claims are hardly exclusive even to recent women's genre filmmaking. Garrett notes that postclassical Hollywood as a whole is often perceived to be characterized by "metageneric" blockbusters and the bending of generic codes (one only has to think of the 2011 *Cowboys and Aliens* to see what she might mean). Moreover, she notes how the emphasis on hybridity in the so-called new genre criticism of Richard Maltby, Steve Neale, and, especially, Rick

Altman points up the historical roots of such practices (since genre-mixing is likely by its nature to make features of particular genres stand out in a more overt fashion).[12] For Garrett, the self-consciousness and irony of chick-flicks is differentiated by virtue of their very "in-your-face" quality, involving allusiveness no longer aimed primarily at cinephiles but at the audience as a whole.[13] Similarly, the overlapping but distinct quality of heightened or over-determined genericity, which revels in its own constructedness, but in this case without only referencing *particular*, highly recognizable other texts, is common in mainstream cinema now. Indeed, as I have argued in a discussion of the films of Richard Linklater, genre can work like pastiche in creating an impression of previous works, or in the words of Richard Dyer, "an imitation you are meant to know is an imitation": as in many of the films by women I have cited, genres can tend to pastiche themselves.[14] However, this takes on particular importance in the context of women's filmmaking.

It is no doubt significant if, as Garrett argues, films directed at women exploiting postmodern referential techniques are proliferating. As she notes, early 1980s accounts of postmodernism were associated with New Hollywood's male directing pantheon, while in the 1980s and 1990s the linkage of postmodernist features with male-oriented cinema applies to both mainstream action filmmaking (such as the *Die Hard* franchise and more experimental indie fare by the likes of David Lynch, Quentin Tarantino, Martin Scorsese, David Fincher, and Michael Mann. Initial discussions of the relationship between postmodernist filmmaking and feminism focused on the form's apparent desire to either exclude or offend the female audience, and even more recent accounts that pay attention to the articulation of gender reveal an underlying assumption of the links between postmodernism and male-oriented, often violent films. Meanwhile, Garrett attributes a critical reluctance to perceive postmodernist strategies at work in female-associated cycles to the traditional association of women's films with affective intensity and female viewers with over-engagement, in contrast to "the more cerebral, distanced 'masculine' pleasures of reference-spotting."[15] While female fan cultures are becoming increasingly prominent in ways that severely challenge the associations identified historically by Garrett, it is true that melodrama and romance remain over-privileged sites for feminist scholarship about films made by and especially for women. The already cited over-privileging of Jane Campion's oeuvre alone exemplifies the trend for prioritizing films that supposedly address not only the female spectator's emotions but also their very sensorium, bypassing concern with conscious cognitive pleasures.[16] Reference-spotting is certainly one of the pleasures of Heckerling's films and it is often, as we shall see, in comparable terms that *Clueless* in particular has been discussed, for example by Lesley Stern and Deirdre Lynch.[17] However, seeing women's use of relatively overt allusionism as transgressive does little to disturb the binaristic logic on

Figure 4.1 Costumes in *Clueless* and *Vamps* evoke Heckerling's exhilaratingly anti-historicist approach.

which such a conception of gendered spectatorship reposes, reversing rather than destabilizing its poles. It strikes me as imperative to consider not only the extent to which such films contribute to the erosion of (always gendered) epistemological categories, but also to question the very status of the category of epistemology—as divorced from embodied, affective sentiment: a realm which has traditionally been gendered feminine.

My approach distinguishes itself at the outset from the strand of feminist criticism, informed by continental philosophy that has sought to associate women with modes of communication beyond a "mainstream" language, such as that of Hollywood genres, weighty with patriarchal cultural accretions.[18] This has more recently been countered by a growing recognition of the limited reach of esoteric "speech" (such as art cinema) and a shift to emphasizing, among other things, the possibility of appropriating (patriarchal) discourse in a self-aware fashion, using, in the words of Roland Barthes cited by feminist film scholar Lucy Fischer, "quotations without inverted commas" to carve out a space particular to women.[19]

This strategy of appropriative rerouting characterizes Heckerling's teen-pics. A number of scholars, including Lesley Speed and Robin Wood, have examined how *Fast Times* introduces a feminine perspective into what was at the time a highly masculine subgenre, characterized by the likes of, from the 1950s to the 1970s, *The Blackboard Jungle* (Richard Brooks, 1955) and *American Graffiti* (George Lucas, 1973), as well as contemporaneously by *Porky's* (Bob Clark, 1982) and *Risky Business* (Paul Brickman, 1983).[20] Thus the film tackles the issue of teenage pregnancy, which has amplified resonance for girls, when Stacy (Jennifer Jason Leigh) is forced to have an abortion entirely unsupported by her easy-come-easy-go sexual partner Mike (Robert Romanus), who fails to show up even to drive her to the clinic. What's more, the film accords equal importance to female friendships as to male ones, in terms of screen time and narrative impetus. In formal terms, it also goes some way to undermining the camera's "male gaze," not only by including a girls' objectifying point-of-view shot of male behinds swathed in tight jeans but, more subtly, by locating its well-known titillating sequence, in which Phoebe Cates' Linda removes her bikini top and kisses Judge Reinhold's Brad, within a fantasy sequence that is, as Wood's analysis notes, comically punctured by her interrupting Brad's masturbatory seclusion in the bathroom in search of a Q-tip. Although a cursory Google search for either Phoebe Cates or *Fast Times* suggests this frame narrative did not prevent viewers from deriving erotic pleasure from the "iconic" scene, it does foreground the distanced authorial positioning theorized by Fischer and others.[21]

If *Fast Times* is widely recognized to have paved the way for many 1990s teen films characterized by a relatively equal focus on both genders, *Clueless*, a standout success in the genre earning just over $50 million at the domestic box office, goes further in its appropriative re-routing of teenpic conventions. The arcane slang used by the narrative's characters provides a *mise en abyme* of the reinvention of generic language itself.[22] This film revises the teenpic even more fully along feminine lines in terms of its narrative focus, after Heckerling resisted proposed changes to the script that would have evened up the representation of the genders.[23] To this end, it blends Jane Austen's *Emma* with vestiges of both *Fast Times* and what Lynch has described as "a cornucopia of visual and aural allusions to the history and prehistory of the teen film genre itself," including salient themes from *Gigi* (Vincente Minnelli, 1958), a James Dean lookalike in the character of Justin Walker's (gay) love interest Christian (Walker also resembles Jason Priestly, an intertextual relay being foregrounded by the fact that Priestly is also referred to in the film), and many 1990s musical covers of 1970s hit pop songs.[24] Additionally, the evocation of a dense network of pop (and high) cultural associations is facilitated by its quintessentially postmodern LA setting, epitomized by Cher's "classic" (as she puts it) neo-classical home, embodying the architectural mixing of styles that is, as Lynch acknowledges, one of Fredric Jameson's targets of condemnation in his well-known theorization of postmodernism.[25] Maureen Turim's assessment of the film's lead character, Cher, as having "a logic all of her own" might well be applied to Heckerling's work, in its refusal to fit pre-existing molds, but such individuation relies precisely on a complex positioning in relation to textual others.[26] Indeed, for all its originality, the film meets seven of the nine criteria for the prominent 1990s cycle of teenpics described by Wood (only departing from the model by including racial and sexual minorities, to an extent).[27]

An insightful analysis of *Clueless* is facilitated by Lynch's focus on the film's negotiation of history. For her, Heckerling's promiscuously referential aesthetic, in which Shakespeare's *Hamlet* and Mel Gibson's embodiment of the latter's protagonist are indistinguishably valid sources of knowledge, spatializes time, deconstructs modernist notions of historical progress, and questions epistemological categories, with a particular emphasis on the gendered character of the latter: witness the joke that sees Cher read "trashy" pop-psychology book *Men Are From Mars, Women Are From Venus*, while Josh, clad in dark clothes and sunglasses, consumes Friedrich Nietzsche. For Lynch, the motif of fashion in *Clueless* (and beyond) is particularly intricately bound up with the eschewal of linear history, given the participation of sartorial trends in temporal and geographical bricolage: Cher and Dionne sport garments ranging from Austenian Empire-line dresses to theatrical outsize hats, evoking a hodgepodge of past styles, and paired improbably with contemporary-looking A-line skirts and fitted jackets. As Lynch explains, the role of fashion in the film is to shun referential power and to "cultivate the untimely."[28] For her, the film rejects a Hegelian view of historical progress encapsulated in the notion that lends Cher's history teacher her name, *Geist*, or spirit and its so-called coming-to-consciousness. It is certainly no accident that, as she notes, history classrooms are prominent targets of exuberant adolescent mockery—and, we might add, creative misunderstanding—in both *Clueless* and *Fast Times*. Moreover, Lynch's observation that the "crisis of historical memory" decried by Jameson has always been banal for women, excluded from official histories in the first place, lends further weight to the act of championing a postmodern referential aesthetic as propitious for exploration of women's concerns.[29]

Yet Lynch's semiotic reading of details of costume does not exclude an apprehension of their simultaneous functioning as sites of psychic and corporeal engagement, as she acknowledges how the intimacy between clothes and bodies over-determines fashion's responsiveness to desires and dreams.[30] These elements of the film thus signify, by alluding to historical eras, in ways that interpellate both conscious and unconscious registering, and also, simultaneously and *through the same process*, address the viewer's senses. Indeed, if Lynch has argued that "costume can [both] introduce anachronism" and also express "a woman's desire to flee the era by which she is captured," this expression is partly achieved through communicating an affectively generated sense of freedom, comparable to the experience of trying on a new outfit, or identity, ourselves. It should be recognized that the costumes in *Clueless* also convey dedication to capitalist consumption. Thus Cher is willing to argue with the gun-wielding mugger that she may soil her designer Alaïa dress if she lay on the ground, while new girl Tai (Brittany Murphy) is not accepted until she is made over through shopping. Such class circumscription—mirroring the association between female progress toward emancipation and women of means—may limit somewhat the affectively generated sense of freedom associated with the sartorial theme. Nonetheless, Heckerling's wildly anti-realist, colorful costumes in *Clueless* communicate a feeling of fun and possibility as much as they address conscious processes of cognition.

This duality of address is equally a feature of the film's soundtrack. Turim has shown how samples from such hits as Coolio's *Rollin' with my Homies*, The Muffs' *Kids in America* (a cover of Kim Wilde's 1981 hit), Supergrass's *Feel Alright*, and, especially, Jill Sobule's *Supermodel*, "consciously mock the innocence of past generations of teenagers, and enclaves that try to retain that innocence, with self-consciousness and a flippant irony."[31] She also argues that prior knowledge of segments of certain tracks, such as Beastie Boys' *Mullet Head* and Radiohead's *Fake Plastic Trees*, endows these tracks with more irony than does simply hearing the snippets featured in the film. In this case, the experience of the songs does not necessarily coincide with a retrospective, considered appraisal of them: the emphasis during viewing is once more on exhilaration and immediacy, evoking the high pitch of the teen years. Importantly, at least as much as it depends on what is said, the vibrancy of listening to these songs is a function of the sounds of the instrumental score alongside the timbre and delivery of the voices heard—not to mention the songs' associations for individual viewers, which may depend, among other things, on familiarity with the music video, as well as a host of personal circumstances linked to previous instances of listening.

Both Turim and Ben Aslinger—the latter in an article that claims Heckerling played a definitive role in the shift to treating film and television scores as authorial flourishes—single out the Sobule track for analysis from this perspective. While Turim underlines simply what she describes as the "New York punk" delivery, for Aslinger, "Sobule's choice to affect a teen girl accent and a particular Californian vocal uptick at the end of phrases combines with her performance on guitar to simultaneously endorse and satirize gender norms."[32] He goes on to cite Leslie C. Dunn and Nancy A. Jones's observation that "To move from voice to vocality . . . implies a shift from a concern with the phenomenological roots of voice to a conception of vocality as a cultural construct."[33] Once again, the inherent qualities of an effect (here a sound) are inextricably bound up with its signifying potential, both of which produce a complex—but initially and primarily affective—response in the viewer. If Eugenie Brinkema's recent study of cinematic and other forms of affect has correctly observed that discussions of the phenomenon of affectiveness have for too long been severed from those of textuality, Heckerling's revisionist teenpics foreground the inseparability of processes of textual signification and embodied address when it comes to film analysis.[34]

I Could Never Be Your Woman is perhaps the Heckerling film that is most explicit about the power of the constructed, or textual, to impact on the body. Highly camp in its aesthetic yet loosely autobiographical in its subject matter, it focuses on the lives and romances in particular of a divorced television writer and her teenaged daughter in Los Angeles. The show on which Rosie (Michelle Pfeiffer) works resembles the *Clueless* television show spin-off (United Paramount Network, 1996–9). This series—of which Heckerling wrote and directed four episodes and executive-produced another eighteen (as well as retaining a credit as series creator on all episodes)—is notable for an increased use, and salience, of formal distancing devices by comparison with the film, including highly stylized costumes, ostentatious uses of non-diegetic sound in connection with particular themes, and an even more extensive use of voiceover, which is occasionally requisitioned by secondary characters. Like its predecessor, it is arch in tone, its opening episode bearing the name that has lent this essay its title quotation: "As If a Girl's Reach Should Exceed Her Grasp." It also features many of the cast members from the film, namely Stacey Dash (Dionne), Donald Faison (Murray), Elisa Donovan (Amber), Twink Caplan (Miss Geist), and Wallace Shawn (Mr Hall), although Rachel Blanchard steps in as Cher. The television show featured in *I Could Never*, however, has Stacey Dash's Dionne in the central role. Given that the mostly white (and upper-middle-class) nature of Heckerling's film worlds, alongside textual naïvety around the intersectionality of issues of race, class, and gender, has been seen as a limitation for the progressive politics of her work, the promotion of Dash to star billing is not insignificant—although featuring an ethnic minority in the lead only in an embedded narrative appears something of a pyrrhic victory.[35] More relevant to the question of the film's blatant artifice is the way in which the cast and crew of the show are almost as improbably mannered and plastic as the world depicted; a stereotypically flamboyant gay hairdresser character in particular. Furthermore, textual and extra-textual worlds are continually leveled by pop cultural references that disrupt the relationship between sign and referent. Thus the character of Screech (Dustin Diamond) from well-known high school television show *Saved by the Bell* (NBC, 1989–93) is referenced within the embedded show; a nonsense acoustic approximation of French, "the language of love," replaces the real thing in Adam's camp courting of Rosie; and most tellingly of all, Rosie is perplexed by the news that her ex-husband is writing the script for a "reality" television show.

In genre terms, *I Could Never Be Your Woman* is perhaps most likely to be seen as what Margaret Tally has called an "older bird" romcom.[36] In addition to this affiliation, it includes rites-of-passage elements by paying a degree of attention to the teenage Izzie (Saoirse Ronan), and it also deploys adolescent themes and aesthetics in relation to its much older main character, in conjunction with overtly deconstructing generational categories. For instance, during an early scene in which Rosie goes jogging, Mother Nature (Tracey Ullman) appears to her as a know-it-all, middle-aged harridan to tell her that no matter how slim and youthful an appearance she maintains, she can't get away from the realities of mutability, her "internal organs [. . .] rotting." The aging theme is developed through Rosie's relationship with actor Adam (Paul Rudd), eleven years her junior (a number made more pronounced by the fact that Rosie is 40 and Adam is 29). While Rosie's anxiety about going to trendy bars with Adam and inhabiting a youthful role at his side speak to the performative qualities of generational identity (when you get to her age, she quips, all your clothes become "vintage"), they also highlight the staged nature of courtship and dating rituals as a whole: the social construction of coupling culture and, to an extent, the most notionally subjective and embodied experience of attraction itself. This idea is expressed formally by the externalization of the process of falling for someone: in a point-of-view shot from Rosie's perspective, Adam fulfills the criterion for love she has earlier elaborated to Izzie, that of appearing to her in slow motion.

This breaking down of the barriers between externally constructed discourse and internal, bodily affect is quintessentially Heckerling. It is noteworthy that the chirpily-cum-inanely delivered theme song to the *Clueless* show describes Cher's life as "*literally a Polaroid* of perfection" (my emphasis). The notion of the literal Polaroid, like that of Mel Gibson's Hamlet, once more evokes the simultaneity of discourse's status as highly fake yet our experience of it as "real" and/or affectively meaningful. Even more extreme in this vein is a metaphor used by Izzie in *I Could Never* when she describes teenage angst as a "wedgie on your soul." Such a conflation of concepts associated with extremes of corporeality and contrastingly "transcendent" immateriality is not incidental to Heckerling's project. Just as Rosie ignores Mother Nature, who evaporates as she doggedly pursues her laps of the running track, earlier fears about, and a brief breaking off of, the relationship with Adam give way by the end of the film to a provisional union and an embrace of living in the immediacy of the present. Although any attempt by the narrative to dispel taboos around relationships between older women and younger men is severely tempered by Michele Pfeiffer's extreme conformity to ideals of feminine perfection in terms of appearance, suggesting that cultural choices can rewrite the script of biological determinism is an act of faith from a feminist perspective.

All these examples bespeak, then, a highly poststructuralist notion of discourse—in this case encompassing both metaphor and indexical image—as supplanting unmediated or referential notions of the real outside representation. This concept is central to Heckerling's work in ways that demonstrate a desire to rescue discursive practices of signification from being dislocated from the lived experience of individual subjects of any gender. Indeed, Stern's analysis of *Clueless* foregrounded the non-contradictory impulses of what she calls ethnography and rhetoric at play in Heckerling's films.[37] This certainly applies to *Fast Times*. The narrative was based on ethnographic research carried out by Cameron Crowe, the writer of the film's source novel and co-writer of the screenplay with Heckerling, who posed as a student to develop characters absolutely rooted in fact.[38] Yet this detail has not prevented them from taking their place within a generic archetypology for teen films, most obviously in Sean Penn's California stoner slacker Jeff Spicoli.[39] Similarly, in an interview, Amy Heckerling has claimed that the keys to successful filmmaking are "to love your characters and to know how to make your audience feel how you want them to": in other words, the generic qualities of her films do not detract from emotional engagement—including with characters even as they are, in the generic framework, inevitably endowed with archetypal qualities.[40] Rather, as in the examples discussed earlier of the fashion motifs and soundtrack in *Clueless*, it is precisely the appeal these elements make to a mass audience that ensures their affective properties, through Tomkinsean generic "sensitization and generalization."

Ideas of collectivity and group address are altogether crucial to the power of Heckerling's genre pieces. Relational models for identity-formation were championed by second-wave feminism and have defined some theorizations—notably psychoanalytic ones—of female experience as a whole. Group dynamics run equally to the heart of teen narratives. Jean Schwind has moreover examined the substitution of horizontal models of "coaching" for vertical ones in *Fast Times*, where older peers are revealed to be as clueless as contemporaries, while Alice Leppert makes similar claims for *Clueless*'s reinvention of the makeover narrative as no longer absorbed through didactic magazine articles but rather enacted and circulated between friends.[41] According to Leppert, indeed, *Clueless* had a considerable impact on retail fashion and most likely magazine culture too: its "glossy look and instruction in the rules of dating, fashion, and popularity helped pave the way for the girly culture of the late 1990s."[42]

This is a typical example of the tendency of Heckerling's work to bleed outside its textual frames. I have already suggested that Heckerling cross-fertilizes between film genres. Moreover, the existence of a serialized television version of *Clueless*, which in turn features in a highly autobiographical film narrative, muddies further both generic boundaries and the parameters of "reality" and text. *Clueless* has furthermore given rise to several spin-offs and thus, as Kyra Hunting has shown, provides a striking example of convergence culture—not to mention a rare instance of a female-focused franchise, many of whose senior production roles were occupied by female executives. The film's success was a platform for "a complete multimedia brand," including, in addition to the television show, a video game and 21 novels, all featuring the film's idiosyncratic, vernacular, and referential linguistic style.[43]

Of particular interest are the interactive properties of the video game, in which players can, for example, take part in makeover and dressing experiences. As Hunting notes, the concept of world-making as integral to convergence may appear to privilege "male-identified genres" such as sci-fi and fantasy.[44] Technological inventiveness and fantasy are key aspects of the new generic directions being taken by recent women's filmmaking as a whole and Heckerling's oeuvre in particular; furthermore, the move into interactive space merely extends the drive I have identified in her creations to involve consumers as much in a (shared) embodied experience as in hermeneutic games. Turim too has observed that the existence of the *Clueless* video interface foregrounds how *Clueless*—like much popular culture—is about the formation of virtual group identities outside a purely textual model of identification or voyeurism.[45]

Lynch's work on the cavalier treatment of history in *Clueless* reprises the same terms, borrowed from Celeste Olalquiaga, to argue that the film replaces vertical paradigms, linked to hierarchies of value that are both generic and gendered, with horizontal integrality. This perspective facilitates understanding of her claim, that the "problem" of the individual's relation to history, one posed by a poster in *Fast Times* reading "History and you," is—as (she notes) recognized by such thinkers as William Robertson, David Hume, and Adam Smith—"one of genre"; it is linked to canons.[46] Certainly the cyclical nature of not only fashions but also the television series format would appear to bear a closer relation to what Julia Kristeva has called "women's time" than to the teleologies of patriarchal consciousness.[47] The interrelated notions of cyclical ahistoricity and generic hybridity, alongside the convergence of fakery and feeling, all of which have been cited in this essay as feminist strategies, come together most fully in Heckerling's most recent film, *Vamps*. For this reason, I will dedicate the remainder of the analysis to a closer examination of a sequence from this film. This is because, for all my attempts to return the question of affect to formal analysis, the usual challenges of describing subjective experiences are multiplied when considering film and other texts as a whole or in their intertextual relay. With this example, my aim is to attempt to unpick in more detail precisely the functioning and nature of the affective address in an instance of highly generic narrative.

Vamps superimposes a female buddy narrative onto a fantasy backdrop by placing at its center a pair of undead but non-violent female vampires (shades of the *Buffy the Vampire Slayer* franchise [film 1992, TV show 1997–2003] and other texts of the female-accented teen fantasy—often vampire—fad epitomized by it and the *Twilight* franchise). The vampires are played by Alicia Silverstone and Krysten Ritter, the latter an actress associated with death through her role in the international hit television show *Breaking Bad* (AMC, 2008–13) and with the Gothic through several of her television and film roles including *Woke Up Dead* (Sony Pictures Television, 2009) and *27 Dresses* (Anne Fletcher, 2008). The presence of various actors from *Clueless* and other Heckerling texts, now familiar as her "muses," points up the extent to which her work pastiches itself. In this case, the narrative conceit is that the two friends are frozen at the age at which they were turned into vampires. For Ritter's Stacy, this is in her twenties. Silverstone's Goody, turned as a married mother-of-two in 1840, is considerably older in both human and vampire years; however, she lies about both ages to make Stacy feel more at ease and spends the narrative posing as a student with the wisdom of a middle-aged woman who has seen the historical shifts of two centuries. This literalizes many of the themes around aging and the discrepancy it introduces between mental self-perception and external appearance that are at the fore in *I Could Never*—as well as affording further possibilities for pan-historical sartorial ensembles, as Goody puts together the styles she likes best from different eras.

At the end of this film, the vampires decide to return to human form, in order to allow Stacy to have a baby. This requires them to kill the egotistical and rapacious vampire who originally turned them, played by Sigourney Weaver, a star whose (gendered) over-determinacy is acknowledged and exploited by the character's temporary transformation, after being stabbed, into a kind of computer graphic skeleton, whose shoddy, superimposed look matches the film's campy collage aesthetic as a whole. This means the vampires assume their real age—Stacy thus becomes 40 but Goody is now 171, so her conversion means her imminent death. In the final moments of the film, in line with its time-bending postmodern approach as a whole, the (cosmetically) aged Goody's life flashes before her in a series of shots of events occurring in New York's Times Square that answer directly to the question of the links between history and the individual subject, including women. Thus we see from her point of view the vista of the square—surely one of the most frequently represented in the history of cinema, as well as one of the most integral to the history of the performing arts in the USA—dissolve into earlier, remembered images of the same location: initially in color, the temporal slippage signaled only by the replacement of contemporary brand advertising with retro avatars, then black and white, with poor and flickering image quality suggesting aged celluloid, redolent of the early years of cinema in the twentieth century, and later sepia for nineteenth-century memories of her husband and children.

Significant moments in Goody's own life—notably around romance and motherhood—are replayed before her eyes, interspersed with cutaways to her face transfixed with wistful longing, which prompts Stacy to squeeze her hand in sisterly comradeship and empathy, all to the gently melancholic strains of

Figure 4.2 A grainy look evokes celluloid memories of former eras in Times Square.

Gene Austin's *A Garden in the Rain* from 1929. The successive layering of different eras in memory is conveyed by the alternation of different periods, marked by differences of costume and graphics, as well as by the gradual dissolving of different sections of the image into other eras in such a way that elements of each temporarily co-exist, mimicking the subjective experience of recollection. Interestingly, these events are interrupted halfway through by an interlude in which Goody eats her first food of the last couple of centuries and appears equally overwhelmed by this experience, conveyed by her widening eyes and a shared smile of incredulity with Stacy, who is doing the same, accompanied only by the banal pronouncement, "Oh, my God." The materiality of bodily subjectivity, which is best expressed both intra- and extratextually (for the viewer) by a (nonetheless discursively coded) exchange of looks, is underscored here as heavily as the materiality of the cinematic image—and even more so, through retroactive contrast, when Goody literally dematerializes into dust at the end of the scene, to leave Stacy in tears: as William James has observed, it is in experiencing thunder that we experience the silence that preceded it.[48]

Online discussion forums testify to the emotive power of this scene, with several viewers reporting being moved to tears, regardless of the film's extreme anti-realism.[49] Clearly onscreen deaths, not to mention scenes of romantic love and maternal intimacy, are classic tear-jerkers; however, it seems to me that part of this sequence's affective force derives from the important role played in it specifically by evocations of pastness and transience, which are further reinforced for many viewers by the presence of *Clueless*'s Silverstone, now herself older at 35, even without cosmetic enhancement. Indeed, while I have suggested that the affective qualities of *Clueless* are frequently linked to exuberance and vitality, at least one exception to this pattern is provided by a moment toward the climax of that film, during the "low" prior to the final act's union of Cher and Josh, when Cher's father tells her he has not seen so much good done around the house since the days of her mother, at which—anecdotally—I have witnessed viewers (including a male friend in his mid-thirties) well up. The loss of the past is of course the defining feature of the affective states of mourning and melancholia theorized by Freud. On this basis, texts that recall other texts, and thus point up the absence of the experiences associated with those earlier texts, partially through recreating them, recreate the experience of such states, including their characteristic fixation on the absent object through trying imaginatively to reconstruct or cling onto it. From this perspective, heightened genericity reveals itself once again to be well equipped to tap into viewers' feelings of nostalgia. The shadowy suggestion of prior texts, whose specificity may well be lost to the conscious mind but whose affective outline endures like the stain on a photographic negative, is likely to create the bittersweet sensation of nostalgia, which is itself characterized by the duality of material absence alongside mental presence. In this light, knowledge contributes to—rather than ameliorating or even working alongside—sentimentality. This may be more or less conscious—less so when it comes to a vague sense of familiarity—in a distinction that parallels Freud's account of the difference between mourning, for a specific object, and melancholia, for an undefined one.[50]

In psycho-physiological terms, the work of both these processes can moreover be seen, in Brinkema's summary, as "the processual labor involved in directing libidinal attachments after a loss." She notes how, because of the revelatory quality attributed to melancholia especially in later Freud, for whom the depressive had a keener eye for the truth than others, recent theorists of loss such as David Eng and David Kazanjian, as well as Judith Butler, have sought to attribute to these experiences a creative and sensual quality.[51] This concept of re-direction of psychic energies chimes with enactive theorizations of emotion, which have defined the latter as a—not necessarily conscious—"endogenous initiation and direction of behavior outward into the world."[52] Viewed from this perspective, empathetic engagement with other subjectivities itself has an affective force, in the sense of implying an opening up onto the world. This statement applies whether the other subjectivities concerned are constructed as fictional (onscreen) or notionally implied through a sense of shared collective identity that transcends textuality to encompass interactive engagement, including fan cultures. But narratives that color this experience with a sense of shifting temporality up the stakes further: loss is surely the catalyst for the most extreme emotional states, demanding the most radical shifts in psychic energies and thus eliciting that familiar sensation of sadness, yet simultaneously a pleasurable, inspirational feeling of opening up to the outside world and others in it, inspired by sequences like the climax of *Vamps*.

The importance of these arguments for gendering discursive communication should be apparent by now. If I have argued that Heckerling's feminist strategy relies on a bold reimagining of material realities through tropes of liberating fantasy, the pertinence of Brinkema's statement that "ongoing struggles with the potentialities of the past enable unique possibilities to imagine the world otherwise, to speak to (or for) and grapple with the new," is clear.[53] As Lynch shows, Heckerling's requisitioning of genre to her own ends is a clear example of what John Frow, building on Michel de Certeau, has called tactics, the "tactful" way in which unauthorized users temporarily occupy culturally valorized discourses.[54] Additionally, the tactical pairing of narratives designed to elicit affect with extreme referentiality—one possible definition of the genre film—demands reading in terms of a move to blur the boundaries between intellectual and bodily engagement, thus contributing to the erosion of the categories of cognition and affect. At one point in *I Could Never*, Rosie tells Izzie's schoolteacher that "her mind works [in] a *different* way." The originality of Heckerling's approach to expressing inexpressible (gendered) difference is to conceptualize it—paradoxically but necessarily—through sameness, and specifically through a conception of shared subjectivity defined by the interpenetration of the mind and the body as sites of imaginative flight. To conclude by giving language the attention it deserves in Heckerling's universe, and to return to my title, we might see Heckerling's teen and related films, then, as strategically reaching via discourse (in the Lacanian sense of language arising from the desire to interact with the external world), reaching through but beyond the potential limits of such codified communication, toward the phenomenological spectatorial response, in a way that makes hazy and thus exceeds the limits of either. This move widens Heckerling's possibilities for addressing a broad public and repositions her as a female auteur on several levels.

NOTES

1   The fact that a feature length teenpic remix featuring clips from over 200 teen films was entitled *Beyond Clueless* (Charlie Lyne, 2014) signals the ongoing urtext status of Heckerling's second key contribution to the genre.
2   Roberta Garrett, *Postmodern Chick Flicks: The Return of the Woman's Film* (New York and Basingstoke: Palgrave Macmillan, 2007), p. 5.
3   Ibid.
4   Frank Krutnik, "The faint aroma of performing seals: the 'nervous' romance and the comedy of the sexes," *The Velvet Light Trap* 26 (1990), pp. 57–62.
5   Similar arguments have been rehearsed in relation to postfeminism, which can in this specific context be seen as a kind of subset of postmodernism. See for example Sarah Projansky, *Watching Rape: Film and Television in Postfeminist Culture* (New York: New York University Press, 2001); Ros Gill, "Postfeminist media culture: elements of a sensibility," *European Journal of Cultural Studies* 10: 2 (2005), pp. 147–66; Yvonne Tasker and Diane Negra, "Introduction," in Yvonne Tasker and Diane Negra (eds.), *Interrogating Postfeminism: Gender and the Politics of Popular Culture* (Durham, NC and London: Duke University Press 2007), pp. 1–25, esp. p. 15.
6   Garrett, p. 7.
7   According to Deborah Jermyn, leaving aside scholarly articles, Potter has been the subject of two monographs and Campion seven (and the Belgian avant-garde director Chantal Akerman four). In "Nancy Meyers: the wrong kind of woman filmmaker?," paper presented at the *Doing Women's Film and Television History Conference*, University of East Anglia, 10–12 April 2014.
8   Melissa Silverstein, "What Bigelow effect? Number of women directors in Hollywood falls to 5 percent," *Indiewire*, 24 Jan. 2012. Available at <http://blogs.indiewire.com/ womenandhollywood/what-bigelow-effect-number-of-women-directors-in-hollywood-falls-to-5-percent#.T_r9RpH_yVo> (last accessed 12 July 2014).
9   Rebecca M. Gordon, "Remakes, genre and affect: the thriller-chiller-comedy as case study," unpublished dissertation, Portland College, Oregon, English Department (2007), p. 1.

10   Cited in Eve Kosofsky Sedgwick and Adam Franks (eds.), *Shame and Its Sisters: A Silvan Tomkins Reader* (Durham, NC: Duke University Press, 1995), p. 65.

11   Evan Thompson, *Mind in Life: Biology, Phenomenology and the Sciences of the Mind* (Cambridge, MA: Harvard University Press, 2007), pp. 321–2.

12   Garrett, p. 27.

13   Given the existence of such ostentatiously self-reflexive genre films as the *Scream* horror franchise (1996, 1997, 2000, and 2011) or the romcom *Date Movie* (2006), it is perhaps more logical to view the directions being taken by the chick-flick as overlapping with, rather than qualitatively distinct from, other recent trends in genre filmmaking.

14   Mary Harrod, "The aesthetics of pastiche in the work of Richard Linklater," *Screen* 51: 1 (2010), p. 23.

15   Garrett, pp. 5–6, citing Barbara Creed, *From Here to Modernity: Feminism and Postmodernism*, *Screen* 28: 2 (1987), pp. 47–58. See Amy Taubin, "The men's room," *Sight and Sound* 2: 8 (1992), pp. 2–4; Jane M. Shattuc, "Postmodern misogyny in *Blue Velvet*," *Genders* 13 (1992), pp. 73–89; and Lynne Layton, "*Blue Velvet*: parable of male development," *Screen* 35: 4 (1994), pp. 374–93, as examples of early discussions emphasizing the exclusion of feminist concerns. See Christopher Sharrett, "End of the story: the collapse of myth in postmodern narrative film," in Jon Lewis (ed.), *The End of Cinema as We Know It* (New York: New York University Press, 2001), pp. 319–32, and Alexandra Juhasz, "The phallus unfetishised: the end of masculinity as we know it in late 1990s 'feminist' cinema," in Lewis, pp. 210–25, as examples of later accounts that attempt to address gender but still betray assumptions about the ties binding postmodernist strategies to male-oriented film forms.

16   See for example Sobchack's well-known analysis of the synesthetic qualities of Campion's art-house melodrama *The Piano* in *Carnal Thoughts: Embodiment and Moving Image Culture* (Oakland, CA: University of California Press, 2004), pp. 61–6. In a different context, several papers at a 2010 conference on contemporary women's filmmaking in France took a comparably material approach, such as Delphine Bénézet, "Eléonore Faucher's haptic cinema in *Les brodeuses* (2004)" and Margrit Troehler, "The atmosphere of *Lady Chatterley* (Pascale Ferran, 2006)," at *Women's Filmmaking in France 2000–2010*, 2–4 December, Institute of Germanic and Romance Studies, London; so too does much criticism focused on French female-directed "extreme" cinema. Many of these critiques are clearly influenced by the elevation of the female body as the key to championing women's specificity in continental feminist philosophy by such writers as Luce Irigaray, Hélène Cixous, and others.

17   Lesley Stern, "*Emma* in Los Angeles: remaking the book and the city," in James Naremore (ed.), *Film Adaptation* (London: Athlone, 2000), pp. 221–38; Deirdre Lynch, "*Clueless*: about history," in Suzanne R. Pucci and James Thompson (eds.), *Jane Austen and Co.: Remaking the Past in Contemporary Culture* (New York: State University of New York Press, 2003), pp. 71–92.

18   For example, in the well-known work of Laura Mulvey, Stephen Heath, Mary-Ann Doane, and early Claire Johnston, as cited in Garrett, p. 27.

19   Lucy Fischer, *Shot/Countershot: Film Tradition and Women's Cinema* (Princeton, NJ: Princeton University Press, 1989), p. 15.

20   Lesley Speed, "A world ruled by hilarity: gender and low comedy in the films of Amy Heckerling," *Senses of Cinema* 22 (2002), available at http://sensesofcinema.com/2002/filmmaker-profiles/heckerling/ (last accessed 12 September 2014); Robin Wood, *Hollywood: From Vietnam to Reagan . . . and Beyond* (New York: Columbia University Press, 2003), pp. 192–7.

21 See Fischer, *Shot/Countershot*, pp. 3–24, for a detailed explanation of the importance of intertextuality and the revision of canons to Fischer's conception of counter-cinema, as well as reference to other feminist writers who have advanced comparable ideas, including Mary Ann Doane, Linda Williams, Patricia Mellencamp, and Annette Kuhn.

22 For a detailed discussion of language in *Clueless*, see Jennifer O'Meara, "'We've got to work on your accent and vocabulary': characterization through verbal style in *Clueless*," *Cinema Journal* 53: 3 (2014), pp. 138–45.

23 Mary G. Hurd, *Women Directors and Their Films* (Westport, CT: Praeger, 2007), p. 27.

24 Lynch, p. 75.

25 Lynch, p. 74. Ben Aslinger also notes that the use of covers "signals the importance of music from youth and early childhood to teenage aesthetics," in "Clueless about listening formations?" *Cinema Journal* 53: 3 (2014), p. 128.

26 Maureen Turim, "Popular culture and the comedy of manners: *Clueless* and fashion clues," in Pucci and Thompson, p. 42.

27 Robin Wood, "Party time or can't hardly wait for that American pie: Hollywood high school movies of the 90s," *CineAction!* 58 (2002), pp. 4–10. These are: the theme of sex; the lack of focus on education, on familial situations, on politics, or on class; relatively equal gender presence; and textual status as a literary adaptation.

28 Lynch, p. 74.

29 Ibid. p. 78.

30 Ibid. p. 87.

31 Turim, p. 43.

32 Ibid.; Aslinger, p.127.

33 Aslinger, p. 129. Aslinger's article furthermore attempts to probe the difficult question of how "the connections between embodiment, visuality and musicality," including their gendered quality, can be framed in music videos, like the Aerosmith video that launched Silverstone to fame, and film. The issue of gendered delivery is picked up explicitly in *I Could Never Be Your Woman* when Rosie advises Izzie not to hold back on the screeching to appear demurely "feminine" for the sake of a boy she admires when delivering a (rewritten) version of Alanis Morissette's *Ironic*.

34 Eugenie Brinkema, *The Forms of the Affects* (Durham, NC: Duke University Press, 2014), p. 30. I do not, however, share her view on the expendability of the spectator in discussions of cinematic affect.

35 See for example Turim, p. 45.

36 See Margaret Tally, "Something's gotta give: Hollywood, female sexuality and the 'older bird' chick flick," in Suzanne Ferriss and Mallory Young (eds.), *Chick Flicks: Contemporary Women at the Movies* (London and New York: Routledge 2008), pp. 119–31; or, on the same topic, Deborah Jermyn, "Unlikely heroines? 'Women of a certain age' and romantic comedy," *CineAction* 85 (2011), pp. 26–33.

37 Stern, p. 229.

38 Janis Cole and Holly Dale, *Calling the Shots: Profiles of Women Filmmakers* (Kingston, ON: Quarry Press, 1993), p. 112.

39 This bears comparison with Sofia Coppola's reality-based endeavor in the nonetheless generic teen narrative *The Bling Ring* (2013).

40 Cited in Cole and Dale, *Calling the Shots*, p. 115.

41 Jean Schwind, "Cool coaching at Ridgemont High," *The Journal of Popular Culture* 41: 6 (2008), pp. 1012–32; Alice Leppert, "Can I please give you some advice? *Clueless* and the teen makeover," *Cinema Journal* 53: 3 (Spring 2014), pp. 131–7.

42 Leppert, p. 137.

43 Kyra Hunting, "Furiously franchised: *Clueless*, convergence culture and the female-focused franchise," *Cinema Journal* 53: 3 (2014), pp. 150, 145.

44 Ibid. p. 147.

45 Turim, p. 49.

46 Lynch, pp. 81–5.

47 Julia Kristeva, *Les Nouvelles maladies de l'âme* (Paris: Fayard, 1993), pp. 297–332.

48 Cited in Thompson, p. 328.

49 For example, see comments by users Maria Onaiza Pelayo and Jenaizaki Deviant on YouTube: "Gene Austin, *A Garden in the Rain* (1929)". Available at <www.youtube.com/watch?v=zMu-6bSCzlM> (last accessed 15 December 2014).

50 Sigmund Freud, "Mourning and melancholia," in *On Murder, Mourning and Melancholia*, trans. Shaun Witeside (London: Penguin, 2005), pp. 201–18. I have made similar claims in the context of Linklater's work in Harrod, p. 36.

51 Brinkema, p. 65–8.

52 Thompson, p. 365.

53 Brinkema, p. 68.

54 Lynch, p. 84.

Ingenuity and Irony
in the Heckerling Lexicon

Introduction to Part II

This book surveys Amy Heckerling's work as a director, yet her skill as a writer has been most evident in her deft use of dialogue among her characters. Weaving together innovations in contemporary lingo with verbal irony, Heckerling has been able to enliven her characters' traits with humorous aplomb: the snarky sarcasm of baby Mikey in *Look Who's Talking* ("Somebody burp me before I blow up!"); the ostentatious outbursts of Cher and her peers in *Clueless* ("Your face is catching up with your mouth!"); and the witty wisdom of middle-aged cynicism in *I Could Never Be Your Woman* ("Tobacco is natural, Prozac's unnatural. Earthquakes are natural, television's unnatural. Natural sucks!").

Heckerling's writing tends toward the comical, but for every *bon mot* tossed between her protagonists, she has offered often poignant comments about culture, class, and, particularly, gender, as the two chapters in this section demonstrate well. The politics of consumption and class that Heckerling first explored through Cameron Crowe's script for *Fast Times at Ridgemont High* (1982) are taken up by Andrea Press and Ellen Rosenman in their distinctive examination of youth identity in Heckerling's writing of *Clueless* (1995). Rather than merely discussing the upper-crust status of the characters in the film, Press and Rosenman set out to consider how the film's messages about economic identity have been received by contemporary teenagers. Theirs is one of the rare film studies that employs a sociological approach, using focus groups, to explore the intersection of cinematic language and class-consciousness, resulting in a provocative argument about the impact of visual and spoken signifiers in understanding cultural positions.

In the latter chapter, Lisa Richards further analyzes the teenspeak of Heckerling's characters, placing their linguistic practices in the wider context of the teen genre to argue for the various hierarchies and nuances of youth culture. Through her investigation, Richards demonstrates the expressive reaches of Heckerling's dialogue, illustrating the means by which the characters are identified in social groups and as cultural tropes. By scrutinizing this use of language in generic and political terms, she reveals unexpected statements that Heckerling's writing evinces about youth in terms of community membership and generational status.

CHAPTER 5

Consumerism and the Languages of Class: American Teenagers View Amy Heckerling's *Clueless*

Andrea Press and Ellen Rosenman

American media and popular culture reflect contradictory ideas about women's class membership. On the one hand, film and television expose us to more and more images of successful working women, as the great popularity of the current television shows *Homeland* (Showtime, 2011–), *Scandal* (ABC, 2012–), and *How to Get Away with Murder* (ABC, 2014–) testify; on the other hand, and not to be minimized, we are bombarded with images, particularly those aimed at adolescent girls, that equate women's sex appeal, and worth on the marriage market, with the whole of their worth. In many popular cultural fantasies, the route to riches for women—or at least the quickest path to class mobility—lies in cultivating their physical and sexual attractiveness, and their appeal to men, particularly marriageable men who can endow them with favorable market connections.[1] The power of some of our most popular cultural symbols—Beyoncé, or *American Idol* stars Kelly Clarkson, Carrie Underwood, or Fantasia Barrino, for example, and indeed the ageless story of *Cinderella*, recently (2015) and periodically remade for film—repackage this fantasy for the present day. The proliferation of the many self-improvement reality television shows such as *The Biggest Loser* (NBC, 2004–), *Extreme Weight Loss* (ABC, 2011), or *Gone Too Far* (MTV, 2009)[2] testifies to the continuing power of the fantasy that ordinary people can achieve extraordinary looks, attention, and often concomitant riches—the latter particularly for women who, by improving their looks, can attract a (preferably affluent, as well as handsome) Prince Charming. Specifically, the idea that any girl or woman with proper self-improvement techniques, regardless of the accidents of beauty or fortune, can attain the beauty and riches enjoyed by any princess remains a staple of many of the most popular women's magazines aimed at adolescent and young women.

These fantasies have changed somewhat in the postfeminist era: after all, Beyoncé is a successful working woman, as are many of the *American Idol* winners—none is simply a princess of leisure! Yet two aspects remain alarmingly similar in them, ensuring continuity even from Jane Austen's day (the era of incipient capitalism at the turn of the nineteenth century) to today: first, the importance of women's physical "appeal," presumably to men-as-viewers; second, the intermingling in these fantasies of the idea that in the conquest of men lies the surest route to material gain for women, a reality in Austen's day but a myth, sociologically speaking, in our own, in that today most women work to support themselves even when they are married.

Austen's enduringly popular *Pride and Prejudice* (1813) lays out the rags-to-riches fantasy for women most clearly.[3] Modern-day fans are still captivated by Elizabeth Bennet's travels from poverty to wealth (or those of Bridget Jones, a heroine some view as the modern-day reincarnation of Elizabeth Bennet)[4]—at least, judging by the enduring popularity of this heroine through its many popular adaptations and the statistic that *Pride and Prejudice* is the most widely read novel in the English language.[5] Austen's later novel *Emma* (1815) interested Amy Heckerling enough for her to adapt it to a current setting in her popular teen film *Clueless* (1995). This novel takes a different, more complicated, and decidedly "shaded" perspective on the importance of marriage to women's social class position. While Lizzy, the heroine of *Pride and Prejudice*, is born somewhat poor but not too low—she is a gentleman's daughter, but has no inheritance of her own to help her procure a good marriage—Emma Woodhouse is born having everything, which in Austen's world (and our own perhaps?) included brains, beauty, and wealth. Austen refers to Emma, in a famous passage from one of her letters, by saying, "I am going to take a heroine whom no one but myself will much like,"[6] presumably because all her readers would either be consumed with envy at her advantages or simply be irritated by her proclivity toward interfering in the lives of her friends.

Emma lives alone with her ailing father. Her older sister and her governess have both married, while her mother has been deceased since her girlhood. She is a close friend to a neighbor, Mr Knightly, whose brother is married to her older sister, and in the course of the novel she befriends a poor girl named Harriet Smith, of unknown parentage. She has many friends in the small village of Highbury, most of lower status than she is herself. The novel focuses on how Emma makes connections, successfully or not, with a series of other characters whom she meets with in this remarkably self-enclosed town, and how she learns to value others both ethically and empathically, despite their personality flaws and often despite their relative poverty and want of social connection.

Of all Austen novels, *Emma* offers perhaps the most ambiguous reading of the social class hierarchy that marked Austen's time.[7] While Emma tries to

achieve friendship across class lines—in particular, with her lower-class associate Harriet Smith, whom she attempts to take under her wing—by the end
of the novel this is shown to be a misguided enterprise, and Emma and Harriet
are both safely returned to their proper class associations and milieu. Emma's
plot to marry off Harriet to the local clergyman Mr Elton is thwarted in part
by his desire to move up socially; he turns up with a more affluent wife of his
own choosing. Harriet mourns him but subsequently becomes engaged to a
local farmer, Mr Martin, with whose family she has become friendly despite
Emma's initial disapproval. Critics argue at great length about the point of
Emma: some contend that it is written to reflect on British class structure, to
both clarify and question it. Others claim that the narrative strongly reinforces
the values underlying the class structure of turn-of-the-nineteenth-century
England. Austen seems both of and apart from her time, and critics are
divided.[8]

As fans of Jane Austen and her various film and television adaptations,
we became even more interested in *Emma* when we viewed Heckerling's
remarkable adaptation, the teen film *Clueless*. We were now both Austen *and*
Heckerling fans. A smash hit, *Clueless* moves Austen's story to a modern
Beverly Hills high school.[9] Heckerling's adaptation—particularly given its
updated setting—remains surprisingly close to Austen's narrative structure
and thematics. *Clueless*'s widespread acclaim, therefore, potentially meant
that modern American viewers were processing some of the same social class
themes present in Austen's British novel. Because of our scholarly interest
in the intersections between gender, social class, and media reception, and
because we believe that reception cannot be studied through textual analysis
alone, we decided to launch an audience study of the film, which we had been
teaching in college "teen film" and British literature classes for the past two
decades.[10]

Moving Austen's 1815 novel to the setting of a present-day high school
in Los Angeles posed some particular problems given the nature of Austen's
original story. Nationality, age, and time period were all necessarily to be
altered beyond recognition. *Clueless* was marketed modestly to teenage girls
by Paramount as a small, offbeat film, the studio holding no particular ambitions for its success, yet it became an unanticipated hit and remains to this day
one of the most universally viewed teen films, almost definitive of the genre.[11]
Clueless's modest budget of $12 million would yield over $77 million at the
global box office.[12] Press always uses it to begin discussion of the teen film
genre in a course entitled *Teen Film*, taken by students drawn from a variety
of majors who have in common, usually, their past viewing of *Clueless*. The
film's popularity sparks some interesting questions for us, as both a sociolo-
gist (Press) and literary scholar (Rosenman). In particular, it asks a question
of central interest to sociologists: at what level is the perception of social class

membership widespread, even in a society that overtly denies the importance of this issue?

Ethnographic work on American high school and college students, and on the US population in general, indicates that most do not perceive the reality of social class difference in US society.[13] Therefore, the popularity of a narrative in which the social class identity of the heroine plays such a central role—we would argue this is as true in Heckerling's adaptation as it was in Austen's original novel—is curious, in our view, given that social class is not in the everyday vocabulary of American teenagers. This feature inspired our interest in studying students' present-day reception of *Clueless*. Of course, many popular films of the last several decades have focused their dramatic tension on the issue of the upwardly mobile lower-class woman, including *Ella Enchanted* (2004), *Working Girl* (1988), and *Pretty Woman* (1990).

Some of Heckerling's other work has also focused on social class issues. Her breakthrough film *Fast Times at Ridgemont High* (1982) is a Los Angeles-based high school film set in a middle-class, and sometimes lower-middle-class, milieu. Heckerling's high school students are concerned with their jobs in fast-food restaurants and at the local mall; losing a job is a major student headache, and working in a particular business is seen to confer identity and status on the film's major characters. Social class stereotyping, as well, is at play in some of the film's characterizations. The "bad guy" in the film—Mike (Robert Romanus), who sleeps with his best friend's crush, impregnates her, and refuses to subsidize or even show up for the abortion—is depicted as the poorest character in the film, living in a downscale, welfare-hotel apartment building, and running a concert-ticket-scalping business that takes advantage of the fandom of small children by overcharging them for the tickets of their musical idols.

Heckerling's follow-up to *Clueless*, *Loser* (2000), concerns a relatively poor scholarship student at a New York City university,[14] Paul Tannek (Jason Biggs), who must continually worry about losing his scholarship money, especially after having trouble with his wealthier roommates and friends. In this film, the class stereotyping works in reverse, as his roommates' low moral character is constantly juxtaposed with Paul's morality and genuine concern for others. Professors don't fare well either, as the one college professor portrayed in depth has multiple callous affairs with undergraduate students.

In the case of Heckerling's *Clueless*, we were particularly interested in examining the transposition techniques that had allowed an American female director and writer to transplant *Emma* to suburban Beverly Hills, and also in determining how American teenagers read this Austenian tale of gender and social class. What makes it so popular? Why are American teenagers still watching Jane Austen's tales of gender and social class in the new millennium? And finally, how did Austen's treatment of social class translate into the present, and were her original meanings understood similarly, or not, by today's viewers? These were the questions we set out to address in this study.

We decided to begin our investigation by interviewing students in a small private high school, and comparing their reception of the film, and remarks about it, to those of public high school and college students drawn more from a more mainstream, middle-class population. In a society like the contemporary USA, where almost everyone in the population considers themselves middle-class, and where the class distinctions that do exist are often invisible and buried,[15] we felt that this comparison of potentially different social class groups would begin to give us a handle on the way young Americans experience social class and its relationship to gender, and perhaps offer some insight into the popularity of Austen narratives as well. We organized five focus group interviews, two with private high school students, two with public college students, and one from a more prestigious public college that drew students from many elite high school settings, to probe these issues. Of course, readers should approach this data cautiously, since at times we are comparing high school students to college students, as well as drawing from members of different social class groups whose boundaries are often indistinct. We gathered demographic information from each of the students that helped us assess their social class backgrounds in a general way. Results are of course tentative, however, as assessments of social class membership in the US context always are.[16]

One of the most interesting features of *Clueless*, which it shares with the indie film version of *Emma* produced in 1996 featuring Gwyneth Paltrow, is the way the class themes in Austen are somewhat "sanitized" as the ocean to the USA is crossed.[17] What is presented as class distinction in the novel is often reduced to a matter of the divergent "styles" which perhaps overlie and even mystify class difference in *Clueless*, and to mere snobbery in the film *Emma*, stripped of much of the import of class hierarchy which characterized Austen's vision (however you interpret her perspective on this hierarchy, it certainly occupied a central position in her storytelling). As one public school student put it, "Class distinction is harder to tell" now; "you can't really class people" today as in Austen's time—a remark that well captures the consciousness of most middle-class Americans. Though most of our respondents could identify Cher as relatively "wealthy," certainly wealthier than they themselves were, this doesn't necessarily translate into an identification of a distinct social class membership, as much social scientific study of the issue has demonstrated.[18]

In fact, scholarly assessments of social class difference in the USA have determined that social class identity is a mixture of the factors of educational attainment (which confers a certain cultural capital), occupational category or position (some occupations confer social or cultural capital over and above the remuneration they yield), and financial capital (this would include access to wealth, perhaps that accrued through inheritance or through business ventures, as well as the salary attendant upon one's own or one's partner's job). Social class identity is a complex phenomenon drawing from the status conferred by each of these categories. For women, the determination of social class identity can be even more complex as some women who do not work for pay gain status from their partner's occupation, salary, and/or family wealth. Children, such as Cher, gain social class status and identity from their parents'—most often, their fathers'—relationship to these variables.

Heckerling's treatment of social class issues in the adaptive process is worth detailing. Notably, she downplayed the screenplay's relationship to Austen's novel out of fear that the product would be perceived as too "intellectual" by the studio and the viewers.[19] Austen is mentioned nowhere in the credits and the only direct allusion to the novel *Emma* is in the name of the character Elton (a dead-ringer for Austen's Mr Elton). The masquerade was so effective that even erudite film critic Roger Ebert seemed unaware of the relationship in his initial review of the piece.[20] Heckerling feared, and rightly so, that a more overt connection to high literary culture would scare off the American mass teen audience, and producers seeking a mass audience for their products as well.

Clueless borrows from the Austen model an amused and tolerant perspective on wealthy leading character Cher. She lives an unusually privileged life ("both of us [friend Dionne (Stacey Dash) and Cher herself] know what it's like to have other people be jealous of us"). Her situation is one that clearly can inspire envy and even contempt. The film takes seriously—but not too seriously—Cher's attempt to grow into a more moral person, capable of transcending petty jealousies and her own envious feelings. It captures well the whimsical feel of the novel, which has a fair amount of comedy in its portrayal of all the various characters of a small community, and their intrigues and gossips. It perhaps captures less well the moral seriousness of the novel, which focuses on Emma's moral growth from a somewhat careless, uncaring neighbor into a nurturing member of her close-knit community. The novel also indicates both the critical aspects of Austen's perspective on the social class hierarchy within which she lived and her conservative support of it (but simultaneous ability to satirize it). Though the most intelligent characters are also the wealthiest (such as Emma herself, and her ultimate love interest, neighboring estate owner Mr Knightly), there are many worthy poorer characters and enough ridiculous rich people to make the novel perennially entertaining. All, however, in the novel *Emma*, end up exactly where they should end up according to the conservative values of the day: Harriet, the daughter of "no one in particular" (no one known), as Austen tells us, is married to modest farmer Mr Martin; the would-be social climbers Mr and Mrs Elton find each other; and Emma, happy in her inherited wealth, finds another, even wealthier partner, cut from similar cloth. The social order is fully supported by the novel's end, though Emma has become a more sensitive and caring friend. Cher undergoes a very similar transformation in *Clueless*.

Heckerling does succeed surprisingly admirably in translating both the cast of characters, and the novel's moral shading of each, into the world of the Beverly Hills High School. In each adaptation (Heckerling's and the Paltrow film), the social climbing aspirations of Mr Elton (represented in *Clueless* by first Tai's and then Cher's would-be boyfriend Elton, played by Jeremy Sisto) mark him out as shallow. While wealth is not vilified in the novel or in the films, "aspiring" to greater wealth through marriage, as Mr Elton does quite overtly, is frowned upon. Mr Knightly/Josh is similarly humorless in each film, a didactic prig, played in *Clueless* (against current type) by burgeoning film star Paul Rudd.[21] Mr Martin, Austen's farmer, is a bit more respectable in the novel than is his counterpart in *Clueless*, Travis (Breckin Meyer), a stoner (who does end up in a rehab program). However, Martin's love interest Harriet, a simple lower-class girl in the novel, is transformed into the grungier Tai (Brittany Murphy) in the adaptation. The Harriet/Tai story in the novel reminds us not to try to enter a milieu above one's own "level," especially when pursuing a romantic relationship. Cleverly, in *Clueless*, Tai is portrayed as simply and naturally having more in common with Travis—a penniless low-life of her own class background—than with the wealthier Elton, and her attraction to Travis naturally flows from this. Though it might be counter-intuitive, the social class narrative still actually operates as such in the current context, but its meanings are inflected with cultural as well as social class differences. In the case of the Cher–Tai relationship, Tai is quite emphatically *culturally* different from Cher, as indicated by her accent, clothing, and allusions to drug use and sexual activity. These traits *hint* that she might hail from a different economic class (her accent is an urban twang, her clothing is less fashionable, she has a proclivity for recreational drugs, and she is not a virgin), as this might follow from these other differences—but this information is left vague. The social class differences so explicit in *Emma* become, in the Heckerling script, cultural differences that *may* be indicative of class. But, according with the much more ambiguous nature of social class identification in the American context, the class inflections of these differences remain abstruse.

Prominent in *Clueless* is the clever way that Heckerling allows consumerist values to represent the social class hierarchy—for instance, the intellectual and moral superiority of the upper class—that is celebrated in the original Austen version. The two versions may not be as divergent as they appear. In Austen's day the consumer dominance of the upper class was certainly also celebrated, along with their superior education and moral sense. Though radical upward mobility was presumed to be impossible (and in fact undesirable, against the normal order of things), in other Austen books female heroines often aspire to greater wealth through marriage—which is celebrated, however, only when accompanied by true love; but true love is represented as being much more pleasant when one falls in love with a rich man rather than a poor one.

Of all the Austen narratives, *Emma* contains perhaps the most conservative set of judgments on social class issues. Emma's desire that Harriet marry well is shown to be entirely misguided because it would drive Harriet to seek someone outside her own class. Indeed, renouncing this notion is part of both Emma's and Harriet's personality development, as depicted throughout the narrative. Of course, Emma ultimately gives up her judgment against Mr Martin, Harriet's lower-class suitor, in part because she realizes that he is in fact a person of some "quality" (good character), and that Mr Elton, her middle-class would-be beau, is not. This recognition that a lower-class or poor person can also be a person of good character is a less conservative aspect of the narrative; it contrasts with Emma's initial evaluation of Mr Martin. At first Emma is repulsed by the idea of her friend marrying such a lower-class man, but she comes to see that he is of good and stable character, which Mr Knightly initially tells her. In turn, Mr Knightly comes to see that Harriet, though "the natural daughter of no one knows who," also possesses many amiable qualities, along with the all-important "good character." This aspect of the novel's story is paralleled in *Clueless* as Cher develops increasing friendship for Travis, and respect for his drug rehabilitation efforts and skateboarding skill. In the end, Tai ends up paired happily with him.

We had students view not only *Clueless*, but a more faithful BBC adaptation of *Emma* as well, which allowed us to investigate these social class themes more directly by asking them to contrast the two adaptations (necessary because few had read the novel).[22] Many had also viewed the independent adaptation of *Emma* featuring Paltrow as well. Focusing on distinctions between the reception of the private school students and that of the public school students, we note the following four thematics that emerged as essential axes of difference between the two groups.

One. Perhaps the main difference between the private school and public school students focused on the distinctive importance to the latter of the theme of the "authenticity of the self," which was more of an issue for the public school students than for the private school ones. In Austen, Emma becomes her "best self"—the self that is worthy of her personality and her class position. While public school students sought "authenticity," this concept did not really inform the Austen novel, in which Emma's "authentic self" is really her "best self," which we see to be more mannerly and caring than the Emma we initially meet—but in the course of the novel, Emma has to learn to be her "true" self; it doesn't come naturally. In the American public school students' sense, then, Emma's "true" self, according to Austen, is not necessarily her "honest" self; it is not encapsulated in her immediate reactions to the events of everyday life. In the case of Austen, Emma's "true" self is also the one that is more true (and more appropriate, in behavior), to her "class," though this theme drops out in the case of *Clueless*.

Public school students from a middle-class background criticized Emma's transformation in all versions they viewed, finding it to be a change in the direction of inauthenticity—that is, Emma learned to be *less* sincere or less honest in her self-presentation—rather than a desirable change, as in the following comment by a woman who had attended a large public high school, who here is commenting on a scene in the Paltrow film of *Emma*. The students did not perceive these "changes" to be in the interests of the kind of authenticity or "truth" that they admired:

> You're obviously supposed to like *Emma*. She is very sweet, she's very pretty. But for instance when she's riding with Harriet in the carriage, she's being all gossipy and making fun of the others in the town. Just talking about things that they said, she couldn't believe that she said them. And then all of a sudden it's "Hi, Mr So-and-So, how are you?" You're kind of going, "Come on, give me a break." Obviously she's insincere. Even though you're *supposed* to like her . . . You're not supposed to like Mrs Elton, but I found her to be the most sincere of them all because at least when she didn't like somebody you knew it . . . As soon as they weren't in the picture for the moment, she was telling the truth about her feeling on them. So as much as I hated Mrs Elton, I liked her. Or at least I could appreciate her actions.

This student shows she admired expressions of honesty from the character of Emma even if they were critical or impolite. For her and her classmates, the "true-to-herself" Cher would become even more preoccupied with shopping and consumption. Environmentalism, and her attachment to Josh, are seen as leading her "away" from herself. The authenticity of the self is not connected, for these students, to any moral set of judgments, or to moral worth. It simply "is" how people are, and they should be true to themselves. Ironically, though Mrs Elton is disliked in the novel and the BBC adaptation, as well as the Paltrow film—her "honesty" being seen as crassness and insensitivity to others—this student nevertheless had a certain respect for a character who could be so forthright and genuine. Other students went so far as to say that it was antithetical to their most important core values to try to change oneself to attract a mate. One student cautioned that one of her life lessons was, "Don't try to change or get another person to go against what they feel."

Another student applied these values to her interpretation of Cher's character in *Clueless*:

In *Clueless* we're all supposed to like Cher's change and transformation. It showed her maturing, but at the same time at its core it was maybe a dangerous precedent to set because what it said was that in order to get what you want you may have to change yourself a little bit. As Americans, we don't like to have to think about that. But you should always be who you are . . . The change could almost be seen as only for the sole purpose of winning Josh over. I suppose it's a bit debatable but I found some of it sort of disingenuous. I didn't really think that she wanted to be [captain of the Pismo Beach Disaster Relief]. Perhaps she was just doing it. (said by a student who had attended a large public high school)

Notably, the climactic scene of the novel, the famous Box Hill picnic where Emma insults the poorer and older Miss Bates and is chastised by Knightly for not realizing her social power, was directly criticized by some of the public school students. The scene appears also in modified form in *Clueless* in the scene between Cher and Lucy (Aida Linares), the maid, when Cher unthinkingly insults her by calling her "Mexican," only to have Josh explain that such a label would insult Lucy, who hailed from El Salvador; and of course, it is also included in both *Emma* films. Reacting to its depiction in the Paltrow version of *Emma*, these students find it to be the first time Emma really speaks her mind, or "tells it like it is." In fact, one woman said that the only problem with Emma's insult to Miss Bates was that it was inconsistent with her earlier polite behavior. If only Emma had been honest with Miss Bates right from the beginning of their relationship! This might have led to a more authentic relationship—and a more positive one, in this student's view. Some of the public school students also commented that they viewed Mrs Elton somewhat positively, despite Austen's decidedly negative representation of this character. Mrs Elton is represented critically by Austen and in the two *Emma* films as a "social climber" (and she appears similarly though rather indirectly in *Clueless* through the character of Amber [Elisa Donovan], a Cher "wannabe" who turns up in the same dress Cher wears and procures Elton as a boyfriend subsequent to Cher's rejection of him). As noted above, at least one woman in our sample felt Mrs Elton spoke her mind, and by some reckonings she was the most honest character in the story. She didn't deserve her negative portrayal. While Mrs Elton's remarks may not have been "pretty" or nice, they were authentic, and therefore indicated that she was an authentic person who did not deserve the level of criticism she received in the film's negative portrayal of her.

It's important to emphasize here that though the students introduced this idea of "authenticity" as one way in which they judged Emma's development, such a notion was not part of Austen's way of valuing individuals. Manners are important for Austen because they express morality, rather than authenticity;

this aspect of Austen is appropriated by Heckerling in her adaptation. Many of the private school students, for the most part, saw the value of refinement in manner and address more clearly. They specifically disliked Mrs Elton for being "too obvious," much as Austen dislikes her and criticizes her for similar reasons. Authenticity, while somewhat discussed, was clearly a less strong value for these students, and was tempered as a value by other considerations. Their comments contrasted strongly with the public school students, who made statements that marked them as disbelievers in the importance of social custom and manners, one of the meanings most clearly supported in the Austen novel that at least in part characterized both adaptations.

Interestingly, an extensive literature on the way Americans' conceptions of authenticity has changed over time indicates that "authenticity" is a concept in flux. Ralph Turner, in 1976, found that few Americans reflected on or worried about the meaning of the "authentic self."[23] By 2009, it had become commonplace for Americans to "reify the 'true'" or authentic self, while many remained cognizant that "being authentic," though desirable, was not necessarily an important "life skill."[24] The middle-class students in our study did not necessarily separate their stress on "authenticity" as a positive value from its utility as a life skill, as did the adult participants in a study by Alexis Franzese.[25] Perhaps they were too young to discern this distinction. Perhaps a more privileged class background made the drawbacks of untempered authenticity more salient to the private school students. It's difficult to explain how these differences in background could have affected their perspective on the role of manners in social life, but this difference in perspective emerged clearly in our interviews.

Other differences were salient as well between students of different class backgrounds. The difference between the two groups of students vis-à-vis their attitude toward distinction of rank and class comes out clearly when we look at a private school student's remark on the Box Hill adaptation scene in *Clueless*: Cher comments to her maid Lucy (Aida Linares) that she "doesn't speak Mexican," which misinterprets Lucy's El Salvadorian identity and essentially trivializes her concerns. The remark is made in the context of Cher's vexation that her clothing was late coming back from the cleaners. A private school student supported Cher's comment to Lucy, stating that "she wants to keep that distinction of upper- vs. lower-class distinction. In my experience, people that have maids or servants that live with them often have the servants become part of the family. She [Cher] wasn't going to let that kind of thing happen. She wanted to maintain class distinction," which apparently was accomplished, in this student's view, by her critical remarks. It's interesting to us that the sensibility around Cher's chastisement of Lucy differs so markedly between the two student groups, and is, potentially, indicative of their different social class positions leading to different types of identification with Cher and her relationship to her "servant," with the private school students finding this "servant"-relationship relatively unproblematic, even desirable.

Two. The level of identification with the heroine of the novel and films (as represented in the A&E adaptation that the public school students saw; none had read the novel, but the A&E adaptation attempted a faithful and straightforward presentation of its heroine) differed between public and private school students. Some of the private school participants—women in particular— mentioned that they actually did identify with the trappings of Cher's life; her problems with her maid and her unlimited ability to spend Daddy's money, for example, struck a chord with some of the wealthy students in this group. For example, one private school female student mentioned that she identified with Cher's vexation with Lucy when her blouse was lost: "I get mad at my maid because she 'hides' my stuff, placing it in drawers [or other places]." She identified with Cher's attitude toward Lucy rather than criticizing it like many of the public school students did. There was an overall feeling among the private school students that they, too, knew what it was like "to have other people be jealous of them" for their advantages.

In contrast, public school students quite consciously identified Cher's life as an ideal—and in some respects, they felt, this cut down on the humor of the film for them, and seemed to cut down on their understanding of Cher as the object of satire. One woman spoke of aspiring to be rich, beautiful, and universally popular, like Cher, and thus she found it hard to read this character and her actions satirically. All mentioned the "ideal" nature of having such a large closet of clothes that one had to organize them by computer. This overt longing for Cher's wealth and glamour is the dimension of clearest contrast between the wealthier private school students, and those from the public school.[26]

Three. Students differed somewhat in terms of which attributes they credited Cher's success and her popularity. Private school students mentioned her looks as primary, seeing them as the attribute from which all others flowed. Public school students were more apt to mention her wealth as a primary attribute, and to connect her wealth—her ability to afford the best clothing, plastic surgery (though Cher herself did not admit to having it, it was referenced in the film vis-à-vis another girl), massages, trainers, and so on, all referenced in the film and identified by these students as essential to maintaining beauty—to her superior looks. The private school students saw Cher's beauty as simply a personal quality which led to her social dominance; the less affluent public school students saw her privilege as leading to her social dominance, as she had access to a multitude of services and products that helped her achieve her beauty, and concomitantly her popularity. In this respect, what remains ambiguous in *Clueless* (Cher *is* beautiful, but why?) was read more in terms of class by public school students, and more in terms of individual attributes leading to success—such as looks and personality—by private school students. The public school students saw wealth and social class; the private school students, in contrast, tended to reduce the social class references in the narrative to a variety of personal attributes.

Four. Students seem unable to read *Clueless* without making mention of their own specific vision, and experience, of high school. The public school students in particular believe that, in high school, students are simply not concerned with life's larger issues, but legitimately obsess over what to wear to the prom, and similar topics which foreground issues of consumption. Their reading of Cher is colored by this vision of what high school is all about, and this is one of the big differences for them between Cher's situation in *Clueless* and Emma's in the novel and the other adaptations. High school is a universe unto itself, with its own "rules." Morality has little place in it. The private school students were more willing to discuss Cher's moral trajectory; they seems less "ground down" by the exigencies of social life in high school, which for the public school students seemed to require unusual behavior adapted to its stresses. Perhaps this connects to the fact that the private school these students attended was relatively small, as compared with the public schools we drew from; perhaps high school society was, legitimately, simply less stressful at this smaller, more sheltered school.

Finally, a coda: we take note of a significant silence in our interviews. We began this study interested in the way women in particular were portrayed vis-à-vis work and family—this is one of the reasons why modern adaptations of Austen, and their popularity, are so interesting from the perspective of feminist media scholars such as Press, or feminist scholars generally such as Rosenman. We suspected that the *Emma* adaptations would inspire tales about women's dependence, or independence, or at least discussion of what Cher and/or the Emmas were preparing themselves to do as regards work in their future lives. But little such talk ensued in our interviews. No remarks were made about what Cher's work future might hold, what the effect of her focus on boys-vs-grades might lead to, or the impact it might have on her college success or later career; this despite the fact that her father explicitly criticizes her in the film for not having the "focus" and serious career-trajectory of her older stepbrother, who later becomes her love interest.

These themes are often absent in current American media that targets adolescent girls, and this absence in itself is noteworthy. Alison Bechdel invented the "Bechdel test" to show that the great majority of current popular Hollywood films rarely showed girls even speaking to other girls, and when they did, their conversations were almost never about issues other than courtship and boys. The specific terms of the test—"two women, talking to one another, about something other than men"—were perhaps intended as a joke, but have been seriously used by feminist scholars to critique popular films because the latter so often, tellingly, fail this test.[27]

Perhaps this indicates that the fantasy lives of American adolescent girls still focus on issues of courtship and marriage to the exclusion of more work-centered issues, even in the age of postfeminism where some argue that equality between the genders has been achieved.[28] Could this account for the recent incident in Press's class where a female college student burst into tears when she announced that, statistically speaking, the vast majority of young women today could expect to work for almost all of their adult lives? Clearly her fantasy of becoming a stay-at-home mom and housewife—a strong fantasy for some, despite the fact that most women in the USA work outside the home for most of their lifespan—had been shattered by learning this statistical reality for the first time.[29] The neo-conservative dreams introduced by the Reagan backlash of the 1980s, which challenged the foothold that progressive ideas of gender, family, and personal life had achieved in 1970s American mainstream culture (including a focus on professional identities for women), may have helped to keep the notion of fixed gender roles alive, despite a socioeconomic reality that belies these notions: the "nostalgia trap" elaborated by Coontz and treated more recently by Gerson.[30]

Are Austen narratives and their adaptations part of a cultural apparatus offering vast fantasies of escape from the realities of contemporary women's lives? The popularity of the film *Bridget Jones's Diary* (2001), a relatively recent adaptation of *Pride and Prejudice*, as well as the extreme popularity of two recent *Pride and Prejudice* adaptions themselves (television in 1995, film in 2005), plus a very popular updating in the recent YouTube series *The Lizzy Bennet Diaries*, supports this thesis. Though Austen's original heroine Elizabeth (Lizzy) Bennet is a strong, intelligent, and outspoken young woman, the film's Bridget is silly and unprepared at work, spending most of her time fantasizing about various boyfriends or talking to her girlfriends about their own romantic disasters. One imagines that if Lizzy lived in the age of third-wave feminism she'd take her work much more seriously, even if she were destined to marry Mr Darcy—though of course it's difficult to imagine what each heroine would do in the context of such different times (here we recommend the 2008 British television mini-series *Lost in Austen*, which offers precisely this fantasy for contemplation).

The machinations wrought on Austen's *Emma* by Heckerling's vision differ fundamentally from the popular *Bridget Jones* transformation of Austen's earlier *Pride and Prejudice*. In *Clueless*, Cher is portrayed to be as intelligent as the novel's heroine. And like Emma, she grows and develops, becoming more serious and socially aware—but of course, as our student respondents noted, it was all in pursuit of Josh, her desired boyfriend, and therefore vulnerable to a Bechdel critique. Heckerling herself, speaking on the DVD commentary of her earlier feature *Fast Times*, notes that she had to tone down the feminism of her work a few years after Reagan came to power and his cultural backlash gained force, shifting the cultural tone of the country (to be more negative on abortion, for example, and possibly more judgmental of teenage sexual activity).[31] Cher becomes a much more postfeminist heroine than the Stacy of *Fast Times*; Cher is much more concerned with consumerism, her fashions, hairdo, body, and so on, while still maintaining at various points in the film— particularly the end—that she is career-oriented and not planning an early marriage since this would be inappropriate to most twentieth-century feminist heroines (or at least Cher herself states this, perhaps sarcastically). While *Fast Times* could be deemed a second-wave feminist tract, following as it does its innocent high school heroine's sexual "quest" (though it ends with placing her squarely in the camp of chaste "romance"), *Clueless* is much more prescient of postfeminism—Cher is still a strong, relatively independent "feminist" heroine, though the feminism is "assumed," as both Gill and McRobbie note in their definitions of "postfeminism."[32]

The reality of Austen's own relative poverty and dependence, as an unmarried woman of little inheritance, remains hidden in her novels behind fantasies of women's upward mobility through marriage (it might be of note that Austen herself rejected an opportunity to do precisely this) or, in the case of *Emma*, good fortune acquired at birth. Are contemporary American students seduced by fantasies of upward mobility through marriage? And if so, how—if at all— do such fantasies impact on their actual futures? Our interviews produced only silence on all issues related to this question. In ethnographic work, silence often indicates either an area too sensitive to be discussed in the interview situation, or a conclusion so obvious that one has not formulated any thoughts or comments on the issue. In this case, might there perhaps be a little of both? In our view, the fantasies offered by the smash hit *Clueless*, a film viewed repeatedly by so many of our interview subjects and our students over the years, serve to shield students from the inherent contradiction for women of a fantasy life focused on romance, that downplays the importance for women of developing other skills, and gaining status, approval, and actual power through their achievements in school and beyond.

In conclusion, American culture in general masks issues of social class behind those of style and individual attainment. Sociologists have remarked that high school is the last American setting where the social classes really mix and socialize.[33] Yet our media portrayals of high school,[34] of which *Clueless* is a prominent and popular example, tend to reduce issues of social class to those of quirky cliques or styles, making it difficult to decode high school stories as having any connection at all with class issues.[35] This mirrors the general lack of class-consciousness and discourse in American popular culture generally. These representations support a general belief in the "American dream," the idea that individuals can overcome class distinctions by dint of hard work and application, despite a preponderance of evidence contradicting this conclusion.[36] Our discussions with students of different social class backgrounds reveal, perhaps surprisingly, that both middle- and upper-class students do perceive distinctions of social class and wealth, though they attach different importance to these qualities, and the public school students value "authenticity" over the trappings of wealth and class in a way the private school students do not. The public school students value authenticity over good manners, and don't see manners as social performances grounded in social class.

Of course, conclusions based on such a small study must remain tentative. Nevertheless, it is interesting that the private school students even went so far as to comment that the world of the public high school, as depicted in *Clueless*, was a place, unlike their world, where individuals could be themselves, expressing their own style without reference to group conformity and social mores; these observations ignored the fact that there are very clear groups in *Clueless*, dictating, for example, Cher's initial reluctance to "allow" Tai to date Travis, a member of an "inferior" group in her judgment. They perceived the public school as a diverse world unlike their own, with diversity ensured by the preponderance of cliques as the film depicts. Essentially, they idealized public school as a place where social class differences were less important than in their world, and where instead individualism reigned. This they contrasted to their own world, a place where conformity, and class distinctions, mattered more. It's interesting that their preconceptions actually lead them to ignore the ways in which this film does emphasize the existence of class groups and distinctions, even in the public high school (but of course, a public high school in such a wealthy location as Beverly Hills has some particularities).

In what ways, if any, can these ideas be traced to popular filmic representations of the world of the public high school? What do we make of the power of American media to create an idealized realm that can be read so differently by different viewers? And in particular, what do we make of the power of these media to suggest that the absence of class distinction is what is ideal about American society, even to those who know better, and even when adapting a story from another century based on supporting the essential nature of social class differences? Finally, do the particular ways in which issues of women's class membership and mobility are presented have a specific impact on women's sense of themselves, and on the decisions adolescent women make about their preparations for the future? These are the questions we will be investigating in the future conduct of these studies.

NOTES

1 See Beverley Skeggs, *Formations of Class and Gender: Becoming Respectable* (London: Sage, 1997); Beverley Skeggs and Helen Wood, *Reacting to Reality Television: Performance, Audience and Value* (London: Routledge, 2012); Diane Negra and Yvonne Tasker (eds.), *Gendering the Recession: Media and Culture in An Age of Austerity* (Durham, NC: Duke University Press, 2014).

2 For a discussion of these issues vis-à-vis British self-help books see Angela McRobbie, *The Aftermath of Feminism: Gender, Culture and Social Change* (Los Angeles, CA: Sage, 2009).

3 In 2003, the BBC conducted the largest poll ever of UK readers' favorite books, in which *Pride and Prejudice* came in second to *The Lord of the Rings*; a 2008 poll of 15000 Australian readers found *Pride and Prejudice* listed first on a list of the 101 most beloved books. See Wikipedia, "Pride and Prejudice". Available at <http://en.wikipedia.org/wiki/Pride_and_Prejudice> (last accessed 14 January 2015). *Pride and Prejudice* was adapted by Hollywood in 1940, 2003, and 2005; by the BBC in 1938, 1952, 1967, 1980 and 1995; and by Bollywood as *Bride and Prejudice* in 2004 (though this was a British film with a Bollywood aesthetic).

4 Bridget Jones was a very popular British character created by Helen Fielding, who first began publishing the heroine's stories as a column in 1995, and then published the first novelization, *Bridget Jones's Diary*, in 1996 (London: Picador). The novel was adapted as a film of the same name in 2001, starring Renée Zellweger, Colin Firth (reprising his Mr Darcy role made popular by the 1995 BBC adaptation of *Pride and Prejudice*), and Hugh Grant, and directed by Sharon Maguire; this too became extremely popular, earning nearly $282 million at the global box office.

5 Robert Clark, "Jane Austen," *The Literary Encyclopedia*, 8 January 2001. Available at <https://www.litencyc.com/php/speople.php?rec=true&UID=5167> (last accessed 15 February 2015).

6 James Edward Austen-Leigh, *A Memoir of Jane Austen* (Create Space Independent Publishing Platform, 2013 [1870]), p. 148.

7 Carol M. Dole, "Austen, class, and the American market," in Linda Troost and Sayre Greenfield (eds.), *Jane Austen in Hollywood* (Lexington, KY: University of Kentucky Press, 1998), p. 67.

8 Adela Pinch discusses the critical debate over *Emma* in her introduction to novel, detailing these opposed interpretations of the work. See Jane Austen, *Emma*, ed. James Kinsley and Adela Pinch (Oxford: Oxford University Press, 2008 [1815]).

9 Interestingly, the late 1990s were the "era" of *Emma*, which was adapted to the large and small screen three different times within the space of one year (1995–6) in the Austen movie mania that followed the success of the BBC television version of *Pride and Prejudice* in 1995. In addition to *Clueless*, a British telefilm of *Emma* was produced in 1996 by A&E Television, and a British theatrical feature widely released in the USA in 1996 was made with Gwyneth Paltrow in the title role, directed by Douglas McGrath.

10 It is scandalous how little audience research exists in the field of film study. Some of the few relatively recent books include Jackie Stacey, *Star Gazing: Hollywood Cinema and Female Spectatorship* (New York and London: Routledge, 1994); Annette Kuhn, *Dreaming of Fred and Ginger: Cinema and Cultural Memory* (New York: New York University Press, 2002); Martin Barker and Ernest Mathijs, *Watching "The Lord of the Rings": Tolkien's World Audiences* (New York: Peter Lang, 2007); and a few of the essays in Melissa Click, Jennifer Stevens Aubrey, and Elizabeth Behm-Morawitz (eds.), *Bitten by Twilight: Youth Culture, Media, and the Vampire Franchise* (New York: Peter Lang, 2010). Press is well

known as a scholar of the media audience focusing on issues of gender and social class; see Andrea L. Press, *Women Watching Television: Gender, Class and Generation in the American Television Experience* (Philadelphia, PA: University of Pennsylvania Press, 1991); Andrea L. Press and Elizabeth R. Cole, *Speaking of Abortion: Television and Authority in the Lives of Women* (Chicago, IL: University of Chicago Press, 1999); Andrea L. Press and Bruce A. Williams, *The New Media Environment* (Oxford: Blackwell, 2010). Rosenman is a scholar of popular and canonical nineteenth-century British literature; see her latest book, *Unauthorized Pleasures: Accounts of Victorian Erotic Experiences* (Ithaca, NY: Cornell University Press, 2003).

11 Press has been asking her university classes for at least the last decade whether they have seen the film *Clueless*. Almost universally the answer is yes; most often the film has been viewed, and repeatedly, by almost every student in her film classes.

12 We derive both of these figures from data provided by IMDb.com. See <http://www.imdb.com/title/tto112697/business?ref_=ttco_ql_4> (last accessed 17 February 2015).

13 Kevin T. Leicht and Scott T. Fitzgerald, *Middle-Class Meltdown in America* (New York: Routledge, 2014); Eric Olin Wright and Joel Rogers, *American Society: How It Really Works* (New York: Norton, 2010); Press (1991).

14 Heckerling's other popular features tend to restrict representation to members of a given social class, as in *Fast Times at Ridgemont High* (1982), which examines the social scene at a middle-class high school, and *I Could Never Be Your Woman* (2007), which focuses on affluent workers in the entertainment field.

15 It is well known that Americans occupying many different socio-economic positions tend to self-identify as "middle-class." A recent Gallup poll finds that only 2 percent of Americans identify as "upper-class," a percentage that remains unchanged over the last decade. See <http://www.gallup.com/poll/159029/americans-likely-say-belong-middle-class.aspx> (last accessed 31 December 2014). However, a recent poll by Rakesh Kochhar and Rich Morin at the Pew Research Center finds that fewer Americans identify as middle-class and more are identifying as lower-class: <http://www.pewresearch.org/fact-tank/2014/01/27/despite-recovery-fewer-americans-identify-as-middle-class/> (last accessed 31 December 2014). See Skeggs (1997) for a somewhat more nuanced version of the way social class distinction operates in the UK; see Press (1991) and Wright and Rogers (2011) for a nuanced discussion of the way social class operates as an "identity category" in the USA.

16 On this point, see Kochhar and Morin (2014); see also Press (1991), and Lillian Rubin, *Worlds of Pain: Life in the Working Class Family* (New York: Basic Books, 1976).

17 Technically this film was actually produced in the UK, but Paltrow's casting reveals an attempt to reach American audiences.

18 See especially Rubin's discussion of the way social class in the USA can be seen as an identity rather than a category, unconsciously inhabited. For a more recent discussion of the "status" of social class identity in the USA, see Leicht and Fitzgerald.

19 Michael Singer, *A Cut Above: 50 Film Directors Talk About Their Craft* (Los Angeles, CA: Lone Eagle, 1998).

20 Roger Ebert, "Clueless," *Chicago Sun-Times*. Available at <http://www.rogerebert.com/reviews/clueless-1995> (last accessed 18 January 2015).

21 See Paul Rudd's recent roles in, for example, *I Love You, Man* (John Hamburg, 2009), *Our Idiot Brother* (Jesse Peretz, 2011), and *Anchorman 2: The Legend Continues* (Adam McKay, 2013).

22 The television version of *Emma* that students viewed was the same version by A&E discussed in note 9. It was directed by Diarmuid Lawrence from a screenplay written by

Andrew Davies, and it remained faithful to the book in most respects by most critical accounts.

23 Ralph Turner, "The real self: from institution to impulse," *American Journal of Sociology* 81 (1976), pp. 989–1016.

24 Alexis T. Franzese, "Authenticity: perspectives and experiences," in Phillip Vannini and J. Patrick Williams (eds.), *Authenticity in Culture, Self and Society* (New York: Ashgate, 2009), pp. 87–102.

25 Ibid. p. 99.

26 It is important to note here that the private school that supplied our informants had almost no scholarship recipients, and none of the students we interviewed from this school was a scholarship recipient. Also, the public school students in our sample came from middle-class homes, with an average, middle-class income level according to questionnaires we distributed before each focus group interview. While it is true we cannot generalize necessarily that all public school students are less affluent than all private school students, this was true of our sample and, overall, is true of many specific private schools when compared with many specific public school districts.

27 See Wikipedia's description of the Bechdel test, available at <http://en.wikipedia.org/wiki/Bechdel_test> (last accessed 15 February 2015).

28 For a brilliant explanation of the contested term "postfeminism," see Rosalind Gill's 2009 essay "Postfeminist media culture: elements of a sensibility," in Mary Celeste Kearney (ed.), *The Gender and Media Reader* (New York and London: Routledge, 2009), pp. 136–48. Gill begins by stating that there are many contradictory definitions of this term, illustrating its current centrality and importance. In her definition, she notes that it is a "sensibility" more than anything else, one which encompasses "the notion that femininity is a bodily property; the shift from objectification to subjectification; the emphasis upon self-surveillance, monitoring and discipline; a focus upon individualism, choice and empowerment; the dominance of a makeover paradigm; a resurgence in ideas of natural sexual difference; a marked sexualization of culture; and an emphasis upon consumerism and the commodification of difference. These themes coexist with, and are structured by, stark and continuing inequalities and exclusions that relate to 'race' and ethnicity, class, age, sexuality and disability as well as gender" (p. 148). See Angela McRobbie, *The Aftermath of Feminism: Gender, Culture and Social Change* (Los Angeles, CA: Sage, 2009) for further discussion of the concept of postfeminism. By these criteria, *Clueless* is a film that overwhelmingly exhibits postfeminist themes, particularly in its focus on consumerism and adherence to a makeover paradigm.

29 For recent statistics on the percentages of "stay at home" moms in current US culture, see Kathleen Gerson, *The Unfinished Revolution* (Oxford: Oxford University Press, 2011). For commentary on the origins of the "nostalgia trap" in ideas about American families, see Stephanie Coontz, *The Way We Never Were: American Families and the Nostalgia Trap* (New York: Basic Books, 1993).

30 Coontz, ibid.; see Gerson, ibid.

31 Amy Heckerling, "Commentary by director Amy Heckerling and screenwriter Cameron Crowe" special feature, on the DVD Edition of *Fast Times at Ridgemont High* ("Awesome special edition," Universal, 2004), 00:04:35–00:04:57. Heckerling's exact words here are: "We got in just ever so slightly before the whole Reagan backlashy [*sic*], although we sort of had a problem with the nudity because we implied that the characters were under eighteen even though they weren't, and that was a big issue." By 1982, the date of *Fast Times at Ridgemont High*'s issue, the "Reagan backlash" was certainly pervasive, and teenage girls—in fact, adult women as well—all but quit having abortions in movies

thereafter. See Press and Cole (1999) for a discussion of television representations of abortion over the decades, and viewer response to them; and Press, *Feminism LOL: Media Culture and "Feminism on the Ground" in a Postfeminist Age* (forthcoming) for a more current discussion of cinematic representations of the abortion issue.

32 See Gill (2009), and McRobbie (2009). See also Diane Negra and Yvonne Tasker (eds.), *Interrogating Postfeminism: Gender and the Politics of Popular Culture* (Durham, NC: Duke University Press, 2007), particularly their Introduction, which lays out the parameters of postfeminism well.

33 See C. J. Pascoe's *Dude, You're a Fag* (Berkeley, CA: University of California Press, 2011) for a recent discussion of cliques and social class in high school. See also Julie Bettie, *Women Without Class: Girls, Race and Identity* (Berkeley, CA: University of California Press, 2003) for a similar discussion of high school girls that focuses on issues of social class, race, and identity.

34 Philip Kaufman's *The Wanderers* (1979) and John Sayles's *Baby It's You* (1983) are notable exceptions to this rule. Both were smaller-scale productions than the star vehicle *Clueless*. See also the John Hughes films of the 1980s, and the three S. E. Hinton adaptations *Tex* (1982), *Rumble Fish* (1983), and in particular *The Outsiders* (1983). More recently, see *The Perks of Being a Wallflower* (Stephen Chbosky, 2012) and *Juno* (Jason Reitman, 2007), both of which portray distinctly classed teenagers without explicit reference to the issue.

35 While many recent teen films do eschew mention of social class issues, there are exceptions; see especially *Assassination of a High School President* (2008), *Precious* (2009), *Winter's Bone* (2010), *Prom* (2011), *The Hunger Games* (2012), *The Spectacular Now* (2013), and *The Bling Ring* (2013). Even in *Clueless*, as we have pointed out earlier, Cher does confront class (and ethnic identity) in the slight altercation she has with Lucy, her maid.

36 See Leicht and Fitzgerald; see Wright and Rogers.

CHAPTER 6

"An Increasingly Valid Form of Expression": Teenspeak and Community Identity in the Work of Amy Heckerling

Lisa Richards

This chapter examines Amy Heckerling's position as a writer and director in the teen genre. Her use of language, and the means of self-expression granted to her teenage characters, reinforce a significant convention of the genre, and allow for distinctive and occasionally mystifying dialogue that can be welcoming for the genre's young audience. The use of teenspeak marks out a generational community separated from the adult characters around them by a boundary of age and references to specific cultural texts. A linguistic generation gap can be seen in Heckerling's first feature film as director, *Fast Times at Ridgemont High* (1982), which was adapted to the screen by Cameron Crowe, from his own book of the same name. However, it is in Heckerling's 1995 film *Clueless* that her role as both writer and director allowed the language of teenagers to become more complex. The essay will analyze the language presented in Heckerling's teen texts using Michael Halliday's theories of social dialects and Mikhail Bakhtin's analysis of speech genres and the "utterance."[1] These theories will not only highlight the style of Heckerling's screenplay but also demonstrate the linguistic structures operating within the community of characters that inhabit her oeuvre.

Linguistically, the worlds of *Fast Times* and *Clueless* may appear straightforward as there is only one language at work: contemporary American English. These movies are also clear examples of the teen genre, with narrative tropes (romance, comedy, the stress of high school) and archetypal characters (the popular and unpopular cliques, the disconnected parents and teachers) that are quite conventional and recognizable from across the genre itself, and from the familiar literary characters in Jane Austen's novel *Emma* (1815) which inspired the film's narrative.[2] However, in the most standout and notable teen films, such as *Clueless*, the use of conventions allow us to see the status of the teen genre and also how the genre adapts and extends itself time and time again. The dialogue may begin from a recognizable point, English, and more specifically a combination of familiar Californian "Valley-speak" and politically correct terminology that became so prominent in the 1990s.[3] The words may be striking and lyrical (while also indicating the intelligence of the speaker), but this language has the power to change a character's social position within a specific film, and to have an influence across the genre, affecting the dialogue in subsequent films.

The teen films that followed *Fast Times* in the 1980s, and those that followed *Clueless* in the 1990s and beyond, feature a prominent use of slang by the teenagers, and this is used not only as a dialect between peers but also to highlight the positions of outsiders. In *Heathers* (Michael Lehmann, 1989), the use of the positive term "very" is fairly consistent and low-key among the characters, while the examples of aggressive imagery in Daniel Waters's screenplay are more heightened among the popular clique, as is Heather Chandler (Kim Walker)'s put-down, "Did you have a brain tumor for breakfast?" The position of outsider is also prominent in the film *Mean Girls* (Mark Waters, 2004), where new student Cady (Lindsay Lohan) arrives at a high school, having previously been home-schooled, and must learn how to socialize with her peers, how to move through the school's social hierarchy, and how to become fluent in the local teenspeak.

The dialogue of Heckerling's teen films is significant, moving from the frankness of the conversations in Crowe's script to the overt stylized nature of Heckerling's banter for the *Clueless* universe across various media;[4] it creates a consistent voice for the teenage characters separating them from the older generations in both subject matter and form. In *Fast Times*, the protagonists demonstrate an attempt to act beyond their years, performing their maturity by doing the things that adults do—engaging in casual sex, drug consumption, and workplace politics—but revealing their youth in the most basic ways, such as being concerned about their sophisticated food orders in "fancy" restaurants while still instinctively ordering Cokes to drink. Their dialogue is concerned with adult themes, while being naïve and acknowledging a lack of certainty about what adulthood might involve. In his thesis on the language of young women, Lucien Hilaire notes that the linguistic patterns of *Clueless* are predominantly found in the dialogue of the film's female characters,[5] and represent a very female-oriented speech following the influence of the Valley Girl stereotype. However, the stylized nature of the teen speech of Heckerling's films crosses gender boundaries, with the language of Cher (Alicia Silverstone), the film's protagonist, matched by the linguistic style of her male and female contemporaries. In *Clueless*, the language expresses a time and place while maintaining a tone which is never entirely naturalistic, and which goes beyond the everyday conversational style of the earlier film. The overtly stylized language of the film reflects the characters' environment, suggesting the decadence of the Beverly Hills lifestyle as opposed to the suburban sprawl of Ridgemont.

The teen protagonists of these texts use familiar contemporary slang that is then built and elaborated upon as the narratives unfold. The difference between the teenagers and the older generations can be highlighted by the use of teenspeak, and this language plays an active part in distinguishing between the generations of characters as well as between the protagonists and antagonists of each film. Although the teenspeak within Heckerling's texts is understood by the young protagonists who speak it, it can elicit utter confusion from the adults around them. This generational linguistic divide presents a speech community as outlined by Halliday's theoretical model:

> The speech community is an idealized construct, and it is one that combines three distinct concepts: those of social group, communication network, and linguistically homogenous population. Each of these three embodies ideas of a norm. A speech community, in this idealized sense, is a group of people who (1) are linked by some form of social organization, (2) talk to each other, and (3) all speak alike.[6]

The use of language and linguistic modification represents the changing dynamics within established groups of individuals. By focusing on the individualized speech of characters, and specifically the language use within groups of teenage characters, it is possible to analyze the ways in which these groups can be defined by their language. In his analysis of language genres, Bakhtin discussed the realization of language as countless individual spoken or written "utterances" from individuals in all walks of life:

> These utterances reflect the specific conditions and goals of each such area not only through their content (thematic) and linguistic style, that is, the selection of the lexical, phraseological, and grammatical resources of the language but above all through their compositional structure. All three of these aspects—thematic content, style, and compositional structure—are inseparably linked to the *whole* of the utterance and are equally determined by the specific nature of the particular sphere of communication.[7]

The utterances within the film are a combination of the elements that Bakhtin discusses. The nature of the sphere of communication in both *Fast Times* and *Clueless* is affected primarily by the location of the dialogue within a fictional context. The relationship between the phrase and the elements noted by Bakhtin (theme, style, and the structure of composition) changes if they are analyzed within the context of a film script rather than in everyday conversation. The film uses language primarily to create a pleasant and credible world, and to capture the interest of the audience. Bakhtin also notes the individuality of an utterance: "Any utterance—oral or written, primary or secondary, and in any sphere of communication—is individual and therefore can reflect the individuality of the speaker (or writer); that is, possess individual style."[8] Therefore the individual members of the speech community are able to demonstrate their personal style and interests with each utterance, despite using the same compositional structures and thematic content in conversation. All teenagers may make numerous references to popular culture in their dialogue, but the specificities of these references highlight the individuality of each character.

In *Fast Times*, there are several significant aesthetic and narrative elements that are integral to the contemporary teen film. The use of locations, character types, the high school's hierarchical structure of popularity, and the importance of sex and education (in life if not in academia), are all present, as with the countless teen films that followed. As Robin Wood notes of the genre, "*Fast Times at Ridgemont High* anticipates almost everything in the later films and must be seen as the cycle's origin and archetype."[9] There is also a distinct generational gap between the teenage protagonists and the somewhat distant adults in their lives. The adults are predominantly represented by teachers, as there are only minimal parental appearances, either in a fleeting domestic moment or as a disembodied voice on the end of the phone. The need for advice or authority is found within the teen group, with the teens readily presenting opinions and advice on various subjects, from sex to careerism, without adult intervention.

Heckerling returned to the teen genre with the film *Clueless* in 1995, which featured many similarities with the earlier film and with wider genre conventions, such as the division of the action between high school, home, and the mall, the use of archetypal characters, and the balance between the characters' expectations of their relationships and the realities. The differences between the two films are more interesting, with a narrative and aesthetic style that is adapted not from a piece of undercover journalism, as Crowe's script was, but from a nineteenth-century novel. Heckerling's script for *Clueless* may draw on observation as much as Crowe's did, but the construction of style in the language of the latter film is far more sophisticated. The teenagers of *Clueless* form a speech community that isolates their speech from the adults around them, and though communication between teenagers and adults is possible and credible, the linguistic ability of the teenagers is far more diverse than in the earlier film.

Clueless is significant as a progression in the genre, described by Jonathan Bernstein as starting a potential "teenpic renaissance" in the 1990s,[10] partly owing to the film's similarity to the popular Hollywood teen films of the 1980s but with significant alterations. Bernstein suggests that *Clueless* modifies the genre's archetypes, by asking "the revolutionary question: what if the pretty, rich, popular girl wasn't the evil witch? What if she . . . saw it as her civic duty to spread the wealth of her knowledge, friendship and taste?"[11] This discussion of *Clueless* as a turning point, and the comparison of it with the Larry Clark film *Kids* (1995), builds a debate around an audience's expectation of the teen genre. The teen film is generally constructed along relatively conventional lines, but by altering the narrative structure by taking in literary influences,[12] or, as in Clark's film, by altering the genre's aesthetic by the use of a more documentary style of filming. However, "both films indicate that the traditional representations of youth that were seen in American cinema since the early '80s were changing considerably by 1995."[13] Timothy Shary discusses the same period of production in terms of an evolution rather than a "renaissance":

> By the mid-'90s, the latest expansion of youth movie production emerged . . . The youth population at the end of the century was clearly witness to a new wave of films that catered to their interests and explored their images, and these films were and will continue to be undoubtedly influenced by and built upon the evolution of cinematic youth representations in previous generations.[14]

Shary includes *Clueless* in a list of equally successful and interesting films from the mid-1990s, but notes the relevance of the clear influence from earlier examples of the genre, and especially how films such as *Fast Times* and John Hughes's *The Breakfast Club* (1985) use familiar character types to reinforce the location and hierarchies of the school experience.[15] Bernstein's comparison of *Clueless* with the films of the 1980s compliments the film for capturing the spirit of that cinematic period. Along with its mainstream peers, *Clueless* is happy to display this influence, and to wrap itself in the genre's conventions. Shary lists *Clueless* among its contemporaries, which include less orthodox examples of the teen genre (*Kids* and *Girls Town* [Jim McKay, 1996]) as well as more mainstream studio films (*Dangerous Minds* [John N. Smith, 1995] and *Scream* [Wes Craven, 1996]), drawing comparisons based on their significance to the audience and their intelligence as pieces of cinema history. Alongside this, Shary notes how these films build upon those of previous generations, making direct references to the evolution of the genre through the narratives, generic hybridity, and character types.[16]

Clueless demonstrates its awareness of the teen genre and its conventions, and highlights them in the dialogue, making the language as significant as the use of iconography. The teenagers' conversations are familiar from other examples of the genre but the dialogue—as with the dialogue of teen films that followed, such as Wes Craven's *Scream*—plays with the form, making the characters' language more noticeably stylized than in the previous generation of films, where it was the subject matter that was more significant. In *Rebel Without a Cause* (Nicholas Ray, 1955), Jim (James Dean) and Judy's (Natalie Wood) first conversation on their way to school features the question "You wanna carry my books?" but in a mocking tone, since even in 1955 the use of such a stock phrase seemed clichéd. The film's overall representation of how the young interact is familiar but made striking by the emotion of the delivery rather than the words themselves.

The leading teen characters of *Fast Times*—Brad (Judge Reinhold), Stacy (Jennifer Jason Leigh), Linda (Phoebe Cates), Mark (Brian Backer), Mike (Robert Romanus), and Spicoli (Sean Penn)—represent various aspects of the adolescent experience, dividing their time between school and the mall, and discussing the issues that are most important to them: sex, work, and relaxation. Spicoli is the only one of these teens without a job of any kind, but he is also the most honest about himself and his ambitions. For example, when Brad suggests that Spicoli should get a job, Spicoli asks why:

Brad: You need money.
Spicoli: All I need are some tasty waves, cool buds, and I'm fine.

Ambition is Brad's primary characteristic, even though for him, as a high school senior, that ambition is channeled into working at various fast food outlets. His dialogue is often concerned with his future and potential, with him referring to himself as a "successful guy." He is often seen in and around his car, and, as is seen when he rehearses a break-up speech, he values the idea of his own personal freedom. However, when his girlfriend breaks up with him first, citing the same reasons and the same argument about personal freedom, he does not react well.

Both Stacy and Mark are mentored in life and love/sex by two older and wiser (though just barely) teens, Linda and Mike, even though the authority they present is not truly representative of either one's actual experience. In their sessions of "cool coaching" as discussed by Jean Schwind, both Linda and Mike state the importance of certain actions and reactions when dating, and the importance of being mature and cool, or "how to avoid looking like a loser."[17] Stacy and Mark find happiness through making their own choices, and, as Schwind notes, "discover that peer coaching is power as well as friendship and that coaches are often more concerned with protecting and augmenting their positions of authority than with providing honest advice or accurate information."[18] Their success is also marked against the fact that their mentors are both single at the end of the film, whereas Stacy and Mark's relationship is seen as a success story in the film's epilogue.[19]

The teenagers do have a need for authority figures; however, they make no attempt to seek guidance from outside of their own peer group. In scenes that Lesley Speed analyzes under the heading of "low comedy," the film is praised for moving beyond the traditions of adolescent male fantasy by offering a female perspective on teenage sexuality through the characters of Stacy and Linda, as well as a "framework for focusing upon issues such as teenage pregnancy, abortion and promiscuity."[20] These scenes, as well as those that address the themes of career and education, are notable for the absence of parental or adult guidance, and, as in many other teen films, the various moments when a teenager does interact with adults often end in a situation of conflict. One example is when Brad tries to deal with a customer complaint when working at All-American Burger, which leads to Brad threatening the customer ("Mister, if you don't shut up, I'm gonna kick one hundred percent of your ass"), before losing his job entirely.

The teen–adult relationship that is explored the furthest is between the surfer and stoner Spicoli and his American history teacher, Mr Hand (Ray Walston). This relationship is contained within the classroom for the most part, beginning with profanity when Spicoli calls Mr Hand a "dick"; developing throughout the academic year as Spicoli challenges the expected behavior of the learning environment by ordering a pizza to class, "learning about Cuba, having some food"; and eventually leading to a mutual understanding between the two characters at the end of the film: "Aloha, Mister Hand." The development of the relationship through the dialogue also provides the film's most notable linguistic contrast, with the formal speech of the teacher and the languid slang of the surfer operating in opposition.

Spicoli is dismissive of almost any authoritative voice, be it that of his teacher, or Brad in his role as an employee of various fast food outlets. Spicoli's place in the school, as an unreliable and uncomprehending student, is similar to his general role in the film's teenage community: he is present but rarely involved. The individuality of his utterance makes him stand out from those around him, even his two regular companions who have very little dialogue. He is recognizable to other students in the school (". . . this guy's been stoned since the third grade"), and stands out to Mr Hand as the only student who appears to actively speak, as well as present a challenge to the rules that have been set out in the classroom environment. He stands out to another teacher, Mr Vargas (Vincent Schiavelli), but passes a brief interrogation by having an unnerving sense of self and place:

Mr Vargas: Hey, are you in this class?
Spicoli: I am today.

His place as a comedic character demonstrates the diversity of the film's teenage group, but his linguistic style is more pronounced and clearer as an expression of teenage opposition than the others. Although the other teenagers are distinguished by the subjects they choose to talk about, Spicoli is distinctive for the specific *way* that he speaks. Spicoli is a character whose life revolves around surfing and recreational drug consumption with his friends, and this is reflected not only in his appearance and attitude but also in his language. He embodies the dangerous apathy against which Mr Hand protests when he asks the question of his silent class, "Are you on drugs?" The answer from Spicoli—if he'd been present—would be a very simple "Yes." He is the figure of the indifferent, addled fool that his teacher dreads: he is wasted potential and simplistic defiance wrapped, if only on occasion, in a Hawai'ian shirt. His speech is littered with familiar terms and idioms, which are now more instantly recognizable. The use of words such as "dude," "bogus," and "totally awesome," marks out his vocabulary as different from his fellow students'. Despite being supported by two companions at various points in the film, Spicoli is the most prominent of the trio, and among the film's leading characters his place as a stoner and surfer allows him an image distinct from the others, an image that is reinforced by his use of language.

It is Spicoli's individual linguistic style, which can be read as an example of the Bakhtinian "utterance," that places him apart from his fellow students, and it is the positioning of this style against the rigidity and formality of Mr Hand's classroom that adds to the conflict initiated by Spicoli's general attitude and behavior. However, linguistic style also unites the two characters without them even being in the same space. When Mr Hand introduces himself to his new class of students, he begins with the Hawai'ian greeting "Aloha," meaning not only "hello" or "goodbye" but also a term of friendly welcome. It is this term that Spicoli uses when they part ways at the end of the school year, signifying the mutual understanding in their relationship. The individualist nature of Mr Hand in comparison with other teachers at the school (something that he himself notes at various points), and Spicoli's connection of Hawai'i with surf culture, may set them apart, but linguistically they have been connected throughout their year of classroom hostility. The shared use of the term in this case creates an understanding between teacher and student that occurs across the teen genre, be it positive or negative. The conflict of John (Judd Nelson) and Mr Vernon (Paul Gleason) in *The Breakfast Club* is emphasized by the continued aggression in their dialogue,[21] but the relationship of Spicoli and Mr Hand is allowed to end on an optimistic note emphasized by their linguistic connection.

The differences in linguistic style in the teen genre are mostly highlighted by the cultural references of the differences shown with Spicoli and Mr Hand. Several films use contemporary slang to provide verisimilitude for the characters and to emphasize their age and generation. In *Clueless*, language and style are significant because they create a relationship between the characters by placing them in specific social groups as well as within a specific generation and location (within a time period and geographically). *Clueless* calls attention to the language of its teenage characters, as in many scenes the teenspeak is positioned as unusual when it is spoken in the presence of adults, who pause in order to interpret what has been said; for example, in the classroom of Mr Hall (Wallace Shawn) when Cher offers "surfing the crimson wave" as an excuse for her tardiness. When the film opened in 1995, several reviews referred directly to the use of slang in the film, and several magazines presented a glossary of terms to allow the audience to keep up with the characters' dialogue.[22] These would provide the definitions of terms such as "Baldwin" and "Betty" as references to attractive males and females, the former based on the popularity of the family of acting brothers at the time and the latter from numerous attractive performers and characters who share the forename.[23]

The film's linguistic style was created by Heckerling, who studied language by researching twentieth-century youth slang, and observing the conversations of real high school students, as well as the linguistic styles of the film's young cast, and then combined them in the final script. In addition to this, Jennifer O'Meara notes that Heckerling attended events—plays, debates, and competitions—at Beverly Hills High School, to gain a sense of the language and interests of the real-life students.[24] According to interviews with Heckerling,[25] her intention was to treat the characters with respect and to provide them with dialogue that flowed clearly, and demonstrated their ability to express themselves creatively. Heckerling also wanted to create a language style that would be specific to each character, and reflect her or his personal attitude and interests. O'Meara provides a significant analysis of the role of verbal traits in the language of various characters, noting the significance of hyperbole and strong vocabulary in Cher's dialogue, as opposed to the understated nature of Christian (Justin Walker)'s dialogue and the contrast of Tai (Brittany Murphy)'s New York accent.[26] However, it is possible to take this analysis further by noting the linguistic patterns at work across the entire film. Returning to the theories of Bakhtin and Halliday, the language of each character not only expresses their individuality, but also creates a functioning speech community among the teenagers.

The characters' dialogue in *Clueless* has to reflect the reality of teen language in the mid-1990s, and so presents the more familiar language of teenagers (the common use of words such as "cool," "totally," and "like") among examples of more creative language (phrases such as "couch commando"), in order to push the film to more lyrical and literary places than one would expect. Daniel Chandler refers to the understanding and use of figurative language that "constitute a rhetorical code, and understanding this code is part of what it means to be a member of the culture in which it is employed."[27] Although the dialogue of *Clueless* is understandable, there are specific terms or phrases that need to be interpreted, either for a new character arriving at the school or for the audience. However, as the film proceeds, the character becomes habituated to them—the assumption is that this is also the case for the audience as they are led through the film by Cher's narration—and the meaning is intuited even though the phrasing may be unfamiliar.

The use of teen language reflects the attitude of *Clueless*, as Heckerling's script acknowledges that there is a difference between the language of the teenagers and that of the older generations, but prioritizes the language of the teenagers as the majority of the dialogue occurs within the teenage community. Heckerling is also willing to use this language to create humor, as her dialogue features some inventive and outrageous phrases among the more familiar terminology, such as the use of the politically correct idiom "hymenally-challenged" to describe the state of female virginity. There is no attempt to use language in order to make the teenage characters seem foolish, and even if the characters' dialogue indicates a certain cultural community outside of the realms of the film, their next lines could easily bring them back into the fold of the film's speech community. Each teenage character individualizes her or his statements, but each statement evokes and reinforces the linguistic style of the community.

In one scene, Murray (Donald Faison) refers to his girlfriend Dionne (Stacey Dash) as "woman," to which she objects. His next line explains his position on the use of the term—"Street slang is an increasingly valid form of expression. Most of the feminine pronouns do have mocking, but not necessarily misogynist undertones." His verbal dexterity and eloquence here undermine the negative aspects of his earlier dialogue and indicate an intelligence and understanding of his appropriation of a known style of linguistic expression. The line is also delivered in front of the new student Tai, allowing her to form a wondrous admiration for the sophistication of her new schoolmates, "Wow, you guys talk like grown-ups." The inclusion of a line to justify the use of street slang by a wealthy black teenager acknowledges the difference in Murray's image and his social position, demonstrating his adoption of a specific identity despite his distance from those whose identity he emulates. Films from the early 1990s such as *Boyz N the Hood* (John Singleton, 1991) and *Menace II Society* (Albert Hughes and Allen Hughes, 1993) represented life in inner-city Los Angeles as filled with violence, gun crime, and drug abuse; alongside the rise of urban black music in the 1980s and 1990s, certain styles of speech were brought into mainstream youth slang. Paula J. Massood's discussion of African American urban identity in relation to *Boyz N the Hood* notes how the film features a contemporary "urban patois" moving the dialect and style of rap music and African American cinema, initially popularized in

Blaxploitation cinema and through the work of filmmakers like Spike Lee in the 1980s and '90s, into mainstream culture.[28] Although Murray may attempt to emulate the language and slang—in a very tame approximation—his obviously privileged lifestyle and attendance at Beverly Hills High School present a heavy contrast with these images.

It is possible to think of the teenagers' language as a generational dialect. Halliday discusses the concept of social dialects as "a configuration of phonetic, phonological, grammatical and lexical features—that is associated with, and stands as a symbol for, some more or less objectively definable social group."[29] The idea of a dialect that characterizes a group or community is appropriate in this context, as it is an effective summary of teenspeak. In these terms, this form of language is a direct means of identifying the teenage group's form of expression. Halliday's statement acknowledges the idea that language changes between groups and events, and that this is a part of organizing everyday life. Different professions, such as medical staff, computer technicians, or academics, require a fluency in languages that would be alien to anyone outside that profession.

Clueless belongs to the subgenre of the school film as defined by Shary, and the characters in the film include students and teachers as well as the students' families.[30] As an adaptation of *Emma*, *Clueless* takes up characters from the novel as a foundation for the characters in the film—not only among the main group of teenagers but also the surrounding figures. Looking at individual characters, we can see how their identities and their language use position them in relation to the film's dominant group led by the main character, Cher. It is her voiceover that opens the film and introduces the audience to her daily life, and therefore it is Cher's voice and language use—reinforced by her role as narrator—that introduce the primary linguistic style of the film.[31] This is the linguistic style of Cher and the language of the speech community, which is part of this generation's means of expression regardless of social clique.

In *Clueless*, Tai compliments her new friends on their apparently mature vocabulary, and although in a later scene Cher is shown to have a strong vocabulary—she describes *The Ren and Stimpy Show* (1991–6) as "way existential"—she does not always understand what she's saying:

Josh: Do you have any idea what you're talking about?
Cher: No, why? Do I sound like I do?

Cher's interest here is in *appearing* intelligent rather than developing her actual understanding: it is only important that her words sound right. At the beginning of the film, we see Cher succeeding in improving her school grades by convincing her teachers to change them without her needing to re-do the work. She is also praised for this skill by her father, Mel (Dan Hedaya). Cher is skillful in her use of language and can use different genres of language easily in order to get her own way. She demonstrates this proudly to Mel, who is himself a manipulator of language in his profession as a lawyer. Cher's adoption of his linguistic skills may be partly due to the lack of a contrasting influence in the home. Cher is the child of a single parent, her mother having died during her early childhood. The constant presence of her father, and the apparent dominance of work in his life (supported by scenes of Mel and his colleagues working in the family home), invite the assumption that his conversation is filled with the jargon and linguistic style of the legal profession. Cher has absorbed this language through years of exposure to her father's work-talk, and incorporated it into her everyday speech.

The life of privilege that Cher has experienced—living in a palatial home with a housekeeper, and great wealth—as well as her verbal abilities has given her great confidence and the self-assurance to protest when she considers herself to have been wronged by those in authority. When she receives a report card with a series of grades that she considers unfair, Cher applies an original approach with each teacher, adapting her performance and tailoring her style of address to suit the teacher's personal interests and politics, and uses flattery effectively to reach her goal. The society of the school is built around divisions among the students as well as between the students and the faculty, constructing a social hierarchy. When Cher and Dionne introduce Tai to the school, Cher refers directly to the cliques:

> That is Alana's group over there. They do the TV station. They think that's the most important thing on Earth. And that's the Persian mafia. You can't hang with them unless you own a BMW. And there's Elton in the white vest, and all the most popular boys in the school . . . If you make the decision to date a high school boy, they are the only acceptable ones.

Every social group has its own characteristics, but beyond this sequence the members of each group only appear in classroom scenes or at parties filling the background. These characters exist only as stereotypes, and representations of a specific type of behavior. In turn, some cliques represent the lower social classes. Within this film, and several others of the genre,[32] the lowest class is the "loadies," the students who spend much of their time involved in recreational drug use.[33] This group is considered a joke, and an easy target for mockery from other cliques within the school. The only member of this group who is developed into a full character is Travis (Breckin Meyer), who becomes involved in the narrative's romantic confusion.[34]

Christian is the second new student to be introduced to the school, but unlike Tai, his position as an outsider goes unchanged, and he makes no effort to join the central group. His language use, clothes, and cultural interests combine to keep him a step apart from the other teenagers, his identity having been formed by his interest in the style and culture of the 1950s. Everything about him reflects this interest, including his clothes, his car, and his love of Billie Holiday music and Tony Curtis films. Despite the fact that Christian discusses cinema, art, music, and fashion, his identity is formed from a different time period from that of every other member of his peer group. Unlike on the numerous occasions when Cher has proven her cultural understanding, here she is unable to follow Christian's references. This is shown clearly on two occasions: first, when Billie Holiday is raised in conversation, and Cher assumes that the singer is male; and second, when she mentions that Christian has brought a copy of the film "Sparaticus" for them to watch.[35]

The use of the 1950s is also significant for that decade's association with the rise of teenage culture, and the origins of the Hollywood teen film. Teen representations of successive generations have given the 1950s a privileged status in film and television, with nostalgic views of the decade used in the musical *Grease* (Randal Kleiser, 1978) and the sitcom *Happy Days* (1974–84). Christian's language is full of period slang, featuring phrases such as "clambakes," "doll face," and "I dig," which stand out from the dialogue of the other teenagers, highlighting Christian's position as an outsider. The use of cultural signifiers from the past also adds to Christian's mystery and appeal, and his chosen identity is as significant and meaningful as that taken by Murray, who attempts to convey a current form of desirable African American masculinity in the language of the inner city. Murray's identity is contemporary and familiar, while Christian distances himself from his peers by choosing an identity associated with the past.

To the teenage community, Christian's language and behavior is colorful and exciting, whereas the adults tend to find him foolish and irritating:

Mel: What's with you, kid? You think the death of Sammy Davis left an opening in the Rat Pack?

The reaction to Christian's persona alters depending on the company he keeps, as the teenagers may find him fascinating for various reasons, though the older characters seem to suffer him more than encourage him. The "permanent" element of Christian's identity, his homosexuality, is made known but is not revealed by Christian himself, and at first this element is disguised while he is presented as Cher's "ideal man." There are suggestions throughout the film that Christian is an unsuitable romantic partner for Cher—such as at a party when he goes to the dance-floor with Cher but then begins dancing with another male—but this becomes clearer still when he spends an evening at Cher's house to watch films: *Some Like it Hot* (Billy Wilder, 1959) and *Spartacus* (Stanley Kubrick, 1960). We are shown a notorious scene from *Spartacus*, featuring Tony Curtis and Laurence Olivier (as Antonius and Crassus), the homosexual subtext of which works as a signifier of Christian's own sexuality—which is then confirmed further by Christian's verbal praising of the scene.[36] Christian is ultimately "outed" by Murray to the surprise of Cher and Dionne, as neither girl had suspected that he was gay. At no point is Christian questioned on his sexuality, and neither does he verbally confirm the assumption, but immediately following Murray's revelation, Christian is seen wearing pink, apparently signifying the truth of the statement.

As with the rest of the teenagers' dialogue, Christian's "outing" is contextualized through references to popular culture. Murray refers to numerous significant gay icons and texts, such as Barbra Streisand, Oscar Wilde, and *The Wizard of Oz* (Victor Fleming, 1939), to emphasize his declaration. Christian's sexuality contributes to his outsider status, and even though his language use does not directly indicate this aspect of his identity, his constant position outside the group and his refusal to compromise his identity reinforce his presence as a gay teenager.[37] Christian does not comply with the social dialect used by his peers, and the construction of his identity around cultural points that are unfamiliar to these peers allows him to stand out.

Clueless is a film where the utterances within the teenage characters' group are highly stylized, creating a standard language that the group maintains. However, on an individual level, their utterances demonstrate individuality through references to different spheres of communication or examples of popular culture. The effect of having individualized language can exclude some characters from joining the main group, because each character must appear to fit in with the film's central community and an overt allegiance to another social clique can cause him or her to stand out too far. As discussed earlier, Murray may use a more urban style of slang at times to prove his independence from his relationship with Dionne, but his behavior and linguistic ability are within the conventions of the main group (he is popular, wealthy, expensively dressed, and uses the language of the speech community). Travis differs from Murray because of his association with the loadies (an undesirable association), and though he uses the language of the speech community as well as the others, it is only when he drops his loadie persona that he can effectively belong to the group.

Heckerling's work in the teen genre provides a coherent and consistent voice for the representation of adolescence. The consistency of style in the utterances of the teenage characters grounds the narratives in a time and location (albeit fictional ones). The constructed nature of each utterance as a piece of film dialogue allows for a state of consistency in the writing process across the different texts, whilst also establishing individual character identities to support and propel the overall narratives. In *Fast Times*, the subjects of conversations as well as the overall lack of an adult presence establishes an authority to the teenage voice in the film. This is developed in the *Clueless* universe through Cher's narration. Bakhtin's theory of the utterance discusses the role of language in conveying period, character history, and the context of the statement. The repetition of conversational structures (Cher's numerous attempts to manipulate her father and her teachers), the individuality of speech patterns (Spicoli's surfing slang, the rhythms of urban slang used by Murray, or Tai's New York accent), and contemporary terminology and cultural references (such as the use of 1990s political correctness argot) provide a context for the events of the various texts.

In her films, Amy Heckerling's use of teenspeak within her adolescent communities demonstrates an engagement with the groups' voices and capacities for self-expression. The characters are allowed individuality of linguistic style or utterance, but reinforce a sense of community by maintaining established speech patterns and subject areas. The language used in *Clueless* has additional functions and can be used to examine the social aspects of the film's narrative. Not only is language responsible for creating distinctions between generations, but it can be used to examine character placement within the film's speech community, which differs from the membership of the social group at the center of the film. Membership of the central group depends on the ability to conform to the speech community.

The role of language in conveying the conventions of the teen genre, and in the contemporary examples of the teen film, provides a sense of self-awareness in each film, in the acknowledgment of the wider genre. Moving through the teen texts of Heckerling's career, we can note the growth in the significance of the characters' dialogue, from expressing teenage fixations to expressing teenage identities. Teen films and television series have always featured slang in the dialogue of their young characters, but by creating an overt linguistic style, which combines references to popular culture, the trading of adolescent insults, and a sophisticated understanding of language as a signifier of community membership, *Clueless* in particular advances the understanding of the genre in the complex utterances of its teenage characters. These are both varied and eloquent as generational markers, and as statements of individuality despite their fleeting lifespans.

NOTES

1   Michael Halliday, *Language as Social Semiotic: The Social Interpretation of Language and Meaning* (London: Edward Arnold, 1978), p. 159; Mikhail Bakhtin, *Speech Genres & Other Late Essays*, trans. Vern W. McGee, ed. Caryl Emerson and Michael Holquist (Austin, TX: University of Texas Press, 2002), p. 63.

2   Cher and Tai stand in for Emma and Harriet, while Josh, Christian, Elton and Travis are equivalent to Mr Knightley, Frank Churchill, Mr Elton and Robert Martin.

3   "Valley-speak" is the term for the linguistic style used by young people—predominantly female—of the San Fernando Valley in California. It features the repetitive use of words such as "like" and "totally," and was famously used in the song "Valley Girl," written and performed by Frank and Moon Unit Zappa in 1982. The voice of the "Valley Girl" may be absent from *Fast Times*, but was explored in *Valley Girl* (Martha Coolidge, 1983), which emphasized the stylistic differences of teens from different areas of Los Angeles, when a popular girl from the valley falls for a punk boy from Hollywood.

4   Kyra Hunting notes how *Clueless* became a multimedia brand, including the film and television series, as well as novels, a CD-ROM game, a line of fashion dolls, jewelry, clothing and make-up. See "Furiously franchised: *Clueless*, convergence culture, and the female-focused franchise," *Cinema Journal* 53: 3 (2014), p. 147.

5   Lucien Hillaire, "*Mean Girls* and the likes: the language of girlhood in American pop culture," MA thesis, Université Denis Diderot (2013), p. 16. Available at <https://www.academia.edu/4038405/Mean_Girls_and_the_likes_the_language_of_girlhood_in_American_pop_culture> (last accessed 8 December 2014).

6   Halliday, p. 154.

7   Bakhtin, p. 60.

8   Ibid. p. 63.

9   Robin Wood, *Hollywood from Vietnam to Reagan . . . and Beyond* (New York: Columbia University Press, 2003), p. 313.

10   Jonathan Bernstein, *Pretty in Pink: The Golden Age of Teenage Movies* (New York: St. Martin's Press, 1997), p. 220.

11   Ibid.

12   *Clueless* predates the surge of teen films that were adapted from literary sources, significantly Shakespeare but also Fyodor Dostoyevsky (*Crime and Punishment in Suburbia* [Rob Schmidt, 2000]) and Pierre Chordelos de Laclos (*Cruel Intentions* [Roger Kumble, 1999]).

13   Timothy Shary, "'The only place to go is inside': confusion about sexuality and class from *Kids* to *Superbad*," *Popping Culture*, Murray Pomerance and John Sakeris (eds.), Pearson Learning Solutions, 2012), p. 11.

14   Timothy Shary, *Generation Multiplex: The Image of Youth in Contemporary American Cinema* (Austin, TX: University of Texas Press, 2002), p. 10.

15   Ibid. pp. 31–2.

16   Ibid. pp. 28–30.

17   Jean Schwind, "Cool coaching at Ridgemont High," *The Journal of Popular Culture*, 41: 6 (2008), p. 1020.

18   Schwind, p. 1026.

19   The film ends with a few snapshots of how the students have progressed since the end of the school year, which was the duration of the film's narrative: Stacy and Mark fall in love, Brad becomes the manager of a mini-mart, Linda goes to college and has an affair with her professor, and Spicoli goes on to save Brooke Shields from drowning.

20   Lesley Speed, "A world ruled by hilarity: gender and low comedy in the films of Amy Heckerling," *Senses of Cinema* 22 (2002). Available at <sensesofcinema.com/2002/22/heckerling/> (last accessed 8 December 2014).

21   Their final conversation features Vernon threatening his student John (Judd Nelson), who is quite surprised: "You think anyone's gonna believe you? You think anyone is gonna take

your word over mine? I'm a man of respect around here. They love me around here. I'm a swell guy. You're a lying sack of shit and everyone knows it."

22 One example can be found in the British film magazine, *Empire* 77 (November 1995).

23 Anna Klassen, "Clueless glossary: buggin', cake boy, & more '90s slang from the film," *The Daily Beast*, 19 July 2013. Available at <http://www.thedailybeast.com/articles/2013/07/19/clueless-glossary-buggin-cake-boy-more-90-s-slang-from-the-film.html> (last accessed 8 December 2014).

24 Jennifer O'Meara, "'We've got to work on your accent and vocabulary': characterization through verbal style in *Clueless*," *Cinema Journal* 53: 3 (2014), p. 138.

25 Notes from the short documentary *Language Arts*, featured among the special features on the DVD version of *Clueless: Whatever! Edition* (2005).

26 O'Meara, pp. 139–40.

27 Daniel Chandler, *Semiotics: The Basics* (New York: Routledge, 2002), p. 124.

28 Paula J. Massood, *Black City Cinema: African American Urban Experiences in Film* (Philadelphia, PA: Temple University Press, 2003), p. 160.

29 Halliday, p. 159.

30 Shary (2002), p. 26.

31 Because the teenage group is the center of the film, I suggest that in terms of a linguistic hierarchy, the teenage linguistic style is the film's primary language, higher in status than the language of the surrounding characters. Therefore, within *Clueless* the teenspeak of these characters is the "correct" form of language, heard most often within the film and by the largest number of characters, and any variation away from this style of speech instantly positions a character outside the main group and speech community, as shown by Tai's confusion by the language of her peers.

32 In *The Breakfast Club* (John Hughes, 1985), John is looked down upon for having marijuana in his locker, even though the group bonds while smoking his stash at a later point in the film; *10 Things I Hate About You* (Gil Junger, 1999) features both stoners and "white Rastas" who are shown to be mocked and apathetic in their attitude; and in *Dazed and Confused* (Richard Linklater, 1993), despite various characters being shown buying and using drugs, it is a habitual stoner who is the most ridiculed.

33 See also: "slackers," "stoners," "burners," "reef-worms," etc.

34 Consider that Travis is the equivalent character to Robert Martin in *Emma*, a tenant farmer who is considered an unsuitable match for Emma's new friend Harriet.

35 Cher is attempting to refer to the film *Spartacus*.

36 As discussed in Vito Russo's *Celluloid Closet: Homosexuality in the Movies* (New York: Harper & Row, 1987), pp. 119–20.

37 The use of a gay character in the conventional teen genre was still fairly rare at the start of the 1990s, despite the fact that the archetype had been established early in the genre's history, such as the character of Plato in *Rebel Without a Cause* (Nicholas Ray, 1955). Gay teenagers appear more regularly on television, where a longer format can devote more time to the exploration of the character. By the end of the 1990s, gay teenagers featured in many of the most influential television dramas of the genre, including Ricky (Wilson Cruz) in *My So-Called Life* (1994–5), Willow (Alyson Hannigan) in *Buffy the Vampire Slayer* (1997–2003), and Jack (Kerr Smith) in *Dawson's Creek* (1998–2003).

Femininity, Aging, and Postfeminism

Introduction to Part III

Akey thread running throughout Heckerling's film and television work has been the exploration of the changing expectations of women's identities during the last three decades. From the start of her directing career, with the release of *Fast Times at Ridgemont High* in 1982, Heckerling's work differed from that of the majority of teen film directors in that she focused her attentions on female rather than male characters. As many contributors in this collection note, the proportion of female directors working in Hollywood remains stubbornly low, and indeed the vast majority of Hollywood films fail to achieve even the meager criteria for Alison Bechdel's infamous test, which requires that a film feature two women talking to each other about something other than men.

Heckerling's films frequently find autobiographical echoes in the director's own life. For instance, the *Look Who's Talking* films (1989, 1990), on which Claire Jenkins focuses, followed soon after the birth of Heckerling's daughter, Mollie Israel, in 1985. Jenkins compares the focus of Heckerling's family films favorably with the contemporary focus on father figures, and finds that, even today, her work possesses a liberal attitude toward motherhood and romance that stands in sharp contrast to the majority of what she terms "mom-coms."

In retrospect, of course, it's possible to see Heckerling's career as reflecting the rise of postfeminism and the concomitant demise, or at least the dimming, of second-wave feminism. Mirroring the contradictory impulses of postfeminist discourses, Mollie (Kirstie Alley) is the self-sufficient breadwinner of her small family, even as she searches for a romantic partner, and thus to recuperate the nuclear family unit. Nonetheless, as Betty Kaklamanidou observes in the second essay of this section, it is in Heckerling's latest work, which deals with the construction of femininity and the aging process, that the postfeminism of her work is most apparent. *I Could Never Be Your Woman* (2007) once again reflects the biography of the director in centering on a television producer of a successful teen show.

The final essay in this section, by Murray Leeder, focuses on the construction of femininity and aging in *Vamps*. Drawing from the vast body of literature and film on the world of vampires, Leeder argues that Heckerling's contribution to the genre provides a reflection on the status of the aging woman, and on the urban landscape, in a world continually fixated on youth.

CHAPTER 7

Look Who's Doing the Caring: Shared Parenting, Subjectivity, and Gender Roles in Heckerling's *Look Who's Talking* Films

Claire Jenkins

The significance of Amy Heckerling's films *Look Who's Talking* (1989) and *Look Who's Talking Too* (1990) emerges most clearly when comparing them to others of the same genre. As attitudes toward the formation and structure of the American family have become more liberal, Hollywood comedies have begun to position the single or expectant mother in romantic comedies. This has been particularly evident in the recent trend of 'mom-coms,' including but not limited to *The Back-up Plan* (Alan Poul, 2010), *The Switch* (Josh Gordon and Will Speck, 2010), *Friends with Kids* (Jennifer Westfeldt, 2011), and *What to Expect When You're Expecting* (Kirk Jones, 2012), where single mothers who have fallen pregnant through non-traditional means combine pregnancy and motherhood with the search for a mate.

In tandem with these films, there is also a trend toward narratives about "accidental" mothers, as in *Raising Helen* (Garry Marshall, 2004), *Knocked Up* (Judd Apatow, 2007), *No Reservations* (Scott Hicks, 2007), and *Life As We Know It* (Greg Berlanti, 2010), where women either fall pregnant unexpectedly, or become mothers by inheriting the children of deceased friends or family members. This latter group of mom–coms have their root in the 1980s, when there was a considerable trend toward comedy films about motherhood and child-rearing, including *Mr. Mom* (Stan Dragoti, 1983), *Baby Boom* (Charles Shyer, 1987), and *Three Men and a Baby* (Leonard Nimoy, 1987), in which parenthood is thrust upon unwitting career women, and men, who learn that it is more fulfilling than their corporate lives. Susan Faludi recognizes the backlash messages of these films in the way they promote a particular idea of motherhood: "These movies aren't really reflecting women's return to total motherhood, they are marketing it . . . The backlash films struggle to make motherhood as alluring as possible. Cuddly babies in designer clothes displace older children on the 1980s screen."[1] *Baby Boom* is a prime example of this, as the film reinstates the initially reluctant mother, J. C. Wiatt (Diane Keaton), in a small town where she is romanced by the local vet and sets up a cottage industry manufacturing baby food.

While *Baby Boom*, and more recent films that have followed such as *No Reservations*, function as a morality tale for women wishing to put work before motherhood, Heckerling's *Look Who's Talking* films buck the trends of mom-coms, allowing the single mother to juggle career and motherhood. Elizabeth Traube suggests that as such, *Look Who's Talking* is "exceptional for its validation of the independent working woman."[2] Traube's assessment of the film contrasts with other scholarship that is more critical of *Look Who's Talking*'s gender roles and familial representation. For example, Sarah Harwood believes the film narrativizes a "search in which the interests of the child are paramount, the desires of the mother sublimated and in which the father acts as tutor."[3] Traube herself cites Lynne Joyrich, who claimed the film offered a "one-sided affirmation of the male role in reproduction and family life."[4] Traube's assessment of the film is set apart from much feminist scholarship that focuses solely on its anti-abortion message (evident, as the fetus is given both a voice and a personality) and the need to reinstate a father figure to complete the family. As Traube explains, "how spectators handle the device of Mikey's prefetal and fetal voice is likely to influence their perceptions of the movie as a whole."[5] She concludes her analysis of the film by arguing that "*Look Who's Talking* seems to me to deserve more credit than it has received from feminist critics for depicting genuinely shared parenting rather than single male mothering and for its playful subversion of its own generic antecedents."[6] Following Traube's lead, then, this chapter reassesses the *Look Who's Talking* films from a contemporary perspective, arguing that beneath a relatively conservative narrative premise, the original film discussed by Traube, and its sequel, are liberal in their depiction of motherhood and the family, something that emerges most clearly when one compares these films with their contemporaries, and, in particular, more recent mom-coms.

The narrative premise of *Look Who's Talking* is that an accountant, Mollie (Kirstie Alley), has fallen pregnant after an ill-advised affair with a married client, Albert (George Segal). Mollie goes ahead with the pregnancy, concealing the details of the affair from friends and family by claiming she was artificially inseminated. Once baby Mikey—whose inner thoughts are voiced by Bruce Willis—has been born, Mollie sets out to find a suitable father figure, all the while resisting the charms of taxi driver James (John Travolta) (whom she met while in the throes of labor), who becomes her babysitter. The film, predictably, ends with Mollie and James united, and the second film sees the two married, but troubles arise following the birth of their daughter Julie, who similarly shares her inner thoughts with the audience, this time through the voice of Roseanne Barr.

LOOK WHO'S TALKING AND "MOM-COMS"

The narrative drive of the *Look Who's Talking* films draws upon the two central tropes of mom-coms: the arrival of an unplanned child (whether biological or "inherited"), and the reinstatement of the single parent into a nuclear, albeit not biological, family. The repudiation of the career woman remains central to narratives of "accidental" motherhood, such as *Baby Boom*, *Raising Helen*, *No Reservations*, *Knocked Up*, and *Life as We Know It*. With the exception of the accidental pregnancy in *Knocked Up*, children are inherited through the death of a relative. In all cases, mothers are not equipped for parenthood and it is distinctly displayed as at odds with their career; for example, in *Raising Helen*, fashion promoter Helen's (Kate Hudson) nieces and nephew disrupt a high-end fashion show when they accompany her to work. Similarly, in *No Reservations*, Kate (Catherine Zeta-Jones)'s job and new role as mother are not compatible. In this film Kate, a chef, takes her young niece to work with her, meaning the child is up late, often helping out in the kitchen, and is subsequently tired during school hours, resulting in Kate being reprimanded by her niece's teacher. Although the career of Alison (Katherine Heigl) does not suffer so readily in *Knocked Up*, there is clearly a tension between her role at a TV station and her impending maternity, played out comically through the character of Jill (Kristen Wiig), who finds the very idea of Alison's pregnancy grotesque. Pamela Thoma suggests that instead of affecting Alison's career, her pregnancy instead disrupts her status as independent woman: "Alison begins to 'unlearn' feminism and to retreat to the regulated modesties of middle-class femininity."[7] This gradual change occurs through consumption: Thoma argues that Alison is transformed "from sexually assertive career woman to choice-making consumer mother,"[8] so although independence is rebuked it is by consumerism rather than conventional familial tendencies.

For Mollie in *Look Who's Talking*, motherhood is similarly accidental, but it does not represent the same blow for her career. Traube notes that Mollie, the independent career woman, is contrasted favorably with the elite dependent wife—the wife of Mikey's biological father, Albert. In comparison to frivolous, flighty, "over-controlled" Beth, Mollie is "practical, rational, and progressive."[9] It is only in *Look Who's Talking Too* that any tension between work and motherhood is visible. Although her male boss is horrified by the presence of Mikey in the office, an incident that only occurs once during the film, there is no reason given for Mikey's presence, and nothing said of it afterwards. Furthermore, a similar scene recurs when Mikey is at work with James, sat in the front seat of his cab. In both instances Mikey causes minor disruption, but the sequences are quickly forgotten. Despite these small moments, there is no tension depicted between work and motherhood; in fact, in *Look Who's Talking*, Mollie is doing a couple's accounts while Mikey happily plays next to her with his own toy calculator. The ease with which work and motherhood are apparently combined contrasts with a more recent film, *One Fine Day* (Michael Hoffman, 1996), where a similar scene recurs when architect Melanie Parker (Michelle Pfeiffer) is forced to take her young son into the office. Both the circumstances leading up to this event, and the fallout from it, are over-played within the narrative; Melanie is forced to deny that the child is her son, for fear of losing her job, and it is only once she is prepared to admit to her boss that the child was her son, and consequently admit that she has been neglecting him, that the narrative can be resolved. Throughout this film Melanie learns that family must come first, the same lesson learnt by J. C. in *Baby Boom*, Helen in *Raising Helen*, and Kate in *No Reservations*. These latter three women all change their jobs to something more flexible, and Melanie agrees to make sacrifices. Although Traube argues that the presence of the male boss in a female-dominated workspace suggests that "only moderate aspirations are acceptable in women,"[10] the film takes working motherhood for granted, not just with Mollie, but also Mollie's own mother, who is similarly an accountant.

The fact that Mollie is an accountant—like her mother—pokes fun at the obsession with male inheritance in 1980s action cinema. In action and adventure narratives such as the first *Star Wars* trilogy (1977, 1980, 1983), the first *Indiana Jones* movies (1981, 1984, 1989), and the *Back to the Future* trilogy (1985, 1989, 1990), the son's inheritance of the father's traits is crucial to his development. Indeed, as Britton argues of the decade, "'patriarchy' is very much the term to describe what gets reaffirmed in Reaganite entertainment: with unremitting insistence and stridency it is the status and function of the father and their inheritance by the son that are at stake."[11] In films of the decade, father–son relationships and male inheritance are serious concerns. However, female inheritance is treated differently; it rarely garners the same interest or importance in Hollywood narratives. As I have argued elsewhere, mother–daughter narratives have tended to focus on the frictions of the relationship, as in *Terms of Endearment* (James L. Brooks, 1983), *The Bridges of Madison County* (Clint Eastwood, 1995), and *One True Thing* (Carl Franklin, 1998), rather than on inheritance of traits. This echoes a Freudian notion of inheritance where mothers feature as obstacles in the development of their children.[12] Heckerling's films have a significant take on issues of inheritance: the theme is not over-played, but all members of Mollie's family are accountants, and as Mikey uses the toy calculator, the link to the next generation is playfully implicit. This breaks down gender boundaries—inheritance is no longer only important between fathers and sons—at the same time as reiterating the importance of inheritance to the families of the decade.

REIMAGINING THE PATRIARCH

Inheritance is further critiqued as the narrative of *Look Who's Talking* sees Mollie keen to find a suitable non-biological father for Mikey. Mollie's need to find a father figure for her son is, of course, in keeping with the tropes that dominated Hollywood cinema of the 1980s. While the need to find a suitable father is not new to the 1980s, it is in this decade that it becomes a central theme of Hollywood production. The need to reconcile the son with an adequate, changed, biological father figure drives the narrative of Hollywood's big action films of the 1980s, but elsewhere in the decade, the surrogate father is celebrated as a figure of masculine authority, as in the first *Star* Wars trilogy, *The Karate Kid* (John G. Avildsen, 1984), and *Back to the Future*. This trend leads Jon Lewis to claim that the decade's teenagers "seek out aged mentors, preferring . . . instruction, discipline and obedience."[13] The need for masculine authority extends beyond the decade into the 1990s, where Arnold Schwarzenegger's killing-machine-turned-protector is deemed the ideal father in *Terminator 2: Judgment Day* (James Cameron, 1991) because, as Sarah Connor (Linda Hamilton) explains, "The Terminator would never stop, it would never leave him and it would never hurt him . . . it would always be there and it would die to protect him." While biological paternity is not necessarily a concern here, the reinstating of a protective father is.

In *Look Who's Talking*, it is Mollie's desire for authority and paternal influence, rather than that of the son, that drives the narrative, in some ways offering a comparable storyline to *Terminator 2*, where Sarah had sought protection for her son (albeit with a very different tone). However, in Heckerling's film, Mollie's search for a suitable patriarch functions primarily as a comment upon the decade's obsession with fatherhood, rather than simply upholding this concern. As Stella Bruzzi notes, the film is actually playful and mocking in its attitudes to fathers: "a baby friend pokes fun at new man paternity as, to a bemused Mikey . . . she defines a Dad as 'you know, the big men types that hang around the mummies. That's a Daddy.'"[14] The playfulness with which the film deals with paternity is similarly evidenced in its portrayal of James, who lacks many of the characteristics of the ideal patriarch of 1980s films inasmuch as he is not a breadwinner, nor a disciplinarian. James's model of paternity is in keeping with Travolta's star persona of the 1980s, which is built upon his musical roles in *Saturday Night Fever* (John Badham, 1977), *Grease* (Randal Kleiser, 1978), and *Staying Alive* (Sylvester Stallone, 1983), where working-class heterosexuality is expressed through music and dance.

Although these performances hide emotion behind bravado, in all instances the masquerade drops, depicting a more emotional version of working-class masculinity that challenges norms concerning gender and class. The costuming of Travolta in the *Look Who's Talking* films, and his brief musical performances in both, clearly reference this star persona, reiterating a soft, classed masculinity. However, in this instance the nod to Travolta as musical star seeks primarily to depict James as a nurturing father: his most tender moments in both *Look Who's Talking* and its sequel are when he is dancing with the children. As Traube notes, by the epilogue of *Look Who's Talking*, Mollie has learnt that "good providing is not the essence of good fathering."[15] From the outset, James is a nurturing father—rather than a breadwinner—having, as he announces, practically raised his (working) sister's children. His nurturing is further celebrated in the film in an altercation with Albert, Mikey's biological father. Albert turns up at Mollie's apartment while James is babysitting, keen to see Mikey. James—who had believed Mikey to be the product of artificial insemination—is clearly shocked that Albert claims to be the biological father. However, James questions Albert's paternity, by suggesting that biology is not enough to make a father:

> James: Okay, if you're the father and that's your son, maybe you can answer a few questions for me, okay? When was he born?
> Albert: July third.
> James: Ok, what's his favorite cereal?
> Albert: I don't know!
> James: Cheerios. What's his favorite stuffed animal, Fred or Barney? (Albert pauses.)
> James: Fred.
> Albert: That's right.
> James: No, no, Barney. How many diapers does he go through a day? About six. Who's his favorite rock star? Michael Jackson. Don't you think a father should know some of these things?

What is pertinent about James's questioning is that he sees the good father as someone who is involved in nurturing (knowing how many diapers Mikey gets through) and knowing the child's personality. This is a soft model of fatherhood that is not interested in either biology or breadwinning. This sets the film apart from numerous films—both contemporary to *Look Who's Talking*, and more recent. Indeed, the 2010 film *The Switch* sees biology as a crucial to paternity. In this film, Wally (Jason Bateman) is anxious when his best friend Cassie (Jennifer Aniston) decides to have a baby through artificial insemination. She throws a party to mark the event and a drunken Wally finds the sperm sample in her bathroom. He accidentally washes this away and replaces it with his own offering, an act he promptly forgets. When, six years later, Wally realizes what happened and confides in a colleague, the response is "congratulations, you're a father." Here biology is the *only* defining factor in paternity. While *Look Who's Talking* is one of a number of films (including, but not limited to, *Jerry Maguire* [Cameron Crowe, 1996], *One Fine Day*, *The Next Best Thing* [John Schlesinger, 2000], and *Maid in Manhattan* [Wayne Wang, 2002]), in which the non-biological father is clearly the better father, the focus here is also on the close nurturing relationship between father (figure) and son.

James's competence as a nurturer sets him apart from his contemporaries. Unlike the fathers of *Mr. Mom* or *Three Men and a Baby*, James does not need to "learn" how to be a father. In both the original film and its sequel, he is a natural parent. When Mollie expresses reservations about him becoming the babysitter, James explains that he is great with kids, and throughout the course of the film proves this to be true. Despite this, some criticism still maintains that this is a transformation narrative in which James must learn what it is to be a good father (and only then can the final romance between him and Mollie occur). If understood in this way, *Look Who's Talking* can be grouped with other films, such as *Kramer vs. Kramer* (Robert Benton, 1979), *Three Men and a Baby*, and *Mrs. Doubtfire* (Chris Columbus, 1993), in which fun fathers have to learn to be responsible parents. Nicole Matthews is one such critic who believes James to be irresponsible—and hence unable to consummate his relationship with Mollie—until he has "transformed" into a more responsible father, demonstrated here in his concern for Mikey when the child is lost in the city, at the climax of the first film.[16] However, if, as Matthews claims, responsibility as a father has come to be recognized as presence,[17] then James proves himself from the start—being present for Mollie's labor. In fact, James is more than just present, although he is often haphazard, and seemingly out of control—never more clearly articulated than in his chaotic charge through the streets of Manhattan when Mollie is in labor. Despite the chaos, James *does* get Mollie to the hospital on time and stays with her through the birth, even coercing a doctor into administering painkillers. Later in the film he takes Mikey for a drive (albeit it without Mollie's knowledge) so that the mother can get some rest. He also entertains Mikey, and as such, James frequently delivers as a patriarch. In proving himself to be a suitable father figure, James contrasts with Mollie's other suitors, who are either presumed to be or proven to be controlling and strict. For example, Mollie worries that a date who shouts at a waitress, and another who complains aggressively about dirty crockery at a restaurant, will unnecessarily reprimand Mikey. When another potential suitor is waiting with Mikey for Mollie to get ready, he refuses to let him watch his chosen television channel, instead changing the channel and belligerently snatching the remote from the child. This scene reiterates the film's playfulness around expectations of male responsibility; Mollie constantly berates

James, even though he proves himself again and again, as she assumes middle-class career men will be more responsible.

As such, in *Look Who's Talking*, James does not transform; he is responsible from the outset, just not in Mollie's eyes. Indeed, Traube notices that it is Mollie's transformation that leads to the final romance as she renounces her previous ideas about what constitutes a good father.[18] James is a good parent—because he is more relaxed than Mollie—who relies on the recommendations of experts such as Dr Spock: "Through Mikey the film supports James's position, which is to return to parents the control that was expropriated from them by the experts over what Ehrenreich and English (1979) call the 'century of the child.'"[19]

The refiguring of the child's role in the family is another liberal discourse that can be teased out of *Look Who's Talking*. Whereas Mollie's obsession with responsibility and protecting Mikey reinforces the notion that the child is at the center of the family, the narrative premise recognizes that both parents require their own professional and personal fulfillment away from the child. This upholds claims made by Jessica Valenti's *Why Have Kids?* (2012), which argues that despite popular rhetoric that promotes children and motherhood as integral to a woman's happiness, child-rearing has not, historically, been about personal fulfillment, and the need to perpetuate the myth that it has is causing guilt in those not completely fulfilled by the role.[20] By celebrating the subjectivity of both male and female characters, and recognizing both mother and surrogate father to be more than just their parental roles, *Look Who's Talking* is liberal and progressive in its depiction of family.

CLASS AND FATHERHOOD

The most striking contrast between James and his 1980s counterparts, and indeed more recent examples of single parents, concerns class and employment status. *Look Who's Talking* follows many of the traditions of single-parent narratives—not least in that it allows the child to choose the "new" stepfather. This is a trope that has been well rehearsed in film such as *The Courtship of Eddie's Father* (Vincente Minnelli, 1963), *The Sound of Music* (Robert Wise, 1965), *Sleepless in Seattle* (Nora Ephron, 1993), *Jerry Maguire*, *Pay it Forward* (Mimi Leder, 2000), or *Maid in Manhattan*. This trope of the child choosing a new suitor for the parent allows parental desires to be seemingly fulfilled while the main concern remains the desires of the child.[21] This is certainly the case in *Look Who's Talking*, although the father that Mikey chooses is also the one that best fulfills the mother's needs, a sentiment that is echoed elsewhere in the film as Mollie's mother tells her "Mikey will like whoever you like."

In recent films concerned with restoring a pseudo-nuclear family, there has been a focus on the chosen father as a middle-class figure, one who brings financial stability alongside completing the unit. *Jerry Maguire*, *As Good As It Gets* (James L. Brooks, 1997), *Pay it Forward*, *Maid in Manhattan*, and *Mamma Mia!* (Phyllida Lloyd, 2008) all refigure the working-class single parent family by instating a middle-class father, a figure that has long been assumed to be the preferred paternal model. Ehrenreich and Bruzzi both argue that working-class masculinity, in Hollywood in particular, has been depicted as physical, often violent, and certainly un-nurturing.[22] This is supported by *Pay It Forward*, where the biological, working-class father is an abusive alcoholic and the preferred surrogate is a middle-class teacher. What is significant, then, about *Look Who's Talking* is the completion of the family with a father who is working-class. This is a point of anxiety for Mollie throughout the film, particularly in one of her many fantasy sequences in which she imagines potential suitors in the paternal role. Mollie assumes James's drinking and smoking will become out of control and envisages a filthy smoke-hewn existence in which the working-class body is overweight and out of control. The working-class father is assumed to be crude and overly sexualized, with his desire to get things free, meaning that he cannot sufficiently provide for his family. Mollie's fantasy is hysterically conservative and is neatly undercut by the film. Traube argues that "Molly's [sic] 'mistake,' in the movie's terms, is not only her attempted denial of her sexuality but also her adherence to what the movie presents as the outmoded breadwinner family."[23]

The parade of unsuitable middle-class men that Mollie dates, while trying to find a suitable father figure for Mikey, consists of unattractive disciplinarians. Mikey's biological father, an upper-middle-class businessman, is seen to be unsuitable precisely because of his sense of privilege and entitlement that is linked to his class status: "Albert is a parody of . . . new masculinity. Although still a breadwinner when we meet him, he no longer identifies himself with the role but is more concerned about the class status asserted though his New Age office décor."[24] Thus wealth and status become corrupting and lead to self-involvement rather than providing. When Mollie finally takes Mikey to meet Albert, the father is comically over-invested in the unnecessary refurbishment of his office, and this affects his interest in Mikey, whom he tries to prevent from playing with the artifacts in his office. The tension between privileged class position and parenting is brought to the fore when Albert complains about Mollie changing Mikey's nappy on his new desk; Mollie protests by slamming the filled nappy down on the desk and storming out.

James's flexible employment as a taxi driver (something Mollie initially equates to irresponsibility and inability to find a more reliable job) allows him to become the ideal father, owing to his ability to work hours that fit around Mollie's schedule. As a result the working-class father can, in contrast to the model put forward by Ehrenreich and Bruzzi, be nurturing and involved. The stability of the working-class father is further evidenced when comparing James to the fathers of comedies about parenthood, including *Mr. Mom*, *Three Men and a Baby*, *Mrs. Doubtfire*, *One Fine Day*, *Cheaper by the Dozen* (Shawn Levy, 2003) and *Daddy Day Care* (Steve Carr, 2003) in which dads—whether biological or not—must *learn* to be parents. Thus, in these films, it is male transformation that leads the narrative. James's lack of transformation separates him, and demonstrates that *Look Who's Talking* is about more than just fatherhood, despite Matthews's claims that it is a parable of fatherhood,[25] and Harwood's belief that the mother is largely evacuated from the family until she has learnt from the father and son.[26]

In more recent mom-coms, it is not necessarily male transformation, but instead male anxiety, that has dominated the narrative. Films such as *The Back-Up Plan*, *What to Expect When You're Expecting*, and *Friends With Kids* see new and expectant fathers struggle to "have it all." The anxiety around men having it all—providing for families and juggling career and family— has been recognized by reports from The Families and Work Institute,[27] an American nonpartisan, non-profit organization that researches shifting tensions between families and work, and the key issues that affect both of these. Despite research into real family experience recognizing the pressures felt by men to be part of wider shifts in work–life structures, within the narratives of these films this concern seeks only to "usurp female/feminist concerns of reproductive freedom and focus on male concerns, removing any sense of shared experience, and exploring parenthood through its effect on the father."[28] In *Look Who's Talking*, anxieties and transformations are reserved for the mother. However, she does not need to transform into a good parent, but instead she must transform so that she can recognize her own desires and James's suitability as a father. When, in *Look Who's Talking Too*, Mollie and her family take it upon themselves to improve James's job prospects by finding him employment as a corporate pilot, the fallout becomes detrimental to their marriage, and James moves out. That said, it is important to note here that although James is a cab driver, he has aspirations beyond this, and therefore upward mobility remains the important characteristic for a father.

Upward mobility is also implicit in the dual-earner family which, while not formed until the end of *Look Who's Talking*, is present—without question— through *Look Who's Talking Too*. As Stephanie Coontz argues, dual-earning families are integral to upward mobility in contemporary America, and upward mobility is, itself, at the heart of the American dream.[29] However, Traube does suggest that James's work ethic is undercut by his more dominant position as a "small-time scam artist,"[30] and his lack of professional progress is reiterated in the second film when Mollie's attempts to mold him into the assumed ideal of fatherhood are again unsuccessful. As a result, the mother's belief in the societal expectations of the good father is undercut in both films. In much the same way, the film has no expectations about good motherhood: while the father is more flexible in his working patterns, the mother has a full-time job and there is never any question of Mollie leaving work once she has had a child. Although there is an imperative for Mollie to find a suitable husband for herself and father for Mikey, the single mother is resourceful throughout and manages to combine the demands of motherhood and work, albeit with hired help. While Mollie does appear to have a nanny/housekeeper, she is never formally introduced into the narrative, and thus neither Mollie's work nor her domestic situation is critiqued by the narrative. The only tensions that do arise, as mentioned, are the brief sequence in which Mollie takes Mikey into the office in *Look Who's Talking Too*, and this is quickly followed by a sequence in which Mikey is also seen at work with James.

It is a point of note that, although the father is not middle-class, both parents do work, and the mother is certainly more upwardly mobile. The family does have financial stability, and James's employment status does improve in the sequel when he becomes an airline pilot. However, the financial status of the parents is deemed to be less important than the flexibility of their working lives. This liberal re-imagining of the family effectively undercuts the notion of the father as breadwinner, offering not only flexible parenting, but also more diverse gender roles in which the mother is the main breadwinner and the father's flexible work conditions make him the ideal carer.

MATERNAL SUBJECTIVITY AND GENDER DIFFERENCE

The celebration of the independent woman is most notable since *Look Who's Talking* seeks to fulfill Mollie's romantic and sexual desires. Criticism of the film has argued that Mollie is punished for transgressing her natural role, and therefore aligns her with the sacrificial mother of melodrama.[31] Conversely, Traube suggests the film demonstrates that "not only can a woman be 'something else besides a mother,' to recall Stella Dallas's famous complaint, she is a better mother for being something else besides, not only a sexually fulfilled wife but also an active, independent working woman."[32] Much of the debate around the film's attitude to the mother centers on the voice given to the baby. As Matthews believes, the subjectivity afforded Mikey decenters the figure of the father who (as noted) tends to dominate parenting comedies.[33] Despite this decentering of the father, both Matthews and Harwood argue that a clear link is drawn between father and male child, one that seeks to oust the mother from the narrative by, again, foregrounding masculine concerns. Harwood claims: "The film solves this not-father dilemma by allocating authorial control to

Mikey who then validates James within the paternal role. The child has the power to confirm the father and it is the paternal role which is more important within this paradigm."[34]

The privileging of Mikey's voice is undoubtedly problematic when read as an anti-abortion narrative, particularly because the fetus has a voice long before he is born, suggesting that personhood begins in the womb. However, as Traube argues, it also provides the necessary "comic convention" the narrative requires.[35] Furthermore, subjectivity is not only reserved for the child. Despite claims of Mollie's marginalization, both *Look Who's Talking* and its sequel are peppered with fantasies and daydreams from Mollie's and Mikey's perspectives (but notably never the father's). This is seen in *Look Who's Talking* in Mollie's daydreams of how various suitors would perform as fathers, and in *Look Who's Talking Too* in her fantasies of reconciliation with James. Mikey's inner thoughts are coupled with similar daydreams of his life as a big brother in *Look Who's Talking Too*. In both Mollie's and Mikey's fantasizes (in the sequel, especially), gender difference is comically unpicked. Mollie fantasies a romantic encounter in which James fawns at her sexual allure, and Mikey sees himself as a protective big brother keeping his sister safe from thuggish toddlers. Both fantasies are quickly debunked by reality. As Mollie, and her daughter, Julie, doll themselves up in advance of a visit from James, Mollie ladders her tights and cannot fit into her glamorous dress. Julie ends up dressed in an androgynous New Romantic-style outfit, all the while ironically accompanied by the song 'Being a Girl' on the soundtrack. The effect of this sequence is to undermine expectations around femininity, and the impossible standards set for women, further celebrating Mollie as a woman who transgresses the expectations of femininity, and placid maternity, in favor of independent womanhood.

In much the same way as *Look Who's Talking* undercuts expectations around gendered parenting, the sequel unpicks expectations around gender division more broadly. Mikey's assertion that his toys are for boys, and that Julie cannot desire the "Cobra Hammer Head" they both see advertised on television, is undone when his assertion of gender division upsets the sister he had wished to protect. Similarly, Uncle Stuart (Elias Koteas) carries a gun and plays war games with Mikey, but does not protect the children when a burglar breaks into the apartment. Instead, he chases the culprit, leaving the children alone, while food on the stove then starts a fire. The playful representation of gender division is evident from the opening of *Look Who's Talking* when the sperm are accompanied by the Beach Boys' "I Get Around" and the egg by a more feminine love song: The Chantels' "I Love You So." Traube argues that the instance "instructs us *not* to assign a realistic motivation to the procreative imagery";[36] it also does the same for the obsessive representation of gender difference.

It is also worth considering the way in which the woman/mother's body is treated in these films. Contemporary mom-coms such as *Knocked Up* or *The Change-Up* (David Dobkin, 2011) treat the mother's body as abject, where the moment of birth (that uses actual footage of childbirth) is one of horror for the male characters (*Knocked Up*), or the sexualized, pregnant body becomes troubling (*The Change-Up*). Although a joke is made at Mollie's expense in *Look Who's Talking*, when James, upon seeing Mollie's swollen, post-partum breasts, responds, 'I see you've got your figure back,' the film is generally more nuanced and sympathetic in its treatment of the mother's body. The film's response when James accidentally adds breast milk to his coffee is most telling. Mollie waits until James has drunk the coffee before she reveals his mistake. Although he initially spits out the drink, he soon laughs along with Mollie, and leaves the scene taking the beverage with him, unperturbed by the provenance of the milk. This is in stark contrast to, say, the television show *Friends* (1994–2004), in which a whole episode is built around Ross (David Schwimmer)'s horror at the prospect of tasting breast milk.

DISRUPTING THE WOMAN'S NARRATIVE

While there is much to recommend about Heckerling's films in terms of their playful exploration of gender roles and family dynamics, in terms of narrative, the original, and to a greater extent its sequel, are somewhat lackluster. *Look Who's Talking Too* has very little narrative drive and even less coherence. It seems, at times, little more than a sequence of scenes rather haphazardly strung together (the conception, Mollie and James trying to potty-train Mikey, Julie's birth), none of which flows smoothly. This strategy affects the quality of the film as narrative cinema, but it opens up interesting questions about the way in which the woman's story is told. Indeed, looking at other films by Heckerling, a similar storytelling strategy occurs, most notably in *Fast Times at Ridgemont High* (1982) and to a lesser extent in *I Could Never Be Your Woman* (2007). *Fast Times* "cleverly undercuts the conventional sexism of the high school coming-of-age cycle,"[37] and rather than constituting a sustained narrative, the film presents the key events that high school students go through in the course of their academic year. The advantage of this strategy of storytelling is that it unpicks the presumed importance of certain events in a woman's life. For example, the pregnancy of Stacy (Jennifer Jason Leigh) and her subsequent abortion are relatively small moments in the film. Instead of these events being imbued with undue sentimentality, they are dealt with in a matter-of-fact way; Stacy is sad, yet she moves on. Rather than dwell on pregnancy, and the resulting decisions a woman has to make, as a defining moment in life, Heckerling refuses to give them undue importance, thus seeing a woman's life as more than just "rites of passage." Indeed, in *Look Who's Talking Too*, although the film begins with Julie's conception, there is never any big announcement of pregnancy; rather, it is brushed over. The conception and birth are significant to Julie's narrative rather than her mother's, because the difficult delivery leaves Julie traumatized, and explains her personality thereafter. Similarly, although *Look Who's Talking* concludes with Mollie and James's romantic union (and a flash forward to Julie's arrival), their wedding is never seen. This allows a woman's narrative to be more than just the milestones that typify heteronormative womanhood, with her subjectivity existing away from these moments, and as such the film sets itself apart from the majority of mom-coms or romantic comedies. It also contradicts the impetus of family-driven sequels such as *Father of the Bride Part II* (Charles Shyer, 1995) or *Meet the Fockers* (Jay Roach, 2004) and *Little Fockers* (Paul Weitz, 2010), where marriage provides the conclusion of a film and its sequel, then becomes about pregnancy and/or parenthood. Although parenthood is a key concern of Heckerling's films, the absence of marriage complicates the expectations of the genre. That said, the films, although not narratively coherent, do adhere to the convention of the romantic conclusion.[38] However, once again, the romantic conclusion of *Look Who's Talking*, in particular, is significant in foregrounding the mother's sexuality and desire, reiterating her subjectivity in its resolution.

Overall, Heckerling's films depict a version of the family that is liberal, particularly in the context of its time. It is through the treatment of nontraditional parenting, and gender roles, that the films' significance emerges. Heckerling's sensitivity in dealing with the non-traditional family underpins the success of the films. Although the problematic narrative drive of the second film affects its quality, both of Heckerling's films are more nuanced than their spin-offs, that include the third film of the series in which talking pets appear, *Look Who's Talking Now* (1993), and the ABC sitcom *Baby Talk* (1991–2). Although the sitcom lists Heckerling as a creator, she only provided the program with its characters and premise. The comic exploration of the working mother's subjectivity in *Look Who's Talking* is superseded in *Baby Talk* by a bland comedy that takes most of its humor from the child's ability to speak. Furthermore, the unruly and forthright Kirstie Alley is replaced by svelte, blonde Julia Duffy (although she was superseded in the second series by Mary Page Keller). It seems, then, that Heckerling's stamp on the *Look Who's Talking* films offers a sensitive portrait of the family, one that depicts tensions between liberal and conservative values, but that ultimately demonstrates an attempt to explore shifting family forms.

NOTES

1   Susan Faludi, *Backlash: The Undeclared War against Women* (London: Chatto & Windus, 1993 [1991]), p. 163.

2   Elizabeth Traube, *Dreaming Identities: Class, Gender and Generation in 1980s Hollywood Movies* (Oxford: Westview Press, 1992), p. 163.

3   Sarah Harwood, *Family Fictions: Representations of the Family in 1980s Hollywood Cinema* (Basingstoke: Macmillan, 1997), p. 133.

4   Lynne Joyrich, cited in Traube, p. 157.

5   Traube, p. 156.

6   Ibid. p. 165.

7   Paula Thoma, "Buying up baby: modern feminine subjectivity, assertions of 'choice' and the repudiation of reproductive justice in unwanted pregnancy films," *Feminist Media Studies* 9: 4 (2009), p. 413.

8   Ibid.

9   Traube, p. 158.

10   Ibid. p. 164.

11   Andrew Britton, "Blissing out: the politics of Reaganite entertainment," *Movie* 31/32 (1986), p. 24.

12   Claire Jenkins, "'You're just some bitch who broke my heart and cut up my mom's wedding dress': the significance of the wedding dress in Hollywood's romantic comedies," *Film, Fashion and Consumption,*2: 2 (2013), p. 163.

13   Jon Lewis, *The Road to Romance and Ruin: Teen Films and Youth Culture* (New York: Routledge, 1992), p. 237.

14   Stella Bruzzi, *Bringing Up Daddy: Fatherhood and Masculinity in Post-War Hollywood* (London: BFI, 2007), p. 148.

15   Traube, p. 161.

16   Nicole Matthews, *Comic Politics: Gender in Hollywood Comedy after the New Right* (Manchester: Manchester University Press, 2000), pp. 114–15.

17   Matthews, p. 116.

18   Traube, p. 162.

19   Ibid. p. 169.

20   Jessica Valenti, *Why Have Kids? A New Mom Explores the Truth about Parenting and Happiness* (Las Vegas: Amazon, 2012), pp. 14–15.

21   Claire Jenkins, *Home Movies: The American Family in Contemporary Hollywood* (London: I. B. Tauris, 2015).

22   Barbara Ehrenreich, *The Hearts of Men: American Dreams and the Flight from Commitment* (London: Pluto Press, 1983), pp. 136–9; Bruzzi, pp. 104–7.

23   Traube, p. 163.

24   Ibid. p. 159.

25   Matthews, p. 114.

26   Harwood, p. 103, p. 132.

27   Galinsky et al., "Times are changing: gender and generation at work and at home," 2008, rev. 2011. Available at <http://familiesandwork.org/site/research/reports/Times_Are_Changing.pdf> (last accessed 16 December 2014); Aumann, Kerstin, Ellen Galinsky, and Kenneth Matos, "The new male mystique," 2011. Available at <http://familiesandwork.org/site/research/reports/newmalemystique.pdf> (last accessed 16 December 2014).

28   Jenkins (2015), p. 174.

29 Stephanie Coontz, *The Way We Really Are: Coming to Terms with America's Changing Families* (New York: Basic Books, 1997), p. 59.

30 Traube, p. 160.

31 See Harwood.

32 Traube, p. 163.

33 Matthews, p. 110.

34 Harwood, p. 133.

35 Traube, p. 157.

36 Ibid.

37 Ibid. p. 156.

38 Ibid. p. 162.

CHAPTER 8

Amy Heckerling's Place in Hollywood: Issues of Aging and Sisterhood in *I Could Never Be Your Woman* and *Vamps*

Betty Kaklamanidou

Amy Heckerling's two most recent films as writer/director, *I Could Never Be Your Woman* (2007) and *Vamps* (2013), constitute a slight departure from her family and teen comedies. The first follows the conventions of the romantic comedy genre with elements of fantasy, and the second is a hybrid narrative, mixing the basic structure of the female friendship film with elements of horror. In this essay, I will examine the ways Heckerling negotiates issues of female aging and sisterhood in these two texts, using textual analysis as well as analysis of specific cinematic codes—mise-en-scène, editing, and cinematography—to reveal Heckerling's preferences and style, while utilizing gender theory to assist in the contextualization of the narratives.[1] I will be basing my arguments mainly on Samantha Holland's *Alternative Femininities* (2004), and Rosalind Gill and Christina Scharff's collection *New Femininities: Postfeminism, Neoliberalism and Subjectivity* (2011),[2] because I find the use of the term "femininities" that the books' authors use inclusive and appropriate in contemporary discussions on gender. Instead of femininity being treated as a monolithic and absolute concept, its plural avoids "notions of essentialism," and "ideas that femininity equates with young, white, slim, heterosexual, able-bodied women."[3] I would add that the plural also assists in the exploration of various fictional feminine performances created by the same agent, in the case of this study a single filmmaker. Heckerling's heroines may share common traits, yet they also contradict themselves and differ in interesting ways, more often than not in the same narrative, performing various aspects of femininities. Second, Gill and Scharff draw useful connections between postfeminism and neoliberalism, stressing that "the autonomous, calculating, self-regulating subject of neoliberalism bears a strong resemblance to the active, freely choosing, self-reinventing subject of postfeminism."[4] Because the representations

I will be discussing were produced and consumed in the same sociopolitical context, it will be useful to examine the interconnections, if any, among the subtle yet pervasive influences of neoliberal principles on female agency. Indeed, as Gill and Scharff argue, "to a much greater extent than men, women are required to work on and transform the self, to regulate every aspect of their conduct, and to present all their actions as freely chosen."[5]

Nevertheless, before I move to the films, it is important to contextualize Heckerling herself in a specific film industry at a specific time in order to observe the influence of socio-cultural and industrial factors on her career. Heckerling's directorial work spans four decades so far, and her career longevity is in itself remarkable, but since the focus of this study is her recent contributions to mainstream cinema, both examples of which met with considerable production and distribution obstacles, I will concentrate on her position in a contemporary context.

HECKERLING VS. CONTEMPORARY HOLLYWOOD

In 2012, "women accounted for 9% of directors" of the top 250 highest-grossing films in the USA, which equals "the percentage of women directors working in 1998," notes Martha M. Lauzen in her study on female employment in the film industry, confirming Hollywood's infamous male-centric nature.[6] In January 2014, the Sundance Institute and Women In Film Los Angeles published the results of a study entitled "Exploring the Barriers and Opportunities for Independent Women Filmmakers Phase I and II," and stated that a mere "4.4% of directors were female across the 100 top box-office films each year from 2002 to 2012."[7] This number accounts for "41 unique females at the helm and 625 unique males at the helm across 11 years and 1,100 movies," resulting in a ratio of 15.24 male directors to every one female director.[8]

Despite these obviously disappointing figures, there is a group of female directors celebrated for commercial success and/or artistic excellence, a kind of endangered species that should be protected and studied. Nora Ephron, Betty Thomas, Penny Marshall, Nancy Meyers, Catherine Hardwicke, Kathryn Bigelow, Jennifer Yuh Nelson, Vicky Jenson, and the focus of this collection Amy Heckerling, are among this valuable, yet largely undervalued, cluster of women, having directed a significant number of both box office hits and multi-award-winning films over the last 40 years.

As a profit-driven industry in a capitalist structure, Hollywood is not really interested in the artistic vision and/or social messages of the films it produces, exhibits, and distributes, but is rather focused on their marketing appeal, which is meticulously taken into consideration starting with the inception of any given film. Therefore, a director's or actor's career record (primarily commercial success and secondarily artistic acclaim) increases the potential bankability of the project and usually constitutes the first step in securing capital for production. Heckerling's "past" would therefore be considered a wise investment, because her lifetime gross in the USA alone, based on nine films since the 1980s, is just shy of $385 million. If one considers the above sum as average or insubstantial, and therefore an indication that Heckerling is not an ideal investment, one should take into account the basic economic parameters of box office success and also place Heckerling in a context of other contemporary directors with a similar number of films and/or financial and artistic achievement. *Look Who's Talking* (1989), Heckerling's most commercially successful film to date, earned more than 39 times its production cost of $7.5 million, taking in an impressive $296 million worldwide. *Clueless* (1995) was also a hit, surpassing $77 million worldwide with a budget of $12 million.[9] Nevertheless, as Annette Kuhn and Guy Westwell rightly note, box office numbers alone cannot confirm the financial success of a film—a number of other parameters must be taken into account, such as distributor fees, exhibition fees, production costs, stars' percentage shares—so a general "rule of thumb" maintains that "to break even box office gross must be 2.5 times production costs."[10] Thus, on the basis of numbers alone, Heckerling should be an important commodity for the industry. Additionally, her lifetime gross total is on par with or higher than that of other less "commercial" contemporary directors who have been celebrated worldwide for the quality of their work. For instance, Danny Boyle's total US box office gross is a little over $280 million with ten films, Richard Linklater's is $197 million with sixteen films, and Alexander Payne's is almost $252 million with seven films. Nonetheless, Heckerling is also acknowledged today as a distinctive cinematic voice, at least academically, in addition to having directed films that placed in the top 100 of the annual US box office (*Fast Times at Ridgemont High* was the 29th highest-grossing film of 1982, *Look Who's Talking* the fourth highest of 1989, and *Clueless* the 32nd highest of 1995). Some of her films are today considered paradigms of transcending generic formulas and providing perceptive commentary on contemporary social attitudes regarding youth.[11]

Of course, one could argue that Heckerling's *Loser* (2000), a film that cost $20 million and failed at the box office, with US admissions around $16 million, is the reason why her subsequent projects were treated with suspicion. However, a single failure in an otherwise financially stable career did not deter her fellow filmmakers from moving on; for instance, Boyle's sci-fi *Sunshine* (2007) cost $40 million but returned only $32 million worldwide, while the director still got $15 million to make the highly successful *Slumdog Millionaire* (2008). Similarly, M. Night Shyamalan secured a budget of $48 million to film *The Happening* (2008) after the commercial failure of *Lady in the Water* (2006), which only returned a little over half of its $70 million dollar budget in US admissions.

On the basis of the above, Heckerling should have been considered a solid investment for the film industry as she continuously released films at a satisfying profit. However, her two most recent films, *I Could Never Be Your Woman* and *Vamps*, met with considerable production and distribution problems. In the case of the former, Heckerling initially sent the screenplay to Paramount Pictures but the studio declined to invest in a film with an older female protagonist.[12] Consequently, Heckerling decided to collaborate with a novice French producer with a problematic past, whose company not only went bankrupt under questionable circumstances but created great difficulty in allowing her to distribute the film.[13] Heckerling explained exactly what went on behind the scenes, revealing the intricacies of film production and the difficulties involved in having her film financed and distributed:

> The company went under and I'm not a thousand percent sure of what happened but this [producer] had sold off—to make other movies—our foreign distribution . . . Meanwhile when we would go to the studios and distributors and show them the movie and ask them what they thought they would say yeah and then they would find out that they wouldn't be getting any foreign or any DVD rights. So it was not worth putting in the money you would need to advertise . . . I don't know what I could have done. I was not in the loop of the deals this guy is making behind my back.[14]

As a result, even with its star casting and budget of $24 million, *I Could Never Be Your Woman* "went straight to DVD in the USA in 2007 despite having been completed in 2005 and [having] earned a little over $9 million in its worldwide release."[15] By comparison, *Vamps* was financed with the help of producer Lauren Versel, with a more modest budget of around $10 million, but was only released in a single US theatre, earning a little less than $4,000.[16] When Heckerling was asked in 2008 whether a successful past facilitates filmmakers' future projects in Hollywood, she replied: "It's always a new river every time you stick your foot in."[17] However, as demonstrated above, her male counterparts don't seem to have had the same experience, either with the modestly-budgeted films Heckerling is usually in charge of, or with high-budget mega-pictures.

I maintain that the reason behind Heckerling's production, and, more importantly, distribution, obstacles is the thematic focus of the female-centered narratives, and especially her recent focus on female aging and sisterhood. Female stories are indeed infrequent in Hollywood's landscape, and initiatives like the recently announced Mentoring Program for Female

Directors, which aims to help "add a female perspective and diverse voices across film, broadcast, cable and digital programming," proves how female voices and stories rarely find their way to the theatre.[18]

FEMALE AGING AND SISTERHOOD IN *I COULD NEVER BE YOUR WOMAN* AND *VAMPS*

I Could Never Be Your Woman is a romantic comedy that focuses on a May–December romance: Rosie (Michelle Pfeiffer), a 40-something divorcee, mother of a pre-teen daughter, and producer and writer of a teen TV show, falls in love with Adam (Paul Rudd), a much younger actor she casts for her show. *Vamps* falls under the subgenre of the female friendship film, as theorized and contextualized by Karen Hollinger in 1998.[19] It is a hybrid horror-comedy where Heckerling explores the relationship between two female vampires, 171-year-old Goody (Alicia Silverstone) and 40-year-old Stacy (Krysten Ritter), who live in New York City and must deal with the former's aggravating need to always behave like a young, frivolous woman, and the latter's dilemma of choosing between eternal life or bearing a child and becoming human again. I contend that without abandoning her unique cinematic traits and her penchant for comedy, and by placing the issue of age and aging at the center of these two narratives, Heckerling adds to her feminist film discourse, and even anticipates an increasing number of similarly themed female-centered films.[20]

The title sequence of *I Could Never Be Your Woman* is indicative of the thematic turn Heckerling takes while remaining faithful to the narrational mode of comedy. A montage of nature shots filled with birds, animals, and landscapes, accompanied by the 1984 song 'Heaven' from British post-punk band The Psychedelic Furs, alternate as the names of Heckerling, Michelle Pfeiffer, and Paul Rudd appear. The music stops and Tracey Ullman appears in the middle of a forest as Mother Nature. She is quite frustrated, for she believes that, despite millennia of co-existence between people and wildlife, the Baby Boomers arrived and disrupted the circle of life. Mother Nature accuses the postwar generation of egotism, obsession with material goods, and indifference to their environment. She also chastises them for their obsession with youth and concludes that no one can tamper with the aging process. The rest of the titles begin rolling again, and media images of men and women having plastic surgery and exercising alternates on the screen. The credit sequence ends with Mother Nature in a matte shot, appearing as a miniature in a close-up of the female heroine, Rosie, introducing her with the phrase: "Here's a pal of mine in her forties trying to moisturize her way back to thirty."

Figure 8.1 Mother Nature introduces Rosie.

In a little less than four minutes, Heckerling not only presents the mode (comedy), the setting (the contemporary urban USA), and the main character of her fictional cosmos (Pfeiffer as Rosie), but also introduces one of the main themes (the need for women over 40 to retain the illusion of youth) while managing to criticize this obsession through Mother Nature's caustic commentary. The leap from the teen comedy genre into adult comedy, and more specifically (as will later be revealed) the romantic comedy universe, is achieved. Or is it?

As the first post-credit scene helps to further establish Rosie's character by introducing her pre-teen daughter, Izzie (Saoirse Ronan), and her ex-husband, Nathan (Jon Lovitz), Rosie's and Nathan's adulthood is immediately put into question. The two characters seem initially on good terms, despite the fact that Mother Nature has already informed viewers that Nathan divorced Rosie to marry a much younger woman. The two converse about everyday things until Rosie asks about a white patch on Nathan's forehead, and he tells her that he had to have some hair plugs removed. Rosie also comments, somewhat irritatedly, on how his always wearing sportswear will not make him fitter unless he really exercises. A little annoyed by this remark, Nathan comments on how Rosie's preference for Doc Martens boots—a symbol of a number of youth cultures in the 1970s, 1980s, and 1990s—will not turn her into a teenager again. Despite being in the presence of their daughter, Nathan and Rosie behave like two frustrated teenagers who talk back to each other in an effort to win an already pointless argument. Both characters, however, can be blamed for the same desire they accuse each other of: their longing to stay young whether by aesthetic/medical procedures (Nathan) or by clothing appropriate for a younger age group (Rosie).

Nathan is a supporting character who appears a couple of times in the film. Nonetheless, it is important that Heckerling shows that men are also interested in retaining a youthful look, and, like women, undergo costly and even painful procedures to achieve the desired result. This condition is corroborated in a study by the American Academy of Facial Plastic and Reconstructive Surgery, which in 2006 measured "a 60 percent increase in men . . . electing to have cosmetic procedures since 2000."[21] In addition, Nathan's perpetual quest for a more youthful appearance, however comedic, constitutes one of the still rare movie depictions of male anxiety over physical appearance. In fact, four years after the release of *I Could Never Be Your Woman*, two "traditional" male makeovers in the romantic comedies *Larry Crowne* and *Crazy, Stupid, Love* appeared, as well as a number of cinematic superheroes who exhibited their virile bodies, prompting Joe Reid to wonder if the summer film season of 2011 could be regarded as the "Golden Age of Male Objectification."[22]

This comment notwithstanding, it is Rosie's concerns about aging and physical appearance that the film text negotiates in detail. The viewer sees Rosie exercising, avoiding unhealthy foods, and also trying to have her daughter, Izzie, follow her dietary habits. At other times, Rosie behaves like an immature individual. For instance, before her first date with Adam, she is visibly anxious and is seen in a number of outfits asking Izzie to help her, acting more as a young girl herself than a mature woman. Heckerling succeeds in presenting the various facets of a single individual and the contradictions that can form a part or the whole of a woman's life. On the one hand, Rosie is represented as a responsible, hard-working, single mother, and on the other as an anxious woman who seems afraid of getting older, and who is highly skeptical about embarking on a sexual relationship with a younger man. The complexities of Rosie's character confirm how the use of femininities is a more useful theoretical tool in exploring onscreen female representations. Rosie is a three-dimensional character who can perform and assume a variety of gender roles given a specific context. In the 97 minutes of the film, Rosie is seen as a sensitive and caring mother, an efficient career woman, a frustrated ex-wife, an attractive and sensual woman, and an apprehensive and even angry woman. Her femininity cannot be determined by the use of a single noun, such as compassion, motherhood, or practicality, but is rather made up of a number of performances, each chosen by Rosie to apply to a specific context.

Heckerling emphasizes that Rosie's preoccupation with aging and dating a younger man does not only originate from within but is to a great extent a result of her immediate environment and social pressures. As a writer of a teenage television show in Los Angeles, the space *par excellence* where youthfulness is sanctified, she is not only surrounded by young, beautiful people, but is bombarded by images of perfectly proportionate individuals, however constructed and fake they may be. Therefore, Rosie can't help but be influenced and try to maintain her youthful appearance. In addition, I would argue that her self-regulation regarding her dietary and exercise regimens is also a result of the general neoliberal climate, which uses popular culture images and advertising to create self-disciplined subjects who consume in order to feel empowered. In her study of contemporary beauty advertising, Michelle M. Lazar underlines how advertisers "link the normative practice of beautification with an emancipated identity," by promoting products and practices "as offering women self-determined choices," and by centering their discourse "on rights, freedoms and choices," which are linked to postfeminism.[23]

Heckerling also highlights the fabricated nature of television, and by extension the Hollywood film industry, both cinematically and narratively, on a number of occasions. The chromatic palette of the studio and the sets where Rosie works is dominated by cold and fluorescent colors, creating an atmosphere of artificiality and unreality as opposed to the warmer colors associated with the scenes at Rosie's home. Although these design choices may go unnoticed, there are several narrative instances that explicitly point to the artificiality of show business. For instance, the teenage protagonist of Rosie's show, Brianna (Stacey Dash), is in fact an actor in her late thirties and has her stomach area sprayed to create the illusion of well-defined abdominal muscles. A little later in the film, Brianna—who is constantly worried about her age and her place in the industry because of it—shoots a public service spot against smoking and lights a cigarette the second the director says "cut."

Older women are actually anathematized in a brief, albeit compelling scene, where Rosie is waiting outside her boss's office, and overhears an executive and a producer speaking about the selection of a female actress. The scene is filmed as a medium three-shot, with Rosie sitting on the left side and actually turning her back and gesturing, hearing the following insults against accomplished women who happen to be of a certain age:

TV executive: Courtney Love?
Producer: Drugged-out hag.
TV executive: Faye Dunaway?
Producer: Don't call us, we'll call you!
TV executive: Sharon Stone?

Figure 8.2 Rosie "attacks" the sexist producers.

Producer: Hag.
TV executive: Geena Davis?
Producer: Hag.
TV executive: Sigourney Weaver?
Producer: Hag.
TV executive: Kim Basinger?
Producer: Hag.
TV executive: Emma Thompson?
Producer: Brit hag.
TV executive: Susan Sarandon?
Producer: Red-state-alienating hag!
TV executive: Meg Ryan?
Producer: Too much plastic surgery.
TV executive: Melanie Griffith?
Producer: Way too much plastic surgery.
TV executive: Patricia Heaton?
Producer: Pointless plastic surgery.
TV executive: Cher.
Producer: Insurmountable amount of plastic surgery.

Rosie is visibly angered at the obvious sexist comments exchanged by the men beside her and, after grabbing the producer by the chin, exclaims:

Listen, you little bird of a man, where do you come off insulting these women? How many hit songs did *you* sing? How many Oscars do *you* have? Could you look cute next to Warren Beatty? Or live with Don Johnson? Or act with Ted Danson? You're not worthy of kissing Cher's tattooed ass!

Rosie's justified outburst is consistent with recent academic discussions on femininity in the twenty-first century, and especially in a neoliberal context. Estella Tincknell claims that the first decade of the new millennium "helped renew the hegemony of beauty culture as the apex of femininity at a historical juncture when women (in parts of Western society at least) are ostensibly more economically independent, socially engaged and politically visible than ever before."[24] Although Tincknell's work centers on the British TV makeover show *Ten Years Younger*, her argument regarding the fragmentation of female bodies and loss of feminine agency through an incessant quest for physical perfection applies to Hollywood female stars, the quintessential paradigms of global beauty trends. In the same vein, Diane Negra and Su Holmes have noted that the discussion of celebrity bodies is "heavily gendered" as "female celebrities . . . can still be enshrined and celebrated as the ultimate example of aspirational fleshed perfection," but "are also positioned . . . as the sites upon which corporeal scrutiny will take place."[25]

Heckerling's inclusion of the way Hollywood male executives invalidate the careers of successful female stars because of their age and/or aesthetically altered features, and the repetitive use of the derogatory term "hag," corroborates Negra and Holmes's argument and further alludes to the prejudice of the industry. The twelve named actresses' combined seven Academy Awards from thirteen nominations, and thirteen Golden Globes from an impressive 39 nominations, among a significant number of other prestigious accolades, are nonchalantly nullified because these women are no longer in their twenties. It seems, therefore, that decades of a successful career and a proven record of awards and honors are simply not enough if they are not accompanied by a youthful physical *emballage*—which begs the question of how one can be considered a seasoned, accomplished thespian and still look like a twenty-something individual. Clearly, this is an impossible task, which still applies to female stars, with the exceptions of Meryl Streep and Helen Mirren. While fifty-something actors, such as Tom Hanks, Tom Cruise, Brad Pitt, and George Clooney thrive at the box office and are offered lead parts in star vehicles, their female counterparts are usually relegated to the narrative periphery, playing the mother, or even grandmother. Susan Sarandon is only 24 years older than Melissa McCarthy but she portrayed her grandmother in *Tammy* (Ben Falcone, 2014); Laura Dern played Reese Witherspoon's mother in *Wild* (Jean-Marc Vallee, 2014), even though she is only nine years older than the film's star; more preposterously, Angelina Jolie was 28 when she played the mother of 27-year-old Colin Farrell in *Alexander* (Oliver Stone, 2004). Natural aging is a forbidden process for women in Hollywood, only reserved for its male population, and many are the times today we read articles that address this blatant discrimination.[26] Voicing their indignation at this double standard, both Sarandon and Kim Cattrall have recently accused the industry of sexist exclusion and the public scrutiny they endure over their physical appearance.[27]

Aging naturally is off limits to fictional female characters as well, and Heckerling makes that clear by having Rosie express insecurities related to age when her character starts dating 29-year-old Adam. She initially lies about her age, feels out of place at the hip club they go to on their first date, and sees younger women as potential competitors. In the club scene, the doorman looks at her identity card, then looks at her and makes a facial expression that connotes surprise. Once in the club, a number of point-of-view shots from Rosie's perspective show some young people who look skeptically at her, while the heroine and the viewer hear their disapproving thoughts: one woman says, "They let *her* in?" implying Rosie's age group does not belong there, while a young man comments, "I guess when you're old all your clothes are vintage."

Rosie feels uncomfortable, and despite Adam's efforts to make her laugh, they leave early. A little later, during a restaurant scene between the couple, Rosie is visibly upset when their young and attractive waitress openly flirts with Adam. Mother Nature appears and freezes time to remind Rosie that it's only natural for the waitress and Adam to be together, because they are both the same age and the young woman is in her reproductive years.

Mother Nature appears sporadically during Rosie's tense and/or contemplative moments. Her presence may act as fantasy, comic relief, and a pause from the action, but it also adds to the discussion on aging, making her a "surreal" commentator. Mother Nature functions as a rather conservative, didactic critic: "You can jump and peel and nip and tuck but your insides are still rotting away," is what she tells Rosie while the latter is running on a track as part of her exercise regimen. "There's an order to this mating business," is her openly voiced opposition to Rosie's attraction to Adam, while during a brief break-up between the couple, Nature comforts her with the phrase, "Now you can settle down and act your age." I argue, however, that this fantastical character, which only Rosie is able to see, is used by Heckerling not as a conveyor and actual proponent of conservatism, anti-feminism, and/or ageism, but rather as Rosie's conscience: a conscience filled with insecurities and anxieties that mainly stem from media and celebrity culture, and that are disseminated at unprecedented speed by the Internet. In our contemporary neoliberal climate, images of female perfection can serve as empowering tools for agency and self-reassertion. Nevertheless, "the kind of agency promised by the display of the sexy body only appears to offer a strong and positive subject position to women, while actually positioning them as an object for others, and indeed, for themselves. In the process, women are reduced to their bodies and subjected to impossible standards of acceptability which are likely to cause enormous anxiety and stimulate endless self-monitoring."[28] In the end, however, and despite all the age-related anxiety, Rosie decides to stay with Adam, accepting not only their age difference but staying perhaps true to her inner voice and ignoring societal norms.

Heckerling's preoccupation with age continues in *Vamps*, a female-friendship film mixed with horror conventions, for which she borrows from the recent popularity of vampires in both film and television.[29] The use of the vampire as a narrative trope is not only a marketing stratagem to entice more admissions but is a most appropriate terrain via which to explore the issue of age, since the overwhelming majority of these undead creatures, especially in contemporary popular culture (from the cinematic *Twilight* franchise [2008–12] to TV's *True Blood* [2008–14] and *The Vampire Diaries* [2009–]), have the eternal gift of youth. On the one hand, as Lorna Piatti-Farnell notes, this trait is "related to the concept of humanity itself, and the 'natural' course of life," and on the other, it has been used to comment on the association between youth and neoliberal capitalism.[30] Heckerling interestingly explores this duality in *Vamps*.

Vamps follows the adventures of 171-year-old Goody and the much younger Stacy, whom she took under her wing in the 1990s. The two women live in New York City, take classes at night pretending they are college students, and survive exclusively on animal blood to spare human lives. As in *I Could Never Be Your Woman*, the two-minute credit sequence of *Vamps* introduces youth as the main theme through a montage of both fictional and real footage, where Goody's voiceover informs the viewer that she became a vampire in 1841. Her narration is accompanied by black-and-white gravures and photographs of the world's progression, depicting technological inventions and social advances. In a similar way to how the shots of nature and plastic surgery are used in *I Could Never Be Your Woman*, media and documentary footage are also used in *Vamps* as a way of anchoring fiction to reality. Archival footage of the New York subway accompanies Goody's remark that with its arrival "you could travel the whole city and still be in your coffin by sunrise," while her description of the 1920s and the apotheosis of youth in the figure of the flapper is illustrated by scenes of young people partying during the decade that roared. "The world belonged to the young and I was an expert at being young," comments Goody before talking about the "flickers," her favorite invention of the industrial age. Heckerling pays a brief homage to the pioneers of the medium, with shots from films directed by George Méliès, Charles Chaplin, and Buster Keaton, or starring James Cagney—icons who, according to Goody, could never get older in the movies. After the 1920s, the narration moves rather quickly, as Goody refers to the 1960s, when she first fell in love, and then to the 1990s, when her stem—the vampire who transformed her—also turned Stacy, her protégée and roommate. Goody concludes with how Stacy taught her about new technology, such as e-mail and Napster, and how to spend their lives in New York as college students.

This use of cultural verisimilitude—incorporating material as a means of invoking authenticity and creating a closer tie to reality—is interesting insofar as both films involve elements of a supernatural nature (the use of Mother Nature and vampires) and belong to genres (romantic comedy and horror comedy) which, by definition, abide by a certain number of generic conventions, resulting in a generic verisimilitude not necessarily based in reality.[31] Steve Neale rightly observes that cultural verisimilitude is generally assessed more positively than generic verisimilitude because its realist connotations are regarded as more important.[32] Indeed, the intertextual references that abound in *Vamps*, from the purely cinematic ones, such as the use of clips from silent US films, German expressionism, and documentary footage, to the casting of Alicia Silverstone (the star of *Clueless*) and Taylor Negron as the pizza guy (Negron was also the pizza guy in *Fast Times*), are the focus of many reviews.[33]

Most critics, however, such as John Anderson, Melissa Anderson, and Rachel Saltz, insist on the nostalgic aspect of the film, underlining how Goody consistently refers to the past and how life used to be.[34]

I claim that Heckerling's preoccupation is not so much nostalgia for the "good old days" as aging and acceptance of this natural process. Goody is not tired of acclimatizing to each era's cultural zeitgeist; she is, rather, exhausted from being obliged to hide her accumulated knowledge for fear of revealing she is not a twenty-something childish woman. Similarly, when Stacy unexpectedly gets pregnant by a human—appropriately the son of Homeland Security vampire hunter Dr Van Helsing (Wallace Shawn)—she faces the dilemma of turning into a human to bring the baby to term in her early forties or to enjoy eternity as a young student. While Goody and Stacy struggle with accepting the concept of time passing by, their maker, Cisserus (Sigourney Weaver), represents their antithesis: a female vampire of "a certain age," who drinks human blood (preferably coming from much younger men), enjoys spending money on couture (despite not being able to see her reflection), and travels all around the world. Through this cougar-like, eccentric, and hyperbolic character, Heckerling comments on how patriarchal capitalist mechanisms transform the individual and lead to a vacant existence. Negra notes that, under postfeminism, "the achievement of a youthful appearance through consumerist 'empowerment' is positively encoded," and has been incorporated in many recent female-centered films.[35] In *Vamps*, however, Cisserus's association with constant consumption of material goods is represented as both a meaningless act—because Cisserus can't see herself in the mirror—and as a consequently monotonous undertaking that can only alleviate boredom in a life of centuries.

Although aging in *I Could Never Be Your Woman* is finally accepted yet not fully welcomed, in *Vamps* it is celebrated. *Vamps* may be a hybrid horror-comedy, but it's also a female friendship film, because the combined desires and decisions of Goody and Stacy move the plot forward. In her study of the female friendship genre, Hollinger explains that her aim is not to view these films as "progressive challenges to the status quo" or "reactionary props of dominant patriarchal ideology, but rather as complex products of an intricate process of negotiation."[36] In later writing, Hollinger poses a number of questions regarding the function of the female friendship film. Centering on their ambiguity, she wonders about whether these narratives "raise questions that challenge women's prescribed gender roles and the role of female friendship in women's lives" or "advocate women's submission to long established gender proscriptions," and stresses that "significant ambiguity remains just under the seemingly progressive surface of all of these films."[37] However, Hollinger infers that these films "undoubtedly shape women's thinking about themselves and about women's role in society," and that continuing examination of these representations can lead to important conclusions about the intricacies of women's relationships.[38]

Demonstrating the complexity of the female friendship film, *Vamps* is not a radical narrative, yet it empowers female sisterhood by offering a representation of a strong and loving female bond that has lasted for over two decades. Moreover, the film's climax finds Goody sacrificing herself for her friend. As it turns out, for Stacy to have her baby and turn back into a human, the stem that converted her and Goody—Cisserus—must die. However, Cisserus's demise means that Goody will also automatically turn human again and die, because she is over 170 years old. "Staying young is getting old," remarks Goody, before she makes her decision to turn into a human and die so that her friend can have her child and a human life. Then once Cisserus is exterminated, both friends instantly become human. Two close-up shots of Stacy's body show the results of gravity as both her breasts and buttocks are now revealed to be in a lower position, while a third close-up on her face reveals the more subtle appearance of a few wrinkles. Stacy immediately turns and stares at her reflection, surprised and content to find that being 40 is not so different from being in her twenties. However, she also witnesses Goody becoming her real age as an old lady, and must come to terms with the inevitability of her death. Goody's final wish is to visit Times Square, as she wants to be "in the center of things." In a very moving three-minute sequence, Goody, Stacy, and her boyfriend stand in the middle of the square, while the camera focuses mostly on Goody and her memories of the same place over the decades. Accompanied by the 1928 standard "Garden in the Rain," sung by Gene Austin, the shots of contemporary billboards and signs alternate with documentary footage of the 1920s through the 1940s, as well as insert scenes of Goody in the 1840s walking the streets with her children. An extreme close-up shows Stacy's hand taking Goody's hand to place it on her [Stacy's] heart. No words are exchanged, and as the song ends, Goody disintegrates into golden ash, which is seen transported over the square before landing on the statue of Broadway pioneer George M. Cohan.

Figure 8.3 Stacy and Goody say goodbye.

CONCLUSIONS

Lesley Speed situates Heckerling's work, especially her teen comedies, in a postfeminist context that abandoned the polemical undertakings of the second feminist wave and became part of mainstream cinema. Speed finds that from an industrial perspective, the modest budgets of the mainly comedic female-helmed films of the 1980s and 1990s, such as *European Vacation* (which Heckerling directed in 1983), *Wayne's World* (Penelope Spheeris, 1992), and *The Brady Bunch Movie* (Betty Thomas, 1995), and their subsequent commercial success, allowed the continuing employment of female directors; on the other hand, from a feminist perspective, these films negotiated traditional gender stereotypes while imbuing generic narratives with potentially subversive elements regarding concepts such as femininity, sisterhood, masculinity, romance, and humor, among others.[39]

It is true that Heckerling has had a long career in Hollywood. However, I would suggest that her narrative insistence on aging and more mature characters in her last two films contributed greatly to the production and distribution obstacles she faced as a writer and director. Lavish studio productions with older protagonists have met with great commercial success (*Sex and the City* [Michael Patrick King, 2008], *Mamma Mia!* [Phyllida Lloyd, 2008], *It's Complicated* [Nancy Meyers, 2009]), but there is still a very long way to go before female stories with either young or mature characters are written—and more importantly told—by female voices, as recent research has concluded.

I Could Never Be Your Woman and *Vamps* do offer interesting observations regarding female aging and sisterhood, and it is unfortunate that those narratives never found their way to a wider audience. The disheartening percentage of female directors in twenty-first-century Hollywood does not easily allow for future optimism (as previously mentioned, only a mere 4.4 percent of the most commercially successful recent films have been directed by women). Despite her long career and success, when asked about the film industry, Heckerling said:

> It's a disgusting industry. I don't know what else to say. Especially now. I can't stomach most of the movies about women. I just saw a movie last night. I don't want to say the name—but again with the fucking wedding and the only time women say anything is about men.[40]

Nevertheless, at this point in history, film schools abound globally, and online platforms allow for every voice to be heard. If one combines these facts with the realization—on the part of industry executives—that female-centered films can return impressive profits (from franchises such as *Twilight*

[2008–12], *The Hunger Games* [2012–], and *Divergent* [2014–][41] to *Bridesmaids* [Paul Feig, 2011], *Brave* [Mark Andrews and Brenda Chapman, 2012], *Frozen* [Chris Buck and Jennifer Lee, 2013], and *Maleficent* [Robert Stromberg, 2014]), more female filmmakers can have opportunities they were not afforded in the past. The future awaits.

NOTES

1 Although Heckerling frequently collaborates with the same individuals, such as composer David Kitay (*Clueless, Loser, Look Who's Talking, Look Who's Talking Too, Vamps*), and editor Debra Chiate (*Clueless, Look Who's Talking, Look Who's Talking Too, Vamps*), she also works with different cinematographers and costume designers. Elements of auteurship are clearly evident in her work, but such an investigation exceeds the scope of this essay.

2 Samantha Holland, *Alternative Femininities: Body, Age and Identity* (Oxford: Berg, 2004); Rosalind Gill and Christina Scharff (eds.), *New Femininities: Postfeminism, Neoliberalism and Subjectivity* (New York: Palgrave Macmillan, 2011).

3 Holland, p. 9.

4 Gill and Scharff, p. 7.

5 Ibid.

6 Martha M. Lauzen, "The celluloid ceiling: behind-the-scenes employment of women on the top 250 films of 2014," Center for the Study of Women in Television & Film. Available at <http://womenintvfilm.sdsu.edu/files/2014_Celluloid_Ceiling_Report.pdf> (last accessed 13 December 2014).

7 Stacy L. Smith, Katherine Pieper, and Marc Choueiti, "Exploring the barriers and opportunities for independent women filmmakers phase I and II," Sundance Institute, 2013, p. 47. Available at <http://www.sundance.org/pdf/press-releases/Exploring-The-Barriers.pdf> (last accessed 13 December 2014).

8 Ibid. p. 53.

9 Budget and income numbers are drawn from data provided by the Internet Movie Database (www.imdb.com) and Box Office Mojo (www.boxofficemojo.com).

10 Annette Kuhn and Guy Westwell, *Oxford Dictionary of Film Studies* (Oxford: Oxford University Press, 2012), p. 42.

11 For discussions on the significance and legacy of *Fast Times at Ridgemont High* (1982) and *Clueless* (1995), two of the films Heckerling's name is most associated with, especially in the course of teen film history, see (among others): Esther Sonnet, "From *Emma* to *Clueless*: taste, pleasure and the scene of history," in Deborah Cartmell and Imelda Whelehan (eds.), *Adaptations: From Text to Screen, Screen to Text* (London: Routledge, 1999), pp. 51–62; Clara Tuite, *Romantic Austen: Sexual Politics and the Literary Canon* (Cambridge: Cambridge University Press, 2002); Roz Kaveney, *Teen Dreams: Reading Teen Film from Heathers to Veronica Mars* (London: I. B. Tauris, 2006); Catherine Driscoll, *Teen Film: A Critical Introduction* (Oxford: Berg, 2011).

12 Missy Schwartz, "Would you dump this woman?" *Entertainment Weekly*, 1 February 2008: <http://www.ew.com/ew/article/0,,20175469,00.html (last accessed 13 December 2014).

13 Ibid.

14 Melissa Silverstein, "Interview with *Vamps* director Amy Heckerling," *Indiewire*, 3 November 2012. Available at <http://blogs.indiewire.com/womenandhollywood/interview-with-vamps-director-amy-heckerling/> (last accessed 13 December 2014).

15 Betty Kaklamanidou, *Genre, Gender and the Effects of Neoliberalism: The New Millennium Hollywood Rom Com* (Oxford: Routledge, 2013), p. 86.

16 For a more detailed account on the production of *I Could Never Be Your Woman* and *Vamps*, see Silverstein (2012).

17 Noel Murray, "Interview with Amy Heckerling," *A.V. Club*, 20 March 2008. Available at <http://www.avclub.com/articles/amy-heckerling,14217/> (last accessed 13 December 2014).

18 Bret Lang, "21st Century Fox launches mentoring program for female directors," *Variety*, 1 July 2014. Available at <http://variety.com/2014/film/news/21st-century-fox-launches-mentoring-program-for-female-directors-1201256061/> (last accessed 13 December 2014).

19 Karen Hollinger, *In the Company of Women: Contemporary Female Friendship Films* (Minneapolis, MN: University of Minnesota Press, 1998).

20 Especially regarding female friendship films, successful productions such as *Mamma Mia!* (2008), *Sex and the City* (2008), *Sex and the City 2* (2010), and *Bridesmaids* (2011) constitute a new chapter in the subgenre's life, after its near obscurity in the late 1990s, as argued by Karen Hollinger, "Afterword: once I got beyond the name chick flick," in Suzanne Ferriss and Mallory Young (eds.), *Chick Flicks: Contemporary Women at the Movies* (Oxford: Routledge, 2008), p. 223.

21 Anonymous, "Men versus women . . . Different cosmetic procedures and their reasoning," *Facial Plastic Surgery* 20: 3 (2006). Available at <http://www.aafprs.org/patient/fps_today/vol20_3/pg2.html> (last accessed 13 December 2014).

22 Kaklamanidou, p. 24; Joe Reid, "Are we living in the golden age of male objectification?" *New York Magazine—Vulture*, 12 September 2011. Available at <http://nymag.com/daily/entertainment/2011/09/are_we_living_in_the_golden_ag.html> (last accessed 13 December 2014). I should add that there is much to be said about the various masculinities represented in the two films examined, but this discussion goes beyond the aims of this essay as it deserves a detailed analysis.

23 Michelle M. Lazar, "The right to be beautiful: postfeminist identity and consumer beauty advertising," in Gill and Scharff, pp. 37–8.

24 Estella Tincknell, "Scourging the abject body: *Ten Years Younger* and fragmented femininity under neoliberalism," in Gill and Scharff, p. 83.

25 Diane Negra and Su Holmes, "Introduction," *Genders Online*, 48, 2008. Available at http://www.genders.org/g48/g48_negraholmes.html> (last accessed 13 December 2014).

26 Melissa Silverstein and Kerensa Cadenas, "Women, aging and Hollywood," *Indiewire*, 12 June 2013. Available at <http://blogs.indiewire.com/womenandhollywood/women-aging-and-hollywood> (last accessed 13 December 2014). Hollywood and sexism have had a long history. In a forgotten interview for PBS, which has recently re-emerged online, Bette Davis spoke openly about sexism and the unjust treatment of women in the film industry. She remarked: "There's deep resentment [against female actors], no question about it, from the male side of the business . . . We all work for men, they're the people in charge. I think they find women easier who don't have the ability to think for themselves. One can make more enemies as a female with a brain, I think." See Amy Argetsinger, "Bette Davis, feminist: 'The real female should be partly male'," 1 October 2014, *The Washington Post*. Available at <http://www.washingtonpost.com/blogs/style-blog/

wp/2014/10/01/bette-davis-feminist-the-real-female-should-be-partly-male-video/>
(last accessed 13 December 2014).

27 Sarandon and Cattrall are not the only women to express their indignation and publicly
address Hollywood's obvious prejudice against female actors over 50. A significant
number of articles are appearing regularly online analyzing research and numbers, such as
Eliana Dockterman, "Lena Dunham has a point: new research documents Hollywood's
sexism," 11 March 2014, *Time*. Available at <http://time.com/19007/lena-dunham-has-
a-point-new-research-documents-hollywoods-sexism/> (last accessed 13 December
2014). Some commentary points at the apparent inequality that exists between female and
male actors. See Paige Morrow Kimball, "Aging out: Hollywood's problem with women
over 40," 27 September 2013, *The Huffington Post*, available at <http://www.
huffingtonpost.com/paige-morrow-kimball/aging-out-hollywoods-prob_b_3999544.
html> (last accessed 13 December 2014); and Sagit Maier-Schwartz, "Hollywood abhors
an aging woman. Too bad for Hollywood," 7 May 2013, *Slate*. Available at <http://www.
slate.com/blogs/xx_factor/2013/05/07/hollywood_is_allergic_to_aging_women_and_
too_bad_for_them.html> (last accessed 13 December 2014). At the same time, however,
both media outlets and blogs alike continue to scrutinize female stars' bodies and faces,
uploading unretouched images to reveal their "flaws" or to ridicule the random famous
woman who happened to gain a couple of pounds. This contradiction is indicative of the
long way the Western world still has to come for women over 40 to be able to age naturally
without having to attempt to construct an unattainable standard of beauty.

28 Feona Attwood, "Through the looking glass? Sexual agency and subjectification online,"
in Gill and Scharff, p. 204.

29 Vampires have been a staple in film history since the silent era, but, as noted by Leon
Hunt, Sharon Lockyer, and Milly Williamson, they have been "given a new lease of life by
the success of the cult TV series *Buffy the Vampire Slayer* (U.S., 1997–2003)." The great
popularity of the show spawned similar representations, and vampires became central
figures in "mainstream popular culture," from the "paranormal romance" of the *Twilight*
novels and films, to Charlaine Harris's "Sookie Stackhouse" novels, adapted as *True Blood*
by HBO in 2008 and running to 2015. See Hunt, Lockyer, and Williamson, "Introduction:
sometimes they come back—the vampire and zombie on screen," in Hunt, Lockyer, and
Williamson (eds.), *Screening the Undead: Vampires and Zombies in Film and Television*
(London: I. B. Tauris, 2014) pp. 1–18.

30 Lorna Piatti-Farnell, *The Vampire in Contemporary Popular Literature* (Oxford: Routledge,
2014), pp. 57–8.

31 In his application of Tzvetan Todorov's two categories of verisimilitude (generic and
cultural) to film, Steve Neale notes that certain film genres such as gangster films, war
films, and political thrillers are characterized more by the cultural via the use of shots/
scenes that include newspapers, specific objects, news reports, etc., enveloping the
fictional universe with an aura of authenticity. On the other hand, as Neale continues,
other genres, such as science fiction, horror, and slapstick comedies, follow narrative
conventions (generic verisimilitude) without necessarily paying attention to "reality."
Steve Neale, "Questions of genre," in Barry Keith Grant (ed.), *Film Genre Reader III*
(Austin, TX: University of Texas Press, 2003), p. 161.

32 Neale, p. 162.

33 See: Andrew Schenker, Review of *Vamps*, *Slant Magazine*, 28 October 2012, available at
<http://www.slantmagazine.com/film/review/vamps> (last accessed 13 December
2014); John Anderson, Review of *Vamps*, *Variety*, 6 November 2012, available at <http://
variety.com/2012/film/reviews/vamps-1117948695/> (last accessed 13 December 2014);

John DeFore, Review of *Vamps*, *The Hollywood Reporter*, 7 November 2012, available at <http://www.hollywoodreporter.com/review/vamps-film-review-387510> (last accessed 13 December 2014).

34   John Anderson, ibid.; Melissa Anderson, "In the undead comedy *Vamps*, Amy Heckerling loses the pulse," 31 October 2012, *The Village Voice*, available at <http://www.villagevoice.com/2012-10-31/film/in-the-undead-comedy-vamps-amy-heckerling-loses-the-pulse/> (last accessed 13 December 2014); Rachel Saltz, "Vampire girls just want to have dates," 1 November 2012, *The New York Times*, available at <http://www.nytimes.com/2012/11/02/movies/vamps-by-amy-heckerling-with-alicia-silverstone.html?_r=0> (last accessed 13 December 2014).

35   Diane Negra, *What a Girl Wants? Fantasizing the Reclamation of Self in Postfeminism* (Oxford: Routledge, 2009), p. 48.

36   Hollinger (1998), p. 6.

37   Hollinger (2008), p. 231.

38   Ibid.

39   Lesley Speed, "A world ruled by hilarity: gender and low comedy in the films of Amy Heckerling," *Senses of Cinema* 22, 2002. Available at <sensesofcinema.com/2002/22/heckerling/> (last accessed 13 December 2014).

40   Silverstein (2012).

41   The first *Twilight* film was directed by Catherine Hardwicke (2008), and it was followed by *New Moon* (Chris Weitz, 2009), *Eclipse* (David Slade, 2010), and *Breaking Dawn Parts 1 and 2* (Bill Condon, 2011–12). The first *Hunger Games* film was directed by Gary Ross (2012), and its three sequels—*Catching Fire* (2013) and *Mockingjay Parts 1 and 2* (2014–15)—were directed by Francis Lawrence. *Divergent* was directed by Neil Burger (2014); its first sequel was *Insurgent* (Robert Schwentke, 2015), and its closing entries, *Alligiant Parts 1 and 2* (2016–17), have yet to appear. All of these films are based on book series written by women.

CHAPTER 9

'Staying Young is Getting Old': Youth and Immortality in *Vamps*

Murray Leeder

The world belonged to the young. And I was an expert at being young.
—Goody Rutherford (Alicia Silverstone) in *Vamps* (2012)

It seems appropriate that such lines appear at the beginning of a film by Amy Heckerling, a director easily described as a specialist in depicting youth. Here, however, they are placed in the mouth of a young woman who was transformed into a vampire in the 1840s and whose identity has long been structured on her being paradoxically aged and youthful at the same time. But note the *was*—though she has not aged externally, Goody's investment in the shifting cultural constellation that is "youth" has frayed over time, leaving her angry and alienated. The film invites being read through Heckerling's status as an aging specialist in youth cinema and a long-time commentator on society's construction of youth.

One need not be a hardline auteurist to interpret *Vamps* as a personal film for Heckerling. In addition to its references to earlier works in her career[1] featuring her daughter's music, some events take place at Heckerling's *alma mater*, the New York University film program. Further, *Vamps* resonates with many of Heckerling's core themes: education, motherhood, slang, fashion, New York City, age-mismatched relationships, and perhaps above all, youth. At a Q&A and screening in April 2012, Heckerling described the genesis of the film in terms of "thinking about what would make [Goody] happy . . . [I] concluded that she didn't want to get old; she just wanted to "horse around with [her] friends." She wanted, in essence, "to be a teenager, at night." But, as she admitted, "The problem is that you really are meant to grow up."[2] *Vamps*, then, both indulges this fantasy and acknowledges its impossibility. The tension between the desire to cling to the trappings of youth and the need to acknowledge youth's inevitable passing is central to *Vamps*, with movie stars and their simultaneous permanence on screen and public aging as a key point of reference.

Next to Heckerling's famous and influential *Fast Times at Ridgemont High* (1982) and *Clueless* (1995), *Vamps* is an obscure film that attracted only a small audience[3] and failed to ride on the recent popularity of cinematic vampires (the final *Twilight* film, *Breaking Dawn—Part 2*, earned \$830 million the same year). If the idea of an Amy Heckerling vampire film is vaguely ludicrous, the film's extensive intertextual interplay with the genre's history[4] suggests a knowledgeable director delivering her own quirky spin on established genre conventions, and using the prism of the vampire story to deliver commentary on the cultural construction of youth. If vampires can "represent a desire for eternal life in a physical body which is impervious to disease . . . and to the 'normal' human aging process,"[5] *Vamps* repurposes this dynamic into a critique of contemporary culture's pathological obsession with youth, and in particular its inability to let women age naturally. This essay will explore two characters in particular, Silverstone's Goody and Sigourney Weaver's Cisserus, as parallel case studies in the unnatural preservation of youth, before moving to an exploration of the film's own reflexive construction of cinema itself as a medium for the preservation of youth that is also inevitably haunted by decay and death.

YOUTH, VAMPIRE STYLE

The convergence of vampires and youth culture existed long before Stephanie Meyer's *Twilight* novels and their associated film adaptations (2008–12); Rob Latham describes the vampire as "literally an insatiable consumer driven by a hunger for perpetual youth."[6] The paradox of being simultaneously young and old is present in numerous literary and cinematic vampires; notable examples include Claudia in Anne Rice's *Interview with the Vampire* (1976; film 1994), Timmy Valentine in S. P. Somtow's *Vampire Junction* (1984), and the young female vampire from the various iterations of *Let the Right One In/Let Me In* (novel 2004; films 2008, 2010). The song "I'm a Vampire," written by Stephin Merritt for his goth-influenced electropop band Future Bible Heroes, contains the lines:

I've survived the Inquisition, been a harlot, been a queen/
I've lived for 700 years and I still look seventeen.

This jokey track, cataloguing many conventional elements of (especially female) vampires, fittingly appeared on an album called *Eternal Youth* (2002).

For women in particular, youth is a space both of power and of imprisonment. Among contemporary vampire narratives, *Vamps* is arguably unrivaled in exploring these ideas through the young/old vampire figure.

The image of a youthful, beautiful exterior that conceals decades or centuries of life is a compelling one, and has particularly proved so in recent decades. For Latham, this vampire constitutes an image of late capitalism's excesses and contradictions.[7] *Vamps* is attuned to the same connections, depicting a shallow world of surfaces and rituals, dominated by meaningless sex and consumption, suggestive of Fredric Jameson's diagnosis of postmodernism's fragmented, disaffected character.[8] So many vampire narratives of recent decades, at least since *Love at First Bite* (1979) and *The Hunger* (1983), have nightclubs as key settings, suited to vampires' (and postmodern culture's) conspicuous consumption[9] and ostentatious style, and in *Vamps*, Goody and Stacy seem to persist in the shallow clubbing lifestyle mostly out of boredom and ritual. *Vamps*'s sensibility is also reminiscent of Jameson's laments on the demise of history: the decline of the historical metanarratives that Goody still identifies with has resulted in a bland, superficial, and affectless world of mindless consumption that reduces its own history to sound bites and ignores the economic base that uneasily sustains the lifestyle of its subjects. If *Clueless* "confirms—albeit in a forgiving spirit—the view of postmodern historiography associated with Fredric Jameson,"[10] more critique is on display in *Vamps*. The film's playful expropriation of rat imagery from *Nosferatu* (1922) positions the rats as humans: overpopulated, overbreeding, and dying of cancers from the products they so eagerly consume.

Despite Goody's claim to be a specialist in being young, it becomes clear that she is finding it increasingly difficult to maintain that position. After all, "youth" has changed dramatically since the 1840s. As Latham writes, youth has "ceased to be a quality inextricably attached to quantifiably aged bodies and instead become a set of values desirable both as a means of production and the end of consumption."[11] In other words, youth exists to be achieved, through fashion, behavior, or surgery. In Heckerling's previous film, *I Could Never Be Your Woman* (2007), Rosie Hanson (Michelle Pfeiffer)—a producer of pandering and phony youth-oriented television—asserts unequivocally, "Young is far superior to old . . . in everything . . . In our society, young outranks old." That film skewers the impossible social promise that youth is achievable for anyone. Mother Nature (Tracey Ullman) insists that "You can jump and peel and nip and tuck, but your insides are still rotting away." *Vamps*, too, plays with the dichotomy of inside and outside with characters whose outward youthfulness belies inner agedness, helping foreground the reconfiguration of youth Latham finds emblematized by vampires.

Heckerling's films show acute awareness of the elasticity of categories of age. Her characters, especially female ones, repeatedly lie about their ages.

In *Fast Times*, Stacy Hamilton (Jennifer Jason Leigh—actually 20 at the time), pretends to be 19 when she is 15, so that she can gain the interest of a 26-year-old stereo salesman. Conversely, *I Could Never Be Your Woman* finds Michelle Pfeiffer (actually 51) playing the 40-year-old Rosie, who pretends to be 36 to attract Adam (Paul Rudd, actually 38), who pretends to be 32 but is in fact 29 (and plays a teenager on TV). *Vamps* pushes this age-passing theme to new extremes: Stacy (Krysten Ritter, actually 31) is made into a vampire around 20 but at the time of the story is chronologically double that age, and then professes to be "a bit older" than her 25-year-old boyfriend guesses she might be; while Goody pretends to be only moderately older than Stacy, she is, in fact, well over a century older. Alicia Silverstone plays simultaneously younger and much older than her roughly 35 years, and sexagenarian Sigourney Weaver plays a vampire who identifies herself as "young" despite all obvious evidence to the contrary. Collectively, these examples expose the increasing unpinning of youth from chronological age, and the pressure on women especially to conform to given age categories through deception (of self or otherwise).

In *Vamps*, Goody's veneer of eternal youth is fracturing. From their first scene, differences between Goody and Stacy are foregrounded in terms of fashion, slang, and technology. Throughout, Goody is positioned as possessing more "legitimate" and "timeless" style, while Stacy is more attentive to the vagaries of fashion. Stacy chides Goody for wearing "Mom jeans" which "mark your age more than a birth certificate"[12] (the irony being that Stacy is herself clueless as to Goody's real age). Goody's combination of a Gibson Girl shirt (1890s), short skirt (1960s), platform shoes (1970s), and a turn-of-the-twentieth-century boater hat (traditionally a piece of men's apparel), earns gentle mockery from Stacy as "the history of fashion." In reference to *Clueless*, Deidre Lynch claims, "Fashion encourages fantasizing. An article of dress can register a woman's desire to flee the era by which she is captured";[13] but the point seems even more applicable to *Vamps*, where fashion facilitates one of Goody's few routes of nostalgic escape into her past. Kaja Silverman values retro fashion as "crossing vestimentary, sexual, and historical boundaries," and "salvaging the images that have traditionally sustained female subjectivity, images that have been consigned to the waste-basket not only by fashion, but by 'orthodox' feminism,"[14] and Goody's clinging to the fashions of the past functions similarly, reflecting her attempts to preserve elements of her own history and identity (if in a tellingly fragmented, disconnected manner, linked to Jameson's loss of history). It is a kind of masquerade that ironically discloses the true identity she hides from Stacy.

In her opening monologue, Goody describes her early embrace of the technologies of modernity: the electric light, the telephone, and the subway all made the life of a vampire easier and more pleasurable. Her favorite invention, she tells us, was the "flickers."[15] Goody finds it dismaying throughout to find that classic movie stars like James Cagney, Fred Astaire, Jack Lemmon, and Paul Newman are largely forgotten, even as New York society fawns over reality stars like The Situation (Michael Sorrentino, of *Jersey Shore* [2009–12]). Throughout, classical Hollywood is constructed as possessing a kind of analogue authenticity superior in contrast to the digital media that Goody disdains.[16]

Goody is also encumbered by changes in language, especially slang. Where the protagonists of *Clueless* are masters of slang and Rosie in *I Could Never Be Your Woman* repurposes it for her TV show, Goody is disdainful of it. When she is informed that the perplexing phrase "G2G" means "got to go," she objects, "Why can't kids say entire words? It takes just as long to say letters." Meanwhile, Goody's use of words like "cornball" and "spiffy" disclose her advanced age to anyone paying close enough attention.[17] Character is revealed through speech patterns as clearly in *Vamps* as in *Clueless*,[18] mainly to reinforce Goody's deepening separation from the world around her.

If Goody's attitude toward modern slang seems old-fogeyish, her attitude toward digital media is damning.[19] Where she once celebrated modern technologies as liberating, she is baffled and dismayed by the wired generation. She wonders, "Why do people even go out if all they want to bond with is their little glowing boxes?" and she disputes the language of "visiting" a website, unable to comprehend the logic of moving through digital space. Goody's harshest reaction is reserved for Renfield (Zak Orth) and his new personal device, an iPad mini:

> So as the day progresses, you can read thousands of unsolicited messages, advertisements, and the mindless brain vomit of acquaintances? . . . You have to keep learning to use new crap that doesn't actually do anything better than the old crap, which is incompatible with the new crap, all so you can have blogs and watch fake teenagers and real housewives? And it's all happening too fast and I'm tired. I'm just sick and tired of it all.

Vamps validates Goody's technophobia, since it is through new media that the government is tracking and persecuting vampires under the banner of Homeland Security. Indeed, Goody uses a *Farmer's Almanac* to learn of a solar eclipse that allows the vampire community to intervene to remove themselves from the government's computers, and thus analogue ingenuity trumps computerized nefariousness.

Goody's reference to "fake teenagers" highlights the links between digital media and the contemporary construction of youth. In a 2013 article for *Psychology Today*, Dale Archer connects the modern American obsession with youth to the technological revolution:

As the world continues to speed up, the wisdom of the ages can be Googled by anyone . . . Who needs to ask an old guy for advice when you can become a superficial expert on any topic after 30 minutes on the computer? . . . This constant access to information leaves the impression that a tidbit of knowledge, or a sound bite, is enough to be relevant. It suggests that a quick ten-minute read or video is equivalent to wisdom gained from years of hard-earned experience.[20]

Archer's diagnosis of society's techno-ills is similar to Goody's, and indeed, that of *Vamps*. Goody's knowledge of the times she lived through, and consequent wisdom about a number of subjects, often invokes suspicion from Stacy. She speaks learnedly on subjects ranging from New York City's history to the Dutch West India Company. When Stacy twice asks how she came to know this information, Goody unconvincingly credits The History Channel. The riddle of Cisserus's hiding place, the "place no New Yorker ever goes," which turns out to be Grant's Tomb,[21] comes to Goody through her knowledge of New York's history and of Groucho Marx's later career as a quiz show host on *You Bet Your Life* (1951–61). As in Archer's article, *Vamps* constructs the wired generation as substituting the easy accessibility of information for genuine, acquired knowledge and experience that proves far more valuable.

When the opportunity for a heroic self-sacrifice arrives, we finally realize that Goody's youthful exterior hides an old woman alienated by a rapidly changing world and ready for death. Late in the narrative, Stacy discovers that she is pregnant and the only way the child will survive is if Cisserus dies and Stacy (and Goody) are restored to their mortal ages. "Staying young is getting old," a resigned Goody tells Stacy, who does not realize that killing Cisserus means dying herself. In what is perhaps a bit of wish fulfillment, Stacy bears her restoration to mortal life comically well, but Goody is transformed into an old woman and has only a small amount of life left to her before she disintegrates into dust. Critically, Goody not only gives herself up to death but also, however briefly, to the old age and decrepitude that her vampirism previously spared her.[22]

Goody earlier revealed to Van Helsing (Wallace Shawn) the reason why she decided to become a vampire: so she could help her children survive a cholera epidemic.[23] There had only been the mildest hint that she was a mother up till this moment, but we realize that her relationship with Stacy was as motherly as sisterly, at least from Goody's perspective. She remained close to her family for decades, but eventually she deliberately distanced herself to avoid scaring her grandchildren. Her rootlessness, it is suggested, stems from her estrangement from her original, maternal, role. Van Helsing reveals the fate of Goody's descendants, showing her a picture of Congresswoman Jane Rutherford (also played by Silverstone), noting, "She looks like you"—an important moment of self-recognition for a vampire older than photography, who has never been able to see her own image. Only after Goody is secure in the knowledge of her bloodline's success can she die happily ("I was able to save my kids," she asserts to Van Helsing. "Let's go and save yours"), and is semi-reincarnated through Stacy's daughter, named "Goody" in tribute.

There is a significant contrast between one Stacy, in *Fast Times*, whose abortion is presented matter-of-factly and without judgment, and this later Stacy, whose preservation of pregnancy drives the film's final conflicts. Motherhood is a major theme in Heckerling's later work (as in the two *Look Who's Talking* films [1989, 1990] and *I Could Never Be Your Woman*), and *Vamps* also foregrounds Heckerling's own motherhood: the band The Lost Patrol, fronted by her daughter Mollie Israel, performs onscreen and its music plays nondiegetically in other scenes. The fact that Heckerling makes *Vamps* into a family affair reflects the valorization of motherhood that runs through the film. At the end of *I Could Never Be Your Woman*, Rosie admits that witnessing her daughter's successes means more to her than anything in her life, and Mother Nature tells her that she is wasting away to make room for her child; likewise in *Vamps*, the inevitable but painful passage from youth into decrepitude and death (here staged over minutes rather than a lifetime) is blunted by the knowledge that there is a girl set to succeed her.

THE MONSTROUS OLDER WOMAN

If Goody is a "good mother," she is contrasted with her own bad one, Cisserus, whom she needs to help destroy in order to save her own symbolic daughter, Stacy. In so doing, she needs to destroy the attitude toward death and aging that Cisserus represents. If Michelle Pfeiffer had been cast as Cisserus in *Vamps* as Heckerling originally intended,[24] the parallels would be all the more apparent between her and Rosie in *I Could Never Be Your Woman*: both powerful older women clinging unhealthily to the trappings of youth. Instead, Cisserus, the "stem" vampire[25] who made both Goody and Stacy, is played by Sigourney Weaver, who was dismissed, along with most of the older women in Hollywood, as a "hag" in *I Could Never Be Your Woman*. While Rosie is tempted into transgressing the norms of Western society by having an affair with a younger man, Cisserus is ruled by unrestrained appetites for blood and sex and consumption, all linked together in her first scene through her casual, sexualized murder of a delivery man: "I feel like a pizza guy." Barbara Creed argues that "The female vampire is abject because she disrupts identity and order; driven by her lust for blood, she does not respect the dictates of the law which set down the rules of proper sexual conduct."[26] Cisserus fulfills this role in *Vamps*, in contrast to the sedate Goody and Stacy; she is unconcerned about the dictates of either human society or the pacified vampire society, presented as a mix of expatriate community and twelve-step program. If the title *Vamps* and the film's intertextual play with the silent era is calculated to evoke the "vamp" star type of Theda Bara, Valeska Suratt, Helen Gardner, and Louise Glaum, then it is certainly Cisserus, not Stacy or Goody, who resembles that type: "women who appropriated the masculine agency utilized in seduction, who refused to restrict their sexuality to procreative heterosexual monogamy . . . and who 'unmanned' their victims by rendering them passive and dependent."[27]

Weaver's role in *Vamps* followed *Paul* (2011) and *The Cabin in the Woods* (2012), both of which feature her as a villainous authority figure, a nameless character alluded to throughout but who remains unseen until the films' final scenes. These third-act cameos by Weaver harness her recognizable star presence and, especially, her association with science fiction and fantasy/horror films (despite her lengthy and varied career, for most, Weaver's presence first summons associations with Ripley, the character she began playing in *Alien* [1979], and Dana Barrett from the *Ghostbusters* films [1984, 1989]). Matt Hills draws the distinction between actors (such as Christopher Lee) whom he identifies as cult stars despite their mainstream visibility, and Harrison Ford, who appeared in cult films and franchises without becoming a cult star per se.[28] Weaver fits uncertainly into these categories and possibly straddles them, but the evidence of *Paul* and *Cabin in the Woods* puts her closer to Lee, since her cameos, and indeed her role in *Vamps*, depend on a certain cultish pleasure of recognition and the intertextual knowledge of previous roles. Note, for example, that Cisserus's flowing red gown closely resembles Weaver's costume from the *Ghostbusters* possession scene.

That Weaver's screen persona never signified "youth" is something rare among postclassical female stars. *Alien*, her first lead, was made when she was 30, and instantly secured her image of capability and maturity. When paired with actors like Mel Gibson, Harrison Ford, Kevin Kline, or Bill Murray, she has signified the older, more serious and mature partner (her considerable stature no doubt playing a role in cementing this dynamic). She regularly played authoritative career professionals of one kind or another. Her Oscar-nominated "boss from hell" role in *Working Girl* (1988) hits many of the same notes as *Vamps*, with Weaver playing the stern, authoritative superior to the more girlish modes of femininity of her respective underlings, Melanie Griffith and Alicia Silverstone respectively.

Vivian Sobchack writes of a particular kind of "scary woman": "one whose scariness, while related to her sexuality, has less to do with power than with powerlessness, and whose scariness to men has less to do with sexual desire and castration anxiety than with abjection and death."[29] This is the middle-aged woman, not yet contained by the category of the "old" but past child-rearing

years, and whose sexual desire is consequently marked as excessive and terrifying. Yet she is also pathetic:

> Objectively felt, she is an *excess woman*—desperately afraid of invisibility,
> uselessness, lovelessness, sexual and social isolation and abandonment
> . . . Objectively viewed, she is sloppy, self-pitying, and abjectly needy
> or she is angry, vengeful, powerful, and scary. Indeed, she is an *excessive
> woman*, a woman in masquerade, in whiteface.[30]

All of these descriptors suit Cisserus perfectly (even the masculine ending
of her name reinforces the fact that she is on some level not a *real woman*, if
only by virtue of being an excessive one), and like the women in the films
Sobchack discusses (such as *The Wasp Woman* [1959] and *The Leech Woman*
[1960]), she needs to die for the narrative to conclude.

Like so many of Heckerling's women, Cisserus is heavily associated with
fashion. Her first lines lament the fact that, although she can purchase high-
end clothing ("Gaultier, Prada, Dries"), she can never see how she looks
wearing them: "What is the point of looking like this, if I can never enjoy it?"
In fact, she has turned Goody and Stacy into vampires to serve as clothing
models, so they can don her clothes and allow her to imagine how much better
they will look on her. The fact that Cisserus is obviously significantly taller
than either of them provides a sly joke, accompanying the fact that Cisserus
believes herself to be young, despite being played by an actress past 60. When
Stacy objects to an outfit on the basis that it is not meant for young people,
Cisserus's response is rich with levels of irony: "Excuse me, are you telling
me about being young? Do you have any idea how long I have been young?"
Here Cisserus echoes a different character in *I Could Never Be Your Woman*:
the aging starlet Brianna Minx (Stacey Dash), who lambasts her upstart rivals
by saying, "I was a teenage girl before any of them!" It takes years to instanti-
ate the complex cultural phenomenon that is youth, Heckerling seems to be
saying, but by then one is no longer young . . . or the definition of "youth" has
shifted in the meantime.

Where Goody's retro costuming helps her reconstruct lost scraps of her
identity, Cisserus's wardrobe is current as "the new fall line," and serves as
evidence of her bottomless vanity and self-deception. Outward displays of
taste and wealth are important to her even though she cannot see them herself.
However, her fixation on Spanish pop star Diego Bardem[31] reveals that she
has been fooled by her own masquerade. Her puzzling insistence on being
young makes one wonder at just what age she became a vampire, and just
how she came to be so self-deluded. Although she has never met Bardem, she
has "mad love for him" all the same, and she decides to seduce him without
hypnotism, her standard seduction technique. Her failure as a seductress (as

a "vamp") awakens her monstrosity, as she massacres everyone in a Chinese restaurant—a violent eruption of that "vengeful, powerful, and scary" aspect of Sobchack's terrifying older woman. This display of gore and death seems wildly out of place in the largely bloodless vampire film *Vamps* has been up till then. Cisserus's excessive appetite is tied to her pathetic neediness, and she defrays the seriousness of her actions with self-help clichés: "Just because you overdid it one day doesn't mean you have to be bad all weekend." When her body is hacked apart during her comic/grotesque death scene, Cisserus's lack of self-awareness is again reinforced: her severed head looks on her body and asks, "When did my ass get so flat?"

Cisserus's self-delusion—her having constructed a self-image far removed from her actual appearance—is simultaneously pathetic, comic, and monstrous. Violent and mercurial at the best of times, she becomes even more monstrous when her illusions of youth are threatened. Importantly, however, the film positions her self-delusion as the self-delusion of all women trained to think that youth can be achieved through effort and money, and maintained indefinitely. Cisserus represents what happens when a woman's denial of the inevitability of abject senescence is pushed to absurd extremes.

THE UNDEATH OF MOVIE STARS

In one intriguing moment, Cisserus implies that she once had a love affair (or at least desired one) with Al Jolson. Stacy asks, incredulously, "The Mammy guy?"—like most film students, she knows Jolson best from *The Jazz Singer* (1927). Cisserus answers, "He was an incredibly dynamic performer. You have no idea because you never saw him live." It is a significant line in a film where "authenticity" is frequently located in classical Hollywood and its stars. For all of their differences, Cisserus and Goody both treasure memories of deceased movie stars, but Cisserus privileges the live experience and alludes to cinema's limitations as a recording mechanism. A reflexive streak runs all through *Vamps*—it is a film fixated on film, and in particular the linkages between film, nostalgia, aging, and memory.

Goody is not the first screen vampire to embrace cinema. In *Interview with the Vampire*, Louis (Brad Pitt) sees it as a modern "mechanical wonder that allowed me to see the sunrise for the first time in two hundred years." Louis's technofetishism is shared by the Count (Gary Oldman) in *Bram Stoker's Dracula* (1992), whose visit to the London cinematograph has inspired plentiful scholarly attention,[32] as well as Max Schreck (Willem Dafoe) in *Shadow of the Vampire* (2000). Theoretical links between film and vampires are plentiful: Lloyd Michaels speaks of film's "unique process of simultaneously deceiving and enthralling the spectator by substituting an illusory presence for an absent referent, rendering as 'undead' a departed object by animating projected shadows and light."[33] This dynamic of presence/absence is often illustrated with reference to stardom, as in Christian Metz's example from *The Imaginary Signifier*:

> At the theatre, Sarah Bernhardt may tell me that she is Phèdre or, if the play were from another period and rejected the figurative regime, she might say, as in a type of modern theatre, that she is Sarah Bernhardt. But at any rate, I should see Sarah Bernhardt. At the cinema, she could make the same two kinds of speeches too, but it would be her shadow that would be offering them to me (or she would be offering them in her own absence).[34]

The complex nature of our relationship with movie stars is that we do not know them, and can only connect with them in their absence, but nevertheless feel an investment in their presence on the screen. At the same time, we recognize that there is an unbridgeable gap: Bernhardt's shadow, or Jolson's, is not the person. As Cisserus implies with respect to Jolson, presence and immediacy and liveness have different kinds of values attached to them; recall Walter Benjamin's famous claim that the "cult of the movie star, fostered by the money of the film industry, preserves not the unique aura of the person but the 'spell of the personality,' the phony spell of a commodity."[35] Ironically, Cisserus has fallen under just that spell from Bardem.

Vamps plays with this vampire/cinema link, but largely evacuates the uncanny dimensions to the illusive semi-resurrection of dead images and people. Clips from *Nosferatu*, *The Cabinet of Dr. Caligari* (1920), *Metropolis* (1927), and *Carnival of Souls* (1962) are playfully pulled out of context and made into ironic counterpoints to the film's plot. Classic Hollywood stars are keystones of Goody's nostalgic worldview, but her assertion that stars "never got any older" ignores all the many ways in which movie stars quite clearly *do* get older, often quite publicly, and speaks to Goody's valorization of permanence and tradition over change and variation. In fact, the very idea that stars (or anyone else) should *not* get older contributes to the plastic surgery culture lampooned in *I Could Never Be Your Woman*.

Strung on the paradox of simultaneous stillness and motion, cinema can likewise arrest aging and document it at the same time. This is evident with respect to the stars of *Vamps*. The many close-ups of Silverstone allow us to study her face in search of signs of both continuity and change. She has aged subtly, but one is hard pressed to imagine the "baby fat siren"[36] of *Clueless* delivering Goody's monologue to Van Helsing about her family and history with such poise and warmth. Just as we learn all of these unexpected details of Goody's history in that sequence, we also learn something about Alicia

Silverstone and the unexpected new depths that she can bring to the role precisely because she has aged. Placing her in the scene with her *Clueless* co-star Wallace Shawn only enhances the effect, as we reflect on both the consistencies with and differences from Silverstone's person of seventeen years previously. Silverstone's graceful aging with her persona and Goody's willingness to forgo her eternal youth contrast with Cisserus's inappropriately clinging to an illusion of youth that all others see through. Weaver, on the other hand, seems preternaturally unchanged with the passing decades.

The curious "lifedeath"[37] of the cinematic image and its stars seems particularly to have resonated with Heckerling early on. A 1985 profile says of her childhood: "Sobbing through [James Cagney's] death scene in *Angels With Dirty Faces* [1938], Amy caught her mother's attention. 'She told me it was only a movie, and you don't die in movies,' says Heckerling, 'so that sounded like a great thing to go into.'"[38] Jocular though this anecdote might be, it touches on a serious subject: cinema as a place where death can be overcome. Rocky Sullivan, Cagney's character in the film, dies, but of course not Cagney himself, and Rocky lives again if you rewatch the film. Cagney is now dead, but he too lives for as long as his star image endures on screen. Thought of only slightly differently, however, *all* photographic and cinematic images are dead, or undead.

Cagney is referenced numerous times throughout *Vamps*, and is even evoked during Goody's bittersweet death/not-death in Times Square. The sequence is framed as a diffusion both into her own past and that of New York City, with her memories peeling back levels of memory before her eyes, and into the history of cinema, since the historical footage of Times Square from different periods is aesthetically distinct from the images marked as her memories, yet commingles with them.[39] After Goody turns to dust, her remnants linger on the statue of George M. Cohan, whom Cagney portrayed in *Yankee Doodle Dandy* (1942). Minutes later, Goody appears on screen again, the first of a series of images that close the film,[40] even as Cohan's "Give My Regards to Broadway" plays on the soundtrack.[41] The reappearance of Goody's image alongside Silverstone's credit (the first live-action image of Goody we saw in the film, in fact) reinforces the idea that no one whose image is captured by the camera is truly dead. The sentiment resembles that displayed by the writer for *La Poste* reviewing the Lumière cinematograph in 1895, who wrote that "when this device is made available to the public, everyone will be able to photograph those dear to them, not just in their immobile form but in their movement, in their action, and with speech on their lips; then death will no longer be absolute."[42] Such an optimistic construction effaces the fact that the immortality bestowed by the camera's gaze is also a brand of living death,[43] but then, as Goody tells us during the opening montage, she's "always looked on the bright side."

CONCLUSION

Vamps's intertextual web with other films privileges *Nosferatu* in a number of ways, even parodying the famous reflexive shot of Count Orlok (Max Schreck)'s shadow as Cisserus descends on the ill-fated pizza guy (Taylor Negron). If Cisserus is associated with the hideous, outwardly monstrous Orlok, then Goody has affinities with Ellen Hutter (Greta Schröder), the virtuous woman who lays her life down to defeat him. Gilberto Perez reads *Nosferatu* as a Heideggerian fable on different ways of responding to death, valorizing Ellen's "self-embracing, anxiously yet freely, the condition of 'being-toward-death,'"[44] and *Vamps* works similarly, contrasting Cisserus's "bad death" against Goody's "good death." I would suggest, however, that *Vamps* modifies *Nosferatu*'s themes of the confrontation with death by foregrounding aging, positioning Goody's clear-eyed resignation against Cisserus's grotesque resistance. And if, in *Nosferatu*, "[as] the body yields to ghost in the film image, so [Ellen's] flesh yields . . . to the specter of death,"[45] Goody and the film ultimately refute the seductive potential for eternal youth that cinema seems to bestow on its subject (notably on movie stars) in favor of the inescapability of change and death. As Goody turns to dust, so shall we all, and *Vamps* asks that we look to those things that survive us (pictures, children, memories, statues) to make life worthwhile in spite of—or because of—this fact.

NOTES

1   In addition to casting Alicia Silverstone and Wallace Shawn from *Clueless*, *Vamps* also features Taylor Negron as the pizza deliveryman from "Mr Pizza Guy," a role he played in *Fast Times*. In *Vamps*, Negron's ill-fated character even delivers the very same order to Cisserus as he did to Spicoli (Sean Penn): double cheese and sausage.

2   Miranda Popkey, "Writer-director Amy Heckerling and her muse Alicia Silverstone discuss *Clueless*, *Vamps*, and filming women," *Capital New York*, 9 April 2012. Available at <http://www.capitalnewyork.com/article/culture/2012/04/5659176/writer-director-amy-heckerling-and-her-muse-alicia-silverstone-discu> (last accessed 7 December 2014).

3   Just how successful it was is difficult to determine. Distributor Anchor Bay only granted it a brief "courtesy release" in New York City and Los Angeles, earning a little over $3,000 altogether. It was already available on demand, with its video release scheduled for eleven days later (Christopher Rosen, "*Vamps*' box office flops: *Clueless* reunion earns $500 from one theater," 5 November 2012. Available at <http://www.huffingtonpost.com/2012/11/05/vamps-box-office-flop_n_2077496.html> (last accessed 7 December 2014).

4   I discuss some of these in Murray Leeder, "Dracula in New York: the comic, anachronistic vampire in *Love at First Bite* and *Vamps*," in Vicky Gilpin (ed.), *Laugh Until You Bleed: Vampires and Comedy* (Jefferson, NC: McFarland, forthcoming).

5 Jean R. Hillabold, "The vampire cult of eternal youth," in Lisa A. Nevárez (ed.), *The Vampire Goes to College: Essays on Teaching the Undead* (Jefferson, NC: McFarland, 2013), p. 79.

6 Rob Latham, *Consuming Youth: Vampires, Cyborgs and the Culture of Consumption* (Chicago, IL: University of Chicago Press, 2002), p. 1.

7 Ibid., esp. pp. 26–95.

8 Most famously articulated in Frederic Jameson, "Postmodernism, or the cultural logic of late capitalism," in Michael Hardt and Kathi Weeks (eds.), *The Jameson Reader* (Malden, MA: Blackwell, 2000), pp. 188–233.

9 Instead of being independently wealthy as so many vampires (often inexplicably) are, Goody and Stacy support their lifestyle with the mendacious work of exterminating pests. In this respect, they are closer to the young middle-class protagonists of *Fast Times*, who have jobs (save for Spicoli, whose lack of employment is commented upon) than the rich kids of *Clueless*.

10 Dianne F. Sadoff and John Kucich, *Victorian Afterlife: Postmodern Culture Rewrites the Nineteenth Century* (Minneapolis, MN: University of Minnesota Press, 2000), p. x.

11 Latham, p. 15.

12 The "jeans/genes" pun pays off when Stacy sees Goody's true age and says, "Maybe your genes aren't as good."

13 Deirdre Lynch, "Clueless: about history," in Suzanne R. Pucci and James Thompson (eds.), *Jane Austen and Co.: Remaking the Past in Contemporary Culture* (Albany, NY: State University of New York Press, 2003), p. 87.

14 Kaja Silverman, "Fragments of a fashionable discourse," in Tania Modleski (ed.), *Studies in Entertainment: Critical Approaches to Mass Culture* (Bloomington, IN: Indiana University Press, 1986), p. 151.

15 A once-pejorative early slang term for moving pictures; according to Lillian Gish, D. W. Griffith once castigated an actress for using the term (Miriam Hansen, *Babel and Babylon: Spectatorship in American Silent Film* [Cambridge, MA: Harvard University Press, 1991], p. 77). The opening mangles the history of cinema: Goody speaks about the 1920s, and says, "And then came my favorite invention: the flickers," as we see a clip from *A Trip to the Moon*, which premiered in 1902.

16 The scene where Stacy creates a digital portrait of Goody runs counter to this trend; on that occasion, Goody admires the ability of computer manipulation to show her what presumably no camera can capture—an image of her own face.

17 Compare *Loser* (2000), where Paul (Jason Biggs) using the word "skosh" is a marker of his rural identity.

18 For a thorough exploration of speech in *Clueless* and its significance, see Jennifer O'Meara, "'We've got to work on your accent and vocabulary': characterization through verbal style in *Clueless*," *Cinema Journal* 53: 3 (2014): pp. 138–45.

19 There is a relationship between the two, as Goody objects to slang terms like "G2G" or "BTW," which represent Internet chatspeak infiltrating verbal discourse. Dora (Mena Suvari) in *Loser* is similarly vocal in her disdain for new media.

20 Dale Archer, "Forever young: America's obsession with never growing old," *Psychology Today*, 2 October 2013. Available at <http://www.psychologytoday.com/blog/reading-between-the-headlines/201310/forever-young-americas-obsession-never-growing-old> (last accessed 18 July 2014). Emphasis in original.

21 This is the burial place of President Ulysses S. Grant in Upper Manhattan. Groucho Marx famously used "Who is buried in Grant's tomb?" as a softball question on the TV show *You Bet Your Life*.

22 Goody's speedy decline into decrepitude echoes the fate of John Blaylock (David Bowie) in *The Hunger* (1983).

23 Extratextual knowledge about Silverstone's motherhood—in recent years, she has been more visible as an advocate for the controversial "attachment parenting" than as an actor—filters through to Goody.

24 Jennifer Vineyard, "*Clueless* writer-director Amy Heckerling on her new Alicia Silverstone movie, *Vamps*," *Vulture*, 9 September 2012. Available at <http://www.vulture.com/2012/04/vamps-amy-heckerling-interview.html> (last accessed 7 December 2014).

25 Within the film's typology, a stem is the only kind of vampire who can create new vampires.

26 Barbara Creed, *The Monstrous Feminine: Film, Feminism, Psychoanalysis* (London: Routledge, 1993), p. 61.

27 Jeffrey Andrew Weinstock, "Sans fangs: Theda Bara, *A Fool There Was*, and the cinematic vampire," in Douglas Brode and Leah Deyneka (eds.), *Dracula's Daughters: The Female Vampire on Film* (Lanham, MD: Scarecrow Press, 2014), p. 37.

28 Matt Hills, "Cult movies with and without cult stars: differentiating discourses of stardom," in Kate Egan and Sarah Thomas (eds.), *Cult Film Stardom: Offbeat Attractions and Processes of Cultification* (Basingstoke: Palgrave Macmillan, 2013), p. 31.

29 Vivian Sobchack, "Revenge of *The Leech Woman*: on the dread of aging in low-budget horror film," in Rodney Sappington and Tyler Stallings (eds.), *Uncontrollable Bodies: Testimonies of Identity and Culture* (Seattle, WA: Bay Press, 1994), p. 80.

30 Ibid. p. 81 (emphasis in original).

31 Bardem is played in a cameo by Mexican actor Gael García Bernal. His name presumably alludes to Diego Luna and Javier Bardem, both of whom have co-starred with Bernal (in *Y Tu Mamá También* [2001] and *Sin noticias de Dios* [2001], respectively).

32 Ken Gelder, *Reading the Vampire* (London: Routledge, 1994), pp. 88–9; Garrett Stewart, *Between Film and Screen: Modernism's Photo Synthesis* (Chicago, IL: University of Chicago Press, 1999), pp. 241–4; Rachel O. Moore, *Savage Theory: Cinema as Modern Magic* (Durham, NC: Duke University Press, 2000), pp. 48–9; Simon Joyce, *Victorians in the Rearview Mirror* (Athens, OH: Ohio University Press, 2007), pp. 105–7.

33 Lloyd Michaels, *The Phantom of the Cinema: Character in Modern Film* (Albany, NY: State University of New York Press, 1998), p. 67.

34 Christian Metz, *The Imaginary Signifier: Psychoanalysis and the Cinema* (Bloomington, IN: Indiana University Press, 1982), p. 44.

35 Walter Benjamin, "The work of art in the age of mechanical reproduction," *Illuminations* (New York: Schocken, 1968), p. 231.

36 Tom Doherty, "Clueless kids," *Cineaste*, 21: 4 (1995), p. 15.

37 To borrow a term used by Alan Cholodenko in "The crypt, the haunted house of cinema," *Cultural Studies Review* 10: 2 (2004), pp. 99–113.

38 Kristin McMurran, "Mixing marriage and movies is a mirthly delight for directors Amy Heckerling and Neal Israel," *People* 23: 19 (13 May 1985). Available at <http://www.people.com/people/archive/article/0,,20090679,00.html> (last accessed 7 December 2014).

39 Elsewhere in the film, cinema, nostalgia, and memory are closely aligned as Danny (Richard Lewis) looks for familiar movies to show to his dying wife Angela (Marilu Henner).

40 Many of Heckerling's films have ended with similar montages, a tradition shared by *Citizen Kane* (1942) and 1980s sitcoms. This one lacks the "what happened next" captions of *Fast Times* or *Loser*.

41 This is neither Cagney's performance from *Yankee Doodle Dandy* nor Al Jolson's famous version (as Cisserus might have preferred), but is rather by Mollie Israel, Heckerling's daughter. This choice underscores the semi-survival of Goody through the namesake child.

42 Quoted in Jon Stratton, *The Desirable Body: Cultural Fetishism and the Erotics of Consumption* (Manchester: Manchester University Press, 1996), p. 83.

43 This distinction, more or less, is the one Laura Mulvey draws between André Bazin's and Roland Barthes's respective positions on the relationship of the photographic image and death (Laura Mulvey, *Death 24x a Second: Stillness and the Moving Images* [London: Reaktion, 2006], pp. 54–66).

44 Gilberto Perez, *The Material Ghost: Films and Their Medium* (Baltimore, MD: The Johns Hopkins University Press, 1998), p. 147.

45 Ibid. p. 148.

Reflections on the Heckerling Oeuvre

Introduction to Part IV

As the preceding chapters have illustrated, Amy Heckerling's work as a writer and director of feature films and television shows has been diverse and important, and these concluding essays reflect on that work in broader terms, presenting a somewhat auteurist perspective on a woman whose extensive creative output is not always recognized for its sophistication and distinction.

Using the film Heckerling is most often associated with, *Clueless* (1995), as their foundation, Stefania Marghitu and Lindsay Alexander consider the director's oeuvre in terms of its vital status as a collection of statements about female empowerment. The two authors uncover, in the commemoration of *Clueless*, how audiences continue to embrace the underappreciated attitudes of women in Heckerling's texts, as they trace the evolution of spectatorial experiences with the film over the past two decades. Their attention to fashion, music, and speech, along with interviews from industry professionals, bolsters their study of Heckerling's special treatment of female characters.

Kimberley Miller then lends further validity to Heckerling's reputation through a comparison with one of her contemporaries, John Hughes, who similarly wrote teen and family comedies in the 1980s and '90s. In fact, Hughes wrote the script for Heckerling's most lucrative film of the 1980s, *European Vacation* (1985), which Miller considers alongside other Hughes movies such as *Sixteen Candles* (1984) and *Ferris Bueller's Day Off* (1986). While Hughes would have somewhat greater glory through the broader profitability of his films until his death in 2009, Miller argues that Heckerling's continuing output of films and television shows that continue their challenge to gender and genre standards—such as *Vamps* (2012) and *Suburgatory* (2011–14)—is well worth further analytical assessment.

We conclude the book with an updated and expanded revision of an essay by Lesley Speed, who provides a comprehensive coda for our study of Heckerling's productions by relocating her films within the pantheon of other female directors and popular comedy conventions. With attention to movie industry traditions and critical reception, Speed celebrates the stylistic and political accomplishments of Heckerling as a director in a field that has often limited women's creative control and dismissed the merits of comedy as a genre. Speed specifically argues for the unique contributions of Heckerling to the concepts of body humor and youth transformation, while she ultimately conveys the enduring significance of Heckerling within American media.

CHAPTER 10

"But seriously, I actually have a way normal life for a teenage girl": The Teenage Female Empowerment Payoff in Amy Heckerling's *Clueless*

Stefania Marghitu and Lindsey Alexander

When fans go online to pay tribute to Amy Heckerling's 1995 cult classic *Clueless*, the film's fashion and slang are often at the forefront. Through the film's styling and language, Heckerling creates a cultural representation of female power. That sense of power and playfulness—achieved via feminine practices—still resonates with women today. *Clueless* commemorations are rooted in an appreciation of Heckerling's pastiche of fashion and slang. For instance, a widely shared YouTube video provides a montage of every outfit that protagonist Cher Horowitz (Alicia Silverstone) wears in the film, while a boutique clothing brand dedicated its 2013 collection to the film's femme-centered styles.[1] Heckerling transformed the pivotal plotlines of Jane Austen's 1815 novel *Emma* into a high school coming-of-age story, and set a new standard for the female-driven teen film. This essay will reveal that the oft-quoted and most culturally-defining components of *Clueless* were, in fact, not particularly representative of teenagers of the time, but instead were molded by Heckerling as a means of ousting the male-centric teen film and grunge era with a cultural collage of decades of feminine fashion and slang as a female-dominant alternative. Rather than giving in to established approaches of the teen film genre, Heckerling proves to be a true postmodern master of pastiche, remaking classic literature under the guise of a present-day setting but with a retro representation that evokes the late 1970s and early '80s, from its bright attire to the lingual resurgence reminiscent of California beach babes and '80s Valley Girls. Cher, memorable for shopping and slang, uses these powers, often denigrated as superficial, to navigate societal hierarchy and gain power. Whether Cher is using a scantily clad outfit as an innocent seducer or her argumentation skills to go from average student to honor roll, Heckerling writes a tongue-in-cheek script that displays how young women can wield power.

Figure 10.1 Cher organizes her immaculate wardrobe with a futuristic computer program on her desktop computer.

Arguing against the Marcusian theory of consumerism as sexist, the feminist cultural critic Ellen Willis writes:

> For women, buying and wearing clothes and beauty aids is not so much consumption as work. One of a woman's jobs in this society is to be an attractive sexual object, and clothes and makeup are tools of the trade . . . When a woman spends a lot of money and time decorating her home or herself . . . it is not idle self-indulgence (let alone the result of psychic manipulation) but a healthy attempt to find outlets for her creative energies within her circumscribed role.[2]

While the grunge era of the late '80s to early '90s—pairing the DIY punk ethos of the '70s raw masculine energy of heavy metal and Generation X malaise—already succeeded in subverting disparate subcultures of different eras, Heckerling continues the same method with a different pattern. She favored designer fashions and pop culture as currency for her teenage characters. For example, Cher wears brands like Calvin Klein and Fred Segal, and can quote *Hamlet* on the basis of the 1990 Mel Gibson movie adaptation. We will explore how Heckerling's inspiration stems from the late '70s to the early '80s, the era of her first high school film, *Fast Times at Ridgemont High* (1982), and how she blended chic aesthetics from the past with current fashion trends to produce a savvy script for *Clueless* that relied on real pop culture references but fabricated slang. Postmodernism is a patchwork of high and low culture, but the director was a pioneer in weaving together eras of style and trends to construct a "contemporary" representation, particularly for teen films. *Clueless* launched fashions and vernacular, and in so doing promoted feminine-dominant culture and provided the standard for female-centered teen media, along with modes of fandom and appreciation.

Heckerling helped create a '90s-styled mainstream femme culture for female teens that celebrated fashion and beauty as well as self-realization and personal growth. Aligned with postfeminist, or post-second-wave or third-wave feminist attitudes, *Clueless* does not question gendered identity as a social construct, and instead chooses to celebrate femininity and feminine modes of consumption as empowering for its protagonists. Throughout the coming-of-age teen narrative, however, Heckerling's film asserts that there is more to life, and room for Cher to develop as a self-actualized adult who cares about larger issues. Cher does not simply transform into a socialite who donates money to good causes. She becomes a vigilante for less fortunate individuals who have lost their homes and possessions during a natural disaster. She is less concerned with her looks and more preoccupied with her causes and helping her father's trial, yet she maintains her beauty and style. She also realizes that saving her virginity for celebrity heartthrob Luke Perry is not the most ideal option, and comes to see that she is in love with her intelligent and thoughtful ex-stepbrother Josh (Paul Rudd), who motivated her to become a better person.

Whereas female-dominated teen films such as John Hughes's *Sixteen Candles* (1984) and *Pretty in Pink* (1986) still focused on boy–girl romances as the narrative focal point, *Clueless* offered more in terms of a female teen lead who was, admittedly, interested in her burgeoning love life, but also friendships, family, cultural pursuits, self-improvement, and personal happiness. While Cher's do-good impulses might be somewhat misplaced in making over Tai (Brittany Murphy), she does subvert the stereotypes associated with a wealthy high school Beverley Hills socialite. She doesn't want to be seen as "a ditz with a credit card." In her quest for self-actualization, Cher doesn't lose her personal style, but she becomes less vapid and more interested in becoming a self-conscious contributing member of society, while still maintaining her femininity and confidence. (Her budding romance with Josh furthers this interest. But it's important to note it does not *spark* her goals of personal betterment, so the film does not solely revolve around the romance between Josh and Cher.)

Future media works such as *Buffy The Vampire Slayer* (WB/UPN, 1997–2003) would go on to challenge *Clueless*'s standard by showing that a pretty, feminine, teenage blonde could be "badass," while the TV series praised the outsiders, nerds, and outcasts over the stylish and beautiful popular kids. *Clueless*'s goal at the time it was released seemed more about showing a confident, empowered, feminine teenage girl as a protagonist, something that was missing from the American zeitgeist. Furthermore, Heckerling does not devalue or condescend to the teenage female experience, and treats her protagonists as young adults rather than children.

When *Splitsider* contributor Alden Ford first watched *Clueless* in 2011, the journalist marveled at the pro-feminine attitude of the film:

> The feminist odds seem starkly against *Clueless*—at first glance there doesn't seem to be much to recommend a movie about a cute, rich blonde that gets her grades, her friends and her man by being cute, rich and blonde. But against those odds, *Clueless* is a film about a girl who takes responsibility for her own actions, takes care of the people she loves, finds what she wants, and makes a series of good choices to get it. What more could you ask of a protagonist of any gender?[3]

Clueless still produces strong feelings for viewers who remember the film in terms of their own youth, as well as viewers who dissect its relevance today. Timothy Corrigan and Patricia White point out that the most notable thing about Heckerling's project is its reception:

> *Clueless* successfully addressed a teenage interpretive community, both in and outside of the United States, which quickly adopted the film's style in fashion and slang. Young women's "use" of the film was generally positive. *Clueless* validated and enabled (coded) communication among young girls, who, far from being treated yet again as know-nothings, were now the only ones fully "clued in."[4]

From an industrial perspective, the film was a monster sleeper hit in the summer of 1995, gaining $56 million at the domestic box office.[5] As Kyra Hunting asserts, the movie made the entertainment industry take notice of the potential financial impact of female audiences and consumers. Hunting cites industry observer Isabel Walcott, who stated that *Clueless* allowed for a new movement of teen films that "opened people's eyes to the fact that if they could get teenage girls to come to a movie, they could make a killing."[6] Hunting proves that *Clueless* precedes films such as *Scream* (Wes Craven, 1996), *Titanic* (James Cameron, 1997), *She's All That* (Robert Iscove, 1999), and *Never Been Kissed* (Raja Gosnell, 1999), as well as TV series like *Buffy The Vampire Slayer*, *Dawson's Creek* (WB, 1998–2003), and *Sex and the City* (HBO, 1998–2004), in this "niche teen programming" trend, not only through its box office success, but through the demand for *Clueless*-related products, including everything from the TV spin-off and book series to the CD-ROM game and Mattel dolls. The film's success thus triggered the film and television industry to further investigate teenage girls as a substantial demographic.

The film's reception and fandom remain remarkable today, twenty years after its original theatrical release. Screenings abound, from the 2014 LA Film Fest to quote-alongs at Austin's Alamo Drafthouse Cinema and London's Prince Charles Cinema. In an e-mail interview, the Prince Charles Cinema's Head Programmer, Paul Vickery, stated that the London landmark has commissioned the screening event "about three or four times over the past few years," yielding an audience over 200 every time, with the first couple of screenings completely sold out at 285 attendees. Audience participation is high, and Vickery states that dressing up and quoting along are encouraged at the event. Vickery asserts that the majority of the crowd, who are 70 percent female, arrive in "their best '90s ensembles,"[7] adding that he believes the film "stands above a *lot* of the films of its kind and time because it had a wider view on things. It's just a great *teen* movie, not a great '90s movie. Which is why it's loved by so many different kinds of people."[8] He also maintains that the age group varies from 18 to 35 years old. This range bridges a generational gap between Generation X and Millennial women; some were Silverstone's contemporaries, growing up in the same era with Cher, while a considerable number of participants were not yet born when the movie was originally released. This splits the audience in two—those who remember coming of age in the mid-'90s and those who do not. However, both groups invest in "re-living" the film. Vickery said one can clearly distinguish between those who grew up with the film and those who are viewing it on the big screen for the first time simply by age. But he claimed that, regardless of this, every fan knew the film equally well.[9]

This ageless appreciation is also evident in online fandom and beyond. An August 2011 YouTube clip posted by *WORN Fashion Journal* entitled "Every Outfit Cher Horowitz Wears in *Clueless* in Under 60 Seconds" yielded over 300,000 hits as of September 2014, and everywhere from popular feminist blog *Jezebel* to *The Huffington Post* quickly shared the video.[10] Brands like LA-based Wildfox Couture pay direct homage to the film's style in new collections and photo shoots. Their Spring 2013 "Clueless Collection" proudly praises the film for changing "girl world forever":

> Everything about the "Clueless" world captured a generation of girls who wanted it all, and who were going to look great getting it. Amy Heckerling created a bold new take on the modern girl amidst the sea of grunge that filled the 90's. Wildfox's Spring 2013 collection pays tribute to Heckerling, capturing the spirit of "Clueless" and their iconic leading ladies. We're the Kids In America![11]

Wildfox designer Kimberly Gordon further touches on how the film impacted on her, and how its fashion functions as a distinct mode of feminine expression:

I have always wanted to express something creatively that is more than just fashion: it's a feeling, a lifestyle, it's about being a girl. It's capturing a moment. I think I felt it first when I was about 12, around when *Clueless* came out, and I was so in love with the characters, I didn't just love the clothes, I loved the girls who wore the clothes—which made me want to wear them even more.[12]

As Gordon implies, the fashions are iconic because of the meaning with which they are imbued. For Gordon at least, and perhaps many other female viewers, that meaning directly corresponds to "being a girl." Wildfox's line, which featured homages to the film's iconic looks as well as shirts emblazoned with sayings such as "I'd Rather Be Shopping," may at some level appeal to a society constructed with sexism, but their irreverent comments also showcase humor, women's buying power, and general ennui. This attitude, also apparent in the film, marks the postfeminist or third-wave era, in which femininity and power are interconnected.

Social media sites such as Pinterest and Tumblr are inundated with fan-created commemorations of *Clueless*; mobile app technologies attempt to mimic the film's computer program that stores personal wardrobes and identifies matching pieces; and link-sharing monolith *BuzzFeed* frequently provides lists that commemorate and deconstruct the cultural facets of *Clueless*. Online tributes in popular press as well as user-generated sites help pinpoint the film's most defining and memorable characteristics for fans.

Online commemorations also help pinpoint that *Clueless* fans pine for the film's fashion and slang above all, while the tenth anniversary *Clueless* DVD (*Whatever!* edition, 2005) shows how Heckerling developed these specific defining characteristics of the film. Special features on the DVD uncover that none of these factors was symptomatic of the '90s. Charlie Lyne, a 23-year-old filmmaker and film journalist who would have been about four years old when *Clueless* premiered, explores how *Clueless* allowed the US film industry to produce a diverse variety of teen films after its surprise success. This increase in more eccentric teen films is evident in his 2014 documentary debut, *Beyond Clueless*, which strings together clips from over 300 movies from the late '90s as the various coming-of-age narrative arcs of the teen film genre unfold. Lyne believes that the success of *Clueless* can be traced to a "sincere interest in really working out who a teenage audience was."[13] Heckerling's conscious choice to place *Clueless* in the present was thus crucial for its connection to teens of the time. Although she essentially created a fantasy world, Heckerling also sat in on Beverly Hills High School classes to gain an understanding of her subjects.[14] After *Clueless*, a boom occurred for the high school film, bringing about individualized and quirky tales, as Lyne states: "The brilliant thing about *Clueless* was that it inspired risk in the teen genre; it gave studios and filmmakers the impetus to take more risks in a genre that was often defined by formulas and traditions."[15]

Though *Clueless* as a coming-of-age comedy points out the ironies inherent among the young, beautiful, and rich, it also does not inherently mock its protagonists' consumption. For instance, while Cher's wardrobe-planning computer program is funny, it's also something many fashionable viewers at the time may have coveted. In recent years, popular press and blogs praise wardrobe organizing mobile applications owing to their likeness to the film's original system, as if *Clueless* fans were waiting for their own since the film's premiere.[16] Cher's insistence on taking photographs of her outfits over simply looking at a mirror nearly foreshadows the surveillance young women hold over their bodies and images through their mobile phones. For Cher, shopping is an outlet for creativity, a reflection of herself, as it is for her peers Dionne (Stacey Dash) and Tai. Cher's focus on fashion—though problematic as regards her cluelessness to class-consciousness—gives her power on the social scene. She also uses language, slang in particular, to negotiate and navigate her way through high society—from arguing for better grades to initiating new members of her tribe. Both offer social mobility that is available to women and minorities.

From Austen's narrative to Cher's iconic namesake, women's storytelling and cultural reverence pervade *Clueless*. In Hollywood, it is still rare for a literary film adaptation, or any film, period or contemporary, to incorporate a female screenwriter, director, and non-sexualized protagonist.[17] Cher's voiceover is established in the opening scenes, and she soon begins her morning routine while scanning her digital wardrobe. Audiences quickly understand that *Clueless* will be seen through her eyes. The '70s are referenced frequently in the film, echoing an era of lifestyle feminism in which popular products were geared toward women consumers with cultural cache and economic means. David Bowie's 1980 anthem "Fashion" plays extradiagetically as Cher explains "but seriously, I actually have a way normal life for a teenage girl." Soon after, she explains in voiceover that she and Dionne are named after "great singers of the past who now do infomercials," that is, Cher and Dionne Warwick. Cher is white and Dionne is black, yet race is otherwise never an issue for the friends as they share a common tie of economic privilege and mutual tastes. Cher later remarks how Dionne and her boyfriend's distinct style and manner of verbally arguing is a result of their multiple viewings of the Ike and Tina Turner biopic, *What's Love Got to Do With It* (Brian Gibson, 1993). Cher returns from school only to ask, "Isn't my house classic? The columns date all the way back to 1972." Defining the '70s as a classical period is funny, but also cues viewers in to what era Heckerling's film will draw from to manufacture "new" trends. Thus, appreciation of the cultural artifacts of the '70s as a "classic" period is established early on.

A newfound '90s appreciation is also applicable to high school students today, as can be seen through the popularity of Nirvana T-shirts coupled with floral prints and Doc Martens boots. For a teenager, and for teens of a digital era—true of Gen-X viewers and certainly of Millennials—time passes extremely quickly. Knowledge of the past is more easily accessible through the Internet. But instead of the surfers, stoners, and Spicolis of *Fast Times*, in *Clueless* we see a feminine and female-dominated culture—shopping, styling, and makeover skills reign. In place of the sexual negotiations girls make in *Fast Times* and other popular teen films, Cher uses her negotiation skills to get better grades in school, while she remains naïve and generally uninterested in how sexuality plays into male–female relationships. She rejects Elton's sexual advances, and is later rejected by a closeted gay friend. And it is important to reiterate the significance of Cher as an active agent, rather than a passive commodity of the male gaze. As Ben Aslinger elaborates on Silverstone's own transition from her sexualized roles in music videos for Aerosmith's "Cryin'" (1993), "Amazing" (1993), and "Crazy" (1994) into a fully-fledged film star: "Heckerling did something interesting by turning the largely silent spectacle into a complicated living, speaking character in a film that challenges rock discourse and its idea about gender."[18]

Male-targeted rock music and its sexualized videos dominated the early '90s. Grunge, a previously alternative rock genre, also infiltrated the mainstream through the success of Seattle natives Pearl Jam and Nirvana. Nirvana front man Kurt Cobain committed suicide just over a year before *Clueless* was released, but Heckerling spent years pitching her film when the malaise of the male-dominated grunge era was still widespread. This era also witnessed a

Figure 10.2 Cher chastises her male classmates' blasé attitude toward fashion.

Figure 10.3 While newcomer Tai (left) serves as the fashion outcast, her style reflects the standard of the time.

decline of female-focused mainstream media, including teen films. Following grunge's decline after Cobain's death, no musical genre or cultural attitude dominated youth culture, leaving an opening for new influences. As Alice Leppert writes, "When Cher and Dionne decide to make Tai over, the film sounds its death knell for grunge."[19] Although this type of makeover is a common trope in teen cinema, such as Ally Sheedy's goth-to-glam transformation in *The Breakfast Club* (John Hughes, 1985) or Rachel Leigh Cook's nerd-turned-homecoming-queen material conversion in *She's All That*, this transition from masculine to feminine is more about a cultural shift toward teenage girls feeling more confident about themselves than just about their validation by the opposite sex. Tai arrived at school as an inarticulate and uncertain tomboy, but her exterior feminine makeover—complete with soft knits, high hemlines, and springy curls—transformed her into a more poised peer of Cher and Dionne. Cher tries to mold Tai into her own disciple, but by the end of the comedy, Tai has defined her own romantic parameters, separate from the strict code of the popular standards, dating a hippie skateboarder (whom Cher initially prohibits). In the meantime, Cher also defies her own rules, falling for someone far from her celebrity crush Christian Slater and far from social acceptability: her ex-stepbrother, Josh. College-aged Josh is initially introduced sporting a flannel shirt and listening to Radiohead, which Cher coins as "complaint rock" that dominated college radio stations of the era.

Despite a predominantly '90s soundtrack largely rooted in new alternative music, four of the fourteen songs in *Clueless* came from the *Fast Times* era, and three of its contemporary anthems are in fact covers of this time. On *Clueless*,

Maureen Turim writes that "compared to earlier teenage high school sagas scored by rock music, this film uses its music less to establish the period and tastes of the teens depicted than to offer other perspectives, some that even comment critically or ironically on their rich enclave."[20] And as Aslinger has noted, the *Clueless* soundtrack is

> timely in in its response to burgeoning indie rock, alternative, and riot grrrl music scenes and modes of production, and it is timeless because it manages to deploy then-contemporary music and cover versions of older songs to represent teen growing pains and identity struggles.[21]

In online tributes, fans commemorate the *Clueless* soundtrack far less than its fashion and slang, yet the film's music also fuses both retro and contemporary styles from different eras. However, Cher and her cohort do not discuss their musical preferences as often or as passionately as they engage with their mutual, perpetual love of fashion, makeovers, and shopping. Therefore, the soundtrack remains on the periphery of the fashion, especially compared to music-centered youth-oriented films of the '90s such as *Empire Records* (Allan Moyle, 1995) and *Wayne's World* (Penelope Spheeris, 1992). While *Clueless* revived the fashion and slang of the '70s into the '90s, *World*'s inclusion of Queen's 1976 "Bohemian Rhapsody" led to the song's rise to #1 and #2 on the UK and US charts respectively.[22]

Instead of primarily being identified through a retro or contemporary rock, pop, or hip-hop subculture, music genre serves as an augmentation or enhancement of each character or social type's fashion style in *Clueless*. In fact, music super-fandom is affiliated with pompous male snobbery through Cher's peer Elton (Jeremy Sisto), whose first line in the film is about his misplaced Cranberries CD. He further name-drops his father's connections in the music industry as a legitimization for his status as an ideal suitor worthy of Cher. While music may not be a primary passion for the film's female leads, it still adds nuance to the principal protagonists. For example, in the film's first scene, The Muffs' "Kids in America" initially introduces Cher and Dionne's popular social group with a glossy, fun, youthful, feminine pop anthem, while Jill Sobule's "Supermodel" follows Tai's makeover. Make no mistake: Sobule's punk track still critiques the vapidity of exuberant femininity and consumerism, yet doesn't serve as a tirade on the women themselves, but instead the culture of female bodies as commodities surrounding it. This song choice also reflects Tai's reluctance to simply mimic her new friends' look, and as the song foreshadows, by the end of the film she establishes her own hybrid style, taking from her past and her peers. Music is again a signifier of a teenager's identity, just as we can tell that the mainstream teen boys are identified with contemporary grunge and alternative rock.

It should come as no surprise, then, that Cher was initially interested in a romantic partner outside these norms. In the DVD special feature "The Class of '95: About Like, Casting and Stuff," the cast and crew discuss how Cher's initial love interest, Christian (Justin Walker), was attractive to her because of his vintage Rat Pack style. This rare refinement was emphasized by his appreciation of retro wear, jazz, classic Hollywood, vintage cars, and 1960s colloquialisms. When Cher is informed he is gay, it emphasizes her virginity and sexual naïvety. The coded talk in which Murray (Donald Faison) informs Cher that Christian is gay operates through that distinct Heckerling mixture of literary and pop culture references, which we will later discuss in detail:

> Murray: Your man Christian is a cake boy!
> Cher and Dionne: A what?
> Murray: He's a disco-dancing, Oscar Wilde-reading, Streisand ticket-
> holding friend of Dorothy, know what I'm saying?
> Cher: Uh-uh, no way, not even!
> Murray: Yes, even! He's gay!
> Dionne: He does like to shop, Cher. And the boy can dress.

Heckerling compresses the signifiers of taste that can define a young gay man into one sentence: disco as a genre; Oscar Wilde as an author; Barbra Streisand as a singer and public persona; and Dorothy (by way of Judy Garland and her status as a gay icon) as the protagonist from *The Wizard of Oz*. Christian functions in contradistinction to his unsophisticated classmates whom Cher chastises in one of her most memorable voiceovers, backed with a 1995 World Party cover of Mott the Hoople's 1972 song written by Bowie, "All The Young Dudes":

> So okay, I don't want to be a traitor to my generation and all, but I don't get how guys dress today. I mean, come on, it looks like they just fell out of bed and put on some baggy pants and take their greasy hair—ew—and cover it up with a backwards cap and like, we're expected to swoon? *I don't think so!*

Yet even the teenagers in this montage are dressed in livelier garb than the typical grunge disciple; perhaps this is a Southern Californian take on the Seattle standard by the film's costume designer/stylist, Mona May. In the DVD special feature "Fashion 101," Heckerling admits that the protagonists' attire was "not really what kids were wearing, it's more hyper style."[23] Throughout *Clueless*, Cher and her fellow fashionistas flaunt the three P's of '70s fashion: polyester, pastels, and platforms. When new girl Tai arrives dressed like her male peers in an oversized black shirt with a troll on it, baggy dark Dickies-style pants, and flannel shirt, she is the anomaly among her class, but true to the era. Any male classmate could also easily wear the same outfit, and it would have been the norm. Teenage girls took on grunge's "alternative" style, as there was no alternative to grunge available.

The film's most ubiquitous ensemble, a near-uniform (both in that it resembles a schoolgirl outfit and in that it cycles through the movie in several variations) is a bright plaid/tartan schoolgirl outfit, consisting of a matching mini-skirt and blazer or cardigan, often with supplemental knee-high socks. We see Cher and Dionne wear their own versions of the look in the protagonists' introductory school scene, and Tai gives her take on the outfit the day after her makeover. The girls thus maintain their own unique flairs within the confines of the uniform. Cher makes fun of Dionne's large Dr. Seuss-like top hat, while Dionne jests that her friend's white furry bag looks like a skinned collie. And while these two maintain a crisp and preppy style, Tai is still looser with her choices, showing she is simultaneously less mature and more approachable. (Likewise, Tai's color palette is darker, maintaining her East Coast roots.)

Further into "Fashion 101," May states that she had no intention of recreating the popular grunge norm, and instead hoped to create a new look inspired by color and femininity, "something fresh and new to emulate."[24] Even the use of the tartan as a pattern and fabric is a female re-appropriation of the popular alternative-rock era's form of plaid and flannel. This "uniform" of Cher and her peers is certainly suggestive of the '60s infantilized "girlish" style; so while the '70s is the root of influence, the overall sartorial attitude of the film is a blend of retro and high fashion design. Even the underground female-dominated riot grrrl movement saw its leaders, such as Kathleen Hanna of Bikini Kill, incorporating the feminine schoolgirl look. So although uniforms do signify conformity, at the time this look conformed to a girlish postfeminist sensibility, and as such, Cher, Dionne, and Tai each tailor the uniform to their individual tastes. Indeed, frequenting vintage shops and incorporating retro wear, mixing high and low designer brands, and generally taking inspiration from eras of the past to create something modern—this still defines today's fashion for young women, with no small thanks to *Clueless*. Cher and Dionne frequent malls in Los Angeles, name-dropping The Galleria and Contempo Casuals in the film, suburban-friendly shopping experiences for teenage girls, while also referencing high-end brands like Fred Segal and Alaïa.

Just as Aslinger describes the careful collection of the *Clueless* soundtrack as both timely and timeless, the film's wardrobe choices adhere to the same mind-set. Heckerling commissioned May to create a bright and hyper feminine style. The stylist, who had an established fashion career, said she consciously transferred runway models' looks to more accessible teenage fashion.

In an interview celebrating the eighteenth anniversary of *Clueless*, May addresses her choices as being based on picking trends that would last beyond the era: "We wanted to make it timeless, and it really stood the test of time. I can watch *Clueless* now and there's still stuff we can wear."[25] Because current trends had little to offer and could become easily dated in retrospect, May turned to history:

> I like to use references from the past, iconic looks like Sophia Loren sexiness and 1960s go-go boots, which are always good no matter what era you put them in. Mini-skirts from the '70s, plaids, the Bonnie and Clyde look with little sweaters, and the 1960s sweater sets that we put Cher in. These timeless, iconic pieces that live forever, that we see our mother[s] wear and then we wear, can be reinterpreted over and over. It's using the past in the best way possible.[26]

In her book *Neo-Feminist Cinema: Girly Films, Chick Flicks and Consumer Culture*, Hilary Radner claims that "*Legally Blonde* [Robert Luketic, 2001] continues a trend established with *Clueless* in which fashion is seen to have an intrinsic interest for the viewer, independently of the manner in which it serves to illuminate and illustrate the character."[27] For Radner, both of these films represent how feminist values of independence and education are popularized and de-politicized in female-centered mainstream Hollywood films, ultimately retaining a postfeminist (or third-wave feminist) attitude, as Cher and Elle (Reese Witherspoon in *Legally Blonde*) preserve their feminine charm and fashion-forward sensibility while achieving their inner goals. Both films fall under what Radner calls neo-feminist cinema, heeding teen coming-of-age narrative tropes as well as classical Hollywood and female empowerment plots. These films challenge viewers' perceptions of young, feminine, and stylish women, suggesting that beauty and intelligence are not mutually exclusive. *Clueless* in many ways accomplished the same thing for the female teen film that *Sex and the City* achieved for female-dominated television shows, formulating a style that Emily Nussbaum used to describe *SATC* in contrast to male-dominated TV programming like *The Sopranos* [HBO, 1999–2007]: "high-feminine instead of fetishistically masculine, glittery rather than gritty, and daring in its conception of character."[28]

Young female audiences are receptive to the style-as-power threads running through *Clueless*. In the following section, we will explore the wide-reaching impact of that reception. Certainly, the most popular, successful, and wide-reaching demonstration of *Clueless* style in recent years is 24-year-old Australian rapper Iggy Azalea's 2014 music video for "Fancy." In less than four minutes, the video recreates a majority of the film's most iconic outfits and scenes. By September 2014, the official YouTube video views stood at a rounded 257 million hits. Azalea's personal stylist and the stylist for the video, Alejandra Hernandez, detailed the collaborative process with Azalea and her own adoration of the film's fashion.[29] As a testament to the pervasiveness of the film's hold on contemporary fashion, Hernandez was able to find a version of every outfit but one, and the video used approximately 275 individual ensembles. Azalea requested that Cher's black-and-yellow plaid schoolgirl outfit be an exact replica, because it was the most iconic, and this was the only ensemble that was made anew, not gathered from vintage collections. Strangely, the most difficult item to find was a yellow sweater vest to accompany the outfit. Hernandez stated that her cousin Franc Fernandez (best-known for making Lady Gaga's infamous "meat dress") created the replica of Dionne's white plastic Dr. Seuss-like top hat with an embellished black bow, as it was the only other difficult item to procure.[30]

Hernandez stated that May always used one clothing item that teenagers could easily find at most clothing stores in order to promote accessibility for young viewers, alongside expensive designer and vintage or retro clothes. Hernandez uses the same approach in all of her styling projects, with Azalea and in the "Fancy" video. Alongside the abundance of vintage wear, they also collaborated with Adidas, Converse All Stars, Doc Martens, and Birkenstocks for the video, all brands popular in the '90s that are witnessing a fierce resurgence today. In 2012, for example, online retailer ASOS reported that its Doc Martens sales jumped more than 200 percent from the previous year.[31] By the summer of 2014, Birkenstocks sales rose 30 percent within a year, and celebrities such as Mary Kate Olsen and Julianne Moore were seen sporting the sandals.[32] The "Fancy" video also united the grunge and feminine aesthetics, rather than bifurcating the two as the film did, illustrating how many of today's teens fuse the '90s styles, especially through the multitude of extras in the video's party sequence. This portrayal accurately depicts today's fashion sense and appropriation of past cultures and aesthetics alongside one another. Post-*Clueless* sensibility evokes a teenager wearing a girly and form-fitting floral dress alongside a pair of bulky, masculine Doc Martens boots. For Heckerling, this is once again challenging understandings of high and low culture and style.

Azalea and Hernandez's collaboration on the "Fancy" video brought together both Azalea and *Clueless* fans. Azalea, of course, didn't merely give a nod to a favorite film or cast of characters, but also banked on gaining notoriety and capitalizing on a young, strong female audience loyal to *Clueless*. Jason Lipshutz of *Billboard* magazine asserts that Azalea's "Instant Classic Music Video" was a key ingredient of the rise of "Fancy" as a number one summer hit, rhetorically asking readers, "Really, who doesn't have a soft spot for *Clueless*?"[33] Upon the video's premiere, Jordan Valinsky of the current and political affairs site *The Week* praised the video's attention to detail:

Children of the '90s, get ready for a flashback: Australian rapper Iggy Azalea and British singer Charli XCX just dropped the music video for "Fancy," and it's an amazing #tbt tribute to 1995 rom-com masterpiece *Clueless*. Shot at the same high school the movie was filmed at, Azalea plays a badass version of Cher Horowitz, decked out in a spot-on version of Horowitz's then-stylish boxy blazer and platform shoes. There's even a shout out to Dionne's near car crash at the 1:20 mark. This will just have to hold us over until there's another rerun on Comedy Central.[34]

In a 2014 interview, Heckerling applauded Azalea's high-budget and spot-on effort, claiming, "It looked like they had more money for the video than I had for the movie," and going on to say she was "extremely flattered" and "thought she [Azalea] was amazing."[35] The brief interview also led Heckerling to discuss her early stages of the *Clueless* Broadway musical, adding that pop star Katy Perry expressed interest, and that maybe even Azalea herself can contribute.[36]

The film's slang is the only facet as influential as the fashion, and it maintains a similar hold on audiences. *Clueless* exported the Valley Girl-style speech Californians are now (in)famous for, and as linguist Carmen Fought explains, the language actually works as a character within the film.[37] Yet, while some of the language is reminiscent of '70s and/or west coast slang, much of it is completely fabricated by Heckerling, not a totally realistic representation of '90s culture. While this layering of new, old, real, and fake may

Figure 10.4 "Oh, as *if!*"

be typical of postmodern pastiche, it is worth noting that the slang Heckerling invented caught on among viewers and infiltrated everyday language. In *Slang: The Topical Dictionary of Americanisms*, Paul Dickson writes that the film was "Hollywood's attempt to package teen slang." He highlights the power of *Clueless*, stating that it "brought an odd new syntax in which 'all' and 'like' became the salt and pepper of a new dialect."[38] This packaging of slang extended to full-on fabrication. For instance, using "Betties" to describe beautiful women drew from contemporary slang, more specifically from *The Flintstones* (ABC, 1960–6). However, this existing (if outdated) slang was intertwined with Heckerling's own choice language, such as "Baldwin" to describe a handsome man, inspired by the famous Hollywood brothers, as established in the DVD special feature "Creative Writing" (2005).[39] Because it fits in believably with the existent slang, this term seamlessly enters the *Clueless* lexicon the director creates, and the pastiche culture, including its lingua franca, is all the more convincing because of its reliance on old terms and new. Though the film presumably was to reflect '90s culture back at audiences, the fun-house mirror added layers of meaning to the language.

So why does Heckerling willfully attempt to invent a language, and why does it catch on like the wildfire that won't be put out? And regardless, why have viewers adopted a language most know didn't predate the film? One obvious answer is that language creation is fun. As previously mentioned, when writing and in pre-production, Heckerling sat in on classes at Beverly Hills High, and got a pulse on the then-contemporary slang, styles, and attitudes of affluent LA teens. She then combined her encyclopedic pop culture knowledge with the mannerisms of present-day teens, including Silverstone's. Codifying a teen language becomes an added obstruction or challenge for the writer: how far will audiences extend their willing disbelief for a comedy? But avoidance of difficult issues isn't Heckerling's style. (She doesn't shy away from more serious social issues that teens confront in *Fast Times*.) Rather, it seems that Cher and her friends' use of slang legitimates teenage speech patterns and vernacular. Similar to the way hippie slang set the counterculture apart from the "squares" of the '60s, the coded speech of teens confounds the grown-ups that surround them. But piecemeal, that language is then taken up by the prevailing pop culture. Likelier, this *Emma* adaptation adopts the many ideas of makeover from the original text, even going so far as to "remake the past . . . in the new fashions, styles, and desires of the present."[40]

It isn't incidental that the film includes this invented language, nor is it hidden. In fact, in marketing the movie, a booklet was released entitled *How to Speak Cluelessly*, which was a short dictionary to define the terms of the film.[41] This guide not only emphasizes the artifice of film as a medium and the language the script promotes, but also acts as a decoder ring for teenagers themselves. This kind of strategizing anticipates the film as a world-building cultural phenomenon, or at least a cult classic, that would penetrate American diction, without seeming too cheesy to be adopted. It plays up the falsity and campiness of such an endeavor, while offering a guidebook for life imitating art supposedly imitating life. (Of course, teens weren't the only ones desirous of being hip to the scene. Scripps-Howard News Service even ran a short article entitled "Don't Go Postal: Here's a Guide to *Clueless* Speak," directed at those over the age of eighteen who might go see the movie.[42]) This reveals that *Clueless* was fun enough for girl viewers, and clever enough for adult audiences. But the intrigue of so-called *Clueless* speak did thoroughly capture teenage interests, according to writers at *The Dissolve*, a film website that is a branch of Pitchfork Media, a noted hub for music aficionados. In a 2014 dissection of the film (which largely focuses on a love of the movie's language and slang), Genevieve Koski remembers:

> When the film first came out, people seemed to fixate on *Clueless'* semi-invented slang—your "Whatevers" and "As ifs!"—to the extent that I remember a "Clueless Glossary" poster for sale at my local Sam Goody, with bubble-letter, candy-colored definitions of terms like "Monet" and "Surfing the crimson wave" . . . The same way Tai is in awe of Cher, my peers and I were similarly dazzled by this funny, quirkily eloquent girl. Even after we stole a couple of *Clueless'* more famous expressions, we never really talked like its characters. But we absolutely *wished* we did.[43]

Like Tai, *Clueless* aficionados were transformed by Cher. Fan appreciation for and interest in the movie's slang didn't end with the film's marketing push. In 2013, *The Daily Beast* published its "*Clueless* Glossary: Buggin', Cake Boy, and More '90s Slang from the Film."[44]

Yet, the very use of the lingo is a form of exclusivity. When Cher, the queen of vernacular, snags flannel-clad Josh, the intellectual must convert, if half-heartedly, to slang. In the film's final scene, he interjects, "I'm buggin' myself," mixing his girlfriend's casual colloquialisms with his college-bound proclivity toward proper grammar. Once initiated into this new world of language, characters become savvier and, at the same time, appear more intelligent. As Cher and Dionne's "project," Tai is a misfit until she is transformed physically through a fashion-and-cosmetics makeover, and also becomes fluent in the culture, which very much includes the language. All the while, our judgment of the newcomer through Cher's perspective allows us to be put on Cher's level of power. Tai even moves from being impressed with Cher's social group ("You guys talk like grown-ups") to turning the language against Cher to one-up her, asking if Cher thinks she's a "mentally-challenged airhead" before calling her a "virgin who can't drive" and saying she's "Audi."[45] Tai has moved to the upper echelons of high school society, or at least uses language to convince her former superior of her newfound status. When the student has become the master, Heckerling employs language—not only a trendy wardrobe—to show it.

This Heckerling brand of cultural understanding and social adeptness serves as an indicator of a "new" kind of intelligence. Cher shows her own cleverness through her understanding of language, particularly when she corrects the date of stepbrother-turned-love-interest Josh about who gives a speech in *Hamlet* (Franco Zeffirelli, 1990). She remembers the language because she's seen the Mel Gibson version. The pseudo-intellectual college-aged woman represents "old" intelligence as a prematurely unhappy academic. She insists she remembers the actual play, and conspicuously uses "proper" English; however, she is proven to be full of hot air, a know-nothing. In the movie, slang such as *whatevers* and *as ifs* flavor discussions ranging from pop philosophy to pop culture. The Valley Girl-isms are put on a par with self-revelation. For instance, in her epiphanic monologue toward the end of the film, Cher uses "totally" and "wigging out" while realizing her deep feelings for Josh. Cher may use language stereotyped as less intelligent, but she is able to discuss literature and recognize existentialism in *The Ren and Stimpy Show* (Nickelodeon, 1991–6). This subverts stereotypes about young women and language. The so-called upward lilt that is much maligned on the Internet today could carry information just as significant as an academic text or a more authoritative, stilted voice. In fact, the young characters who don't use the same slang, such as pre-makeover Tai, are shown to be less intelligent and less self-aware than those that do.

In capturing a femme-centric perspective, *Clueless* revealed one of the culturally recognized powers of teenage girls and young women: social fluency. The movie itself serves as spoof and guide of social fluency. By learning the lingo and wearing the right shoes, knowing when it's OK "to spark up" but not to sit on the lawn, the movie delivers a popularity primer. While Cher's change of heart—her realization that this focus on status is "clueless"—undercuts this somewhat, the film still illustrates the importance of Cher's skillset, and the marketing for the film served as a how-to guide on coolness, especially the pamphlets and posters that worked as slang decoders. As Willis implies, this traditionally feminine role, as consumer, as socialite, isn't totally vapid: it's one of the ways a woman can assert her power. The script's dialogue and vocabulary, real and coined, were so effective that some have been sewn into everyday conversation. Some viewers emulated the styles the movie showed, and adopted the Valley Girl-isms. The most convincing example may be the use of full lines of dialogue—not just select words—to respond to situations in real life. Now possessing cult resonance, the mashed-up language of *Clueless* crosses generational bounds that continue to pervade pop culture. Anecdotally, "That's way harsh, Tai," serves as a quick, humorous response to severe commentary.

WHATEVER.

Figure 10.5 "Whatever."

Heckerling's manufactured slang and styles resonated with female audiences. Through repeat viewings, quoting the movie in everyday life, and even copying the costumes, it may be that some viewers don't simply yearn for high school glory days or the fun of a favorite comedy, but for a woman-controlled culture. In fact, even men in the film must submit to women as rulers of language. When Murray calls Dionne "woman," she says, "Murray, I have asked you repeatedly not to call me woman." He excuses himself, then must explain: "Okay, but street slang is an increasingly valid form of expression. Most of the feminine pronouns do have mocking, but not necessarily misogynistic undertones." This interplay works triple-time: it holds up the woman as the leader in the relationship and in cultural policing, while nixing anti-woman sentiment; it underscores the importance of pop culture and slang in the film; and it displays wit as a social requirement. Arguably, for the 97-minute run time, men in the audience—not just male characters in the film—must also submit to, or at least must tolerate, women's rule of language and cultural policing, too. In *Clueless*, Heckerling's inventive language and dress code make the world run topsy-turvy, with young women at its helm. There, being conspicuously quick and charming are just as important as nabbing the best designer dress.

The draw of the lingo is the power it gives its speaker. This exclusivity, the secret language of the beautiful, of the popular, of the young, might be what viewers find themselves yearning for, even though the language isn't totally historically accurate regarding pre-1995 American life. While it's not by any means a "nostalgia film," as a cult classic it has in some ways come to represent the "Girl Power"[46] movement of the '90s.

Yet, *Clueless*'s representation of female empowerment is not problem-free. While the language is classed through references to designer brands and expensive locales, arguably anyone can learn to use slang. But fashion is a different story. Though grunge culture and the pop scene following Cobain's death may have left a vacuum, virtually all American teenagers could afford ripped flannel shirts and flip their caps backwards. The dandy fashions Cher requires of herself, her friends, and her suitors require serious cash.

However, in *Clueless*, class supersedes other forms of heterogeneity. Though the movie features women as the key players and a relatively ethnically diverse cast, there is little, if any, class difference. Cher, her posse, and their families are obviously moneyed, and Cher drives a new Jeep and resides in a palatial mansion. If clothes are markers, Tai may be the one female representative of the middle-earners in the film,[47] but Cher, in her condescending act of charity, can help Tai rise in social rank if she gives her the proper tools: hair dye, a belly shirt, lingo, and a seat at the right lunch table. *Clueless* may showcase '90s aesthetics and the postmodern quality of drawing on many twentieth-century eras, but it also may appeal to some viewers' desire for less complicated socio-economic hierarchies, in which anyone can move up or down the social ladder by playing by the rules. Language may be used for verbal sparring within the film, most notably between Cher and Josh, but even gender-based epithets, such as when Elton calls Cher a "bitch," are deflected. Race, class, and gender boundaries are easily transcended in Cher Horowitz's world, and they are rarely addressed within the film as an issue.

Heckerling establishes a rare privileging of the female teenage narrative: Cher is a precocious virgin who has no interest in finding a mate, but is involved in improving her own self-worth, scheming to improve her grades, having a relationship with her father, and connecting to her female friends. She maintains her beauty and fashion sense while transforming into a do-gooder, and falls in love with her goofy, intellectual stepbrother instead of finding the most generically ideal partner. While there is a narrative romantic closure for Cher, she pokes fun at the idea of her marriage in the film's final scene. The director created a vibrant space for female audiences to emulate in their everyday lives, establishing an empowering female-focused landscape that changed the way they could perceive high school and its onscreen potential. Heckerling's adaptation reached cult status through her innovative use and distinctive materialization of youthful fashion and language. She provided an unprecedented attentiveness to the state of the experience of female American teenagers, acknowledging that they are closer to adulthood than childhood at such a critical transitional stage.

NOTES

The authors would like to thank Paul Vickery, Charlie Lyne, and Alejandra Hernandez for their interviews in this chapter.

1 Marielle Bingham, "'Clueless' fashion: every outfit in just 60 seconds (VIDEO)," *The Huffington Post*, 24 August 2011, available at <http://www.huffingtonpost. com/2011/08/24/clueless-outfits-video_n_935610.html> (last accessed 4 November 2014); Whitney Jefferson, "Every single outfit worn by Cher in *Clueless*, in under 60 seconds," *Jezebel*, 25 August 2011, available at <http://jezebel.com/5834382/every-single-outfit-worn-by-cher-in-clueless-in-under-60-seconds> (last accessed 4 November 2014); Kimberley Gordon, "The kids in America, SS 13 Wildfox," *I Love Wildfox*, 2 January 2013, available at <http://ilovewildfox.com/iloveyouwildfox/2013/1/2/the-kids-in-america-ss-13-wildfox.html> (last accessed 3 November 2014).

2 Ellen Willis, "Women and the myth of consumerism," in Nona Willis Aronowitz (ed.), *The Essential Ellen Willis* (Minneapolis, MN: University of Minnesota Press, 2014), p. 41. Originally published in *Ramparts*, 1970.

3 Alden Ford, "Watching *Clueless* for the first time," *Splitsider*, 26 January 2011. Available at <http://splitsider.com/2011/01/watching-clueless-for-the-first-time/> (last accessed 17 November 2014).

4 Timothy Corrigan and Patricia White, *The Film Experience: An Introduction* (New York: Bedford/St. Martin's Press, 2008), p. 505.

5 *Clueless*, IMDB.com: <http://www.imdb.com/title/tt0112697/?ref_=nv_sr_1> (last accessed 17 November 2014).

6 Kyra Hunting, "Furiously franchised: *Clueless*, convergence culture, and the female-focused franchise," *Cinema Journal*, 53: 3 (2014), p. 145.

7 Stefania Marghitu, interview with Paul Vickery, by e-mail; 12 March 2014.

8 Ibid.

9 Ibid.

10 Bingham; Jefferson.

11 Kimberly Gordon, "The kids in America, SS 13 Wildfox," *I Love Wildfox*, 2 January 2013. Available at http://ilovewildfox.com/iloveyouwildfox/2013/1/2/the-kids-in-america-ss-13-wildfox.html (last accessed 20 August 2015).

12 Ibid.

13 Stefania Marghitu, telephone interview with Charlie Lyne, 12 September 2014.

14 Amy Heckerling, "Creative Writing" feature, *Clueless* DVD, *Whatever! Edition*, Paramount Video, 2005.

15 Marghitu, Lyne interview.

16 Erica Swallow, "The 'Clueless' closet is real, and you can own it," *Mashable*, 4 March 2013, available at <http://mashable.com/2013/03/04/clueless-closet-fashion/?geo=AU> (last accessed 12 January 2014); *Dazed Digital*, "Cher's virtual wardrobe from *Clueless* is now a reality," *Dazed Digital*, 2 July 2014, available at <http://www.dazeddigital.com/fashion/article/20643/1/chers-virtual-wardrobe-from-clueless-is-now-a-reality> (last accessed 12 January 2015).

17 Stacy L. Smith, Marc Choueiti, and Katherine Pieper with assistance from Yu-Ting Liu and Christine Song Media, "An investigation of female characters in popular films across 11 countries," Geena Davis Institute on Gender and Media, Diversity, & Social Change Initiative USC Annenberg, 2014. Available at <http://seejane.org/wp-content/uploads/gender-bias-without-borders-executive-summary.pdf> (last accessed 14 February 2015).

18 Ben Aslinger, "Clueless about listening formations?," *Cinema Journal* 53: 3 (2014), p. 128.

19 Alice Leppert, "Can I please give you some advice? *Clueless* and the teen makeover," *Cinema Journal* 53: 3 (2014), p. 132.
20 Maureen Turim, "Popular culture and the comedy of manners: *Clueless* and fashion clues," in Suzanne R. Pucci and James Thompson (eds.), *Jane Austen and Co.: Remaking the Past in Contemporary Culture* (New York: State University of New York Press, 2003), p. 31.
21 Aslinger, pp. 127–8.
22 Queen biography, *Billboard*. Available at <http://www.billboard.com/artist/277241/queen/biography> (last accessed 13 February, 2015).
23 Amy Heckerling, "Fashion 101" feature, 00:25–00:32; *Clueless* DVD, *Whatever! Edition*.
24 Mona May, "Fashion 101" feature, 00:35–00:41; *Clueless* DVD, *Whatever! Edition*.
25 Andi Teran, "*Clueless* turns 18 tomorrow! We interviewed costume designer Mona May," *MTV Style*, 18 July 2013. Available at <http://style.mtv.com/2013/07/18/clueless-mona-may-interview/> (last accessed 17 November 2014).
26 Ibid.
27 Hilary Radner, *Neo-Feminist Cinema: Girly Films, Chick Flicks and Consumer Culture* (New York and London: Routledge, 2011), p. 76.
28 Emily Nussbaum, "Difficult women: how *Sex and the City* lost its good name," *New Yorker*, 29 July 2013. Available at <http://www.newyorker.com/magazine/2013/07/29/difficult-women> (last accessed 17 November 2014).
29 Stefania Marghitu, interview with Alejandra Hernandez; Los Angeles, CA, 30 August 2014.
30 Ibid.
31 Bibby Sowray, "Sales of Dr. Martens soar," *The Telegraph*, 20 July 2012. Available at <http://fashion.telegraph.co.uk/article/TMG9414487/Sales-of-Dr.-Martens-soar.html> (last accessed 12 December 2014).
32 Kurt Soller, "Birkenstocks are still ugly—but at least now they're cool," *Businessweek*, 26 June 2014. Available at <http://www.businessweek.com/articles/2014-06-26/birkenstocks-are-fashionable-as-sales-rise-celebrities-wear-them> (last accessed 4 November 2014).
33 Jason Lipshutz, "Iggy Azalea's 'Fancy': 10 key ingredients to a no. 1 summer smash," *Billboard*, 29 May 2014. Available at <http://www.billboard.com/articles/columns/pop-shop/6099425/iggy-azalea-fancy-song-of-summer-10-reasons-charli-xcx-hot-100> (last accessed 5 November 2014).
34 Jordan Valinsky, "Iggy Azalea just made the most amazing music video homage to *Clueless*," *The Week*, 4 March 2014. Available at <http://theweek.com/speedreads/index/257367/speedreads-iggy-azalea-just-made-the-most-amazing-music-video-homage-to-clueless> (last accessed 4 November 2014).
35 Adrienne Gaffney, "Katy Perry is interested in the *Clueless* musical," *New York* magazine *Vulture* blog, 11 July 2014. Available at <http://www.vulture.com/2014/07/amy-heckerling-loved-iggys-clueless-video.html> (last accessed 4 November 2014).
36 Ibid.
37 Fought quoted in Nathan Bierma, "It's been like, 10 whole years since *Clueless* helped spread Valley slang," *Chicago Tribune*, 20 July 2005. Available at <http://articles.chicagotribune.com/2005-07-20/features/0507190293_1_clueless-slang-amy-heckerling> (last accessed 4 November 2014).
38 Paul Dickson, *Slang: The Topical Dictionary of Americanisms* (New York: Walker Publishing, 2006), pp. 3–4.

39 Amy Heckerling, "Creative writing" feature, *Clueless* DVD, *Whatever! Edition*.

40 Suzanne R. Pucci and James Thompson, "Introduction: the Jane Austen phenomenon: remaking the past at the millennium," in Pucci and Thompson, p. x.

41 IMDB *Clueless* entry, under "Trivia". Available at <http://www.imdb.com/title/tt0112697/trivia> (last accessed 4 November 2014).

42 Scripps Howard News Service, "Don't go postal: here's a guide to "Clueless" speak," *Chicago Tribune*, 26 July 1995. Available at <http://articles.chicagotribune.com/1995-07-26/news/9507260241_1_clueless-audi-majorly> (last accessed 4 November 2014).

43 Genevieve Koski, Noel Murray, Nathan Rabin, Tasha Robinson, Matt Singer, and Scott Tobias, "1990s pop culture and teen slang, as seen through *Clueless* eyes," *The Dissolve*, 9 April 2014. Available at <https://thedissolve.com/features/movie-of-the-week/502-1990s-pop-culture-and-teen-slang-as-seen-through-c/> (last accessed 19 January 2015).

44 Anna Klassen, "'Clueless' Glossary: buggin', cake boy, & more '90s slang from the film," *The Daily Beast*, 19 July 2013. Available at <http://www.thedailybeast.com/articles/2013/07/19/clueless-glossary-buggin-cake-boy-more-90-s-slang-from-the-film.html> (last accessed 19 January 2015).

45 Though some would maintain the line is "outtie," simply a means of saying goodbye or "I'm out," we would assert that because it's a homophone of luxury car-brand Audi and because it is in a film with a significant focus on social mores, it is a substantially classed dismissal. Supporting this, the closed captioning on the DVD also lists the line as "Audi," not "outtie."

46 "Girl Power," a sort of pop feminism that emphasized a girly aesthetic and gender equality, is an idea that the Spice Girls, a female British power-pop group, brought to mainstream consumers, and was popularized in the 1990s For more, see McDermott, Maeve, "The Girl Power Philosophy of the Spice Girls," *Nat Geo TV Blogs*, 20 June 2014. Available at <http://tvblogs.nationalgeographic.com/2014/06/20/the-girl-power-philosophy-of-the-spice-girls/> (last accessed 30 January 2015).

47 Travis and his friends could potentially serve as a male middle-class counterpart; however, the correlation between savvy or expensive clothes and status is less remarkable for men in the movie. Cher's famous monologue about the popular male fashions of "baggy pants," "greasy hair," and "backwards cap[s]" underlines this point.

CHAPTER 11

Clueless Times at the Ferris Bueller Club: A Critical Analysis of the Directorial Works of Amy Heckerling and John Hughes

Kimberly M. Miller

Amy Heckerling perfected a style of filmmaking that influenced both the teen and the family film genres. Films like *Fast Times at Ridgemont High* (1982), *Clueless* (1995), and the first two *Look Who's Talking* films (1989–90) revealed Heckerling to be a versatile filmmaker who is willing to take risks. Heckerling pushed the boundaries of humor into an area of low comedy that had not been used before by any mainstream director. Through her unique style, Amy Heckerling set the pace for teen films and paved the way for modern examples like *She's All That* (Robert Iscove, 1999) and *Mean Girls* (Mark Waters, 2004), which include both overt and subtle homages to Heckerling's work in the form of, among other things, makeover sequences and humorous, yet realistic, teenaged drama.

Heckerling's work parallels and intersects the work of likeminded teen and family director John Hughes, who was the creative force behind such films as *Sixteen Candles* (1984), *Ferris Bueller's Day Off* (1986), and the *Home Alone* films (1990–2002). Like Heckerling, Hughes did much to establish and impact on the teen and family genres, though his style is all his own. For instance, Hughes's musical tastes and ability to make characters who would typically be outcasts into heroes allowed his films to secure their own place in film history.[1]

This analysis argues that Amy Heckerling and John Hughes are unique directors whose individual works (and one collaboration) have defined and furthered the teen and family film genres. Although some similar characteristics of Hughes's and Heckerling's works are noted, there are numerous other ways in which each director is distinct. Because each director has created films that can be specifically tied to later films that fit in the same genres, it is possible to state that each could be called an "auteur." Andrew Sarris states that a seminal aspect of auteur theory is that of a "distinguishable personality of the director as a criterion of value. Over a group of films, a director must exhibit certain recurrent characteristics of style, which serve as his signature."[2] I argue that this criterion applies to both Heckerling and Hughes in their defined bodies of work in the teen and family film genres.

Lesley Speed notes that "*Clueless* has resulted in [Heckerling] being positioned as a teen film auteur, thus suggesting a shift in the generic hierarchy toward the admission of forms that had been perceived to lack cultural value."[3] Perhaps it is the number of formulaic teen films that were made after the release of Heckerling's *Fast Times* that give validity to this statement—or it could be that critics ignored and dismissed such films quickly. Whatever the reason, a "lack of cultural value" was not enough to end the development and continuation of the teen genre. Further, while Speed's comment rings true, as evidenced by the many teen films that were made *after* the release of *Clueless* (among them *Can't Hardly Wait* [Harry Elfont and Deborah Kaplan, 1998], *Varsity Blues* [Brian Robbins, 1999], and *Mean Girls*), this point ignores the dramatic impact of Heckerling's *Fast Times*, which predates Hughes's *Sixteen Candles* and *Ferris Bueller's Day Off* as well as the numerous other teen films released in the 1980s, including *Better Off Dead* (Savage Steve Holland, 1985), *Girls Just Want to Have Fun* (Alan Metter, 1985), and *Can't Buy Me Love* (Steve Rash, 1987), among others.

John Hughes, on the other hand, can be regarded as an auteur most recognizably through his ability to utilize many "stock teen characters: the jocks, geeks, alternative misfits, popular cheerleader/captain-of-the-football-team types, snobby rich kids and rough 'delinquents.'"[4] This method of characterization is noted in many of Hughes's teen films, including *Sixteen Candles* and *The Breakfast Club* (1985). But this is not the extent of his contribution to the film industry. Hughes's creation of the "Brat Pack"—a key troupe of young actors he molded into stars—is an achievement that helped establish him as a director. Additionally, Hughes's ability to create a new kind of family film—one where the kids take center stage and the adults are merely pawns for them—solidified his auteur status.

This chapter will provide an analysis of the films of Amy Heckerling and John Hughes from the 1980s and 1990s, focusing most specifically on each director's personal, technical, and narrative style. Speed states that Heckerling uses "comedy to address themes such as gender difference, adolescent sexuality and parenthood" while, according to Rebekah Brammer, Hughes's films "explore a number of themes relevant to teenagers, including alienation and peer group identification, bullying, the role of parents and other authority figures, and romance."[5] These directors impacted on genres that are both appreciated and popular today, and as such are worthy of critical examination.

THE WEIRD SCIENCE OF THE HECKERLING AND HUGHES TEEN FILMS

The films of Hughes and Heckerling have many overlapping characteristics, some of which include a narrative about youthful characters, parents (and other "authority figures") who are out of touch, and a soundtrack of popular music. But an analysis focusing on these aspects would ignore the complexities that can arise when one factors in audience perceptions, narrative structures, and of course the interests of the film industry overall.

Tom Doherty states that "despite the periodicity of teen-oriented cinema (in pinpointing the year of release, the slang, fashion, and rock soundtrack are more accurate than carbon dating), the best of that generation [the late 1970s/early 1980s] has aged well."[6] Doherty's statement indicates that insightful, well-made teen films—whether early in this era or made later with the benefit of adhering to a more standard teen film formula—can find a place in film history that impacts not only on the generation viewing the film for the first time but on the generations that follow too. Many of Hughes's and Heckerling's teen films address issues such as relationships (romantic and social), as well as sexuality and independence—all of which continue to be relevant to modern teen audiences, and as such are viewed by new fans years after their original release. For instance, "Save Ferris" shirts still appear in high school hallways across the country, and "As if!" can be heard peppering teen conversations today. Clearly, modern teens still find these films to be relevant.

Alissa Quart argues that "teen films are a genre that now offers critics one of the best opportunities to straddle the low culture–high culture divide."[7] And yet most critics seem to fall on the "low culture" side of the divide. As Jeanette Sloniowski notes, "The quality [of discussions/criticisms of teen films] is rather low," and critics have "little regard for the genre."[8] While it may be easy to dismiss teen films as merely entertainment, this foolish, surface-oriented analysis fails to consider the heart of such films, and even Sloniowski is quick to acknowledge this point. She argues that, "rather amusingly, and despite critical disdain, teen films have been among the highest-grossing of films."[9] A fine example can be found in the response to the film *Ferris Bueller's Day Off*, which received criticism for being too similar to *Risky Business* (Paul Brickman, 1983), as well as "lacking in irony,"[10] and yet *Ferris* has become ingrained in the popular culture—even being ranked number ten on *Entertainment Weekly*'s "Fifty Best High School Movies" list (2012),[11] in addition to being quoted by teens who see Ferris as a role model of "cool" despite the nearly thirty years that have passed since he took his day off.

Brammer noticed that "teen films often highlight the struggle between different character "types" and the alienation suffered both within and outside peer groups."[12] In *Pretty in Pink* (1986, written by Hughes, directed by Howard Deutch), the trouble is both economic and social between Andie (Molly Ringwald) and her love interest, Blane (Andrew McCarthy), whose wealth and popularity provide the perfect character conflict with ostracized, working-class Andie. Andie is embarrassed of her home—telling Blane to drop her off elsewhere, while he in turn must deal with friends like Steff (James Spader) who consider Andie useless for anything beyond a quick good time. Other teen films feature similar social and economic dynamics, including *Clueless* and *Sixteen Candles*. Such onscreen alienation may be a reflection of the real-life conflicts some teens face.

Quart states that "Teen blockbusters—among them *Clueless*, *Bring It On* (Peyton Reed, 2000), *She's All That*, *Legally Blonde* (Robert Luketic, 2001), and *Varsity Blues*—had become the stories of insiders: sports stars, beauties, rich kids, and cheerleaders," which is not to say that those outside the "in crowd" don't get their time onscreen as well.[13] Hughes clearly distinguishes different kinds of stock characters in his films, as evidenced in *Ferris Bueller's Day Off*, when the school secretary, Grace (Edie McClurg), states that "The sportos, the motorheads, geeks, sluts, bloods, wastoids, dweebies, dickheads" (all of whom are represented throughout the film) adore Ferris.

Teen films may present teenagers as stereotypes, but focusing on this tactic would be unfortunately shortsighted. For example, Quart says of Hughes's *The Breakfast Club*:

> Sure it's overacted and broad, like a summer-stock theater production. But it also has the ring of a diary entry, of what life is really like when our parents or teachers leave the room. Raging against high school cliques and hierarchies, it puts forth an appealingly sappy proposition: that all strata of kids should unite against two common enemies, their parents and a future of soullessness.[14]

While it can be accurate to stereotype teen characters in these films, stopping the analysis there could miss the point. At least where Hughes's *Breakfast Club* is concerned, the characters don't necessarily act in stereotypical ways as they band together to defeat common enemies. And further, the film suggests that in real life, teens could successfully do the same.

Another example of teen stereotypes emerges in *Clueless* as Cher (Alicia Silverstone) carefully defines various groups for a new student, Tai (Brittany Murphy). Cher points out the students who run the TV station, the "Persian Mafia," the "most popular boys in school," and the "loadies." Here, as in *The Breakfast Club*, seemingly incompatible groups work together, this time in an effort to help those affected by the "Pismo Beach disaster"—collecting goods for those in need. And yet these two examples are not an exhaustive list of teen films that challenge the notion of accepting or embracing stereotypes. Films like *Can't Buy Me Love*, *Can't Hardly Wait*, and *Easy A* (Will Gluck, 2010) have, in their own unique ways, fought against accepting characters staying within the boundaries of a stereotyped group, despite such groups being defined in the films.

Utilization of stereotypical cliques and characters in teen films isn't restricted to youthful protagonists, however; adult characters often face a similar fate. Jean Schwind explains, "A stock figure in teen movies is the parent who inadvertently demonstrates abysmal ignorance while claiming to be hip. These claims of coolness are usually couched in hopelessly dated and mangled slang."[15] In *The Breakfast Club*, Principal Vernon (Paul Gleason) has no desire to relate to his students, and in *Clueless*, every adult in the film is portrayed as removed from the teens they are supposed to guide and teach. It is possible that Heckerling and Hughes are representing adults in this manner in an attempt to reject adulthood. Thomas Leitch clarifies that "The problem for Hughes's teens is not merely that particular adults offer inadequate role models; the whole system they represent is so hypocritical, alienating and meaningless that growing up would mean the end of the world."[16] Both Heckerling and Hughes's films offer much in this area. For instance, in *Weird Science* (Hughes, 1985), the grandparents of Wyatt (Ilan Mitchell-Smith) truly think he would love for them to visit him, while the grandparents in *Sixteen Candles* gauchely comment on how Samantha (Molly Ringwald) is developing physically and even encourage her to take an uncouth exchange student to her school dance. The adults in these examples reveal how removed they are from their teen relatives.

Heckerling likewise establishes a distinct difference between parents (and other authority figures) and the teens featured in her films. For instance, in *Fast Times*, Spicoli (Sean Penn) and Mr Hand appear to be on opposite ends of the responsibility spectrum, with Mr Hand seemingly unable to understand why his student can't make it to class on time, while Spicoli has little or no interest in anything beyond "tasty waves and a cool buzz," and can only say "I don't know" when asked to explain his absences from class. This same sort of disconnect continues in *Clueless* as Cher's father, Mel (Dan Hedaya), repeatedly asks her typical parenting questions only to get responses that reveal a divide between generations. For instance:

Mel: So, what did you do in school today?
Cher: Well, I broke in my purple clogs.

Or this exchange:

Mel: What the hell is that?
Cher: A dress.

Mel: Says who?
Cher: Calvin Klein.

In all of the preceding examples, it is clear that Hughes and Heckerling are highlighting the distance between the generations. And while the parents/authority figures in these examples seem to have the desire to relate to their teenage offspring, there appears to be no crossing the chasm that lies between them.

Teen films also enhance the difference between generations by replacing out-of-touch authority figures with strong teen characters who seem to have it all together. Doherty states that teen films (in the 1990s at least) held that "notwithstanding absent, inattentive, or neurotic boomer parents, the kids are well-adjusted and responsible, everything Mom and Dad aren't."[17] In order to guide the struggling teen protagonist through difficult situations, directors utilized knowing characters to instruct protagonists through "cool coaching" that neatly circumvented the ever-apparent divide between teens and their parents or other authority figures. Schwind states:

> The most interesting form of positive peer socialization at Ridgemont High is cool coaching, which occurs when a more experienced or savvy friend (or, as is more often the case, a friend who pretends to be more experienced or savvy) imparts vital information to a peer about how to avoid looking and acting like a loser.[18]

This type of relationship is evident in many teen films. Heckerling uses "cool coaching" in *Clueless* (Dionne [Stacey Dash] and Josh [Paul Rudd] advise Cher, who in turn advises everyone), while John Hughes uses this tactic in *Sixteen Candles* (Randy [Liane Curtis] advises Samantha, "Geek" [Anthony Michael Hall] advises Jake [Michael Schoeffling]), and *Weird Science* (Lisa [Kelly LeBrock] advises Gary [Anthony Michael Hall] and Wyatt).

Schwind claims that "effective cool coaching balances honest criticism and uncritical support, the selfless desire to help a friend and the urge for self-exaltation, cooperative problem-solving and the competitive satisfaction of knowing that a friend has more problems than you do."[19] The intent of "cool coaching" is to give a character advice that will alter his or her future success—often in terms of popularity or relationships with the opposite sex.

Schwind states that "films about high school girls frequently reduce cool coaching to beauty lessons."[20] In *Clueless*, Cher's first response upon meeting the newly-transferred student, Tai (Brittany Murphy), is to tell her friend Dionne that Tai could make a wonderful "project," and a short time later Cher and Dionne also help transform Ms. Geist (Twink Caplan) into a more desirable woman for Mr Hall (Wallace Shawn).

Figure 11.1 Dionne helps Tai with her make-up in *Clueless*.

John Hughes also includes makeovers in his teen films—including *The Breakfast Club*, where Claire (Molly Ringwald) helps Allison (Ally Sheedy) to soften her harsh look so Andy (Emilio Estevez) will notice her as a prospective love interest. Brammer asserts, "there's no obvious attraction between Andy and Allison until she's been 'prettied up,'"[21] which might lead audience members to wonder exactly how long such a superficial relationship could last. Because makeovers have become a staple in teen films, Brammer calls them an "unfortunate teen-film cliché."[22] And yet, the number of films to employ this tactic continues to grow. Some of the many titles include *Never Been Kissed* (Raja Gosnell, 1999), *She's All That*, *A Cinderella Story* (Mark Rosman, 2004), *Mean Girls*, and even *The Princess Diaries* (Garry Marshall, 2001).

With makeover sequences and teen mayhem intact, teen films transitioned successfully into the 1990s. Doherty states, "The nineties teenpics display a generous, good-natured attitude, rejecting the in-group smugness and revelry of humiliation that typified their predecessors."[23] While it can be argued that many 1990s teen films held to the core tenets of the genre—with makeover sequences, cool coaches and the like, the idea that, like real teens, this genre may be "growing up" isn't far-fetched. However, as Leitch explains, "teenpix, even if they are designed to appeal exclusively to an adolescent audience, are still produced and marketed by the very adults whose values the films so directly impugn."[24] In light of this, it is also true that the changes and growth may be slow to occur and that, like westerns and science fiction film genres, typical conventions of teen films may become more entrenched before they are challenged and tossed aside for new ones.

FAST TIMES BECOME FAMILY FILM TIMES

Heckerling's family fare included comedies like *Johnny Dangerously* (1984), *European Vacation* (1985), and the first two *Look Who's Talking* films (on a third film, *Look Who's Talking Now*, directed by Tom Ropelewski in 1993, Heckerling served only as a co-producer, which is typically a token title). Similarly, John Hughes boasted several films in this category as well—notably *Planes, Trains, and Automobiles* (1987), *She's Having a Baby* (1988), *Uncle Buck* (1989), and *Curly Sue* (1991), all of which he wrote in addition to *Christmas Vacation* (Jeremiah Chechik, 1989), *Home Alone* (Chris Columbus, 1990), and many more into the 1990s.

Speed states that "the films of Amy Heckerling use comedy to address themes such as gender difference, adolescent sexuality, and parenthood."[25] Heckerling tackles difficult subjects openly in her films, without concern for offending her audience, by using humor commonly referred to as "low comedy," which Speed describes as a "means of rendering palatable potentially confrontational themes."[26] In *European Vacation*, Heckerling uses low comedy even as she changes the character dynamic to revolve around a family rather than teenagers. Rachel Abramowitz observes that "Heckerling's sensibility [is] comic and broad. It was well-suited for mainstream Hollywood comedies except for the fact that she often liked to put girls at the center of her stories."[27] Women had been the center of a comedic film plot before, but not using Heckerling's style of low comedy. Speed states that "the films of Amy Heckerling use low comedy as a means of reconciling a male-centered generic framework with the portrayal of female perspectives."[28] As an example, in *Look Who's Talking* and *Look Who's Talking Too*, it is Mollie (Kirstie Alley) who navigates the difficulties involved in pregnancy, birth, and single parenting, as well as other relationship issues. In these films, Heckerling doesn't utilize euphemisms but portrays life as it is, or at least as it can be. Speed notes:

> In its focus upon female perspectives of the traditionally feminine concerns of pregnancy and parenthood, *Look Who's Talking* can be seen to develop a style of low humor that is relatively unfettered by male-defined generic constraints. *Look Who's Talking*'s positioning of maternity as a catalyst for humor can be linked to a long-standing relationship between women and comedy.[29]

In the *Look Who's Talking* films, Heckerling engages the subject of pregnancy in an honest way that before had hardly been seen. As comparison, Hughes's *She's Having a Baby* (1988) was made a year earlier and dealt with pregnancy in a comedic way, yet even he failed to approach the subject matter from the baby's point of view, as Heckerling does.

The use of low comedy in Heckerling's films—both family and teen—also reveals the influence of feminism. Speed states, "Paralleling the popularization of feminist values, the use of low comedy in Heckerling's films helps to banish an outdated equation between female achievement and humorlessness by expanding the range of genres through which female perspectives can be conveyed."[30] Heckerling uses low comedy and female protagonists in many of her films, giving characters the freedom to respond in ways that had not been seen before, as evidenced in *Johnny Dangerously* when Ma Kelly (Maureen Stapleton) admits to "going both ways," or in *Clueless* when Murray (Donald Faison) says, "Woman, lend me fi' dolla's," to which Dionne replies, "I have repeatedly asked you not to call me 'woman.'" Here, however, Dionne doesn't get the last word, as Murray retorts, "Street slang is an increasingly valid form of expression. Most of the feminine pronouns do have mocking, but not necessarily misogynistic undertones." In each of these cases, Heckerling develops her characters to have freedom in addressing life in a humorous and honest way that might surprise the audience.

Heckerling's true passion, however, is in featuring female characters in a way that has hitherto rarely been seen. For instance, many studios passed on the opportunity to make *Clueless* because they were worried that a female-centered film would fail; executives encouraged Heckerling instead to make the film an ensemble piece with the male characters having more prominent roles.[31] But for Heckerling, this tactic "Didn't make any sense."[32] While some executives questioned the financial viability of the film, Heckerling forged ahead and found success at a franchise level. Indeed, the film spawned a television show, video game, and an array of novels, impacting on, as Kyra Hunting observed, "the language, fashion, and style of a generation."[33] Prior to the success of *Clueless*, Heckerling's *Look Who's Talking* film franchise became a television show (*Baby Talk*). And, later, Heckerling continued developing strong female characters in her films *I Could Never Be Your Woman* (2007) and *Vamps* (2012).

John Hughes also used comedy to change and revitalize the family genre. In Hughes's case, he aimed for a younger audience with his scripts for the *Home Alone* films, as well as *Uncle Buck* and *Curly Sue*. Nina De Gramont argues that the audience should "Forget *Uncle Buck*. When we consider John Hughes, that's not the sort of film that comes to mind"[34]—a dismissal that may be understandable but at the same time unfair. Although Hughes's family fare failed to reach the iconic status of his teen films (excepting his *Home Alone* films), his family films were successful in entertaining the teen film audience, many of whom had grown up and moved on from the 1980s genre.[35] As an example, the *Home Alone* films used a physical humor that allowed Hughes to branch out from the more character-driven humor he'd become known for in his teen films. Because he was attempting to reach a new audience, it was the physical humor of Kevin McAllister (Macaulay Culkin) fighting off the bad guys that brought the family audience back to the theatres for subsequent sequels. And Hughes employed similar tactics in numerous other films of this genre, including *Curly Sue* (1991), *Dennis the Menace* (1993), and the *Beethoven* films (1992–2003).

PLANES, TRAINS, AND AUTEURS

Hughes and Heckerling did much to further the teen and family film genres, becoming auteurs in the classical sense that had been established by auteur theory in the 1950s under the auspices of film critics and scholars like François Truffaut, Peter Wollen, and Andrew Sarris. An essential argument of this theory was that the final cut of a film was most heavily influenced by one person: the director. Sarris argued that auteur theory consists of three basic premises: the technical competence of the director, the personality of the director, and the interior meaning that can be gleaned from the intersection of these areas.[36]

Both Heckerling and Hughes utilize technical film tools to their own advantages, and have a tendency to work with some of the same people. Heckerling, Jane Mills notes, worked with composer David Kitay on the *Look Who's Talking* films and *Clueless* (TV and film)[37] in addition to using some of the same actors in *Clueless* and *Vamps* (Alicia Silverstone and Wallace Shawn) and again in *Clueless* and *I Could Never Be Your Woman* (Paul Rudd, Stacey Dash, and Twink Caplan). Likewise, Hughes was known to work with similar talent across his films. For instance, Hughes used the talents of Paul Hirsch to edit *Ferris Bueller's Day Off* and *Planes, Trains, and Automobiles*.[38] And then there was the iconic "Brat Pack," which included stars like Molly Ringwald and Anthony Michael Hall, both of whom starred in multiple Hughes films. Interestingly, however, Heckerling and Hughes have also shared creative personnel across their films. For instance, Thomas Del Ruth was the director of photography on both of the *Look Who's Talking* films after he worked first on *The Breakfast Club*. Additionally, Matthew Leonetti served as director of photography on both *Fast Times* and *Weird Science*.[39]

Stylistically, Heckerling was nearly pigeonholed at the start of her career. She states that she was turning down "all these preppie movies"[40] after directing *Fast Times*, because it seemed that many in the industry thought she was capable of handling only teen films. Rather than bow to this notion, Heckerling sought out a different type of picture in *Johnny Dangerously*, followed by *European Vacation*. Still, each of these films fits within the comedy genre, a point that is supported by Heckerling herself when she states, "left to my own devices I will think of very morbid things all day," which is why she makes comedies, as they are a "great diversion. They're a great way to go out and not think about what's troubling you when you're watching them. But for the people who are making them, they're a great way not to deal with the horrors of life."[41]

Heckerling's auteur status may be called into question when she states, "I don't want to do anything like what I've done before."[42] However, Heckerling's style of low comedy, strong female characters, and her willingness to work with different kinds of scripts continue to set her directing style apart. She explains, "What works for me is not necessarily something I could recommend for anyone else."[43] But, according to Joe Morgenstern, Heckerling's style evolved over time. He claims that in *Fast Times*, Heckerling had "erratic pacing and had to make the best of someone else's script," while in *Clueless* the script "was her own," creating a brisk pace and a "brilliant fantasy version of Beverly Hills High."[44] Morgenstern continues his argument, stating:

> Many comedies these days leave bruises; they want you to feel good but they beat you up in the process, like massage therapists with a sadistic streak. That's not Amy Heckerling's style. With *Clueless*, she has found another state of comic energy, just as American physicists earlier this month found a new state of matter. It isn't satire, parody or irony, since she evinces little interest in passing judgment on her young people, but pure unadulterated glee.[45]

Similar to her work in *Fast Times*, Heckerling's comedic style in *Clueless* allowed the audience to be both entertained and challenged as characters dealt with real-life issues in humorous and sometimes shocking ways.

Figure 11.2 Ferris (right) and his friends enjoy the day off in *Ferris Bueller's Day Off*.

Hughes also has trademark technical elements in his teen films, and has been both writer and director on films like *Sixteen Candles*, *Weird Science*, *The Breakfast Club*, and *Ferris Bueller's Day Off*; his influence is also seen in films he wrote and produced but did not direct, like *Pretty in Pink* (Howard Deutch). Hughes's love of music shines in his films. Songs like "Oh Yeah," "If You Leave," and of course "Don't You (Forget About Me)" may never have made popular radio play without the help of Hughes's films. And yet Hughes's signature style goes further than musical influences. *Ferris Bueller's Day Off* featured "direct address to the camera; on-screen graphics; the prominent use of background songs to create de facto music videos; the sudden, exhilarating blur of fantasy and reality,"[46] and thus Hughes revealed a style that was developed in his previous teen films like *The Breakfast Club* and *Sixteen Candles*. In *Ferris Bueller*, Hughes utilized tools he'd developed in his earlier films to great effect—creating one of the most popular teen films of all time.[47]

At a crossroads for these directors lies *European Vacation*, part of the *National Lampoon* franchise, which was written by Hughes and directed by Heckerling. In *European Vacation*, Clark Griswold (Chevy Chase) becomes the stereotypical American international tourist—culturally insensitive, tremendously ignorant. Speed observes:

> Nevertheless, there is undeniable satiric power in the film's pervasive tendency to position the Griswolds, especially Clark, as objects of ridicule. Heckerling's use of comedy as a means of rendering social tensions accessible to general audiences is symptomatic of the satiric potential of humor that privileges the physical world over the verbal and spiritual.[48]

While Hughes conceived the Clark Griswold character, and inevitably developed the initial positioning to which Speed refers, it is Heckerling's comedic insight that develops him viscerally for the audience through privileging physical comedic stunts over the dialogue that draws them into the narrative. In using such low humor tactics, Heckerling asks the audience to see through the laughter and examine itself to consider whether it, like Clark, has been insensitive and ignorant of other cultures.

THE PERSONALITY CLUB

Sarris states that the second characteristic of auteur theory is the "distinguishable personality of the director as a criterion of value. Over a group of films, a director must exhibit certain recurrent characteristics of style, which serve as his signature."[49] As such, a director's background, ideologies, and preferences are expected to be seen in the final film. The personalities of Heckerling and Hughes can easily be seen in their work from the 1980s and 1990s.

The drive to work in the film industry began early for Heckerling, who states, "I can't remember a time when I was not interested in movies because they were always a part of my life."[50] As a child, Heckerling was immersed in classic films. Abramowitz explains that "James Cagney, Clark Gable, and the Three Stooges had practically served as her baby-sitters during the long afternoons spent as a latchkey child."[51] The time spent with classic films likely had a distinct influence on Heckerling's style, as evidenced in the *Look Who's Talking* films' ability to use slapstick humor while tackling serious subjects like giving birth, dating, and single parenthood. The influence of classic films can be seen further still in *Johnny Dangerously*'s obvious homage to James Cagney, star of many gangster films in the 1930s and 1940s that are parodied in Heckerling's film.

At fifteen years old, Heckerling decided to pursue a film career when a fellow student said that was what he wanted to do. Heckerling thought, "You said you can make movies. I love them more than you do. And besides, you cheat off of me on your tests, so I'm smarter, so I should do it."[52] While this attitude might be applicable to many filmmakers, it is revealing of Heckerling's success as a woman in a traditionally male-dominated field. Further still, Heckerling carried this perspective into her films like *Clueless*, where Cher works on everything from makeovers to grade-changes with the same level of prudence as her director. But Heckerling's tenacity doesn't stop there. Speed states that the use of low comedy in *Look Who's Talking* "suggests a defiance of the difficulties of single motherhood, in a society in which individualism and materialism have eclipsed the traditional carnivalesque values of collectivity and regeneration."[53] Where other films on pregnancy and motherhood like *"For Keeps"* (John G. Avildsen, 1988) and *Father of the Bride Part II* (Charles Shyer, 1995) opt for a softer approach, Heckerling used low comedy to make the audience cringe when, for instance, James (John Travolta) asks Mollie why she doesn't "look so hot," to which she replies, "Why don't you try squeezing something the size of a watermelon out of an opening the size of a lemon and see how hot you look?" Here, Heckerling challenges previous representations of pregnancy in a blunt, open way that continues today in films such as *Juno* (2007) and *Knocked Up* (2007). Heckerling accomplishes this, Speed postulates, because she challenges a traditionally male view of pregnancy with a female perspective.[54]

It is not surprising that Heckerling rails against tradition given that she was one of the few women in her film program in the 1970s. Abramowitz states, "By the time Amy Heckerling started at NYU in the early seventies, filmmaking had become a kind of jihad that she pursued over a variety of inner and external obstacles."[55] But Heckerling's drive led her to make strides in the portrayal of women in her films beyond the boundaries of motherhood. Speed asserts that "in Heckerling's films, women are as likely as men to actively participate in sequences involving low humor."[56] This point can be seen in *Fast Times* and in *European Vacation*, where women are as likely as the men to engage in low humor.

But Heckerling's personal style is most clearly seen in her ability to include herself in her films, as in *Fast Times*. Heckerling maintains, "So there's a lot of the real girls that he [Cameron Crowe] knew, and there's a lot of me, and a lot of him. I think that is clear in the movie, the male and female points-of-view."[57] In considering her own high school experience, Heckerling increases the ability of her films to reach audiences. Heckerling states, "Cameron Crowe and I sat down and talked about our own childhood experiences and teen years and figured out how to work certain characters into the story."[58] This desire for verisimilitude increases the reach of Heckerling's films. Stephen Tropiano observes that "[*Fast Times*] is in a league of its own because it is the first film to truly capture that modern-day teenagers were really growing up . . . faster than their ancestors without passing judgment on them" and because of this, the film may be "the best teen comedy of the eighties."[59]

Like Heckerling, Hughes had a personal influence on his films. Brammer states that in the making of *Ferris Bueller's Day Off*, "the central trio of Ferris, Sloane (Mia Sara) and Cameron (Alan Ruck) is based on [Hughes's] own high school relationships—the classic third wheel scenario of a boy, his girlfriend and his best friend."[60] In admitting that his high school relationships inspired even part of this film, Hughes shows that he understood what his characters were going though and was able to empathize with the audience too.

Additionally, Hughes's strong connection to his hometown in Illinois is seen in the Chicago setting of *Ferris Bueller's Day Off*.[61] Susannah Gora explains that "Hughes's own experiences as a teen would be imprinted in all of his youth films; in his characters' misplaced passions, their desire to distinguish themselves, their desperate need to connect."[62]

Hughes's personal style is revealed best in *Ferris Bueller's Day Off*, which Gora states truly brought his filmmaking "full circle."[63] Many personal touches are included in the film, not the least of which are Ferris's promise to marry Sloane (Hughes similarly married his high school sweetheart). Further, Ferris's address is 2800 (as it was for Hughes), and the interior of Ferris's high school, Shermer High, was actually the interior of John Hughes's alma mater, Glenbrook North High School.[64] Hughes and Heckerling each display personal touches in their films that make them truly unique. But it is the interior meaning that emerges from the collision between their technical and personal styles that reveals the impact of these filmmakers on the medium.

LOOK WHO'S GOT INTERIOR MEANING

When brought together, a director's technical style and personal influence over the film create a deeper, interior meaning for the astute audience. Sarris notes that interior meaning is "extrapolated from the tension between a director's personality and his material."[65] One way to note this "tension" is in the narrative structure itself. Brammer observes that Hughes contrasts intelligent teens with pathetic authority figures, and the protagonists in his films reveal a need to survive the teen years without help from those authority figures.[66] Add to this Heckerling's *Clueless*, where Cher's father tries to encourage her to dress appropriately but he is little more than acknowledged by his daughter, who dons a sheer "jacket" to appease him. And in the same film, Cher argues with teacher Mr Hall over her grade and then manipulates him until it is changed.

Mary Sullivan explains that "Hughes's parents just don't get it. They are forgetful, busy, uncaring, shallow, overbearing, in denial, or just not there. All of them are fools."[67] This could, at least initially, be a representation of Hughes's own parents, who didn't seem to understand or encourage his need to create.[68] And just as Hughes seemingly feared trusting adults to advise him, relying instead on input from the daughter of one of his mentors,[69] *Ferris Bueller's Day Off* "was the film where he [Hughes] explored the angst of *leaving* high school, and of jumping into the unknown challenges of young adult life,"[70] revealing a fear of growing up that seemed to be reflected in many of Hughes's teen films.

Relationships with peers are also a core issue for teen films. Whether in friendships or romances, or among rivals and villains, teens featured in Heckerling and Hughes films struggle to understand each other and get along. Raging hormones, social status, and economic forces all work together (and sometimes against one another) to cause friction between teen characters. Brammer observes that in *Sixteen Candles*, "the stereotypical bullying of the geeks is turned on its head by the hero's need for their help."[71] Likely, it is Hughes's own experience that influenced this change. Gora states that because Hughes "never forgot what it truly feels like to be young, he possessed a unique and singular gift as a filmmaker, one that would enable him to lead a new age in youth cinema."[72] As a teen, Hughes had an amazing talent for creative writing, and while he had many friends, he wasn't considered "popular."

While Heckerling's success as a filmmaker seemed predictable because of her childhood immersion in films as well as her driven nature, it was her understanding of comedy that provided the basis for her career. Abramowitz observes that Heckerling's talent was "well-suited for mainstream Hollywood comedies except for the fact that she often liked to put girls at the center of her stories."[73] Heckerling's ability to bring women to the center of her films made a statement about the independence and ability of women socially, sexually, and interpersonally. But it wasn't just teen films or the strict use of female leads that allowed Heckerling to shine in low comedy. Speed remarks, that in *European Vacation*:

> There is an undeniable satiric power in the film's pervasive tendency to position the Griswolds, especially Clark, as objects of ridicule. Heckerling's use of comedy as a means of rendering social tensions accessible to general audiences is symptomatic of the satiric potential of humor that privileges the physical over the verbal and spiritual.[74]

This style of comedy in Heckerling's films likely finds its roots in her early immersion in classics such as *Blazing Saddles*, *Three Stooges* shorts, and *MAD* magazine.[75]

Heckerling and Hughes showed that the teen years are a valuable time of development in a person's life. Allison Lynn states that "Hughes would eventually teach me that it was okay to be myself. He'd insist that the jocks and prom queens weren't the only cool kids on the block—and that if I wanted to date one of those jocks anyway, they weren't, truly, out of my reach."[76]

CLUELESS CONCLUSIONS AND FURTHER RESEARCH

Amy Heckerling and John Hughes were instrumental in reigniting the teen genre in the 1980s and 1990s, and influencing the family film genre during this time as well. While there are a striking number of similarities between these two filmmakers, they have made their own distinct marks on the film industry, and more specifically on the teen film genre where each, arguably, became an auteur. Gora declares that "Amy Heckerling's savvy, critically acclaimed *Fast Times at Ridgemont High* understood teens in ways few films had before, and dealt with societal issues that not even Hughes dared touch."[77] While Hughes centered his films on seemingly mundane teen problems (that actually weren't)—prom dates, social invisibility, and out-of-touch parents— Heckerling utilized a different approach, using low humor to allow her characters to deal directly with weightier issues like sexuality and abortion, while at times venturing into areas of social and physical makeovers.

Gora reveals, however, that the 1980s teen films movement would not have been the same without Heckerling and Hughes. She states, "*Fast Times* would, in many ways, open the door for the youth films John Hughes and his contemporaries would make in the mid and late 1980s, by proving early on that youth audiences of that decade were hungry for entertainment that was amusing but that still took their struggles seriously."[78] While some may disregard teen films as "easily recognizable and yet usually given little respect,"[79] as Timothy Shary postulates, there are issues worthy of exploration, such as gender and relationship issues, as well as the range of teen experiences, that can so often be glossed over or even ignored by currently existing critiques of the teen film genre.

Inevitably, the works of Heckerling and Hughes will be remembered as seminal to the teen film genre, but their work in the family film is worthy of mention. While Hughes's work in this area is often dismissed, Macaulay Culkin, with his wide, grimacing mouth, hands on his cheeks, horrified that his family has left him "home alone," likely will be engrained in the cultural memory for years to come. Similarly, Cher's "As if!" remains as culturally relevant today as it was in the 1990s. For Heckerling's part, she was the first female filmmaker to reveal a potential for using low humor in her work—both teen and family films—to showcase female protagonists who weren't afraid to tell a seemingly inappropriate joke, or make an off-color reference for the sake of laughter, or perhaps, for something greater, that might be called understanding. Speed states:

> While this association is redolent of a traditional hierarchy of film genres, Heckerling's teen films are also products of a period in which this genre has acquired greater cultural value. Moreover, her work helps to counteract the male domination of low screen comedy through positioning women as active participants in comic scenarios. Far from being limited by genres which traditionally lack prestige, Heckerling's films use comedy as a means of communicating, through entertainment, diverse experiences of pleasure and pain.[80]

While Hughes's body of work came to an end in 2009 when he died of a heart attack, Heckerling continues to write and direct films like *Vamps* and television shows such as *Suburgatory* (2011–14). Critics would be wise to further explore the impact of these filmmakers' work beyond the teen and family film genres. Possible areas of further exploration might include feminist interpretations of their work, considerations of the impact of authority on teen protagonists, and the impact of parents-as-friends in the family film genre.

NOTES

1 Susannah Gora, *You Couldn't Ignore Me If You Tried: The Brat Pack, John Hughes, and Their Impact on a Generation* (New York: Crown, 2010), pp. 14 and 160.
2 Andrew Sarris, "Notes on the auteur theory in 1962," in Leo Braudy and Marshall Cohen (eds.), *Film Theory & Criticism* (New York: Oxford University Press, 2010), 7th edn, p. 452.

3 Lesley Speed, "A world ruled by hilarity: gender and low comedy in the films of Amy Heckerling," *Senses of Cinema*, 22. Available at <http://sensesofcinema.com/2002/22/heckerling/> (last accessed 26 February 2014).

4 Rebekah Brammer, "Left of center: teen life, love and pain in the films of John Hughes," *Screen Education* 56 (2009), p. 23.

5 Ibid.

6 Tom Doherty, "Clueless kids," *Cineaste*, 21: 4 (1995), p. 14.

7 Alissa Quart, *Branded: The Buying and Selling of Teenagers* (New York: Basic Books, 2003), p. 93.

8 Jeannette Sloniowski, "A cross-border study of the teen genre," *Journal of Popular Film & Television* 25: 3 (1997), p. 130.

9 Ibid.

10 Patrick Goldstein, "A director's off day in his superteen's 'Day Off,'" *LA Times*, 11 July 1986, Calendar Section, 1.

11 EW staff, "Fifty best high school movies," *Entertainment* Weekly 22, September 2012. Available at <http://www.ew.com/ew/gallery/0,,20483133_20632183_21216415,00.html> (last accessed 12 March 2014).

12 Brammer, p. 23.

13 Quart, p. 78.

14 Ibid.

15 Jean Schwind, "Cool coaching at Ridgemont High," *The Journal of Popular Culture* 41: 6 (2008), p. 1023.

16 Thomas Leitch, "The world according to teenpix," *Literature Film Quarterly* 20: 1 (1992), p. 45.

17 Doherty, p. 14.

18 Ibid. p. 1020.

19 Ibid. p. 1030.

20 Ibid. p. 1029.

21 Brammer, p. 28.

22 Ibid.

23 Doherty, p. 14.

24 Leitch, p. 47.

25 Speed.

26 Ibid.

27 Rachel Abramowitz, *Is That a Gun in Your Pocket? Women's Experience of Power in Hollywood* (New York: Random House, 2000), p. 143.

28 Speed.

29 Ibid.

30 Ibid.

31 Bernard Weinraub, "A surprising hit about rich teen-age girls," *New York Times*, 144, 24 July 1995, p. 2.

32 Ibid.

33 Kyra Hunting, "Furiously franchised: *Clueless*, convergence culture, and the female-focused franchise," *Cinema Journal* 53: 3 (2014), p. 141.

34 Nina De Gramont, "Which John Hughes character are you?," in Jaime Clarke (ed.), *Don't You Forget About Me: Contemporary Writers on the Films of John Hughes* (New York: Simon Spotlight Entertainment, 2007), p. 98.

35 Gora, p. 276.

36 Sarris, p. 453.

37 Jane Mills, "*Clueless*: transforming Jane Austen's *Emma*," *Australian Screen Education* 34 (2004), p. 103.

38 IMDB profile, *John Hughes*. Available at <http://www.imdb.com/name/nm0000455/?ref_=nv_sr_2> (last accessed 12 November 2014).

39 Ibid.; and IMDB profile, *Amy Heckerling*, available at <http://www.imdb.com/name/nm0002132/?ref_=nv_sr_1> (last accessed 12 November 2014).

40 Michael Singer, *A Cut Above: 50 Film Directors Talk About Their Craft* (Los Angeles, CA: Lone Eagle, 1998), p. 83.

41 Ibid. p. 81.

42 Janis Cole and Holly Dale, *Calling the Shots: Profiles of Women Filmmakers* (Kingston, ON: Quarry Press, 1993), pp. 116–17.

43 Ibid. p. 118.

44 Joe Morgenstern, "Film: funny times at Beverly Hills High," *Wall Street Journal*, 21 July 1995. Available at <http://online.wsj.com/news/articles/SB877043990821887000> (last accessed 27 February 2014).

45 Ibid.

46 Steve Almond, "John Hughes goes deep: the unexpected heaviosity of *Ferris Bueller's Day Off*," in Clarke, p. 5.

47 EW staff.

48 Ibid.

49 Sarris, p. 452.

50 Nicholas Jarecki, *Breaking In: How 20 Film Directors Got Their Start* (New York: Broadway Books, 2001), p. 143.

51 Ibid. p. 142.

52 Abramowitz, p. 143.

53 Speed.

54 Ibid.

55 Abramowitz, p. 142.

56 Speed.

57 Cole and Dale, p. 116.

58 Ibid. p. 150.

59 Stephen Tropiano, *Rebels and Chicks: A History of the Hollywood Teen Movie* (New York: Back Stage Books, 2006), p. 173.

60 Brammer, p. 28.

61 Ibid.

62 Ibid. p. 10.

63 Ibid. p. 186.

64 Ibid. pp. 186–7.

65 Sarris, p. 453.

66 Ibid. p. 27.

67 Mary Sullivan, "Make a wish: the first kiss lasts forever," in Clarke, p. 175.

68 Gora, p. 14.

69 Ibid. p. 188.

70 Ibid. p. 196.

71 Brammer, p. 26.

72 Gora, p. 10.

73 Ibid.

74 Speed.

75 Jarecki, p. 143.

76 Allison Lynn, "Ferris Bueller: an infatuation, a life lesson, and one harmless family adventure," in Clarke, p. 118.
77 Gora, p. 5.
78 Ibid. p. 21.
79 Timothy Shary, "Course file for 'Film genres and the image of youth,'" *Journal of Film and Video* 55: 1 (2003), p. 39.
80 Speed.

CHAPTER 12

Way Hilarious: Amy Heckerling as a Female Comedy Director, Writer, and Producer

Lesley Speed

Beneath their surface frivolity, the films of Amy Heckerling use humor to explore such fundamental themes as gender, parenthood, aging, sexual relationships, and the idiosyncrasies of social life in a changing society. As a director, writer, and producer whose work includes prominent and financially successful films, Heckerling is an important figure in women's expanded influence in comedy. Among the distinctive elements of her work are comedic social observation, a focus on youth and age difference, body humor, and an inclusive approach to characterization. Spanning more than three decades, Heckerling's career is a model for women's development of the comedy and teen genres in film and television beyond their traditional masculine preoccupations.

FEMALE AUTHORSHIP AND GENRE

Heckerling's career can be situated within a generation of prominent American female directors, producers, and writers that includes Penny Marshall, Penelope Spheeris, Martha Coolidge, Nora Ephron, Betty Thomas, and Nancy Meyers. Having establishing their careers in various capacities, from acting to behind-the-scenes work in Hollywood and independent films, these women came to prominence in production roles during the 1980s. This was a period in which the widespread social impact of feminism led to opportunities for women in a growing range of occupations. The accomplishments of these women include some of the most prominent comedy films of recent decades, such as *Valley Girl* (Coolidge, 1983); *Big* (Marshall, 1988); Ephron's screenplay for *When Harry Met Sally* (Rob Reiner, 1989); *Wayne's World* (Spheeris, 1992); *Sleepless in Seattle* (Ephron, 1993); *The Brady Bunch Movie* (Thomas,

1995); *You've Got Mail* (Ephron, 1998); *Something's Gotta Give* (Meyers, 2003); *Julie & Julia* (Ephron, 2009); *It's Complicated* (Meyers, 2009); and Heckerling's *Fast Times at Ridgemont High* (1982), *Look Who's Talking* (1989), and *Clueless* (1995). As will be seen, these films also form a precedent for the subsequent prominence of female comedic writers and producers in film and television, including Tina Fey, Diablo Cody, Kristen Wiig, and Amy Poehler.

The significance of female filmmakers has been shaped inevitably by industry factors. Opportunities for women to direct films in Hollywood increased in the 1980s, but the industry's growing emphasis on marketing and blockbusters was often "less conducive to the freedom of the individual director"; the industry's use of the package system, where personnel are assembled on a film-by-film basis, benefited directors with "existing clout" but few female directors were able to get a film made on the basis of their name alone.[1] However, the female director or writer can serve as a marketing entity that generates "extra-textual discourse," notes Christina Lane, and may attract female viewers.[2] Feminism has embraced female authorship as a political strategy, a means of addressing "the reinvention of the cinema that has been undertaken by women filmmakers and feminist spectators."[3]

At the same time, women directors have tended to be "pigeon-holed" in Hollywood and limited to genres such as comedy, melodrama, and teen film.[4] This reflects a gendered hierarchy of genres in which thrillers, historical dramas, and gangster films are traditionally accorded more prestige than teen films, broad comedies, and contemporary melodramas, reflecting what Richard Maltby identifies as a propensity for film criticism to "valorize . . . patriarchal and masculine concerns."[5] By contrast, the scarcity of female directors who specialize in action films is highlighted by the prominence of Kathryn Bigelow, whose association with traditionally masculine subject matter can be linked to her status as the only woman to receive an Academy Award for Best Director (for *The Hurt Locker*, 2010). As a director with a "star persona," however, Bigelow is an anomaly among female filmmakers,[6] her fame contrasting with the lower profile of another respected female director of action films, Mimi Leder (*The Peacemaker* [1997], *Deep Impact* [1998]).

Heckerling's career developed in a period when female directors were usually restricted to projects with middle-range budgets, which are dependent on the success of big-budget films and are "less likely to be financed in years when high-budget films yield low returns."[7] This seems to have changed by 2008, when films employing at least one woman as director, producer, or writer had budgets comparable to films with only men in these roles,[8] but the overall number of female film directors still remains low. Inequality of gender in employment is reflected in *The Celluloid Ceiling*, a report about female employment on the highest-grossing American films between 1998 and 2012. In 2012, "women comprised 18% of all directors, executive producers,

producers, writers, cinematographers, and editors" on those films, reflecting "no change from 2011 and an increase of 1 percentage point from 1998."[9] Not only is Heckerling relatively unusual as a female director whose career spans more than three decades, but her films have contributed to the development of the teen genre and the expansion of the range of subject matter associated with women in comedy.

The relationship between female filmmakers and comedy refutes the view that women, particularly feminists, are "not funny."[10] Heckerling's directorial career was fueled by her preference for comedy and her willingness to work in the genre of teen film, with which few established directors traditionally choose to be associated.[11] Her debut feature, *Fast Times at Ridgemont High*, is remembered particularly for its comedic episodes.[12] It is also notable for being among the first teen comedies to be taken seriously by film scholars, as evidenced in Robin Wood's description of the film as "disarming," "exhilarating," "enlightened and intelligent."[13] Moreover, by reaping a profit far in excess of its modest budget, *Fast Times* became the first of Heckerling's films to vindicate the view that films with low- to middle-range budgets not only are an economic staple of the Hollywood system,[14] but can lead to further career opportunities. Lane suggests that Heckerling's success in gaining studio support for her projects is linked to her ability to complete films within budgetary constraints.[15]

The following decade, Heckerling brought increased critical praise and cultural value to teen comedy by returning to the genre, as an established director, with *Clueless*. In contrast to the teen film's historical origins in the "controversial content, bottom-line bookkeeping, and demographic targeting" of exploitation film, *Clueless* is central to the genre's acquisition of increased critical recognition and respect.[16] This is exemplified by Lesley Stern's account of the film's "genius" for renovating "old rhetorical devices in the service of new insights and pleasures."[17] The film's impact for two decades is encapsulated in Melissa Lenos's observation that *Clueless* "transcended its original target audience and is not a relic of 1990s pop culture but a manufacturer of that culture [and] an important influence on later films."[18] Heckerling's work in the 1980s and 1990s has contributed to the lexicon of teen slang and the canon of teen films.

While *Clueless* confirmed Heckerling as a teen film auteur, the tradition of the individual author is both evidenced and effaced in her films. An important dimension of the cultural significance of *Clueless* is the fact that Heckerling's screenplay is adapted from Jane Austen's novel *Emma* (1815). The film is one of the first and most prominent in a Hollywood cycle of teen-targeted adaptations and updatings of literary works that also includes *Romeo + Juliet* (Baz Luhrmann, 1996), *Cruel Intentions* (Roger Kumble, 1999), *10 Things I Hate About You* (Gil Junger, 1999), *O* (Tim Blake Nelson, 2001), and *She's the Man*

(Andy Fickman, 2006). *Clueless* thus marks an intersection of female author-ship with the teen genre's development as a medium for self-conscious cultural commentary and reinvention of the literary canon.

At first glance, the novels that are the sources of *Fast Times* and *Clueless* appear to undermine Heckerling's entitlement to principal credit (the former is adapted from Cameron Crowe's novel *Fast Times at Ridgemont High: A True Story* [1981]). Yet these films are more significant for how they deviate from these sources. For example, William Paul argues that *Fast Times* presents an "imbalance" between male and female perspectives of sex in which the female perspective is more developed than in the novel.[19] The fact that Heckerling "worked closely" with screenwriter Cameron Crowe to develop the narrative may be seen to have shaped the scene in which Stacy (Jennifer Jason Leigh) loses her virginity, where the use of camera angles and point-of-view shots conveys her sense of being "divorced from the experience of her own body."[20] Equally, Lesley Stern argues that in *Clueless* the theme of the "impulse . . . to remake or refashion the world" is an ingenious departure from Austen's novel that stems from Heckerling's "generic choices" as writer and director.[21] Reflecting Heckerling's influence, these films' remodeling of existing nar-ratives is consistent with the collaborative and market-driven orientation of Hollywood entertainment. Authorial authenticity is indistinguishable from the multiplicity of viewpoints in Heckerling's films, which are not only about "what it is like to be young and female"[22] but also explore the medium's capac-ity to transport the viewer into the lives of other people.

Fast Times and *Clueless* reflect the increased involvement of women direc-tors in Hollywood's production of films targeted at its "core audience of teenagers and young adults."[23] Heckerling's career parallels that of Martha Coolidge, who also began her Hollywood career by directing teen films, such as *Valley Girl* and *Joy of Sex* (1984). Later youth films directed by Fran Rubel Kuzui (*Buffy the Vampire Slayer*, 1992), Penelope Spheeris (*Wayne's World*; *The Little Rascals*, 1994), Betty Thomas (*The Brady Bunch Movie*), and Gina Prince-Bythewood (*Love and Basketball*, 2000; *The Secret Life of Bees*, 2008) suggest a continuing association between female directors and youth-targeted films. Rachel Abramowitz actually identifies teen comedy as "the one genre permitted to female directors" in Hollywood, where *Fast Times* was a product of "the cinematic age of the male adolescent . . . the era of *Porky's* [Bob Clark, 1982] and *Risky Business* [Paul Brickman, 1983]."[24] For the industry, the significance of the genre was that it "was cheap and relatively commercial, and it didn't require stars. Teens were not considered quite full people in Hollywood . . . and neither were women."[25] The relationship between women directors and youth films thus echoes a "legacy of cultural pessimism" in which "the mass/youth and the female spectator" are seen to be easily seduced into "degraded types of collective identification."[26] Although the vast majority

Figure 12.1   Stacy (left) endures Linda's advice about relationships in *Fast Times*.

of teen films are still directed by men, the genre continues to be significant in building the careers of high-profile female screen professionals, including Tina Fey, who adapted the screenplay for *Mean Girls* (Mark Waters, 2004) from Rosalind Wiseman's book *Queen Bees and Wannabes* (2003), and Diablo Cody, who received the 2008 Academy Award for Best Original Screenplay for *Juno* (Jason Reitman, 2007). Women have contributed to the teen genre's capacity to reflect on and challenge stereotypes of young people and women.

Female filmmakers have expanded the range of gendered portrayals of narrative agency onscreen. Before *Fast Times*, girls in teen films were "subject to a double domination, firstly by adults and secondly by male teenagers who are themselves consumed by the need to challenge adult authority in a quest for mastery."[27] The films of Heckerling present more complex views of adolescent experience by juxtaposing female and male perspectives. In *Fast Times*, for instance, conflicting gendered responses to the vulgar comedy's staple theme of masturbation are presented. When the character of Brad (Judge Reinhold) masturbates in a bathroom while gazing out a window at Linda (Phoebe Cates), who is by the swimming pool, a shot from his point of view is displaced by another shot from a more objective angle when the camera follows Linda into the house. The scene thus replaces male fantasy with female agency. The culmination of this shift is then an embarrassing encounter between the two when Linda accidentally intrudes upon Brad in the bathroom. The way in which the scene both acknowledges male fantasy and positions the actions of the female character as an alternative plotline is a departure from conventions of the vulgar teen comedy, as exemplified in male-centered films such as *Porky's*, *The Last American Virgin* (Boaz Davidson, 1982), and *Losin' It* (Curtis

Hanson, 1983). Moreover, the significance of female agency in *Fast Times* prefigures the increased importance of female characters in later versions of vulgar teen comedies that center on males. In *American Pie* (Paul Weitz, 1999), for example, scenes in which female characters advise male characters on how to achieve their hedonistic goals were foreshadowed by Linda's role as Stacy's mentor and defender in *Fast Times*.[28] As well as incorporating female perspectives on experiences traditionally associated with male teenagers, Heckerling's films position body humor as universal.

LOW COMEDY AND POSTFEMINISM

The films of Amy Heckerling allay social tensions through somatic humor. In *European Vacation* (1985, a.k.a. *National Lampoon's European Vacation*), for instance, the Griswolds are positioned as stereotypes of culturally ignorant American tourists. They are unaware that the staff at their Paris hotel ridicule their passport photographs, in which the Griswold children appear surly, and Clark (Chevy Chase) and Ellen (Beverly D'Angelo) pull comical faces. "I don't believe it," one clerk says in subtitled French, "typical American assholes." The film thus seems complicit in the ridiculing of Americans, perhaps daringly so, given that the latter formed a large part of the audience. However, the film also directs humor at European locals. *European Vacation*, co-written by teen film auteur John Hughes, highlights the abilities of both Hughes and Heckerling to explore social difference in non-confrontational ways. While a waiter denigrates the family's incomprehension of his language by making sexual comments in French about the Griswold women, for instance, the kitchen staff are shown to be serving French meals from supermarket packets.

A common characteristic of Heckerling's work is the depiction of contrasting responses to bodily experiences. In *Fast Times*, the scene of a school excursion to a hospital combines universal themes of birth and death with the teen film conventions of gross-out humor and romance. When biology teacher Mr Vargas (Vincent Schiavelli) inserts his hand into a corpse in the morgue and removes the heart, Jeff Spicoli (Sean Penn) exclaims enthusiastically, "Oh, gnarly!" Spicoli is not even enrolled in the class but has joined the excursion for his enjoyment. Meanwhile, the sight of the cadaver prompts Stacy to become nauseated and leave the room. While positioning Spicoli as the center of the film's boisterous humor, the film exhibits equal sympathy for Stacy, who has recently had an abortion. The juxtaposing of body humor and vulgarity with an inclusive approach to characterization is a distinctive aspect of Heckerling's work.

Heckerling has expanded screen depictions of body humor to include female perspectives. Echoing her youthful aspirations to be "a writer or artist for *MAD* magazine" and to make "a female version of *Carnal Knowledge*" (Mike Nichols, 1971), her films respond to an imbalance in screen comedy, in which humor about sex and bodily functions is traditionally associated with male comedians and male filmmakers.[29] In his study of the tradition of low comedy, William Paul demonstrates that "the vulgar" encompasses a range of comedic styles, from the slapstick of Charlie Chaplin and the bawdy comedy of Lenny Bruce to the depiction of adolescent sexual strivings in *Porky's*.[30] Although diverse in form and context, these examples have in common a propensity to derive humor from the functions of the lower body, particularly the genitals and the digestive system. Paul identifies this humor with the spirit of medieval folk theatre, as outlined by Mikhail Bakhtin.[31] In Bakhtin's analysis of the medieval folk carnival, lower body humor is linked to the "material bodily principle," which is "universal, representing all the people" and predates the modern individualization of the body.[32] The material bodily principle underpins the festive spirit of medieval folk theatre in its variously satirical, bawdy, and profane forms. Although the carnival has origins in a feudal social order that has long been succeeded by a consumer society in which popular culture and universal bodily experiences are contained, the spirit of Bakhtin's "grotesque realism" remains residually evident in entertainment. For instance, the use of body humor to satirize the social hierarchy and conventions of propriety can be seen in such films as *M*A*S*H* (Robert Altman, 1970), *Porky's*, *Weekend at Bernie's* (Ted Kotcheff, 1989), *Private Parts* (Betty Thomas, 1997), *Austin Powers: The Spy Who Shagged Me* (Jay Roach, 1999), and *Death at a Funeral* (Neil LaBute, 2010).[33] However, body humor onscreen has usually been associated with male comedians and often with aggressively masculine styles of humor. Heckerling's films contribute to counteracting this male dominance.

Heckerling is among an increased number of female directors of low comedy films, including Coolidge (*Joy of Sex*), Spheeris (*Wayne's World*; *Black Sheep*, 1996; *Senseless*, 1998), and Thomas (*Private Parts*). On the one hand, the fact that some of these films center on men challenges the notion that female filmmakers are incapable of working with masculine subject matter. On the other, women film directors have contributed to extending low comedy to include female characters. *Fast Times*, for example, uses the vulgar teen comedy as a framework for focusing on teenage pregnancy, abortion, and female promiscuity. Robin Wood observes that the film's relationship to vulgar teen comedy involves fulfilling "certain bottom-line generic conditions that must be satisfied for such a film to get made at all" while extending, varying, or subverting conventions and stereotypes.[34] The use of this strategy to appeal to female and male viewers is also evident in Martha Coolidge's teen films.[35]

The practical omnipresence of sexuality in young people's lives is a recurrent theme of Heckerling's work. *European Vacation* gives equal attention to the desires of Audrey Griswold (Dana Hill), who thinks of her boyfriend when she sees a plate of German sausage, and her brother Rusty (Jason Lively), who is ecstatic when a young German woman shows him her breasts. In *Loser*, college students Paul (Jason Biggs) and Dora (Mena Suvari) overhear a man's phone conversation about a sexually transmitted disease. "Well, you didn't get it from me," the man tells the other party; "Is it burning and itchy?" Even *Clueless*, a romantic comedy with a virginal protagonist, includes a verbal joke about fellatio. Heckerling's work in this regard has been central to female film-makers' revising of low comedy.

Her films also prefigure the body humor of a later generation of female directors and writers. Whereas the teen films of Heckerling and Coolidge were unusual in the 1980s for their overt exploration of female perspectives on sex, a shift subsequently occurred in public perceptions of women in comedy. This can be attributed partly to the popularity of the television series *Sex and the City* (1998–2004), adapted from the writings of Candace Bushnell, in which female characters pursue sex that is "recreational" or casual, rather than "relational" or emotionally intimate and committed.[36] *Sex and the City* thereby "challenges commonly held cultural beliefs about what constitutes appropriate sexual desires and behaviors for women."[37] Female screenwriters have since explored sexual themes and toilet humor about women in *The Sweetest Thing* (Roger Kumble, 2002), written by Nancy Pimental, and the very profitable *Bridesmaids* (Paul Feig, 2011), written by Annie Mumolo and Kristen Wiig. Indeed, Helen Warner notes that some critics identified *Bridesmaids* as a feminist work on the basis that it offers a female counterpart to the "raunch comedy" of *The Hangover* (Todd Phillips, 2009).[38] The most frequently cited example in *Bridesmaids* is a scene at a bridal store where the characters experience the effects of food poisoning. However, women's participation in toilet humor remains controversial among critics.[39] The films of Heckerling prefigure screen texts and critical debates that continue to challenge established ideas about acceptable modes of performance for women.

The work of female directors and writers in comedy since the 1970s can be understood in relation to postfeminism. Identified as "a cultural sensibility" that occupies an "ambiguous" relationship to feminism, postfeminism can "represent both a repudiation and an affirmation of feminist politics, depending on how it is deployed within a certain cultural context."[40] Among the traits of postfeminism are the espousal of values of "equality, inclusion and free choice" in ways that have a capacity to empower the individual, but which also tend to obscure and "deem inconsequential" the existence of "social constraints upon contemporary girls and women."[41] Whereas second-wave feminism was "anti-consumption, often in a quite puritanical manner," postfeminism is linked to the more widespread consumption of representations that can be understood in terms of feminist values.[42] The relationship between consumer culture and postfeminism is central to the significance of women in comedy. In particular, postfeminism embraces humor, whereas second-wave feminism places emphasis on political concerns and tends not to invest overtly in humor.[43]

Postfeminism in cinema is also strongly associated with young women. Joel Gwynne and Nadine Muller note that although "female adolescents have always embodied powerful feminist potential[,] the figure of the girl has been resurrected in contemporary popular culture and utilized to demonstrate the empowering possibilities of reconfigured femininity."[44] An example is the film *Legally Blonde* (Robert Luketic, 2001), which juxtaposes the feminist theme of equal career opportunity with a celebration of "the poise, panache, and performance of the 'girly woman.'"[45] While postfeminist girlhood is often portrayed optimistically, however, some established theorists of youth culture take a more pessimistic view. For instance, Angela McRobbie writes that postfeminism makes feminism seem "aged" and "redundant."[46] Heckerling's work combines the optimism of postfeminist humor, consumerism, and youth with acknowledgment of the continuing relevance of earlier feminist principles.

The postfeminism of Heckerling's films reveals the persistence of social constraints upon women. Cher in *Clueless*, for instance, is a precursor to Elle Woods (Reese Witherspoon) in *Legally Blonde*. Both protagonists use their feminine wiles to advance themselves academically and struggle when they are not taken seriously. Yet Heckerling's work differs from the postfeminism of *Legally Blonde*, which has a more ambitious protagonist and an overt feminist agenda. Whereas Elle attends Harvard Law School, Cher displays little ambition beyond matchmaking and makeovers, and is reprimanded by her father for lacking direction. In *Clueless*, as in most of Heckerling's films, the emphasis is on struggle rather than attainment of success. In *Look Who's Talking*, for instance, James (John Travolta) sabotages Mollie (Kirstie Alley)'s date with Harry (Nicholas Rice) by telling him Mollie is "tough" and independent, a description that the conservative Harry equates with the idea of a "liberated" woman. Although James's action is motivated by his own attraction to Mollie, the exchange implicates both men in a stereotyping of independent women that is consistent with a contemporaneous backlash against feminism.[47] However, the film ultimately distances itself from this view by positioning Harry as the only character with a clear aversion to feminism, and he is depicted as boring, rejected by Mollie, and endorsed only by her mother, whose approval aligns Harry with values that predate second-wave feminism.

In Heckerling's other films, references to feminism suggest that its goals remain unfulfilled. When cheerleaders in *Fast Times* voice a public objection to being called "Spirit Bunnies," which they consider to be "a put-down," their diegetic audience is uninterested and inattentive. In *Loser*, student Dora's attempt to assert herself in her relationship with the corrupt Professor Alcott

Figure 12.2 In *Look Who's Talking*, Mollie thinks James is an irresponsible thrill-seeker.

(Greg Kinnear) prompts him to respond sarcastically: "I'm sure . . . Betty Friedan would applaud your little epiphany." At a parent–teacher meeting in *I Could Never Be Your Woman* (Heckerling, 2007), Rosie (Michelle Pfeiffer) asserts that girls are disadvantaged by standardized testing. In Heckerling's work, liberation—feminist or otherwise—is counterpoised by the difficulties of achieving it.

Heckerling's films address the problems as much as the freedoms of contemporary life for young women and other characters. In *Fast Times*, both female and male teenagers are anxious about the prospect of sexual relationships and what is expected of them. The film reveals the spuriousness of claims made by Linda, Brad, and Mike (Robert Romanus) about their sexual experience, while the more circumspect characters of Stacy and Mark (Brian Backer) learn that they cannot always trust their peers. Just as most of Heckerling's films explore the freedom for women to have sex, they also reveal through humor the complications that can arise. Indeed, the idea that men benefit more from sexual freedom than women do—a view consistent with second-wave feminism—is suggested by the sexually opportunistic selfishness of Mike in *Fast Times*, Albert (George Segal) in *Look Who's Talking*, and Professor Alcott in *Loser*. As comedies, however, Heckerling's films are less concerned with political stances than with the complexities of how characters navigate their social environments. In *Fast Times* and *Clueless*, respectively, Linda and Cher distance themselves from high school boys by forming a commitment to a long-distance relationship or virginity. However, the inescapability of the social world of the school is reinforced when Linda has no date for the school dance and Cher envies Tai (Brittany Murphy)'s interest in Josh (Paul Rudd).

In contrast to youth films that mythologize the freedoms of college life, *Loser* presents a bleakly absurd view of students' poverty and isolation. For instance, Dora misses the last train and sleeps at Grand Central Station, works at a bar where she is asked to sell her panties and short-change intoxicated patrons, loses her job, is refused another job because she is female, is invited to a party where she is given a drugged drink, falls unconscious and is hospitalized. Heckerling explores the absurdity of worlds in which characters' experiences are often confusing and unsatisfying.

MATERNITY AND AGE DIFFERENCE

The films of Amy Heckerling develop comedic scenarios around female experiences of pregnancy, childbirth, weight fluctuations, breastfeeding, and the physical manifestations of aging. Whereas *Bridesmaids* has been accused of linking women to toilet humor that "is coded as masculine," the same cannot be said about Heckerling's comedic exploration of experiences that are distinctively linked to female experience.[48] In *Clueless*, for example, Cher explains her absence from class by informing her teacher that she was "surfing the crimson wave," a reference to menstruation. The character of Audrey Griswold in *European Vacation* responds to her boyfriend's rejection by embarking on an eating binge. Middle-aged Rosie in *I Could Never Be Your Woman* is so self-conscious about dating a much younger man that she snatches her identification card back from a nightclub doorman after he looks at it for a long time. During Mollie's pregnancy in *Look Who's Talking*, she vomits in the middle of a conversation, swigs stomach medicine, and gulps a quantity of apple juice.

It is significant that Heckerling's most profitable film centers on pregnancy and childbirth. One of the most prominent comedies ever about human procreation, *Look Who's Talking* expands the genre's range of subject matter and affirms the potentially universal appeal of bodily experiences that are not specific to men. While the film's attraction of a wide audience can be attributed partly to its inclusion of prominent male actors—John Travolta as James and the voice of Bruce Willis as Mikey—this is also consistent with the inclusiveness of Heckerling's humor, which typically encompasses sympathetic male as well as female characterizations. Whereas the film's topics of parenthood and the complexities of adult relationships are universally familiar, its humor has origins in the experiences of women.

The positioning of maternity as a catalyst for humor is part of a longstanding relationship between women and comedy. For instance, Mikhail Bakhtin identifies the bodies of pregnant women as emblems of the "ambivalent" and "contradictory process" of life in medieval folk theatre.[49] Bakhtin's comment that, moreover, "the old hags are laughing" has been embraced by feminists as a traditional configuration of female defiance through mirth.[50] For example, Kathleen Rowe draws on Bakhtin's work in her study of the feminist value of screen comedy. Central to her analysis is the unruly woman, an "ambivalent figure of female outrageousness and transgression with roots in the narrative forms of comedy and the social practices of carnival."[51] Rowe writes that the unruly woman

> is willing to offend and be offensive. As with the heroines of the romantic film comedy . . . her sexuality is neither evil nor uncontrollable . . . nor sanctified and denied . . . Associated with both beauty and monstrosity, the unruly woman dwells close to the grotesque. But [she] often enjoys a reprieve from those fates that so often seem inevitable to women under patriarchy, because her home is comedy and the carnivalesque, the realm of inversion and fantasy where . . . the ordinary world can be stood on its head.[52]

Brazenness without retribution is central to female agency in comedy. Just as the laughter of Bakhtin's pregnant women is "loaded with . . . connotations of fear and loathing around the biological processes of reproduction and of aging," humor in *Look Who's Talking* exists in counterpoint to despondency, pessimism, and self-criticism.[53] Mollie's experiences of childbirth and child-rearing are depicted through humor that is often tormented, invoking laughter's capacity to allay negative emotions. When Mollie is in labor, for instance, she responds to a midwife's instruction by roaring "Fuck my breathing!" in a voice resembling that of the possessed girl in *The Exorcist* (William Friedkin, 1973). Motherhood is a locus of the grotesque when Mollie apologizes to Mikey for looking "like I could play the lead in *Night of the Living Dead*"[George Romero, 1968]. Body humor in *Look Who's Talking* is a foil for despair that is linked to maternity.

The likening of adult masculinity to a childlike state can be viewed as an extension of the grotesque. Sarah Harwood identifies *Look Who's Talking* as an example of the "highly privileged" status that childhood had in Hollywood films of the 1980s, when the family was a "site of political, social and cultural struggle" involving the search for "a moral framework."[54] Yet the significance of the theme of childhood is not limited to biological infancy. Sometimes, Harwood notes, the theme of childhood takes the form of "the adult 'child' [who is] represented within a familial structure, still working through the Oedipal scenarios of their own maturation while initiating that of the next generation."[55] Within this context, the positioning of male characters as embodiments of suspended development has been attributed to screen industries' attempts to attract male viewers while avoiding stereotypes that might offend other social groups, as Anita Gates explains: "As long as men are in power, they are the one group that [screen industries] can ridicule without fear of reprisal."[56]

In *Look Who's Talking*, the likening of contemporary masculinity to a childlike state is exemplified by the characters of two prospective fathers for Mikey, James and Albert, who are presented as being highly susceptible to instant gratification and spontaneous sexual urges. For instance, Albert confesses that he can't make a commitment to the pregnant Mollie because he is "going through a selfish phase." Similarly, Mollie's perception of James as an irresponsible thrill-seeker is reinforced when he shows her how to fly a plane and issues a jocular invitation for her to place her hand on his "stick." The film's theme of arrested male development is underscored by the portrayal of Mollie's father, who has no dialogue and is shown laughing inanely while turning the pages of an accountancy magazine. Whereas male characters are portrayed as infantile in *Look Who's Talking*, however, Heckerling's other work positions youthfulness as an experience shared by all.

Far from it being limited to negative portrayals of men, an ambiguous distinction between adulthood and youth is widely evident in Heckerling's work. Consider that her career developed in a period when media theorist Joshua Meyrowitz observed that adults in contemporary films are "often outsmarted by children," who are "sometimes portrayed as more mature, sensitive, and intelligent."[57] Meyrowitz sees these developments as reflecting a wider diminution of "traditional dividing lines" between the social identities of adults and children, a change he links to the shift from print media to television, the latter of which places less emphasis on skills accumulated with age.[58] He argues that age-determinism has thus become less relevant than how social change shapes childhood.[59]

These ideas resonate in Heckerling's films in the form of a degree of homogeneity between the behavior of young people and adults. For instance, intergenerational exchange is highlighted in *Fast Times* in a subplot involving the relationship between inattentive Spicoli and his teacher Mr Hand (Ray Walston). When Spicoli has a pizza delivered to him in class, Mr Hand responds by emulating the student's casual demeanor and offering the pizza to other students. In *Clueless*, Cher's success in making a match between Mr Hall (Wallace Shawn) and Miss Geist (Twink Caplan) forms part of the film's portrayal of teenagers as having cordially familiar relationships with adults. The likening of adults to teenagers is extended in Heckerling's later film, *I Could Never Be Your Woman*, in which forty-something Rosie embarks on a sexual relationship with Adam (Paul Rudd), who is in his late twenties. While Adam exhibits a childlike propensity for spontaneous dancing and other antics, Rosie is reluctant to "act her age" and is more attached to her tween daughter's Barbie dolls than her daughter is. In Heckerling's work, the postfeminist

Figure 12.3 In *Fast Times*, Mr Hand invites the class to share Spicoli's pizza.

embrace of girlhood and consumer culture extends to themes of youthful adulthood and intergenerational exchange.

Comedic observation of social environments is a distinctive trait of Heckerling's work. In *Clueless*, Cher and Dionne's introduction of Tai to the cliques populating the schoolyard can be seen to form a link between the school hierarchy in *Heathers* (Michael Lehmann, 1989) and the more explicit social mapping of the cafeteria in *Mean Girls*. The title sequence of *Fast Times* presents the mall as an intricate social order in which characters seek to maintain or advance their status. In Heckerling's writing, comedic dialogue serves as social commentary. The pastiche of historical architectural styles in Beverly Hills is encapsulated in *Clueless* when Cher declares, "Isn't my house classic? The columns date all the way back to 1972." In *Look Who's Talking*, James's aside to the infant Mikey can be read as an astute observation of male behavior or of a universal psychological condition: "It's weird, isn't it? You spend the first nine months trying to get out and the rest of your life trying to get back in." Within the worlds they depict, Heckerling's films reflect on current social developments that often prefigure the wider exploration of these issues in other feature films. Examples are the topics of artificial insemination by a single woman in *Look Who's Talking*; plastic surgery and mobile phone use among teenagers in *Clueless*; emancipation of minors and human egg farming in *Loser*; a sexual relationship between a middle-aged woman and a younger man in *I Could Never Be Your Woman*; and infringement of civil liberties through interception of private communications in *Vamps* (Heckerling, 2012). Her comedies reflect on a society shaped by technologies from television to mobile phones.

HECKERLING AND TELEVISION

Television is integral to Amy Heckerling's contributions to the comedy and teen genres. She has worked with alumni of the television series *Saturday Night Live* (*SNL*)—Joe Piscopo on *Johnny Dangerously* (Heckerling, 1984), Chevy Chase on *European Vacation*, and Will Ferrell and Chris Kattan on *A Night at the Roxbury* (John Fortenberry, 1998), which she co-produced. Heckerling's work is a precursor to the work of Tina Fey and Diablo Cody (creator of *United States of Tara*, 2009–11) in both film and television. Tina Fey, in particular, is significant for being the first female head writer on *SNL*, an achievement reinforced by her role as executive producer, writer, and star of the television sitcom *30 Rock* (2006–13) in which she plays the head writer on a television sketch comedy show. Ironically, the success of *30 Rock* coincided with *I Could Never Be Your Woman*, about an aging female television comedy producer who is prompted by the axing of her show to question whether she is too old to do relevant work in the medium.

Indeed, after three decades, Heckerling's career offers insight into the options available to an established female director in the film and television industries, where very few careers, female or male, are unaffected by fickle audience preferences and industry economics. A report by the Writers Guild of America West (WGAW) suggests that employment in these industries is affected by age as much as gender: writers "aged 41 to 50 . . . claimed the largest share of employment in television and film" whereas the "status of older writers tends to decline rather rapidly beyond the age of 60."[60] Although Heckerling's increased television output in the 2010s may be linked to her recent films' lack of success, this shift can also be understood in relation to a decline in employment in the film industry because of "reduced levels of theatrical film production" during and immediately following "the Great Recession."[61] At the same time, the fact that she has worked in television since the 1980s positions this medium as a more important component of her whole career than has traditionally been acknowledged.

That Heckerling's work spans film and television is not unusual. Television now rivals the prestige of film, as reflected in the number of successful film directors who have gone on to work in television, including Martin Scorsese, David Fincher, David Lynch, Harold Ramis, Jason Reitman, and Jon Favreau. Similarly, television has become a more common field of employment than film for many female comedy directors of Heckerling's generation, including Penny Marshall, Penelope Spheeris, Martha Coolidge, and Betty Thomas. Indeed, industry statistics reflect that television is a significant area of women's influence on screen. For instance, the Directors Guild of America reports that women form a higher percentage of directors on primetime television than in film, and women are more likely to hold other key production roles in television than in film.[62] Women are more likely to be writers for film than directors, and are considerably more likely to write for television than for film, according to the WGAW.[63] The *2014 Hollywood Diversity Report* notes that the writing staffs of about half of all comedies and dramas in broadcast television are more than 30 percent female.[64] At first glance, the higher numbers of women working in television than film are consistent with a view that television "has always . . . particularly tried to attract female viewers" because women form a larger part of the television audience than men.[65]

On closer examination, however, employment of women in television is not necessarily abundant or linked to audience demographics. Robert S. Alley and Irby B. Brown note that the number of female television producers has always been disproportionately low in comparison to women's share of the television audience.[66] Denise D. Bielby asserts that opportunities for women in television are limited by the fact that "network executives who make decisions about program procurement and scheduling and those at the production companies who determine financing are almost always males."[67] Women are also disadvantaged by "typecasting of writers," reflected in the relatively high employment of women at "networks that specialize in genres . . . that are targeted to women viewers."[68]

In recent decades, women's achievements in television can also be linked to changes in the structure of the American television industry. The government's deregulation of television in the 1990s led to an increase in the number of networks and a shift from mass programming to "niche-marketing and narrowcasting strategies," including the targeting of youth audiences.[69] Between 2006 and 2012, employment for writers in television increased significantly, by 18.4 percent, and included an increase in the number of female writers; however, women as a percentage of writers dropped because men were the main beneficiaries of the increased opportunities.[70] Nevertheless, the success of Tina Fey suggests that women can surmount traditional barriers to working in genres such as situation comedy, which is traditionally the work of teams of writers that have tended to be overwhelmingly male. As Bielby notes, the work-demands associated with sitcoms are "premised on co-workers sharing common sensibilities about male humor and related considerations" that have been "difficult for outsiders such as women to penetrate."[71] Equally, the relative abundance of youth-targeted television series in the 1990s and 2000s has the potential to provide opportunities for female directors and writers, given their contributions to the teen genre in film.

Heckerling's early work in television precedes this proliferation of youth-targeted television series. Indeed, *Clueless* was originally conceived as a television pilot. The film led to a television spin-off, *Clueless* (1996–9), of which Heckerling was the creator as well as an executive producer, writer, and director. She was also a producer, writer, and director of the television series *Fast Times* (1986) and creator of *Baby Talk* (1991–2), a spin-off from *Look Who's Talking*. However, these series are usually overlooked in surveys of Heckerling's career and in the history of television. Although she gained early experience from these spin-offs, Heckerling's television career reflects the tenuousness of success in culture industries, where genres are "susceptible to . . . cycles of popularity."[72] In particular, the spin-offs from Heckerling's films received less acclaim than the films themselves and tended to be short-lived. In contrast to the film of *Buffy the Vampire Slayer*, which was eclipsed by the popularity of its eponymous television spin-off (1997–2003), Heckerling's films have been so profitable and acclaimed that the spin-offs would have had to be very successful to match their popularity. To date, her films have been better known than her television work.

Nevertheless, Heckerling's early work in television foreshadows the subsequent wave of teen-targeted television series, such as *Beverly Hills, 90210* (1990–2000), *Gilmore Girls* (2000–7), and *The O.C.* (2003–7). In this context, the spin-off from *Fast Times* can be considered to be remarkably ahead of its time. This series appeared in a period when network television was more often targeted at families than specifically at teenagers, and censorship meant that film was more able to address topics unsuitable for children, such as adolescent sexuality and uncontrolled hedonism. It was the "post-network" period of the 1990s that witnessed the growing popularity of "quality" television series,[73] influenced by the productions of cable channel Home Box Office (HBO). Merri Lisa Johnson writes that HBO series such as *Six Feet Under* (2001–5) and *The Sopranos* (1999–2007) were innovative for grappling with "feminist-influenced conflicts over gender, sex, desire, and power" with a degree of depth and complexity that had been unusual in television, while making use of the medium's capacity to reach a wide audience.[74] Quality television aimed at youth audiences includes the movie spin-offs *Buffy the Vampire Slayer*, *Parenthood* (2010–), *Teen Wolf* (2011–), and the television spin-off *The Carrie Diaries* (2013–14), which have come to overshadow earlier spin-offs such as *Fast Times* and *Baby Talk*. For young people who have been raised with post-network television, the films and television shows of the 1980s are within the culture of a previous generation. Nevertheless, the sensibilities of these young people have been shaped partly by popular culture of the 1980s and 1990s, which in some instances has acquired cult status.

The continuing relevance of Heckerling's experience in the teen genre is reflected in her work as a director on youth-targeted quality television series, specifically *Gossip Girl* (2007–12), *The Carrie Diaries*, and *Suburgatory* (2011–14). For example, *The Carrie Diaries* displays superficial affinities with Heckerling's teen films. A spin-off from *Sex and the City*, the series is set in the 1980s and pays homage to the period by incorporating pop songs and references to films. However, *The Carrie Diaries* also infuses the teen genre with the sensibility of a later generation of youth that is presented as being far more knowledgeable about adult relationships. Its narrative about the teenage years of Carrie Bradshaw (Anna Sophia Robb) and her friends involves the premise that their activities exhibit the early stages of a sexual knowingness that is a central theme of *Sex and the City*. *The Carrie Diaries* is characteristic of post-network television in its reflexivity, emphasis on verbal expression of complex emotions, and the fact that the teenagers' lives are barely distinguishable from those of the adult characters.

For example, in the episode "Express Yourself" (2013), Carrie is 17 and has a job in New York City, where she shares an apartment with Walt (Brendan Dooling) and Samantha (Lindsey Gort). While Samantha is a phone sex worker and gives advice to the inexperienced Mouse (Ellen Wong), Carrie's widower father is shown embarking on a new sexual relationship. In another plotline about Walt's interest in Bennet (Jake Robinson), the open expression of a developing homosexual relationship is more consistent with the twenty-first century than with the 1980s, in which few teen films included an openly gay character. Equally, the focus of *Gossip Girl* on privileged young New Yorkers echoes the social world of the Beverly Hills teens in *Clueless*. However, the flirtatious narration by the "gossip girl" (Kristen Bell) is more cynical than Cher's bubbly commentary, and the behavior of the teenage characters in this series is more like that of adults than in Heckerling's films. While Heckerling's work in teen television can be read as an extension of the subject matter of her films, the themes of sexual knowledge and gossip in these series suggest that the distinction between youth and adulthood has since been further undermined by the "exposure" of adult "secret-keeping and the secret of secrecy."[75]

Heckerling's television work also draws on her decades as a director of a wider range of comedies. For instance, she worked as a director on the comedy series *The Office* (2005–13), a mockumentary that satirizes the interaction between office workers, and the comedy-drama series *Rake* (2014–), about a lawyer who engages in unrestrained professional and hedonistic behavior. Both series serve as reminders that Heckerling's professional experience has not been limited to the teen genre. Indeed, on her earliest films she worked with some of the most prominent comedic performers of the day, such as Chase and Eric Idle (on *European Vacation*) and Piscopo, Michael Keaton, and Danny DeVito (on *Johnny Dangerously*). In *The Office* and *Rake*, respectively, Heckerling's direction of Steve Carell and Greg Kinnear is indicative of her considerable skill in working with actors. This is evidenced in the typically convincing performances in her films, in which even the less likable characters tend to have depth. Indeed, she previously directed Greg Kinnear as another unscrupulous character in *Loser*. In contrast to the notion that women in film and television have been marginalized through association with genres targeted at female audiences, recognition of the full range of Heckerling's work provides evidence for why she is a significant elder to the generation of female television comedy professionals that includes Fey, Cody, and Poehler (producer of *Parks and Recreation*, 2009–).

As a director, writer, and producer, Amy Heckerling has developed the genres of comedy and teen film to encompass more complex gendered perspectives and acquire greater prestige. Exploring body humor and the ambiguous social distinction between adulthood and youth, Heckerling's screenplays and films are characterized by comically incisive social observation. The influence of her work over more than three decades is echoed in the exploration of similar themes by a subsequent generation of female comedy writers and producers in film and television.

NOTES

1 Geoff King, *New Hollywood Cinema* (London: I. B. Tauris, 2009), pp. 28, 86, 92.
2 Christina Lane, *Feminist Hollywood from Born in Flames to Point Break* (Detroit, MI: Wayne State University Press, 2000), p. 49.
3 Judith Mayne, *The Woman at the Keyhole: Feminism and Women's Cinema* (Bloomington, IN: Indiana University Press, 1990), p. 97.
4 Lane, p. 37.
5 Richard Maltby, *Hollywood Cinema* (Oxford: Blackwell, 1995), p. 132.
6 Lane, p. 49.
7 Ibid. p. 37.
8 Martha M. Lauzen, *Women @ the Box Office: A Study of the Top 100 Worldwide Grossing Films* (San Diego, CA: Center for the Study of Women in Television and Film, School of Theatre, Television and Film, San Diego State University, 2008), p. 1. Available at <http://womenintvfilm.sdsu.edu/research.html> (last accessed 10 December 2014).
9 Martha M. Lauzen, *The Celluloid Ceiling: Behind-the-Scenes Employment of Women in the Top 250 Films of 2012* (San Diego, CA: Center for the Study of Women in Television and Film, School of Theatre, Television and Film, San Diego State University, 2013), p. 1. Available at <http://womenintvfilm.sdsu.edu/research.html> (last accessed 10 December 2014).
10 Christopher Hitchens, "Why women aren't funny," *Vanity Fair*, January 2007. Available at <http://www.vanityfair.com/culture/features/2007/01/hitchens200701> (last accessed 10 December 2014); see also L. R. Franzini, "Feminism and women's sense of humor," *Sex Roles* 35: 11–12 (1996), pp. 811–14.
11 Nicholas Jarecki, *Breaking In: How 20 Film Directors Got Their Start* (New York: Broadway, 2001), p. 143; Michael Singer, *A Cut Above: 50 Film Directors Talk About Their Craft* (Los Angeles, CA: Lone Eagle, 1998), pp. 81–2.
12 Mary G. Hurd, *Women Directors and Their Films* (Westport, CT: Praeger, 2007), p. 23.
13 Robin Wood, *Hollywood from Vietnam to Reagan* (New York: Columbia University Press, 1986), pp. 192–4.

14 King, pp. 140–1.

15 Lane, p. 231, n7.

16 Thomas Doherty, *Teenagers & Teenpics: The Juvenilization of American Movies in the 1950s* (Boston, MA: Unwin Hyman, 1988), p. 10.

17 Lesley Stern, "*Emma* in Los Angeles: remaking the book and the city," in James Naremore (ed.), *Film Adaptation* (London: Athlone, 2000), p. 223.

18 Melissa Lenos, "In Focus: *Clueless*," *Cinema Journal* 53: 3 (Spring 2014), p. 125.

19 William Paul, *Laughing Screaming: Modern Hollywood Horror and Comedy* (New York: Columbia University Press, 1994), p. 192.

20 Ibid.

21 Stern, pp. 225–37.

22 Ibid. p. 237.

23 Peter Krämer, "Would you take your child to see this film? The cultural and social work of the family-adventure movie," in Steve Neale and Murray Smith (eds.), *Contemporary Hollywood Cinema* (London: Routledge, 1999), p. 294.

24 Rachel Abramowitz, *Is That a Gun in Your Pocket? Women's Experience of Power in Hollywood* (New York: Random House, 2000), p. 144.

25 Ibid. p. 144.

26 Vicky Lebeau, *Lost Angels: Psychoanalysis and Cinema* (London: Routledge, 1995), p. 22.

27 Lesley Speed, "Good fun and bad hair days: girls in teen film," *Metro*, 101 (1995), p. 24.

28 Lesley Speed, "Loose cannons: white masculinity and the vulgar teen comedy film," *Journal of Popular Culture* 43: 4 (August 2010), p. 835.

29 Jarecki, pp. 143, 148.

30 Paul, p. 3.

31 Ibid. p. 45; see also Mikhail Bakhtin, *Rabelais and His World* (Bloomington, IN: Indiana University Press, 1984), p. 19.

32 Bakhtin, p. 19.

33 Ibid.

34 Wood, pp. 217–20.

35 Lane, p. 66; Abramowitz, p. 149; Michelle Citron, "Women's film production: going mainstream," in E. Deidre Pribram (ed.), *Female Spectators: Looking at Film and Television* (London: Verso, 1988), p. 60.

36 Gail Markle, "'Can women have sex like a man?': sexual scripts in *Sex and the City*," *Sexuality & Culture* 12: 1 (Winter 2008), pp. 47–8.

37 Ibid. p. 46.

38 Helen Warner, "'A new feminist revolution in Hollywood comedy?': postfeminist discourses and the critical reception of *Bridesmaids*," in Joel Gwynne and Nadine Muller (eds.), *Postfeminism and Contemporary Hollywood Cinema* (New York: Palgrave Macmillan, 2013), pp. 232–3.

39 Ibid. p. 234.

40 Joel Gwynne and Nadine Muller, "Introduction: postfeminism and contemporary Hollywood cinema," in Gwynne and Muller, p. 2.

41 Ibid.

42 Charlotte Brunsdon, *Screen Tastes: Soap Opera to Satellite Dishes* (London: Routledge, 1997), p. 84.

43 Franzini, p. 811.

44 Gwynne and Muller, p. 3.

45 Chris Holmlund, "Postfeminism from A to G," *Cinema Journal* 44: 2 (Winter 2005): p. 117.

46 Angela McRobbie, *The Aftermath of Feminism: Gender, Culture and Social Change* (Los Angeles, CA: Sage, 2009), p. 11.
47 Susan Faludi, *Backlash: The Undeclared War Against Women* (London: Chatto & Windus, 1992).
48 Warner, p. 231.
49 Bakhtin, pp. 25–6.
50 Ibid. p. 25; see also Mary Russo, *The Female Grotesque: Risk, Excess and Modernity* (New York: Routledge, 1995), p. 63.
51 Kathleen Rowe, *The Unruly Woman: Gender and the Genres of Laughter* (Austin, TX: University of Texas Press, 1995), p. 10.
52 Ibid. pp. 10–11.
53 Ibid. p. 63.
54 Sarah Harwood, *Family Fictions: Representations of the Family in 1980s Hollywood Cinema* (Basingstoke: Macmillan, 1997), pp. 124–5; 3.
55 Ibid. p. 124.
56 Anita Gates, "Boors on the box," *Age* (Melbourne), 20 April 2000.
57 Joshua Meyrowitz, *No Sense of Place: The Impact of Electronic Media on Social Behavior* (New York: Oxford University Press, 1985), p. 229.
58 Ibid. p. 239.
59 Ibid. pp. 231–2.
60 Darnell M. Hunt, *Turning Missed Opportunities Into Realized Ones: The 2014 Hollywood Writers Report* (Los Angeles, CA: Writers Guild of America [West], 2014), p. 11. Available at <http://www.wga.org/subpage_whoweare.aspx?id=922> (last accessed 10 December 2014).
61 Ibid. p. 21.
62 Directors Guild of America, "DGA report finds director diversity in episodic television remains static," 2 October 2013. Available at <http://www.dga.org/News/ PressReleases/2013/100213-DGA-Report-Finds-Director-Diversity-in-Episodic- Television-Remains-Static.aspx> (last accessed 10 December 2014).
63 Hunt, p. 11.
64 Darnell Hunt, Ana-Christina Ramon, and Zachary Price, *2014 Hollywood Diversity Report: Making Sense of the Disconnect* (Los Angeles, CA: Ralph J. Bunche Center for African American Studies at UCLA, 2014), pp. 7, 13–15. Available at <http://www. bunchecenter.ucla.edu/index.php/2014/02/new-2014-hollywood-diversity-report- making-sense-of-the-disconnect/> (last accessed 10 December 2014).
65 Lynn Spigel and Denise Mann, "Introduction," in Lynn Spigel and Denise Mann (eds.), *Private Screenings: Television and the Female Consumer* (Minneapolis, MN: University of Minnesota Press, 1992), p. vii; see also Robert S. Alley and Irby B. Brown, *Women Television Producers: Transformation of the Male Medium* (Rochester, NY: University of Rochester Press, 2001), pp. 16–18.
66 Alley and Brown, p. 18.
67 Denise D. Bielby, "Gender inequality in culture industries: women and men writers in film and television," *Sociologie du Travail* 51: 2 (April–June 2009), p. 244.
68 Ibid. p. 245.
69 Ibid. p. 244.
70 Hunt, p. 17.
71 Bielby, p. 245.
72 Ibid.
73 Anikó Imre, "Gender and quality television," *Feminist Media Studies* 9: 4 (2009), pp. 392–3.

74 Merri Lisa Johnson, "Introduction: ladies love your box: the rhetoric of pleasure and danger in feminist television studies," in Merri Lisa Johnson (ed.), *Third Wave Feminism and Television: Jane Puts It in a Box* (London: I. B. Tauris, 2007), pp. 2–3.

75 Meyrowitz, p. 249.

Appendix:
Other Films and Television Shows Cited in this Collection

Alien (Ridley Scott), 1979
Anchorman 2: The Legend Continues (Adam McKay), 2013
American Graffiti (George Lucas), 1973
American Idol (Fox), 2002–
American Pie (Paul Weitz), 1999
Angels with Dirty Faces (Michael Curtiz), 1938
Assassination of a High-School President (Brett Simon), 2008
Austin Powers: The Spy Who Shagged Me (Jay Roach), 1999
Avatar (James Cameron), 2009
Baby Boom (Charles Shyer), 1987
Baby It's You (John Sayles), 1983
Baby Mama (Michael McCullers), 2008
Bachelor Party (Neal Israel), 1984
Back to the Future (Robert Zemeckis), 1985
Back to the Future Part II (Robert Zemeckis), 1989
Back to the Future Part III (Robert Zemeckis), 1991
The Back-Up Plan (Alan Poul), 2010
Beaches (Garry Marshall), 1988
Better Off Dead (Savage Steve Holland), 1985
Beverly Hills, 90210 (Fox Network), 1990–2000
Beyond Clueless (Charlie Lyne), 2014
Big (Penny Marshall), 1988
The Biggest Loser (NBC), 2004–
The Blackboard Jungle (Richard Brooks), 1955
Black Swan (Darren Aronofsky), 2010
Blade (Stephen Norrington), 1998

The Bling Ring (Sofia Coppola), 2013
Boyz N the Hood (John Singleton), 1991
The Brady Bunch Movie (Betty Thomas), 1995
The Breakfast Club (John Hughes), 1985
Breaking Bad (AMC), 2008–13
Bridesmaids (Paul Feig), 2011
The Bridges of Madison County (Clint Eastwood), 1995
Bridget Jones's Diary (Sharon Maguire), 2001
Bridget Jones: The Edge of Reason (Beeban Kidron), 2004
Bring It On (Peyton Reed), 2000
Buffy the Vampire Slayer (Fran Rubel Kuzui), 1992
Buffy the Vampire Slayer (WB Network), 1997–2001; (UPN), 2001–3
The Cabinet of Dr. Caligari (Robert Wiene), 1920
Cabin in the Woods (Drew Goddard), 2012
The Carrie Diaries (The CW), 2013–14
Carnival of Souls (Herk Harvey), 1962
Can't Buy Me Love (Steve Rash), 1987
Can't Hardly Wait (Harry Elfont and Deborah Kaplan), 1998
The Change-Up (David Dobkin), 2011
Cheaper by the Dozen (Shawn Levy), 2003
Un Chien Andalou (Luis Buñuel), 1929
Christmas Vacation (Jeremiah Chechik), 1989
Cinderella (Kenneth Branagh), 2015
A Cinderella Story (Mark Rosman), 2004
Citizen Kane (Orson Welles), 1942
The Courtship of Eddie's Father (Vincente Minnelli), 1963
The Craft (Andrew Fleming), 1996
Cruel Intentions (Roger Kumble), 1999
Curly Sue (John Hughes), 1991
Daddy Day Care (Steve Carr), 2003
Dance of the Damned (Katt Shea), 1989
Dangerous Minds (John N. Smith), 1995
Dawson's Creek (WB Network), 1998–2003
Dazed and Confused (Richard Linklater), 1993
Death at a Funeral (Neil Labute), 2010
Deep Impact (Mimi Leder), 1998
Desperately Seeking Susan (Susan Seidelman), 1985
The Devil Wears Prada (David Frankel), 2006
Down with Love (Peyton Reed), 2003
Dracula (Francis Ford Coppola), 1992
Easy A (Will Gluck), 2010
Emma (A&E Television), 1996

Emma (Douglas McGrath), 1996
Empire Strikes Back (Irvin Kershner), 1980
The Exorcist (William Friedkin), 1973
Extreme Makeover (ABC), 2002–7
Father of the Bride Part II (Charles Shyer), 1995
Ferris Bueller's Day Off (John Hughes), 1987
The Flintstones (ABC), 1960–6
"For Keeps" (John G. Avildsen), 1988
The Fountain (Darren Aronofsky), 2006
Foxfire (Annette Haywood-Carter), 1996
Frasier (NBC), 1993–2004
Fried Green Tomatoes (Jon Avnet), 1991
Friends (NBC), 1994–2004
Friends with Kids (Jennifer Westfeldt), 2011
Fright Night (Tom Holland), 1985
From Dusk Till Dawn (Robert Rodriguez), 1996
Frozen (Chris Buck, Jennifer Lee), 2013
Get Over It (Tommy O'Haver), 2001
Getting It On (William Olsen), 1983
Ghostbusters (Ivan Reitman), 1984
Ghostbusters II (Ivan Reitman), 1989
Gidget (ABC), 1965–6
Gigi (Vincente Minnelli), 1958
Gilmore Girls (Warner Bros. Television), 2000–7
Ginger Snaps (John Fawcett), 2000
Girl Meets World (Disney), 2014–
Girls Just Want to Have Fun (Alan Metter), 1985
Girls Town (Jim McKay), 1996
Go Fish (Rose Troche), 1994
Gone Too Far (Destin Ekaragha), 2013
Gossip Girl (The CW), 2007–12
Grease (Randal Kleiser), 1978
Hamlet (Franco Zeffirelli), 1990
The Hangover (Todd Phillips), 2009
Happy Days (ABC), 1974–84
Heathers (Michael Lehmann), 1989
Hey Arnold (Nickelodeon), 1996–2004
Homeland (Showtime), 2011–
Home Alone (Chris Columbus), 1990
Homework (James Beshears), 1982
How to Get Away with Murder (ABC), 2014–
The Hunger (Tony Scott), 1983

The Hunger Games (Gary Ross), 2012
The Hurt Locker (Kathryn Bigelow), 2008
Idle Hands (Rodman Flender), 1999
I Love You, Man (John Hamburg), 2009
Indiana Jones and the Last Crusade (Steven Spielberg), 1989
Indiana Jones and the Temple of Doom (Steven Spielberg), 1984
Innocent Blood (John Landis), 1992
Interview with a Vampire: The Vampire Chronicles (Neil Jordan), 1994
It's Complicated (Nancy Meyers), 2009
The Jazz Singer (Alan Crosland), 1927
Jerry Maguire (Cameron Crowe), 1996
Jersey Shore (MTV), 2009–
Joy of Sex (Martha Coolidge), 1984
Joysticks (Greydon Clark), 1983
Julie & Julia (Nora Ephron), 2009
Juno (Jason Reitman), 2007
The Karate Kid (John G. Avilsden), 1984
Kids (Larry Clark), 1995
Knocked Up (Judd Apatow), 2007
Kramer vs. Kramer (Robert Benton), 1979
The Last American Virgin (Boaz Davidson), 1982
Legally Blonde (Robert Luketic), 2001
Let Me In (Matt Reeves), 2010
Let the Right One In (Tomas Alfredson), 2008
Life As We Know It (Greg Berlanti), 2010
Little Fockers (Paul Weitz), 2010
Little Johnny Jones (Mervyn LeRoy), 1929
The Little Rascals (Penelope Spheeris), 1994
Little Women (Gillian Armstrong), 1994
Losin' It (Curtis Hanson), 1983
The Lost Boys (Joel Schumacher), 1987
Love and Basketball (Gina Prince-Bythewood), 2000
Maid in Manhattan (Wayne Wang), 2002
Maleficent (Robert Stromberg), 2014
Mamma Mia! (Phyllida Lloyd), 2008
M*A*S*H (Robert Altman), 1970
Mean Girls (Mark Waters), 2004
Meet the Fockers (Jay Roach), 2004
Menace II Society (Albert Hughes and Allen Hughes), 1993
Metropolis (Fritz Lang), 1927
Mr. Mom (Stan Dragoti), 1983
Mrs. Dalloway (Marleen Gorris), 1997

Mrs. Doubtfire (Chris Columbus), 1993
My Fair Lady (George Cukor), 1964
My So-Called Life (ABC), 1994–5
Mystic Pizza (Donald Petrie), 1988
Never Been Kissed (Raja Gosnell), 1999
A Night at the Roxbury (John Fortenberry), 1998
Night of the Living Dead (George A. Romero), 1968
Noah (Darren Aronofsky), 2014
No Reservations (Scott Hicks), 2007
Nosferatu (F. W. Murnau), 1922
O (Tim Blake Nelson), 2001
The O.C. (Warner Bros. Television), 2003–7
The Office (NBC Universal), 2005–13
One Fine Day (Michael Hoffman), 1996
One True Thing (Carl Franklin), 1998
Only Lovers Left Alive (Jim Jarmusch), 2013
Orlando (Sally Potter), 1992
Our Idiot Brother (Jesse Peretz), 2011
Parenthood (Universal), 2010-
Parks and Recreation (NBC), 2009–15
Paul (Greg Mottola), 2011
Pay it Forward (Mimi Leder), 2000
PCU (Hart Bochner), 1994
The Perks of Being a Wallflower (Stephen Chbosky), 2012
The Piano (Jane Campion), 1993
Planes, Trains, and Automobiles (John Hughes), 1987
Police Academy (Hugh Wilson), 1984
Porky's (Bob Clark), 1982
Porky's II: The Next Day (Bob Clark), 1983
Pretty in Pink (Howard Deutch), 1986
Pretty Woman (Garry Marshall), 1990
Pride and Prejudice (BBC), 1995
The Princess Diaries (Garry Marshall), 2001
Private Parts (Betty Thomas), 1997
Prom (Joe Nussbaum), 2011
The Public Enemy (William A. Wellman), 1931
Pump Up the Volume (Allan Moyle), 1990
Ragtime (Milos Forman), 1981
Raiders of the Lost Ark (Steven Spielberg), 1981
Raising Helen (Garry Marshall), 2004
Rebel Without a Cause (Nicholas Ray), 1955
The Ren and Stimpy Show (Nickelodeon), 1991–6

Return of the Jedi (Richard Marquand), 1983
Risky Business (Paul Brickman), 1983
Romeo + Juliet (Baz Luhrmann), 1996
Rumble Fish (Francis Ford Coppola), 1983
Sabrina, the Teenage Witch (ABC), 1996–2000; (WB Network), 2000–3
Saved by the Bell (NBC), 1989–93
Scandal (ABC), 2012–
Scream (Wes Craven), 1996
The Secret Life of Bees (Gina Prince-Bythewood), 2008
Sex and the City (HBO), 1998–2004
Sex and the City (Michael Patrick King), 2008
Sex and the City 2 (Michael Patrick King), 2010
Shadow of the Vampire (E. Elias Merhige), 2000
She's All That (Robert Iscove), 1999
She's the Man (Andy Fickman), 2006
Single White Female (Barbet Schroeder), 1992
Sin noticias de Dios (Agustin Diaz Yanes), 2001
The Sisterhood of the Travelling Pants (Ken Kwapis), 2005
Six Feet Under (HBO), 2001–5
Sixteen Candles (John Hughes), 1984
Sleepless in Seattle (Nora Ephron), 1993
Slumdog Millionaire (Danny Boyle), 2008
Some Like It Hot (Billy Wilder), 1959
Something's Gotta Give (Nancy Meyers), 2003
The Sopranos (HBO), 1999–2007
The Sound of Music (Robert Wise), 1965
Spartacus (Stanley Kubrick), 1960
The Spectacular Now (James Ponsoldt), 2013
Star Wars (George Lucas), 1977
Suburgatory (WB Network), 2011–14
Steel Magnolias (Herbert Ross), 1989
Summer of '42 (Robert Mulligan), 1971
Sunshine (Danny Boyle), 2007
Superbad (Greg Mottola), 2007
The Switch (Josh Gordon and Will Speck), 2010
The Sweetest Thing (Roger Kumble), 2002
Teen Wolf (MGM Television), 2011–
10 Things I Hate About You (Gil Junger), 1999
Terminator 2: Judgement Day (James Cameron), 1991
Terms of Endearment (James L. Brooks), 1983
Tex (Tim Hunter), 1982
Thelma and Louise (Ridley Scott), 1991

30 Rock (NBC), 2006–13
Three Men and a Baby (Leonard Nimoy), 1987
Titanic (James Cameron), 1997
A Trip to the Moon (George Méliès), 1902
True Blood (HBO), 2008–
27 Dresses (Anne Fletcher), 2008
Twilight (Catherine Hardwicke), 2008
The Twilight Saga: Breaking Dawn—Part 1 (Bill Condon), 2011
The Twilight Saga: Breaking Dawn—Part 2 (Bill Condon), 2012
The Twilight Saga: Eclipse (David Slade), 2010
The Twilight Saga: New Moon (Chris Weitz), 2009
Uncle Buck (John Hughes), 1989
United States of Tara (Showtime Networks), 2009–11
Valley Girl (Martha Coolidge), 1983
Varsity Blues (Brian Robbins), 1999
Vamp (Richard Wenk), 1986
Vampire Junction (Jesus Franco), 2001
Veronica Mars (UPN), 2004–6; (CW Television), 2006–7
Wayne's World (Penelope Spheeris), 1992
Weekend at Bernie's (Ted Kotcheff), 1989
Whatever It Takes (David Raynr), 2000
What's Love Got to Do With It (Brian Gibson), 1993
What to Expect When You're Expecting (Kirk Jones), 2012
Winter's Bone (Debra Granik), 2010
When Harry Met Sally (Rob Reiner), 1989
The Wizard of Oz (Victor Fleming), 1939
Woke Up Dead (Sony Pictures Television), 2009
The Women (Diane English), 2008
Working Girl (Mike Nichols), 1988
The Wrestler (Darren Aronofsky), 2008
Yankee Doodle Dandy (Michael Curtiz), 1942
Y Tu Mamá También (Alfonso Cuaròn), 2001
You've Got Mail (Nora Ephron), 1998

Bibliography

Abramowitz, Rachel (2000), *Is That a Gun in Your Pocket? Women's Experience of Power in Hollywood*, New York: Random House.

Alley, Robert S., and Brown, Irby B. (2001), *Women Television Producers: Transformation of the Male Medium*, Rochester, NY: University of Rochester Press.

Almond, Steve (2007), "John Hughes goes deep: the unexpected heaviosity of *Ferris Bueller's Day Off*," in Jaime Clarke (ed.), *Don't You Forget About Me: Contemporary Writers on the Films of John Hughes*, New York: Spotlight Entertainment, pp. 5–14.

Anderson, John (2012), Review of *Vamps*, *Variety*, 6 November 2012: http://variety.com/2012/film/reviews/vamps-1117948695/

Anonymous (2006), "Men versus women . . . Different cosmetic procedures and their reasoning," *Facial Plastic Surgery*, 20: 3: http://www.aafprs.org/patient/fps_today/vol20_3/pg2.html

— (2009), "Clueless director 'shocked, angry' over Brittany Murphy's death," *US Weekly*, 22 December 2009: http://www.usmagazine.com/celebrity-news/news/clueless-director-brittany-murphy-was-pressured-to-be-thin-20092212

— (2011), "Every outfit Cher Horowitz wears in *Clueless* in under 60 seconds," *WORN Fashion Journal*, 22 August 2011: http://www.youtube.com/watch?v=F6eLxe5hMzg

Archer, Dale (2013), "Forever young: America's obsession with never growing old," *Psychology Today*, 2 October 2013: http://www.psychologytoday.com/blog/reading-between-the-headlines/201310/forever-young-americas-obsession-never-growing-old

Arthurs, Jane (2003), "*Sex and the City* and consumer culture: remediating postfeminist drama," *Feminist Media Studies*, 3: 1, pp. 83–98.

Aslinger, Ben (2014), "Clueless about listening formations?," *Cinema Journal*, 53: 3, pp. 126–31.

Aumann, Kerstin, Galinsky, Ellen, and Matos, Kenneth (2011), "The new male mystique": http://familiesandwork.org/site/research/reports/newmalemystique.pdf

Austen, Jane (1813), *Pride and Prejudice*, New York: Anchor, 2012.

— (1815), *Emma*, ed. James Kinsley and Adela Pinch, Oxford: Oxford University Press, 2008.

Austen-Leigh, James Edward (1870), *A Memoir of Jane Austen*, Create Space Independent Publishing Platform, 2013.

Bakhtin, Mikhail (1984), *Rabelais and His World*, Bloomington, IN: Indiana University Press.

— (2002), *Speech Genres & Other Late Essays*, trans. Vern W. McGee, ed. Caryl Emerson and Michael Holquist, Austin, TX: University of Texas Press.

Barker, Martin, and Mathijs, Ernest (2007), *Watching "The Lord of the Rings": Tolkien's World Audiences*, New York: Peter Lang.

Benjamin, Walter (1968), *Illuminations*, New York: Schocken.

Bernstein, Jonathan (1997), *Pretty in Pink: The Golden Age of Teenage Movies*, New York: St. Martin's Press.

Bettie, Julie (2003), *Women Without Class: Girls, Race and Identity*, Berkeley, CA: University of California Press.

Bielby, Denise D. (2009), "Gender inequality in culture industries: women and men writers in film and television," *Sociologie du Travail*, 51: 2, pp. 237–52.

Bierma, Nathan (2005), "It's been like, 10 whole years since 'Clueless' helped spread Valley slang," *The Chicago Tribune*, 20 July 2005: http://articles.chicagotribune.com/2005-07-20/features/0507190293_1_clueless-slang-amy-heckerling

Bolte, Caralyn (2008), "'Normal is the watchword': exiling cultural anxieties and redefining desire from the margins," in Sharon Marie Ross and Louisa Ellen Stein (eds.), *Teen Television: Essays on Programming and Fandom*, Jefferson, NC: McFarland.

Braithwaite, Andrea (2008), "'That girl of yours—she's pretty hardboiled, huh?': detecting feminism in *Veronica Mars*," in Sharon Marie Ross and Louisa Ellen Stein (eds.), *Teen Television: Essays on Programming and Fandom*, Jefferson, NC: McFarland, 2008.

Brammer, Rebekah (2009), "Left of centre: teen life, love and pain in the films of John Hughes," *Screen Education*, 56, pp. 22–8.

Braudy, Leo, and Cohen, Marshall (2009), *Film Theory and Criticism*, 7th edn, Oxford: Oxford University Press.

Brinkema, Eugenie (2014), *The Forms of the Affects*, Durham, NC: Duke University Press.

Britton, Andrew (1992), "Blissing out: the politics of Reaganite entertainment," *Movie* 31/32, pp. 1–42.

Brode, Douglas, and Devneka, Leah, eds. (2014), *Dracula's Daughters: The Female Vampire on Film*, Lanham, MD: Scarecrow Press.

Brunsdon, Charlotte (1997), *Screen Tastes: Soap Opera to Satellite Dishes*, London: Routledge.

Bruzzi, Stella (2007), *Bringing Up Daddy: Fatherhood and Masculinity in Post-War Hollywood*, London: BFI.

Byers, Michelle, and Lavery, David, eds. (2007), *Dear Angela: Remembering* My So-Called Life, Lanham, MD: Lexington Books.

Cartmell, Deborah, and Whelehan, Imelda, eds. (1999), *Adaptations: From Text to Screen, Screen to Text*, London: Routledge.

Chandler, Daniel (2002), *Semiotics: The Basics*, New York: Routledge.

Cholodenko, Alan (2004), "The crypt, the haunted house of cinema," *Cultural Studies Review*, 10: 2, pp. 99–113.

Citron, Michelle (1988), "Women's film production: going mainstream," in E. Deidre Pribram (ed.), *Female Spectators: Looking at Film and Television*, London: Verso, 1988, pp. 45–63.

Clarke, Jaime, ed. (2007), *Don't You Forget About Me: Contemporary Writers on the Films of John Hughes*, New York: Spotlight Entertainment.

Click, Melissa, Stevens Aubrey, Jennifer, and Behm-Morawitz, Elizabeth, eds. (2010), *Bitten by Twilight: Youth Culture, Media, and the Vampire Franchise*, New York: Peter Lang.

Cole, Janis, and Dale, Holly (1993), *Calling the Shots: Profiles of Women Filmmakers*, Kingston, ON: Quarry Press.

Coontz, Stephanie (1993), *The Way We Never Were: American Families and the Nostalgia Trap*, New York: Basic Books.
— (1997), *The Way We Really Are: Coming to Terms with America's Changing Families*, New York: Basic Books.
Corrigan, Timothy, and White, Patricia (2008), *The Film Experience: An Introduction*. New York: Bedford/St. Martin's Press.
Creed, Barbara (1993), *The Monstrous Feminine: Film, Feminism, Psychoanalysis*, London: Routledge.
Cunningham, Erin (2013), "Amy Heckerling's three favorite scenes in 'Clueless' on its 18th birthday," *The Daily Beast*, 19 July 2013: http://www.thedailybeast.com/articles/2013/07/19/amy-heckerling-s-3-favorite-scenes-of-clueless-on-its-18th-birthday.html
Davis, Glyn, and Dickinson, Kay, eds. (2004), *Teen TV: Genre, Consumption and Identity*. London: BFI.
De Gramont, Nina (2007), "Which John Hughes character are you?" in Jaime Clarke (ed.), *Don't You Forget About Me: Contemporary Writers on the Films of John Hughes*, New York: Spotlight Entertainment, pp. 96–105.
DeFore, John (2012), Review of *Vamps*, *The Hollywood Reporter*, 7 November 2012: http://www.hollywoodreporter.com/review/vamps-film-review-387510
Deleyto, Celestino (2003), "Between friends: love and friendship in contemporary Hollywood romantic comedy," *Screen*, 44: 2, pp. 167–82.
Dickson, Paul (2006), *Slang: The Topical Dictionary of Americanisms*, New York: Walker Publishing.
Doherty, Thomas (1988), *Teenagers & Teenpics: The Juvenilization of American Movies in the 1950s*. Boston, MA: Unwin Hyman.
— (1995), "Clueless kids," *Cineaste*, 21: 4, pp. 14–17.
Dole, Carol M. (1998), "Austen, class, and the American market," in Linda Troost and Sayre Greenfield (eds.), *Jane Austen in Hollywood*, Lexington, KY: University of Kentucky Press, pp. 58–68.
Donadoni, Serena (2000), "Hormonal pyrotechnics 101," *Detroit Metro Times*, 26 July 2000: http://www.metrotimes.com/detroit/hormonal-pyrotechnics-101/Content?oid=2168746
Dresner, Lisa M. (2010), "Love's labor's lost? Early 1980s representations of girls' sexual decision making in *Fast Times at Ridgemont High* and *Little Darlings*," in Tamar Jeffers McDonald (ed.), *Virgin Territory: Representing Sexual Inexperience in Film*, Detroit, MI: Wayne State University Press, pp. 174–200.
Driscoll, Catherine (2011), *Teen Film: A Critical Introduction*. London: Berg.
Ebert, Roger (1982), Review of *Fast Times at Ridgemont High*, *Chicago Sun-Times*: http://www.rogerebert.com/reviews/fast-times-at-ridgemont-high-1982
— (1995), Review of *Clueless*, *Chicago Sun-Times*: http://www.rogerebert.com/reviews/clueless-1995
Egan, Kate, and Thomas, Sarah, eds. (2013), *Cult Film Stardom: Offbeat Attractions and Processes of Cultification*, Basingstoke: Palgrave Macmillan.
Ehrenreich, Barbara (1983), *The Hearts of Men: American Dreams and the Flight from Commitment*, London: Pluto Press.
Faludi, Susan (1992), *Backlash: The Undeclared War Against Women*, London: Chatto & Windus.
Ferriss, Suzanne and Mallory Young, eds. (2008), *Chick Flicks: Contemporary Women at the Movies*, New York and London: Routledge.
Feuer, Jane (1992), "Genre study and television," in Robert C. Allen (ed.), *Channels of*

Discourse, Reassembled: Television and Contemporary Criticism, second ed., London: Routledge.

— (1993), *The Hollywood Musical*, second ed., Bloomington, IN: Indiana University Press.

— (2010), "The international art musical: Defining and periodising the post-1980s musical," in Steven Cohan (ed.), *The Sound of Musicals*, London: BFI.

Fielding, Helen (1996), *Bridget Jones' Diary*, London: Penguin.

Fischer, Lucy (1989), *Shot/Countershot: Film Tradition and Women's Cinema*, Princeton, NJ: Princeton University Press.

Franzese, Alexis T. (2009), "Authenticity: Perspectives and experiences," in Phillip Vannini and J. Patrick Williams (eds.), *Authenticity in Culture, Self and Society*, New York: Ashgate, pp. 87–102.

Franzini, L. R. (1996), "Feminism and women's sense of humor," *Sex Roles*, 35: 11–12, pp. 811–19.

Freud, Sigmund (1917), "Mourning and melancholia," in Sigmund Freud, *On Murder, Mourning and Melancholia*, trans. Shaun Whiteside, London: Penguin, 2005, pp. 201–18.

Galinksy, Ellen; Aumann, Kerstin; and Bond, James T. (2011), "Times are changing: Gender and generation at work and at home": http://familiesandwork.org/site/research/reports/Times_Are_Changing.pdf

Garrett, Roberta (2007), *Postmodern Chick Flicks: The Return of the Woman's Film*, New York and Basingstoke: Palgrave Macmillan.

Gateward, Frances, and Pomerance, Murray, eds. (2002), *Sugar, Spice, and Everything Nice: Cinemas of Girlhood*, Detroit, MI: Wayne State University Press.

Gelder, Ken (1994), *Reading the Vampire*, London: Routledge.

Gerson, Kathleen (2011), *The Unfinished Revolution*, Oxford: Oxford University Press.

Gill, Rosalind (2009), "Postfeminist media culture: Elements of a sensibility," in Mary Celeste Kearney (ed.), *The Gender and Media Reader*, New York and London: Routledge, pp. 136–48.

Gill, Rosalind, and Scharff, Christina, eds. (2011), *New Femininities: Postfeminism, Neoliberalism and Subjectivity*, New York and Basingstoke: Palgrave Macmillan.

Gilpin, Vicky, ed. (forthcoming), *Laugh Until You Bleed: Vampires and Comedy*. New York: McFarland.

Goode, Ian (2003), "Value and television aesthetics," *Screen* 44: 1, pp. 106–9.

Gora, Susannah (2010), *You Couldn't Ignore Me If You Tried: The Brat Pack, John Hughes, and Their Impact on a Generation*, New York: Crown.

Gordon, Rebecca M. (2007), "Remakes, genre and affect: The thriller-chiller-comedy as case study," unpublished dissertation, Portland College, Oregon (English Department).

Grant, Barry K., ed. (2003), *Film Genre Reader III*, Austin, TX: University of Texas Press.

Gwynne, Joel, and Muller, Nadine (2013), "Introduction: Postfeminism and contemporary Hollywood cinema," in Joel Gwynne and Nadine Muller (eds.), *Postfeminism and Contemporary Hollywood Cinema*, New York: Palgrave Macmillan, pp. 1–10.

Halliday, Michael (1978), *Language as Social Semiotic: the Social Interpretation of Language and Meaning*, London: Edward Arnold.

Hansen, Miriam (1991), *Babel and Babylon: Spectatorship in American Silent Film*. Cambridge, MA: Harvard University Press.

Hardt, Michael, and Weeks, Kathi, eds. (2000), *The Jameson Reader*, Malden, MA: Blackwell.

Harrod, Mary (2010), "The aesthetics of pastiche in the work of Richard Linklater," *Screen* 51: 1, pp. 21–37.

Harwood, Sarah (1997), *Family Fictions: Representations of the Family in 1980s Hollywood Cinema*, Basingstoke: Macmillan.

Helford, Elyce Rae, ed. (2000), *Fantasy Girls: Gender in the New Universe of Science-Fiction and Fantasy Television*, Oxford: Rowman & Littlefield.

Hillabold, Jean R. (2014), "The vampire cult of eternal youth," in Lisa Nevárez (ed.), *The Vampire Goes to College: Essays on Teaching the Undead*, New York: McFarland, pp. 78–91.

Hills, Matt (2004), "*Dawson's Creek*: 'quality teen TV' and 'mainstream cult'?" in Glyn Davis and Kay Dickinson (eds.), *Teen TV: Genre, Consumption, Identity*, London: BFI.

— (2013), "Cult movies with and without cult stars," in Kate Egan and Sarah Thomas (eds.), *Cult Film Stardom: Offbeat Attractions and Processes of Cultification*, Basingstoke: Palgrave Macmillan, pp. 21–36.

Hitchens, Christopher (2007), "Why women aren't funny," *Vanity Fair*, January 2007: http://www.vanityfair.com/culture/features/2007/01/hitchens200701

Hollinger, Karen (1998), *In the Company of Women: Contemporary Female Friendship Films*, Minneapolis, MN: University of Minnesota Press.

— (2002), "From female friends to literary ladies: the contemporary woman's film," in Steve Neale (ed.), *Genre and Contemporary Hollywood*, London: BFI.

— (2008), "Afterword: once I got beyond the name chick flick," in Suzanne Ferriss and Mallory Young (eds.), *Chick Flicks: Contemporary Women at the Movies*, London: Routledge.

Holmlund, Chris (2005), "Postfeminism from A to G," *Cinema Journal*, 44: 2, pp. 116–21.

Hunt, Leon, Lockyer, Sharon, and Milly Williamson, eds. (2014), *Screening the Undead: Vampires and Zombies in Film and Television*, London: I. B. Tauris.

Hunting, Kyra (2014), "Furiously franchised: *Clueless*, convergence culture, and the female-focused franchise," *Cinema Journal*, 53: 3, pp. 145–51.

Hurd, Mary G. (2007), *Women Directors and Their Films*. Westport, CT: Praeger.

IMDB profile (2015), *Amy Heckerling*: http://www.imdb.com/name/nm0002132/?ref_=nv_sr_1

IMDB profile (2015), *John Hughes*: http://www.imdb.com/name/nm0000455/?ref_=nv_sr_2

Imre, Anikó (2009), "Gender and quality television," *Feminist Media Studies*, 9: 4, pp. 391–407.

Jameson, Fredric (2000), "Postmodernism, or the cultural logic of late capitalism," in Michael Hardt and Kathi Weeks (eds.), *The Jameson Reader*, Malden, MA: Blackwell, pp. 188–233.

Jarecki, Nicholas (2001), *Breaking In: How 20 Film Directors Got Their Start*, New York: Broadway.

Jenkins, Claire (2013), "'You're just some bitch who broke my heart and cut up my mom's wedding dress': the significance of the wedding dress in Hollywood's romantic comedies," *Film, Fashion and Consumption*, 2: 2, pp. 159–73.

— (2015), *Home Movies: The American Family in Contemporary Hollywood*, London: I. B. Tauris.

Jermyn, Deborah (2014), "Nancy Meyers: the wrong kind of woman filmmaker?," paper presented at the *Doing Women's Film and Television History Conference*, University of East Anglia, April 10–12, 2014.

Johnson, Merri Lisa (2007), "Introduction: ladies love your box: the rhetoric of pleasure and danger in feminist television studies," in Merri Lisa Johnson (ed.), *Third Wave Feminism and Television: Jane Puts It In a Box*, London: I. B. Tauris, pp. 1–27.

Joyce, Simon (2007), *Victorians in the Rearview Mirror*, Athens, OH: Ohio University Press.

Kaklamanidou, Betty (2013), *Genre, Gender and the Effects of Neoliberalism: The New Millennium Hollywood Rom Com*, London: Routledge.

Kaveney, Roz (2006), *Teen Dreams: Reading Teen Film from Heathers to Veronica Mars*, London: I. B. Tauris.

Kearney, Mary Celeste (2002), "Girlfriends and girl power: female adolescence in contemporary U.S. cinema," in Frances Gateward and Murray Pomerance (eds.), *Sugar, Spice, and Everything Nice: Cinemas of Girlhood*, Detroit, MI: Wayne State University Press, pp. 125–42.

—, ed. (2009), *The Gender and Media Reader*, New York and London: Routledge.

King, Geoff (2009), *New Hollywood Cinema*, London: I. B. Tauris.

Kochhar, Rakesh, and Morin, Rich (2014), "Despite recovery, fewer Americans identify as middle class," Pew Research Center, 27 January 2014: http://www.pewresearch.org/fact-tank/2014/01/27/despite-recovery-fewer-americans-identify-as-middle-class/

Krämer, Peter (1999), "Would you take your child to see this film? The cultural and social work of the family-adventure movie," in Steve Neale and Murray Smith (eds.), *Contemporary Hollywood Cinema*, London: Routledge, pp. 294–311.

Kristeva, Julia (1993), *Les Nouvelles maladies de l'âme*, Paris: Fayard.

Kuchich, John, and Sadoff, Dianne, eds. (2000), *Victorian Afterlife: Postmodern Culture Rewrites the Nineteenth Century*, Minneapolis, MN: Minnesota University Press.

Kuhn, Annette (2002), *Dreaming of Fred and Ginger: Cinema and Cultural Memory*, New York: New York University Press.

Kuhn, Annette, and Westwell, Guy (2012), *Oxford Dictionary of Film Studies*, Oxford: Oxford University Press.

Lane, Christina (2000), *Feminist Hollywood from Born in Flames to Point Break*, Detroit, MI: Wayne State University Press.

Lang, Bret (2014), "21st Century Fox launches mentoring program for female directors," *Variety*, 1 July 2014: http://variety.com/2014/film/news/21st-century-fox-launches-mentoring-program-for-female-directors-1201256061/

Latham, Rob (2002), *Consuming Youth: Vampires, Cyborgs and the Culture of Consumption*, Chicago, IL: Chicago University Press.

Lauzen, Martha M., and Dozier, David M. (2002), "Equity time in prime time? Scheduling favoritism and gender on the broadcast networks," *Journal of Broadcasting & Electronic Media*, 46: 1, pp. 137–53.

Lauzen, Martha M. (2014), "The celluloid ceiling: behind-the-scenes employment of women on the top 250 films of 2014," Center for the Study of Women in Television & Film: http://womenintvfilm.sdsu.edu/files/2014_Celluloid_Ceiling_Report.pdf.

Lebeau, Vicky (1995), *Lost Angels: Psychoanalysis and Cinema*, London: Routledge.

Leeder, Murray (forthcoming), "Dracula in New York: the comic, anachronistic vampire in *Love at First Bite* and *Vamps*," in Vicky Gilpin (ed.), *Laugh Until You Bleed: Vampires and Comedy*, New York: McFarland.

Leicht, Kevin T., and Fitzgerald, Scott T. (2014), *Middle-Class Meltdown in America*, New York: Routledge.

Leitch, Thomas M. (1992), "The world according to teenpix," *Literature Film Quarterly*, 20: 1, pp. 43–7.

Lenos, Melissa (2014), Introduction to "In Focus: *Clueless*," ed. Melissa Lenos, *Cinema Journal*, 53: 3, pp. 123–6.

Leppert, Alice (2014), "Can I please give you some advice? *Clueless* and the teen makeover," *Cinema Journal*, 53: 3, pp. 131–7.

Levine, Elana, and Parks, Lisa, eds. (2007), *Undead TV: Essays on* Buffy the Vampire Slayer, Durham, NC and London: Duke University Press.

Lewis, Jon (1992), *The Road to Romance and Ruin: Teen Films and Youth Culture*, New York: Routledge.

Lynch, Deirdre (2003), "Clueless: about history," in Suzanne R. Pucci and James Thompson (eds.), *Jane Austen and Co.: Remaking the Past in Contemporary Culture*, Albany, NY: State University of New York Press, pp. 46–61.

Lynn, Allison (2007), "Ferris Bueller: an infatuation, a life lesson, and one harmless family adventure," in Jaime Clarke, *Don't You Forget About Me: Contemporary Writers on the Films of John Hughes*, New York: Spotlight Entertainment, pp. 116–27.

Maltby, Richard (1995), *Hollywood Cinema*, Oxford: Blackwell.

Marghitu, Stefania (2014), Interview with Paul Vickery, e-mail, 12 March 2014.

— (2014), Interview with Charlie Lyne, phone, 13 August 2014.

— (2014), interview with Alejandra Hernandez, Los Angeles, CA, 30 August 2014.

Markle, Gail (2008), "'Can women have sex like a man?': sexual scripts in *Sex and the City*," *Sexuality & Culture*, 12: 1, pp. 45–57.

Maslin, Janet (1982), Review of *Fast Times at Ridgemont High*, *New York Times*, 3 September 1982: http://movies2.nytimes.com/mem/movies/review.html?_r=1&res=9507E7DA143B F930A3575AC0A964948260&oref=slogin

Matthews, Nicole (2000), *Comic Politics: Gender in Hollywood Comedy after the New Right*, Manchester: Manchester University Press.

Mayne, Judith (1990), *The Woman at the Keyhole: Feminism and Women's Cinema*, Bloomington, IN: Indiana University Press.

McCabe, Janet, and Akass, Kim, eds. (2007), *Quality TV: Contemporary American Television and Beyond*, London: I. B. Tauris.

McKinley, E. Graham (1997), *Beverly Hills 90210: Television, Gender and Identity*, Philadelphia, PA: University of Pennsylvania Press.

McMurran, Kristin (1985), "Mixing marriage and movies in a mirthly delight for directors Amy Heckerling and Neal Israel," *People*, 23: 19, 13 May 1985: http://www/people/com/ people/archive/article/0,,20090679,00.html

McPhee, Ryan (2014), "As if! Amy Heckerling's *Clueless* musical could be coming to Broadway, starring Katy Perry," *Broadway.com*, 11 July 2014: http://www.broadway.com/ buzz/176693/ as-if-amy-heckerlings-clueless-musical-could-be-coming-to-broadway-starring-katy-perry/

McRobbie, Angela (2009), *The Aftermath of Feminism: Gender, Culture and Social Change*, Los Angeles, CA: Sage.

Metz, Christian (1982), *The Imaginary Signifier: Psychoanalysis and Cinema*, Bloomington, IN: Indiana University Press.

Meyrowitz, Joshua (1985), *No Sense of Place: The Impact of Electronic Media on Social Behavior*, New York: Oxford University Press.

Michaels, Lloyd (1998), *The Phantom of Cinema: Character in Modern Film*, Albany, NY: State University of New York Press.

Mills, Brett (2009), *The Sitcom*, Edinburgh: Edinburgh University Press.

Mills, Jane (2004), "*Clueless*: transforming Jane Austen's *Emma*," *Australian Screen Education*, 34, pp. 100–5.

Mittell, Jason (2004), *Genre and Television: From Cop Shows to Cartoons in American Culture*, New York: Routledge.

Moore, Rachel O. (2000), *Savage Theory: Cinema as Modern Magic*, Durham, NC: Duke University Press.

Morgenstern, Joe (1995), "Film: funny times at Beverly Hills High," *Wall Street Journal*, 21 July 1995: http://online.wsj.com/news/articles/SB877043990821887000

Moseley, Rachel (2002), "Glamorous witchcraft: gender and magic in teen film and television," *Screen*, 43: 4, pp. 403–22.

Mulvey, Laura (2006), *Death 24x a Second: Stillness and the Moving Images*, London: Reaktion.

Murray, Noel (2008), "Interview with Amy Heckerling," *A.V. Club*, 20 March 2008: http://www.avclub.com/articles/amy-heckerling,14217/

Nashawaty, Chris (2012), Review of *Clueless*, *Entertainment Weekly*, 5 Oct. 2012, http://www.ew.com/ew/article/0,,20639761,00.html

Neale, Steve (2000), *Genre and Hollywood*, London: Routledge.

— (2003), "Questions of genre," in Barry Keith Grant, *Film Genre Reader III*, Austin, TX: University of Texas Press.

Negra, Diane (2009), *What a Girl Wants? Fantasizing the Reclamation of Self in Postfeminism*, London: Routledge.

Negra, Diane, and Holmes, Su (2008), "Introduction," *Genders Online*, 48, 2008: http://www.genders.org/g48/g48_negraholmes.html

Negra, Diane, and Tasker, Yvonne, eds. (2007), *Interrogating Postfeminism: Gender and the Politics of Popular Culture*, Durham, NC: Duke University Press.

— (2014), *Gendering the Recession: Media and Culture in an Age of Austerity*, Durham, NC: Duke University Press.

Nelson, Robin (2007), "Quality TV drama: estimations and influences through time and space," in Janet McCabe and Kim Akass (eds.), *Quality TV: Contemporary American Television and Beyond*, London: I. B. Tauris, pp. 38–51.

Nevárez, Lisa, ed. (2014), *The Vampire Goes to College: Essays on Teaching the Undead*, New York: McFarland.

Nussbaum, Emily (2013), "Difficult women: how *Sex and the City* lost its good name," *New Yorker*, 29 July 2013: http://www.newyorker.com/magazine/2013/07/29/difficult-women

O'Meara, Jennifer (2014), "'We've got to work on your accent and vocabulary': characterization through verbal style in *Clueless*." *Cinema Journal*, 53: 3, pp. 138–45.

Pascoe, C. J. (2011), *Dude, You're a Fag*, Berkeley, CA: University of California Press.

Paul, William (1994), *Laughing Screaming: Modern Hollywood Horror and Comedy*, New York: Columbia University Press.

Perez, Gilberto (1998), *The Material Ghost: Films and their Medium*, Baltimore, MD: The Johns Hopkins University Press.

Pfeifle, Tess (2013), "5 trends from *Clueless* that pass the test of time: Cher Horowitz go out of style? As if!" *BuzzFeed*, 12 May 2013: http://www.buzzfeed.com/themessupstairs/5-trends-from-clueless-that-pass-the-test-of-time-aoy3

Piatti-Farnell, Lorna (2014), *The Vampire in Contemporary Popular Literature*, London: Routledge.

Pomerance, Murray, and Sakeris, John, eds. (2012), *Popping Culture*, 7th edn, London: Pearson Learning Solutions.

Popkey, Miranda (2012), "Writer-director, Amy Heckerling and her muse, Alicia Silverstone discuss *Clueless*, *Vamps* and filming women," *Capital New York*, 9 April 2012: http://www.capitalnewyork.com/article/culture/2012/04/5659176/writer-director-amy-heckerling-and-her-muse-alicia-silverstone-discuss-clueless-vamps-and-filiming-women

Press, Andrea L. (1991), *Women Watching Television: Gender, Class and Generation in the American Television Experience*, Philadelphia, PA: University of Pennsylvania Press.

— (forthcoming), *Feminism LOL: Media Culture and "Feminism on the Ground" in a Postfeminist Age*.

Press, Andrea L., and Cole, Elizabeth R. (1999), *Speaking of Abortion: Television and Authority in the Lives of Women*, Chicago, IL: University of Chicago Press.

Press, Andrea L., and Williams, Bruce A. (2010), *The New Media Environment*, Oxford: Blackwell.

Projansky, Sarah, and Vande Berg, Leah R. (2000), "Sabrina, the teenage . . .?: Girls, witches, mortals, and the limitations of prime-time feminism," in Elyce Rae Helford (ed.), *Fantasy Girls: Gender in the New Universe of Science-Fiction and Fantasy Television*, Oxford: Rowman & Littlefield.

Pucci, Suzanne, R. and Thompson, James, eds. (2003), *Jane Austen and Co.: Remaking the Past in Contemporary Culture*, Albany, NY: State University of New York Press.

Quart, Alissa (2003), *Branded: The Buying and Selling of Teenagers*, New York: Basic Books.

Rabin, Nathan (2008), "My year of flops: the new batch: case file #105, *I Could Never Be Your Woman*," *A.V. Club*, 12 February 2008: http://www.avclub.com/article/my-year-of-flops-the-new-batch-case-file-105-ii-co-2163

Radner, Hilary (2011), *Neo-Feminist Cinema: Girly Films, Chick Flicks and Consumer Culture*, New York and London: Routledge.

Reid, Joe (2011), "Are we living in the golden age of male objectification?" *New York Magazine—Vulture*, 12 September 2011: http://nymag.com/daily/entertainment/2011/09/are_we_living_in_the_golden_ag.html

Rosen, Christopher (2012), "*Vamps* box office flops: *Clueless* reunion earns $500 from one theater," *Huffington Post*, 5 November 2012: http://www.huffingtonpost.com/2012/11/05/vamps-box-office-flop_n_2077496.html

Rosenbloom, Stephanie (2012), "Log on, coordinate, pose: virtual closet web sites revise online fashion shopping," *New York Times*, 29 February 2012: http://www.nytimes.com/2012/03/01/fashion/virtual-closet-web-sites-like-pinterest-and-stylitics-revise-online-fashion-shopping.html?pagewanted=all&_r=0

Rosenman, Ellen B. (2003), *Unauthorized Pleasures: Accounts of Victorian Erotic Experiences*, Ithaca, NY: Cornell University Press.

Ross, Sharon Marie, and Stein, Louisa Ellen, eds. (2008), *Teen Television: Essays on Programming and Fandom*, Jefferson, NC: McFarland.

Rowe, Kathleen (1995), *The Unruly Woman: Gender and the Genres of Laughter*, Austin, TX: University of Texas Press.

Rubin, Lillian (1976), *Worlds of Pain: Life in the Working Class Family*, New York: Basic Books.

Russo, Mary (1995), *The Female Grotesque: Risk, Excess and Modernity*, London: Routledge.

Sadoff, Dianne F., and Kucich, John (2000), *Victorian Afterlife: Postmodern Culture Rewrites the Nineteenth Century*, Minneapolis, MN: University of Minnesota Press, 2000.

Sappington, Rodney, and Stallings, Tyler, eds. (1994), *Uncontrollable Bodies: Testimonies of Identity and Culture*, Seattle, WA: Bay Press.

Sarris, Andrew (1962), "Notes on the auteur theory in 1962," in Leo Braudy and Marshall Cohen, eds., *Film Theory and Criticism*, 7th edn, Oxford: Oxford University Press, 2009, pp. 451–4.

Schenker, Andrew (2012), Review of *Vamps*, *Slant Magazine*, 28 October 2012: http://www.slantmagazine.com/film/review/vamps

Schwind, Jean (2008), "Cool coaching at Ridgemont High," *The Journal of Popular Culture*, 41: 6, pp. 1012–32.

Scripps Howard News Service (1995), "Don't go postal: here's a guide to *Clueless* speak," *Chicago Tribune*, 26 July 1995: http://articles.chicagotribune.com/1995-07-26/news/9507260241_1_clueless-audi-majorly

Searle, Elizabeth (2007), "*The Scream*, with lip gloss," in Jaime Clarke, ed., *Don't You Forget*

About Me: Contemporary Writers on the Films of John Hughes, New York: Spotlight Entertainment, pp. 162–72.

Sedgwick, Eve Kosofsky, and Franks, Adam, eds. (1995), *Shame and Its Sisters: A Silvan Tomkins Reader*, Durham, NC: Duke University Press.

Shary, Timothy (1997), "The teen film and its methods of study," *Journal of Popular Film and Television*, 25: 1, pp. 38–45.

— (2002), *Generation Multiplex: The Image of Youth in Contemporary American Cinema*, Austin, TX: University of Texas Press.

— (2005), *Teen Movies: American Youth on Screen*, London: Wallflower Press.

— (2010), "Virgin springs: a survey of teen films' quest for sexcess," in Tamar Jeffers McDonald, ed., *Virgin Territory: Representing Sexual Inexperience in Film*, Detroit, MI: Wayne State University Press, 2010, pp. 54–67.

— (2011), "Buying me love: '80s class-clash teen romances," *The Journal of Popular Culture*, 44: 3, pp. 563–82.

— (2012), "'The only place to go is inside': confusions about sexuality and class from *Kids* to *Superbad*," in Murray Pomerance and John Sakeris, eds., *Popping Culture*, 7th edn, London: Pearson Learning Solutions, pp. 5–13.

— (2014), *Generation Multiplex: The Image of Youth in American Cinema Since 1980*, Austin, TX: University of Texas Press.

Silverman, Kaja (1986), "Fragments of a fashionable discourse," in Tania Modleski (ed.), *Studies in Entertainment: Critical Approaches to Mass Culture*, Bloomington, IN: Indiana University Press.

Silverstein, Melissa (2012), "What Bigelow effect? Number of women directors in Hollywood falls to 5 percent," *Indiewire*, 24 January 2012: http://blogs.indiewire.com/womenandhollywood/what-bigelow-effect-number-of-women-directors-in-hollywood-falls-to-5-percent#.T_r9RpH_yV0

— (2012), "Interview with *Vamps* director Amy Heckerling," *Indiewire*, 3 November 2012: http://blogs.indiewire.com/womenandhollywood/interview-with-vamps-director-amy-heckerling/

Singer, Michael (1998), *A Cut Above: 50 Film Directors Talk About Their Craft*, Los Angeles, CA: Lone Eagle, 1998.

Skeggs, Beverley (1997), *Formations of Class and Gender: Becoming Respectable*, London: Sage.

Skeggs, Beverley, and Wood, Helen (2012), *Reacting to Reality Television: Performance, Audience and Value*, London: Routledge.

Smith, Frances (2013), "Rethinking the norm: Judith Butler and the Hollywood teen movie," unpublished PhD thesis, University of Warwick.

Smith, Stacy L., Pieper, Katherine, and Choueiti, Marc (2013), "Exploring the barriers and opportunities for independent women filmmakers phase I and II," Sundance Institute, 2013: http://www.sundance.org/pdf/press-releases/Exploring-The-Barriers.pdf

Sobchack, Vivian (1994), "Revenge of the *Leech Woman*: on the dread of aging in low-budget horror film," in Rodney Sappington and Tyler Stallings (eds.), *Uncontrollable Bodies: Testimonies of Identity and Culture*, Seattle, WA: Bay Press, pp. 78–92.

Sonnet, Esther (1999), "From *Emma* to *Clueless*: taste, pleasure and the scene of history," in Deborah Cartmell and Imelda Whelehan (eds.), *Adaptations: From Text to Screen, Screen to Text*, London: Routledge.

Speed, Lesley (1995), "Good fun and bad hair days: girls in teen film," *Metro*, 101, pp. 24–30.

— (2002), "A world ruled by hilarity: gender and low comedy in the films of Amy Heckerling," *Senses of Cinema*, 22: sensesofcinema.com/2002/22/heckerling/

— (2010), "Loose cannons: white masculinity and the vulgar teen comedy film," *Journal of Popular Culture* 43: 4, pp. 820–41.

Spigel, Lynn, and Mann, Denise, eds. (1992), *Private Screenings: Television and the Female Consumer*, Minneapolis, MN: University of Minnesota Press.

Stacey, Jackie (1994), *Star Gazing: Hollywood Cinema and Female Spectatorship*, New York and London: Routledge.

Stern, Lesley (2000), "*Emma* in Los Angeles: remaking the book and the city," in James Naremore (ed.), *Film Adaptation*, London: Athlone, pp. 221–38.

Stewart, Garrett (1999), *Between Film and Screen: Modernism's Photo Synthesis*, Chicago, IL: University of Chicago Press.

Stratton, Jon (1996), *The Desirable Body: Cultural Fetishism and the Erotics of Consumption*, Manchester: Manchester University Press.

Sullivan, Mary (2007), "Make a wish: the first kiss lasts forever," in Jaime Clarke (ed.), *Don't You Forget About Me: Contemporary Writers on the Films of John Hughes*, New York: Spotlight Entertainment, pp. 173–83.

Tasker, Yvonne (1998), *Working Girls: Gender and Sexuality in Popular Cinema*, New York: Routledge.

Teran, Andi (2013), "*Clueless* turns 18 tomorrow! We interviewed costume designer Mona May," *MTV Style*, 18 July 2013: http://style.mtv.com/2013/07/18/clueless-mona-may-interview/

Thoma, Pamela (2009), "Buying up baby: modern feminine subjectivity, assertions of 'choice' and the repudiation of reproductive justice in unwanted pregnancy films," *Feminist Media Studies*, 9: 4, 409–25.

Thompson, Evan (2007), *Mind in Life: Biology, Phenomenology and the Sciences of the Mind*, Cambridge, MA and London: Harvard University Press.

Tincknell, Estella (2011), "Scourging the abject body: *Ten Years Younger* and fragmented femininity under neoliberalism," in Rosalind Gill and Christina Scharff (eds.), *New Femininities: Postfeminism, Neoliberalism and Subjectivity*, New York: Palgrave Macmillan.

Traube, Elizabeth (1992), *Dreaming Identities: Class, Gender and Generation in 1980s Hollywood Movies*, Oxford: Westview Press.

Tropiano, Stephen (2006), *Rebels and Chicks: A History of the Hollywood Teen Movie*, New York: Back Stage Books.

Truffaut, François (1954), "Une certaine tendence du cinéma Français," *Cahiers du Cinéma*, #31, January 1954.

Tuite, Clara (2002), *Romantic Austen: Sexual Politics and the Literary Canon*, Cambridge: Cambridge University Press.

Turim, Maureen (2003), "Popular culture and the comedy of manners: *Clueless* and fashion clues," in Suzanne R. Pucci and James Thompson (eds.), *Jane Austen and Co.: Remaking the Past in Contemporary Culture*, New York: State University of New York Press, pp. 33–52.

Turner, Ralph (1976), "The real self: from institution to impulse," *American Journal of Sociology*, 81, pp. 989–1016.

Valenti, Jessica (2009), *The Purity Myth: How America's Obsession with Virginity is Hurting Young Women*, Berkeley, CA: Seal Press.

— (2012), *Why Have Kids? A New Mom Explores the Truth About Parenting and Happiness*, Las Vegas: Amazon.

Vineyard, Jennifer (2012), "*Clueless* writer-director Amy Heckerling on her new Alicia Silverstone movie, *Vamps*," *Vulture*, 9 September 2012: http://www.vulture.com/2012/04/vamps-amy-heckerling-interview.html

Wald, Gayle (2002), "Clueless in a neocolonial world order," in Frances Gateward and

Murray Pomerance (eds.), *Sugar, Spice, and Everything Nice: Cinemas of Girlhood*, Detroit, MI: Wayne State University Press, pp. 103–23.

Warner, Helen (2013), "'A new feminist revolution in Hollywood comedy?': postfeminist discourses and the critical reception of *Bridesmaids*," in Joel Gwynne and Nadine Muller (eds.), *Postfeminism and Contemporary Hollywood Cinema*, New York: Palgrave Macmillan, pp. 222–37.

Weinstock, Jeffrey A. (2014), "Sans fangs: Theda Bara, *A Fool There Was*, and the cinematic vampire," in Douglas Brode and Leah Deyneka (eds.), *Dracula's Daughters: The Female Vampire on Film*, Lanham, MD: Scarecrow Press.

Wilcox, Rhonda, and Lavery, David (2002), *Fighting the Forces: What's at Stake in* Buffy the Vampire Slayer, Oxford: Rowman & Littlefield.

Wildfox Couture (2013), *Kids in America Collection*, 2 January 2013: http://ilovewildfox.com/iloveyouwildfox/2013/1/2/the-kids-in-america-ss-13-wildfox.html

Williamson, Lisa (2008), "Contentious comedy: negotiating issues of form, content and representation in American sitcoms of the post-network era," unpublished PhD thesis, University of Glasgow.

Winch, Alison (2012), "'We can have it all': the girlfriend flick," *Feminist Media Studies*, 12: 1, pp. 69–82.

— (2013), *Girlfriends and Postfeminist Sisterhood*, London: Palgrave Macmillan.

Wood, Robin (1986), *Hollywood from Vietnam to Reagan*, New York: Columbia University Press.

— (2002), "Party time or can't hardly wait for that American pie: Hollywood high school movies of the 90s," *CineAction!*, 58, pp. 4–10.

— (2003), *Hollywood from Vietnam to* Reagan . . . and *Beyond*, New York: Columbia University Press.

Wright, Eric Olin, and Rogers, Joel (2010), *American Society: How It Really Works*, New York: Norton.

Index